Rachael

Porch Swings and Spearmint Tea

Eunice J Filler

in collaboration with

Mike Fields
Marilyn Fields
Juanita Stigen
Jean Wood

Copyright ©2011 Eunice J. Filler
All Rights Reserved
ISBN-13:9781491014691

To Rachael, our Granny.

After raising her own six daughters, she had a big hand
in raising almost all of her grandchildren. This book is a
collection of tales she heard from her mother and grandmother,
stories from her childhood, and the adventures
of raising her own children and grandchildren.
You added much wisdom,
love and richness to our lives.
We love you, Granny.

Forward

My purpose in writing this book is to record the stories that Granny told to me when I was a little girl. They convey the values of a way of life that is becoming considered so obsolete that it is deemed unimportant, and might otherwise be forever lost. It is my desire that my children, grandchildren and great-grandchildren know the strong but gentle people from whom they are descended and learn to love them as I do.

This is a saga of the family life of four generations; the inquisitive little girl on the front porch with Granny is me, the fifth generation. Instead of presenting Granny's tales as isolated events, my cousins have given me permission to string them together with conversations and emotions, creating a saga in which the true stories unfold as a continuous adventure.

To depict the quiet love with which she remembered her childhood and raising her daughters and add to the flavor, I have used incidents that my cousins and I remembered. At the quilting party, the funny story of my mother and her oldest sister, Bessie, was actually me and Bessie's daughter, Jean. And the adventure with the treadle sewing machine was actually me and my cousin Mike.

I pray that you enjoy the reading as much as I enjoyed the writing. I hope I have portrayed the emotion of the situations so that you laugh and cry along with them, as I did while writing it.

Other than people who are my direct ancestors, all names are purely fictional.

My thanks to my cousins for their contributions and interest in relating our family history. Thank you, Mike, Marilyn, Jean and Juanita.

Rachael
Porch Swings and Spearmint Tea

Chapter One
The War

In the spring and summer of 1861, there is a sense of urgency in the air in northwestern Georgia. Tension between the northern and southern states has grown to a point that seems insurmountable. Wherever people gather, there are no longer whispers of seceding; talk of seceding from the Union has become the main topic of conversation.

Burrell Barnett was returning home from Rome, Georgia in the early evening. In the quietness of the gathering dusk, he enjoyed the fresh, green beauty of the country lane as he neared home. His thoughts drifted to the events of a very satisfactory meeting with the Quartermaster General of the Georgia Militia. He had just closed a very lucrative deal to sell horses to the militia -- or the southern army if it comes to that. "I really do not want my beautiful grays going into battle," he thought, "I have worked a long time breeding up the only herd of gray horses in the south. If one of my mares throws something other than a gray foal, I really have to wonder.

"But, I guess, if men have to go to war, so do horses."

The buggy horse whinnied, slinging his head and dancing between the shafts of the wagon. His short jumps jostled the buggy forward and back. Burrell had heard the rat-tat-tat as the beeline hit the side of the horse. He spoke soothingly to calm the horse and had the horse back a short way up the lane to be out of the way of the bees. He was a patient man; and the bees have their appointed rounds to make also.

He watched the bees, heavily laden with the bright yellow pollen, as they instinctively followed in line returning to the hive. Burrell let his eye follow the beeline to where it entered the trees; then he looked around for markers to identify the location. That high outcropping of sand rock would be good. Later he would come back and try to find the hive. It would be nice to take some honey home to Minerva. It's always good to make some points with that saucy little woman.

As he sat enjoying the cool of the early evening, Burrell let his mind drift to the woman with whom he had made his life. In their younger years she had worked right alongside him as he cleared fields and built their first house. She was just a little slip of a girl then, quite an eyeful. And she was as feisty and fearless as a bantam hen with chicks. He smiled and nodded to himself, "She still is."

As they began accumulating property and having children, Minerva showed her strength in other ways. She had become an energetic manager, teaching the children respect and manners, directing the house and servants. She was very skillful and graceful as a hostess for social events. A smile drifted across his face. "She always makes me looks good," he thought happily.

The horse stamped his hoof impatiently, bringing Burrell back to the present. He lazily slapped the reins on the horse's rump and clucked a few times. He looked back at the area to check landmarks, and then his mind jumped back to his appointment this afternoon with the horse buyer who was in town. "The state government is stockpiling supplies and horses. Doesn't look good," he shook his head, "but I have some fine horses to sell," he said out loud.

****

The lane into town had taken on a different kind of beauty. Leaves of red and yellow dressed up the lane like the billowing skirts of women dressed for a social gathering. The late blooming flowers hung their heads as they sensed the weather changing.

"Suddenly things are moving so fast," Burrell thought as he drove the buggy down the lane toward town. "It is less than a year since I sold those first horses to the Georgia Militia. Now we are the Confederate States of America. I never really thought it would go this far.

"And what of my family? Leaving them to face the dangers of war alone? The boys are too young for this kind of responsibility, but there's no way around it. They will have to run the farm.

"Minerva is a strong woman. I have no doubt that she can manage the family in whatever situations that arise. I pity anyone who crosses her. My Minerva… she is right here beside me and yet I miss her already."

Minerva sat silently beside him, her hand gently resting inside the bend of his elbow, maybe gripping a little stronger than usual. He glanced down at her gloved fingers tucked inside his arm, and again he noticed the elegantly tailored uniform Minerva had sewn for him by hand. The brass buttons and gold braid contrasted with the gray wool, a shade or two darker than the beautiful gray horses he had spent twenty years breeding.

"John William; Robert," he called, and his sons rode up alongside the carriage. "John William, twelve years old is very early to ask a young man to take on this kind of responsibility." He paused to collect his thoughts. "You have helped me with the farming. You have been a lot of help to me with the work, son. We have discussed the breeding program. I trust your judgment. I know you won't have the strength or enough helpers to geld the young horse colts. Just be careful about separating the bloodlines well before the fillies are yearlings.

"Well, you may not have much to worry about there. The army may take them as soon as they are old enough to ride. We will have to see how this thing goes. Just be sure to keep the broodmares and the studs hidden in those central pastures where no one can see them unless they go looking for them.

"You will have full responsibility for the farm, now. Your mother will help you. Do you think you can deliver a foal alone if a mare has trouble? Most of the able-bodied men are leaving; you won't have much help."

John William nodded in response to each of his father's directions, thinking hard to digest and retain them. Burrell looked at ten year old Robert and studied him for a moment.

"Robert, running this horse farm is up to you and John William while I'm gone. Now, John William is in charge. He is the boss, and you are the straw boss, understand? So you pay very close attention to what is going on. Your input will be valuable to John William.

"Now, John William, being the boss does not mean you can act big and boss everybody around. It means that you have the responsibility for the planning while I'm gone. Planning how and where everyone can best help to get the job done, and keeping this farm running is no small task. As second in command, Robert's observations and suggestions may be very valuable; take him seriously and work together."

He turned his head to look at the girls in the back of the buggy. "Do you girls see your place in this picture? I expect you to help your mother without a lot of arguing and fighting between yourselves. Now, you may… no, you will have new chores with me gone. I expect you both to act older than you are and be a lot of help. Your mother is in charge of the family, but if John William needs your help, do your best to help him, okay?" The two older girls stared at him as if frozen by fear and nodded obediently. The baby girl smiled at her papa and reached out to him. He smiled and caressed her soft reddish blond hair.

Burrell turned back to the road ahead and for a while they rode in silence. "John William," he said, pointing to a spot ahead and to the left. "Mark that rock outcropping. About 20 yards from the lane, you will find a bee hive in a hollow tree. Looks as if lightning struck it. When your mother needs honey for baking; you'll know where to find it. Protect yourself. Take some smoke with you." He touched Minerva on the knee and smiled fondly at her.

The outskirts of Rome, Georgia, came into view, and they could see that the town was full of people. The streets were lined with buggies and wagons. Women were dressed in their Sunday best. Children played along each boardwalk, while mothers called out cautions to stay out of the street. Many men on horseback rode up and down the main street visiting with friends, saying their good-byes. Today the unit was forming up and moving out to fight for the South.

Burrell stopped the buggy near the Emporium. He sat looking at Minerva, his eyes saying more than he would ever have been able to put into words. John William untied his father's favorite gray gelding from the back of the buggy and brought him alongside. Slowly Burrell pulled his gaze away from Minerva and held the baby to him for a moment.

The children lined up beside the buggy horse, and Burrell slowly worked his way down the line, talking individually to each child before giving each a long hug. The last was John William. He looked John William in the eye for a long moment; he nodded as a faint smile spread across his face. "I believe you can do it, son. Make me proud." They hugged, then shook hands as men passing the mantle of responsibility.

Burrell mounted his horse, nodded to Minerva and touched the brim of his hat; then he rode toward the center of town. Most of the mounted men took their cue and also drifted toward the town square. As he reached the square, a man in uniform looked up and saluted, "Major?"

"Have the company form up, Captain."

There were shouted orders, rattling of sabers, and a few horses nickered and danced around with anticipation. Burrell glanced at Minerva, standing in the buggy. He touched the brim of his hat once again and turned his horse east. Three companies of the Georgia Militia rode out of town at a trot.

The town sat in total silence for several minutes after the militia was out of sight, adjusting to the gigantic void that suddenly appeared in their lives. They were dealing with thoughts such as, "How will we manage our lives without them?" "When will they be coming home?" "Will they be coming home?"

Mothers began calling their children back to the wagons. A few wagons began to move slowly down the street toward home. But Minerva just sat there, transfixed. John William asked, "Mama, do we need anything from the Emporium before we start home?" She looked at him as if he were a stranger and blinked a few times. Then she caught a quick breath as if startled and said, "Oh, yes, it would be good to get a sack of flour and a sack of sugar. And get a stick of peppermint for each of the children." She handed him money from her purse and didn't move from the buggy, her eyes straight ahead.

As she stared, her eyes seeing nothing in particular, a friend walked up and touched her arm, "Minerva, are you all right? I didn't see you say 'good-bye' to Burrell."

Minerva drew a startled breath, "Oh, Lydia, I didn't see you." Minerva looked at her for a moment. Lydia's eyes were swollen; her face was red-blotched and tear-streaked. Minerva nodded slightly, her eyes softened and she patted the hand of her friend, "We said our good-byes last night."

Shouldering the sack of flour John William said, "And four sticks of peppermint, too."

"Don't you mean five, John William?" "No. Just four. None for me. Thanks."

He loaded the supplies in the back, climbed into the buggy and picked up the reins. Robert had tied his horse to the back of the buggy for him. John William looked around to be sure everyone was settled in the buggy. He slapped the reins on the horse's rump, clucked a few times and they began a slow, silent ride home.

****

Within a week of Burrell's leaving, Minerva assembled her children, Jessie and her family. Everyone gathered in the parlor; when the chairs were all filled, the younger children sat crossed legged on the floor….there were wall to wall children. Everyone knew from Minerva's demeanor that this was a solemn occasion; there was no giggling or twittering.

Minerva went to the dining room to retrieve a straight backed chair for herself. She took a deep breath and sat down very slowly and gracefully. She smoothed the fabric of her skirt; then gently she patted her knees with just her fingers. She solemnly studied each face in the room.

"When I was just a girl in South Carolina," she began, "my sisters and I would sit on the porch shelling peas with my Grandma Spalding. It was sort of fun just being together, talking and laughing. Grandma sometimes told us tales she remembered from her youth. She was a young girl during the Continental War, the War of Independence from England.

"Her parents were instrumental in organizing the colonists in South Carolina. Meetings were held in their home to make plans and direct the war effort. Her father was a major target for the Red Coats.

"The Red Coats were sweeping through their area, killing and burning, showing no mercy for women and children. Her father was captured by a small squad of English soldiers and they were about to hang him from the big Magnolia tree in front of his house. The thing that saved his life was that he had taught his wife and seven daughters to shoot.

"The girls sneaked out behind the shrubbery and began firing just before they slipped the noose over his head. They were good shots, too. And catching the Red Coats unaware, there really was not much of a fight.

She hesitated for a minute, thinking about the enormity of that situation. "I asked Grandma if she really killed a man. She said, 'Two.'

"'But Grandma,' I said, 'Didn't you feel bad for killing them?'

"'No, darling,' she said. 'Men do terrible things during war times. My sisters and I were to be their prize once they had hanged my papa. We would not have lived until the morning.'"

She sat very quietly, looking back in her mind, picturing the scene as her grandmother had described it.

She slowly studied the face of each of the girls. "Do you girls understand what I mean by 'prize'?"

Stony silence filled the room.

"Well, now," she drew in a deep breath, "the thing for us to do is make sure that we learn how to shoot well in case we need to defend ourselves.

"Before he left, Burrell made sure that we have six rifles and six pistols, plenty of powder and shot.

"John William and Robert will be instructors for anyone who wants to learn. Libby and Mary Elizabeth, I would not expect you to be strong enough to shoot a rifle, but you both need lessons with a pistol.

"Jessie, I know Mr. Burrell taught you to shoot a pistol, but I think you and I both need to practice a little to be sure. If it is okay with you, let's teach William and Mose to shoot a rifle. Would you want your older girls to learn to shoot a pistol?"

Her gaze fell directly on Jessie's older girls. "Would you girls be afraid to shoot a gun?" Everyone of any size looked at Jessie and slowly shook their heads 'no', they were not afraid.

"Does anyone have anything to add?"

"Okay, then. John William, when you and Robert have a little time, start taking one student each out to an empty pasture to practice. I will teach the girls how to load for those who can shoot."

****

As things turned bad, then worse for the Southern army, the fighting came ever closer to their house. Because there was an iron foundry in Rome, which made locomotives and also rifle balls and cannonballs, the Union army made a spearhead to capture Rome. For almost two years there was a garrison there.

At first they took all the horses old enough to ride and all the livestock they could find. They took all the young horses and left the Barnetts two old geldings to pull the wagon. But John William and Robert kept the breeding stock hidden in the central pasture so they weren't found. Old Mose's main job was to hide their one old milk cow and her bull calf in the central pasture every time Union soldiers came around looking for livestock and food. When the soldiers took all the chickens, Big Jessie managed to hatch a big setting of eggs in the oven. Minerva gave William instructions to hide whenever soldiers came up or else they would take a young black man like him, too.

****

"Robert, have you checked lately to see that the bred mares in the central pasture have water?"

"Three days ago, I think, why"

"This has been a dryer that usual summer, I think," John William paused to wipe the sweat from his brow. "The last time we were up there, the creek had almost stopped flowing. The mares may be drinking from pools by now. We need to keep a close watch. We may have to move them soon, don't you think?"

"Yes, you are probably right. I'll go right now, if you can finish here okay."

"I'll finish here. Thanks, Robert."

Robert straightened his back and stretched it a bit. He slowly walked to the barn door, took his hat from a wall peg and stepped out into the bright sunlight of a hot August afternoon. It was a long walk over to the central pasture, but not worth saddling a horse.

He kicked rocks as he walked along thinking about that central pasture. He had always wondered why Papa cleared around the edges and left such a big area in trees. "Guess I know now," he thought. "He was not too tired or too lazy to clear it. He must have known it might be important someday for folks not to know exactly how many horses we have. Why, if those mares were out in plain sight, the Union army would have taken them, too, just like they took the geldings they saw from the lane. Well, we have been blessed that General Sherman finally moved his men out of Rome. But, I really don't know if you can call it a blessing since he burned the foundry and most of the other businesses in town. But, I sure am glad they are gone."

He reached where the horses were grazing and walked down to the stream. "John William was right. There is not much water left here. We need to move these mares tomorrow, but they will be okay overnight." He petted a couple of the heaviest mares and felt their bellies. "See you tomorrow, girls."

There would be more breeze if he walked on top of the ridge down by the lane, so he walked straight toward the lane, then he would turn toward home. "I can check the fence from up there, too," he thought.

Walking along, Robert replayed his previous conversation with John William in his mind. "Well, John William and I have been doing this for nearly four years. He has not been demanding about who does the work or when to do it. But he sure has learned how to frame a suggestion with good enough reasons to make me volunteer. I'll really be glad when Papa gets home so I can go back to being just a kid!" He thought for a minute. "Now, that really is a childish thought, Robert Barnett!" he said out loud. He began surveying their true situation. The South is losing the war; there is no pretending there. We are in real danger here, and we haven't heard from Papa in months. He could be dead or captured. We have been really lucky that the Yankees took only horses and food from us while they were stationed so close. It could have been much worse."

As he reached the top of the ridge, his foot slipped on some dry grass and he fell flat of his face. Raising his head, he heard horse's hooves on the lane, not fast, just the plot, plot, plot of a gentle trot. "What is this?" he thought. "Six, maybe seven horses. On the lane! I see blue! Yankee blue!" his mind was screaming at him. "Yankee soldiers are coming!"

He shinnied back down the incline and ran across the meadow to the house. With any luck he could get there before the soldiers. "Run faster, Robert," he thought, "there is the barn."

"John William! John William!" he shouted, "Yankees are coming! Yankees are coming!"

John William stepped outside the barn and blinked at the sunlight. He heard, "Yankees are coming! Run for the house! Tell Mama! I'll close all the gates to slow them down!"

Running toward the house, John William waved his arms wildly and yelled, "Everybody into the house! Yankees are coming! Everybody in the house! Yankees are coming!" People looked up from their chores and began to run for the house, herding children as they went. Chickens and geese flapped their wings and squawked, scrambling to get out of the way.

Inside the house things were moving fast. Minerva and Libby gathered all the rifles, powder and shot onto the front porch to make a stand there. Mary Elizabeth was put in charge of the 'baby', five year old, Ella Anne. "Now, come here Ella Anne. There is something very important I have to tell you. Yankee soldiers are coming. We don't know how they will act, so we all have to do exactly as Mama laid out. Do you remember how Mama made us practice? I am to stand behind Mama, and you are to stand behind me. At all times, Ella Anne, you are to stand behind me! Will you hold on to the back of my skirt for me? If I move, you move, but stay behind me, okay?" Ella Anne stared, wide-eyed, frozen with fear, and slowly nodded her head. "Good girl, now help me carry these powder horns and patches to the porch. You are being such a big girl."

Hurriedly, Robert climbed the twelve steps to join his family on the front porch. Everyone was taking their assigned positions; Robert took his place to the left of his mother, holding a rifle by the barrel. John William was on her right, holding a rifle by the barrel. Libby stood behind the gap between Mama and John William, holding a rifle by the barrel, ready to hand it to Mama should she need it. Mary Elizabeth stood behind the gap between Mama and Robert, holding a rifle by the barrel. Ella Anne stood behind Mary Elizabeth, with a tight grasp on the back of her skirt. And Minerva stood in the middle of her family with a rifle cradled in her arm, her eyes slightly narrowed, ready for the worst.

Slightly to the left and back stood Big Jesse with her family crowded behind her. Her big arms reached out and back of her, marking the boundary for her children, much as a hen spreads her wings in protection of her chicks.

As the soldiers rode into the large yard, the Yankee Captain surveyed the area. Seeing no men, he gave the order to dismount. He touched the brim of his hat and said, "Begging your pardon, ma'am. My men and I have ridden a long way. We are tired and hungry, and our horses need a rest." A fat, red hen, singing quietly to herself, ventured close to the horses. The nearest soldier grabbed the hen and quickly rung her neck, then stood there holding the hen by the feet.

At the noise of the squawking hen, Ella Anne leaned her head to the side, trying to see around Mary Elizabeth's skirt. Mary Elizabeth quickly pushed her head back.

"You are not welcome here," Minerva said, shouldering the rifle.

"If you think one woman with a rifle is going to stop us, you are as dumb as that old hen," the Captain sneered.

John William and Robert shouldered their rifles. Big Jesse slipped her hand into the big pocket of her apron and slowly pulled out a cocked pistol.

The Captain was so surprised at this that he demanded, "What are you doing, letting a fat, black slave have a gun?"

"I am not a slave!" Jesse shot back. "Mr. Burrell gave me and my husband our freedom twenty years ago. Wrote it on a paper, saying I am free! I work here 'cause I want to! He taught me how to shoot, too. Said someday I might need to defend myself. And that is what I am doing today."

The soldiers, who thought they were going to have easy access to this house and women, were getting tired of waiting. "Let's rush 'em, Captain!"

Minerva held a steady bead on the Captain. "Sir, you will be the first one to fall."

They all hesitated. The Captain slowly lifted his hand and motioned for his men to mount.

Little black Toby, wearing a short shirt and sparkling white diaper toddled out near the big Magnolia tree in the yard. He had been following the hen. The burly Sergeant, who was nearest to the boy, grabbed him by the ankles and swung his head hard against the tree. Blood and brains covered the tree trunk, the ground and the Sergeant's boots.

A rifle ball ripped into the tree just above the man's head. On the porch, there was a scramble of rifles changing hands, and instantly Minerva held a fresh rifle. The boys shouldered their rifles and Libby began reloading the spent one. No one else moved.

"The next one is yours, Captain!" Minerva promised. "Boys, the Captain is mine! Each of you pick a target, and remember the only way to stop them is to shoot to kill!"

One by one the sullen soldiers mounted and turned their horses toward the road. The Sergeant stood there for just a moment, looking at what he had done; then he quickly mounted and followed his companions as they rode away.

****

They all stood there in shock for a few minutes, then Big Jesse ran to her baby and cradled him to her. "I should have shot him, Miss Minerva. I had the gun in my hand, but it all happened too fast. I couldn't see what was going to happen!" She began to weep and sob; the deep, moaning sobs of a mother whose heart was breaking. She finally found an avenue to vent the pain she felt, and for long minutes she held her baby to her and rocked back and forth, wailing loudly, releasing the anguish inside of her.

"Mama, we should have done something!" Mary Elizabeth was saying. "We should have shot him! Shot them all!"

"No, child." Minerva stared with a blank look on her face and shook her head slightly. "We did the only thing we could do. If we had shot one of them, they would all have rushed us. And, I'm afraid we could not have gotten them all." She thought a minute and added, "Protecting ourselves is one thing, but 'Retribution belongs to the Lord.'"

Minerva opened the front door and began motioning for all the children to go inside. Big Jesse's children stood in shock, hesitant to leave the sight of their mother holding her baby and moaning. "Come on inside, children, and let her have her time to grieve."

"Mama, would you have shot him? Could you really shoot a man?" John William asked.

"Yes, son, I would have shot him. To save my children, I could have shot him. If you point a gun, you have to know in your heart that you intend to use it." She sat down on a chair, and said "Ella Anne, come here to me, baby. Let me hold you for a while."

"Well, the milk cow is still tied up in the barn. I'll bet by now she has kicked over the milk bucket or stepped in it. I'd better go out and turn her loose. Robert, will you sneak down toward the lane and make sure they don't decide to turn and come back? Stay well hidden in the brush, now."

The girls began putting the rifles back in the cabinet. Suddenly Robert was back at the door. "Mama, the soldiers rode east. Come look!" Everyone hurried onto the porch.

Billows of black smoke rose above the trees. Everyone stood in stunned silence. Finally, Minerva said, "The Grossmann place! Lydia was not a really strong woman. And she had three half-grown daughters." As she stood looking at the smoke, she said very quietly, "Thank you, Lord. That could have been us." Her grip on the porch post relaxed and she slowly sank down on the steps.

Chapter Two
Papa's Home!

Burrell Barnett felt like an old man; he was bone weary. The horse beneath him was weary, too. "Sure not the fine young horse I rode out on," he thought. That beautiful gray gelding had been blown out from under him by a 32 pounder cannon round at St. Mary's Church. A bad day for the South! He had lost most of his unit that day. Really took a whipping.

"We were given bad information. In the two battles before that our information was right, and we surprised the Yankees. Maybe we were too confident. But this time we were caught in an open field, no brush to cover us. This time they knew we were coming, and they were ready for us. They had cannons hidden near the church and twice as many riflemen as we were told. I lost most of my company in that charge. Men and horses were strewn all across that field."

Since then he had ridden whatever horse he could catch.

He noticed the tattered gray coat, held closed with only two brass buttons. He addressed the coat, "Yes, we have been through the thick of it, haven't we? And yet, we did come through it! That is the miracle!"

He slowly passed the burned out Grossmann place, nothing left but the black, charred corners. The chimneys stood as lonely sentinels over the carnage that took place here. "Wilhelm fell in Virginia, too," he thought, "at St. Mary's Church when we were attached to Maj. Gen. Wade Hampton. Well, I'm glad he doesn't have to come home to see this. Lydia gave Minerva some potato eyes for our garden when they came here."

He thought of his own home and family and pressed the horse on a little faster. But the animal was worn completely out and soon slowed down again. "There are the rocks marking the way to the bee hive. Oh, that seems like a lifetime ago."

He finally reached the little lane that lead to his home and saw that the house was still standing. He breathed a deep sigh of relief and his heart began to pound. He wanted to spur the horse to a gallop. He wanted to wave his hat and yell at the top of his lungs, "I'm home! I'm home!" He wanted to see his family streaming out of the house with arms raised to greet him.

But none of that happened. Plop…plop…plop…he slowly drew closer, and still he could not raise his voice to yell, "I'm home!"

He saw Robert chopping wood and headed for him. Finally, between swings of the axe, Robert noticed him and stood stock still for a moment. He dropped the axe and yelled, "Papa's home! Papa's home!"

The children began running to him from all directions, yelling, "Papa's home! Papa's home!" And finally, Minerva appeared at the door of the house and stood on the porch looking at him, her eyes filled with tears and she, too, ran to meet him. The horse stopped when the children reached him, but Burrell sat there looking at them, drinking in the sight of his wife and his children. He felt them patting him on the legs, holding on to his boots, reaching for his hands. Finally, he wearily dismounted and reached out his arms to hold as many of them as he could. "I'm home," he whispered. "I'm finally home."

Big Jesse came running, too, with questioning eyes. "Mr. Burrell, do you know where he is? Is my Henry coming home?"

"We lost most of our men at St. Mary's church in Virginia, Jessie." He put his arms around her shoulders and they wept together.

****

Several days later, Burrell and Minerva held hands as they sat in the porch swing. "The boys did a fine job of keeping things running," she ventured. "The war has taken away their childhood, but they are fine young men."

He smiled and nodded. They swung in silence for a little while.

"What happened to the big Magnolia that used to be right out there?" Burrell asked.

She thought a few moments, then answered, "We needed it to make little Toby's casket."

The porch swing creaked for a few more minutes. "Well, I always thought we should have a circular flower garden there. Wisteria, azaleas." He looked at the vacant spot for a few minutes then nodded his head, as if he could see just how it would look.

****

It seemed as if it took a month or more for Burrell to get back his strength…and his will to do anything more than sit on the porch swing. He had gone four years with never quite enough food or rest. It had taken a big toll on him.

His family had been very understanding. Everyone continued with their regular busy routine during the day; they let him have time and space to relive memories of the war and to bury them. Minerva had given strict instructions never to ask Papa about the war. "When he feels like it he will tell us," she had explained.

****

Jessie took a glass of spearmint tea to him as he sat in the porch swing, rocking it slowly. She stood there a minute; then she slowly sat down in the chair nearest to him. "I sure do miss my Henry, Mr. Burrell.

"I still remember the day your papa, Mr. William, brought him home from Atlanta. He was tall and strong; he had a real handsome face.

"He didn't understand a word of English at the time, but when our eyes met, I knew that he was going to be mine. I had just turned 15 then, and it was looking like I was going to have to marry my cousin, Jim.

"Mr. William winked at me and said, 'Jessie, look what I brought you.'

"After a couple of months, we knew we was ready, and we said the words and jumped the broom. Wouldn't no minister marry black folks at that time, but we knew in our hearts that God heard us.

"We had six strong, healthy babies. Don't you think my William looks a lot like him, Mr. Burrell?" He nodded.

"I named him after your papa 'cause he brought my Henry to me."

For a while there was silence except for the sounds of nature around them. Burrell finally said, "I remember your wedding day, Jessie. You were beautiful in that white dress that you made. And I don't think I ever saw a happier man than Henry was that day when he could call you his own."

They thought about that day for a while; then Burrell said, "Jessie, what are you cooking for dinner tonight?"

"What do you want for dinner, Mr. Burrell?"

"Do we have any young roosters that we can spare? I have been so hungry for your fried chicken, I just can't seem to get my fill," and they laughed together.

Minerva sat inside looking through the lace curtain at her husband as he sat in the porch swing. It was good to see him laugh. Seemed like sitting in that swing was all he had the will to do ever since he got home.

His face was still handsome, but gaunt. He had a broad forehead, full round cheeks and a square jaw, which he kept neatly covered with a short beard. And those cheeks! When a smile spread across his face, his cheeks jumped up high and made round, rosy mounds beneath his eyes. And his soft brown eyes were so gentle, they shone with love.

"Well, that was the way he used to look," Minerva thought. "He is so thin now that his face sinks in between his cheeks and his jawbone. Rest and Jessie's cooking will fix that part of him. I'll just be so glad when he gets his spirit back."

****

After dinner every evening, the family would gather on the front porch and tell him about things they had done during his absence, decisions they had made, and "Do you think we did the right thing, Papa?"

"Papa, we gave one of our best gray geldings to General Nathan Bedford Forest after he saved Rome from that Yankee, 'Lightning Mule Brigade'," John William ventured.

"Good," Burrell nodded with a tired, half smile. "He was a good soldier."

"We have been very careful about the bloodlines on the horses, Papa," Robert put in. "But we had to cross fence that central pasture to try to keep the young horse colts from fighting. We have a bunch of them that need gelding.

Robert thought a minute. "You did a good thing, Papa, leaving that big central pasture in trees. The Yankees took all of our stock they could see from the road. They even came and took everything that was up around the house. But I guess they never figured there would be livestock in those dense trees."

"And Papa, the Yankees took all of our grain from the barn so there was no way we could raise a crop of wheat or oats," Mary Elizabeth wanted to help tell the story. "Then we had no flour for bread. But Jessie sent her boys out to harvest the buckwheat that grows wild. We ground it ourselves right here. She kept us in buckwheat biscuits and pancakes the whole time," Mary Elizabeth smiled and beamed at Jessie who had just walked out the door.

Ella Anne, always the impulsive one, said, "Papa, tell us what you did during the war." Minerva shot her a look that would crack a rock!

"Well," Burrell began slowly, "I'll tell you about one skirmish I was in somewhere along the Chickamauga in Tennessee.

"There had been a lot of fighting all along that creek, and everybody was so tired. We were hiding in a barn to rest up a bit. Someone up in the hay loft saw some Yankees coming from way off. We knew we were outnumbered; we couldn't just go out and fight them.

"I had everyone strip off their pants and coats and stuff them with hay… some of them naked as a Jay Bird!" he chuckled. "We set them around in several places like men talking or eating. Some of them we stood up with pitchforks and brooms. Then we hid behind a low rock wall not far out in front of the barn.

"The Yankees thought they were sneaking up on us. And when their commander ordered, 'Fire!' we waited for their rifle volley; then we jumped up and fired. When the smoke cleared, there was not a Yankee standing."

The children all clapped their hands and cheered. Burrell slapped his leg and smiled, nodding his head. That was the first real smile they had seen on their papa's face since he came home.

After that he seemed to be not so bottled up inside about the war. His eyes began to take on new life, and he started walking out with John William and Robert in the mornings.

****

On a soft summer evening just before dusk, Burrell and Minerva sat in the porch swing, slowly rocking back and forth. Conversation came even slower. Hints of wisteria, honeysuckle and jasmine wafted by as the soft breeze swirled then fell. It felt good just to rest...just to be together.

"We have made good strides in building the farm back up since the war," Burrell said as the porch swing creaked lazily. "Don't you enjoy that big flower garden right out in front of the house? I do. We needed a circular drive in front of the house. I don't know why I didn't do it sooner."

Minerva nodded. His hand rested on her big tummy as they continued to swing.

"Oh, I felt him kick again."

"Why are you so sure this is going to be a boy?" Minerva asked. He thought a few minutes. "I've seen you carry two boys, then three girls. We are back to the boy shape again. I'm sure of it! What will we name him? We have used up the standard names already."

They swung in silence for a while. "My mother's maiden name was Garrett," Minerva said. "I've always thought that had a pretty flow to it, a manly sound."

"And my mother's maiden name was Aycock. Garrett Aycock Barnett has a real nice rhythm to it, don't you think? All the Barnett families have Williams, Johns and Roberts. He will surely stand out in the crowd."

She looked thoughtful for a minute. "Garrett Aycock Barnett. That has a good feel to me. Garrett Aycock Barnett it is then."

They sat in silence again. Burrell said, "You know that gentle old mare you like so well is due about the same time you are. Could be that would make a good saddle horse for young Garrett when he is old enough to need a horse of his own.

"Minnie, I've been thinking." He knew she did not like to be called that. He just did it once in a while to get her riled up. "I've been watching the boys. John William is 16 now. Since he doesn't have the responsibility of running the farm, I see him taking an interest in what is going on in the government. Reconstruction has been hard on everyone, but John William studies the laws word for word. He knows what is really legal for them to do and what is not. Right now there is nothing he can do about it, but times will get better.

"The boys did a fine job running the farm while I was gone so that our taxes are all paid. That is why nobody has been able to grab our house and land. You know, people I talk to just have a hard time understanding how those two boys held this all together.

"Well, anyway, I want you to help me watch him. He may have the calling for a law profession. We'll have to think on that."

Minerva nodded thoughtfully, "He sure kept things straight while you were gone. Kept track of what money we had to spend and what needed to be paid. Made sure legal things were taken care of in a timely manner. I just had not noticed that he was interested in law on a bigger realm."

They continued to swing in silence for a while. "Robert likes working with the horses and the land. It might be good for him to study at an agriculture school, learn the newest methods and ideas on farming and breeding. Even if a man knows his trade, he needs some basic education behind him. We'll watch them for a year or two and see what develops."

****

Robert had seen the doctor's buggy out front as he walked up. He came in the back door just in time to hear the girls' excited voices, "It's a boy. It's a boy, just like Papa said. Young Garrett it is!"

"Is Mama okay?"

Burrell answered that as he came down the stairs, "She will be okay. This was a pretty hard delivery for her. We knew her age would be a factor in this one."

"But she is going to be all right, isn't she?"

"Yes, it will just take a little time for her to get her strength back, but she has the girls to take over for her. She and Jessie can keep them organized and everything will be just fine."

"It's a horse colt, Papa. Old Delta delivered this morning. The colt looks fine, but Delta delivered pretty slowly this time. I think we ought to give her a good year to rest before breeding her back.

"Young Garrett, huh? How about that? I'm no longer the youngest son!"

Chapter Three
John William Comes Home

Burrell, Minerva, and the girls rode in the buggy. Robert and young Garrett drove the buckboard with two extra grays tied behind. John William was bringing a friend home from law school. They rode along talking excitedly about seeing him after so long a time. They were early enough to get a place right beside the platform at the train station. They would be able to see him when he first stepped from the train.

They could see the smoke in the distance. They could hear the whistle; then they heard the steam hiss as the train began to stop. The horses danced around, jerking the buggy back and forth. And then, there he was!

Slender, dark haired and handsome, young John William Barnett had recently graduated with a Law Degree from Yale Law School. He was dressed in the latest fashion, sporting a new black bowler hat. Grandpa Barnett's gold pocket watch and chain draped across the front of his brocaded vest let everyone know they were seeing someone important. People at the station just kept glancing at him.

After hugs and kisses for all of his family, John William remembered to introduce his friend. "Everyone, this is my friend, John Bailey from North Carolina. We kind of gravitated together because we're both from the South, and we became very good friends. John, this is my father, Burrell; my mother, Minerva; my sister, Mary Elizabeth; my sister, Ella Anne; my brother, Robert, and this is my brother, young Garrett. He couldn't resist tussling young Garrett's hair.

"Why does everyone call me 'young' Garrett? I'm twelve years old now!"

John Bailey was a true gentleman of the South. He shook hands with the men, even young Garrett, and tipped his hat to the ladies, but his eyes never completely left Mary Elizabeth. She had her papa's soft brown hair, and big brown eyes that were gentle. They seemed to say that she was at peace. She had an easy smile that spread across her whole face. When her lips smiled, her eyes smiled too.

The whole family was beginning to notice the attraction between these two. John William broke the silence, "We come bearing gifts! Let's go see if they have unloaded our luggage yet."

There was a lot of baggage. These two young men were leaving school after six years. There were two steamer trunks, several valises, and between them they had a pretty good sized law library.

"Young Garrett, will you drive the ladies home? I'll ride in the buckboard and talk with the men."

Young Garrett missed that one altogether. He did not feel a bit slighted because this was his time to shine. He knew he could handle a team and buggy. He just did not get the opportunity to show his skill very often. With his dad and Robert around, he always had to do the little chores. Why, when John William and Robert were his age they were running the farm while Papa was away in the war! No, sir, he did not mind chauffeuring the ladies in the least.

****

Pulling away from the train station, Burrell said, "Now in about a week – after yall get settled in and rested – we will have a big welcome home party."

"Well, give me all the news," John William said as they started home. Robert and Papa looked at each other; the smile of a shared secret crossed their faces. Papa spoke first. "Robert is planning to marry soon," and he shot Robert a big grin.

"Hey, that's great, Robert. Who is the lucky girl?"

"Do you remember that skinny little Masters girl? Well, she isn't so skinny anymore!"

John William's eyebrows shot up. "Whooo, hooo. She grew up good, did she?"

"I'll say. You'll meet her at the party. Now you remember, she's mine!

"You know I've been home from college for over two years now and saving every dime. Papa helped me buy the old Grossmann place just up the lane from home. The carpetbaggers passed it over because the big house was burned down. I figure we can start out like Mama and Papa did; build a little house to live in while we get started."

"When is the wedding?"

"We haven't set a date yet, but soon. We just closed the deal on the land. I've got to get a house built first. I don't want to spend my honeymoon in Papa's house!"

"You can count on me to help. How about you, John? Can you handle a hammer and saw?"

"You bet I can!" John was delighted to be included. He had been thinking that he really did like this family.

"With four of us working on it, we should have you a nice little house built in no time. You might have a bride sooner than you thought, Robert."

"What is new with the girls? I see they surely have grown into young ladies," John William asked.

"Well, aside from growing up, they are still the same. Mary Elizabeth is as gentle and lady-like as ever. She is very much in demand. With beaus calling several times a week, she keeps the household in a perpetual uproar. And we must mind our manners and dress for dinner every evening.

"Ella Anne is still the spitfire she always was, although she is beginning to purr once in a while. But she still has a mind of her own. She rides a lot and sews a little. Just like always. She has been reading Robert's books on terracing, crop rotation and fertilizing; and she argues with him sometimes about the way he does things. That girl will push some man into being well-to-do someday. He will have to work hard to stay ahead of her."

Things were quiet for a moment; then John William asked a burning question, "Pa, have you had any word from Libby?"

"No, Son. We did hear that there had been a bad outbreak of smallpox in that area of Missouri where she and Bill settled. Last we heard she was expecting her first child. Your mother has been really worried. I'm worried! I guess I will have to make a trip out there soon to find out for sure, but with no letter from her, I'm afraid the news is bad."

Conversation fell away and they rode in silence, thinking of all the possibilities…trying to find some positive reason there had been no word.

Finally Burrell broke the silence, "Well, I've talked half the way home. Tell me about law school."

"The studies were tedious; the beds were hard; the food was bad; the house mother was old; but those Connecticut women will give you an education that you won't forget!" They had a big laugh out of that.

"So now you are a barrister! What about you boys? What are your plans? You have to find a place to hang that new shingle on the wall."

"We have been considering being partners, Papa. We get along well together. We have been study partners for some time now, and our thinking seems to complement each other. You know, we seem to catch the weak spots in each other's logic.

"What does it look like around here, Papa? Do you think Rome could support another law firm?"

"An honest one, it could!"

****

Young Garrett had taken the lead on the way home so the ladies would not have so much dust in their faces. He was having a grand time being the chauffeur while Mama and the girls made plans for the evening. Papa had given him a big responsibility, handling a team, taking care of the women. It would have been nice to be included with the men, but there he would feel like a boy…here he felt he was doing a man's job.

25

"Mary Elizabeth, did you see the way John William's friend kept looking at you? And he is real nice looking, too." Mary Elizabeth blushed.

"Oh, hush now, Ella Anne. Don't you try to get something stirred up," Minerva put in.

"Now when we get home, I want you girls to get freshened up as quickly as possible; then set the table. I'm sure Jessie will have dinner almost ready, and I'll see what I can do to help her." Minerva's thoughts were on her duties as a hostess. "Your papa has been fattening a calf to roast for the party. We could bake one of those young turkeys for tomorrow. Anyone have any suggestions for the rest of the week?"

Ella Anne was quick to contribute, "One of those young geese has been very fresh! Chasing me every time I go outside the yard! I would like to see him on the table!"

Young Garrett spoke what was in his heart, "I suppose since we are having company, Jessie will keep us in those good pies she makes, won't she? I'll bet the blackberries have put on enough for one pie already."

Mary Elizabeth chimed in, "I think she is making sweet potato pie tonight. That is John William's favorite."

When they reached home, Big Jessie and her whole family came running out to greet John William. He gave her a big hug and commented on how much each of the children had grown. Big Jessie had grandchildren now, and she wanted to show off each one.

Then Minerva was back in charge. "Now, John William, things have changed a little while you have been away. Young Garrett has your old room, so I thought we would put you and John in the room next to him for the time being. It has two beds in it, and yall have been roommates for a long time. Is that all right with you?" She looked from one young man to the other searching for some sign of approval or disapproval.

"That will be real fine, Mrs. Barnett," John Bailey offered. "Now that I've met John William's family, we have a lot to talk about."

Minerva looked toward Big Jessie's group and asked, "Will some of you boys take their luggage up to their room?"

****

"Tell us about your home in North Carolina, John," Burrell said. Seeing the color rise in his face, Burrell realized he had interrupted the young man's gazing at Mary Elizabeth across the table. The color rose in her face, too. "She had been gazing back," her father thought with a twitch of his eyebrow. He looked at Minerva and smiled.

Later, Ella Anne elbowed John Bailey and reminded him to eat.

After dinner was finished and everyone had chatted awhile, Minerva announced, "We will have pie and coffee in the parlor." John William brought a big box downstairs in which he had stored gifts he brought home for each member of the family. Everyone was seated and waited expectantly. This was like a birthday party!

First, for Mama was the latest fashion in hats: small and black with sassy, satin-black feathers at one side. In a certain light, the feathers had an iridescent hint of the darkest green. Very dressy! "Is this what ladies are wearing in the North, now?" she asked as she removed the long hat- pin and stepped to a wall mirror to try it on.

For Papa, a curved stem smoking pipe with scroll carved into the bowl, imported from Ireland.

For each of the girls, a bolt of cloth -- pink for Mary Elizabeth and mint green for Ella Anne.

For Robert, a brocaded waist coat. "This will look real sharp under your black coat, Robert. I'm glad to see you are still about the same size as me. I think it will fit."

"Just in time for my wedding!"

Last he brought out the most exciting gift of all. For young Garrett, a Louisville Slugger baseball bat. "This is the latest rage, young Garrett. A bat like this nearly won the World Championship Series this year. The finest bat made, and the wood is almost guaranteed not to split."

He had everyone's attention. "<u>Nearly</u> won the World Championship Series?" someone asked.

"Yes, came very close. You see, Pete Browning was the star player for the Louisville Eclipse. The game was really close and in Browning's last at-bat, his bat broke! This 17 year old kid was there that day, and he took Browning home with him to his father's woodworking shop. Browning told him exactly how he wanted a bat to be and the kid built it. The next day Browning got three hits with it! If he had had that bat earlier, Louisville might have won the series."

"Hey! With you in law school, how do you know so much about baseball?" Burrell reasoned.

"Aw, Pa, don't be unhappy with me. With all that studying, you have to get away once in a while to clear your head."

"That is the truth, Mr. Barnett. We did not go very often, but when we did, we were ready to study when we got back. He did excellent on his Barr Exam."

Burrell broke out in a big laugh; then the two younger men gratefully joined in.

As everyone oowed and ahhed over their gifts, John William looked around the room. "Jessie?" he called. "Jessie, can you come in here for a minute?"

In a few seconds Big Jessie showed up, still drying her hands on her apron. "Yes, John William? What can I do for you?"

"It's what I can do for you, Jessie." He brought out a snow white, knitted shawl and placed it around her shoulders. "This will make you look extra special on Sunday mornings, Jessie."

She lovingly touched his hands as he placed the shawl on her shoulders; then her hands slid down to feel the softness of the shawl. As she pulled the ends across her big bosoms, big tears welled up in her eyes. "Mr. John William, you are too good to me," she said, hugging the shawl tightly to her, "Too good."

"Jessie, you are family!" He grinned mischievously, "Now where is my sweet potato pie?"

Her smile spread across her whole face and down into her soul as she hurried off to oversee things in the kitchen.

****

Early next morning, Robert woke John William about the crack of dawn. "If we hurry, we can have the feeding all done before breakfast, brother," he whispered. "Do you want to wake your friend, John, too?"

"It's all right, I'm awake, and I'd like to go."

"Okay, meet you downstairs. Jessie has coffee made."

****

While Robert was locking the feed barn door John William had his first opportunity to ask Robert about his college experience. "What was Agricultural College like, Robert? You have been doing this all your life. Did you learn anything new?"

"I learned a lot of new things that have worked out good here. Things like rotating crops every year so that they don't take the same nutrients out of the soil year after year. I plant vetch for winter grazing; it returns potassium to the soil. Did you know that planting peas in your field can actually be profitable? It gives Mama and Jessie a lot of peas to can for winter. Cows and horses can graze them, and at the end of the season, you plow the vines under. It returns nitrogen to the soil. Quite a slick trick, don't you think?

"And they are learning more about genetics all the time. You know, what makes the foal take certain of the mare's characteristics, and take certain of the stud's characteristics. I was really interested in that. That is something Papa has worked on all his life. He did it by instinct, but now they are beginning to understand why.

"And I studied a little bit of literature, mostly, well, everything we studied was written in English. We did not go into Latin or Greek, like I'm sure you did. I understand you studied Hebrew, also.

"And we had a lot of math courses. Got to know if you are making a profit or not!" he laughed.

"It sounds pretty balanced, but concentrated on what you really are interested in."

"That's right. And Papa let me pick out six mares to take with me when I move onto my place. That was two years ago; now I have eight mares and two young geldings. I may need your help in breaking them. Are you still tough enough to stay on a young horse?" he said with a broad smile.

John Bailey was drinking all this in.

****

After dinner that evening, the young people took over the porch, and Burrell and Minerva sat in the Parlor quietly. Minerva took up her hand work from the sewing basket that always sat by her chair. Burrell sat pensively drawing on his new pipe and waited for his coffee to cool a bit. Finally he reached for his cup and said, "You know, Min, we won't

have a lot of young people around very much longer, and that's sad. I do enjoy their nonsense and watching them grow. We may lose Robert and Mary Elizabeth both this summer. And I don't know yet what John William's plans are."

"That is very true. We know Robert is getting married as soon as he can get his house built; that is already set. Mary Elizabeth is mature enough to know her own mind. But don't forget your spitfire is just now beginning to blossom. I predict things will be lively around here for a while yet."

****

Hendersonville, North Carolina was a fairly peaceful little town. The families that lived around there were settled, having lived there for years, and very seldom did a newcomer move into town. Occasionally, a Saturday night brawl broke out at the local saloon. But after spending a night in jail, and with throbbing heads, each side usually went their ways without too many hard feelings.

This particular Monday morning, Jeff Dodd hurried home from town and started up the stairs to his room with saddlebags across his arm. The quick cadence of his steps caught his mother's attention.

Jeff was searching through drawers and folding things to fit into the saddlebags. He looked up when his mother appeared in the doorway. "Now, exactly where in Georgia does John live, Ma?"

"Not far across the state line into Georgia," she answered. "Near a little town called Habersham – in Habersham County. He said it was good, rich farm land, supposed to be a pretty little valley with the Blue Ridge Mountains off to the north. It shouldn't be more than three or four days ride.

"John sure has a lot of guts. He didn't say much when he left. Just said he had a new bride, took six mares from our string and headed out. The mares were all bred at the time, but I guess by now he would be happy to see you riding up on that big sorrel stud of yours.

"What has you suddenly wanting to visit John?"

"Well, Ma, I have done pretty good buying off the ships that dock along Pamlico Sound and freighting things inland. I'll keep doing the same thing. I just need a little change of scenery."

She raised an eyebrow and cut her eyes at him. "I know you, Jeff Dodd. You need to get out of the country because of some angry father or a jealous husband. Well, when you get there, you remember that John has his young sister-in-law living with them. And you leave her alone, do you hear me?

"I've been trying to get you to marry Dora Alcott for several years now. She loves the ground you walk on. I don't see why you don't…."

"Ma," he interrupted, "I'm going to leave my wagons here until I find out where I'm going to set up. Now, don't you get mad and sell them. I'll be back to get them, okay?"

Twenty seven year old Jeff Dodd did attract the ladies, sometimes too easily for his own good.

****

Ma was right, John was happy to see Jeff and his big stud. The mares had all foaled and it would be time to breed them again soon.

John was happy to see his brother and catch up on all the news from home. Jeff pitched right in helping with the work, and John was overjoyed with the fast progress they made building up his new horse farm. So enthused was he, that he didn't notice anything was wrong. His wife, Sarah, pointed out that she had seen the glances Jeff was exchanging with her little sister, Maribelle.

"Maribelle is way too young to stir up that kind of feelings, especially about a man more than ten years older than her. Why, he has such easy ways around a woman, she would be easy pickings for him. You've got to do something, John. He can't stay here."

Next evening after dinner, John noticed a perky little swish in Maribelle's skirt as she carried dishes from the table to the kitchen. And he could see that Jeff was enjoying it.

"Jeff, let's walk down and look at the mares while the women clean the dishes."

"Sure, I'll get my hat."

When they got to the small trap where John was holding the mares to watch for them to come back in season, John put his foot on the bottom rail and stood looking at the horses. "I am beginning to believe all of them took, don't you?"

"Well, you won't be able to tell for sure for another month," Jeff said.

"I know, but I can't wait that long. I'll have to take my chances with the mares."

"What do you mean?" Jeff asked.

Sarah and I have noticed your eyeing Maribelle, and I can't take that chance, Jeff. You have been a lot of help to me, and I appreciate the use of your stud. But I can't help it if you are my older brother; I'm going to have to ask you to leave."

"Well, I..." Jeff stammered.

"Tonight!" John said flatly. "I'll help you pack your gear, and Sarah will pack you some food. I don't know how far you will want to ride before you stop." John looked at his brother for a few seconds, then turned sharply and walked toward the house.

****

Spring, 1888, in Georgia held a beauty too rich to compare. One simply had to stop a moment and absorb the quiet splendor of the countryside. Burrell pulled his team of matched gray mares in and just sat in the buggy looking at and listening to the country he loved. Wildflowers growing along the roadside and peach trees in blossom nearby filled the air with nature's own perfume. Bees busily dipped their tails into this flower and that, sampling a number of flowers until they were so heavily laden with pollen they could barely fly. One by one they joined the beeline back to the old hollow tree.

"Yup, there are the rocks that mark the trail into the woods. This old country has come a long way since the war," he thought. "The years have covered the scars of the land and softened men's hearts just a little. When I came home from Appomattox and saw the waste and ruin, I thought my heart would surely break."

A mocking bird scolded him for his gloomy reverie; then quickly changed and sang four different tunes before the team began to dance

around and the rattling harness chains frightened it away. "We certainly live in a land of promise," he thought as he started on down the lane.

He thought, too, of the happy occasion prompting his trip to town. It was so good to have his family together again, and this would be a big party for John William's homecoming. "Yes, we are a very affluent people," he said aloud.

Burrell was almost enjoying his time alone as he drove into town to get supplies for Minerva. His thoughts trailed off to the excitement of having John William home, and getting to know his friend, John. "I think I like that young man," he thought. "He seems to be pretty well grounded and responsible."

He passed the old Grossmann place and remembered the sad memories connected with it. "Well, we will start making some new, happy memories there soon. I think Robert picked a really good girl to marry. Sue Ellen seems very amiable, not demanding at all. They should have a good life together."

When he reached town, he went directly to the Emporium. Mr. Goldman was talking to a man Burrell had not met before, a very tall, broad shouldered man with thick reddish-brown hair, trimmed very neatly. He was very well dressed, too, nicely cut jacket, fitted trousers and English riding boots. Not the dress of a professional man. Burrell thought he might be a successful merchant.

Mr. Goldman looked up as the bell above the door rang. He nodded and spoke to Burrell. Burrell handed him the list Minerva had made, and said, "We'll be having a welcome home party for John William this weekend. Minerva needs extra. You and Mrs. Goldman come and bring your family. Oh, and help me spread the word, will you. You see almost everyone. I'll be over at the livery for a while."

Mr. Goldman began filling the order, and Burrell and the stranger exchanged names. "I haven't seen you around these parts. Where do you come from, Jeff Dodd?"

"I'm from western North Carolina. I'm in the freighting business. I buy directly from the ships that dock along Pamlico Sound, and I'm looking to extend my business further inland."

"Well, if you are still in town this weekend, be my guest at the party we are having for my son, John William. He has just come home from Yale."

Out of the corner of his eye, Burrell recognized a figure walking past the Emporium, and he hurried to the door. "Oh, Judge. Do you have a minute?"

****

When Burrell went to pick up his buggy at the livery stable, Jeff Dodd was currying his horse. "Hello, again," Jeff called out across the horse's back.

Always with an eye for good horseflesh, Burrell walked over to have a look. "This is a magnificent animal! What is he, 16 hands...16.2? Well-muscled, well-balanced, straight legs, good head."

"He is a Morgan, sir. My family breeds them. I can document his parentage for four generations. He stands at stud, if you want to use him," Jeff said.

"The only thing I see wrong with him, son, is his color. I have bred up a line of grays. There is not a colored horse on my farm. Well, I had better stop by the Emporium and be on my way home."

"Would you tell me how to get to your house in case I want to come to the party?"

"I'll do you one better. Ride along with me and have dinner with us. I would like for Robert to see that horse." He thought for a minute, "And we usually have a horse race when everyone gets together for a party such as this will be."

****

"Mama, Ella Anne is putting soot from the lamp chimney on her eyebrows again!" Mary Elizabeth called out.

"Shush, Mary Elizabeth, please don't tell on me. I don't put much, and it makes my eyes look better. You have such big brown eyes, you have no need. My hair and face are so pale, I need some help."

"Okay, but you leave John Bailey alone, you hear?"

"I'll be good, I promise. But I've seen how he looks at you. He wouldn't notice me if I were the Queen of Sheba."

"Girls, come on down and set the table now. Your father will be home soon," Minerva called up the stairs.

As Ella Anne was putting out the plates, she heard voices outside. Moving the lace curtain just slightly, she peeked out the window. "Mary Elizabeth, come here and look at this sorrel horse! Oh!...look at that man!"

Mary Elizabeth was at her side immediately to see what had Ella Anne so excited. She saw the big red horse, and that was a big man; but she had already made her pick so she was not interested. "I don't know why you are going on so at your age."

"I'm almost 17!"

"You are not. You were 16 in December, and this is March. Mama, Ella Anne is peeking out the window at Papa and some man!"

"Ella Anne, where are your manners? Come away from that window!" Minerva scolded as she scurried toward the window. "And set another place at the table; it seems as if your father has brought home a guest. Good Heavens, Ella Anne, he must be ten years older than you!"

****

"Jeff Dodd," Minerva said, as if to herself, when dinner conversation lulled, "Thomas Jefferson Dodd, no doubt."

"No ma'am. Jefferson O'Neal Dodd. There is a wee bit of the Irish in my mother's family."

This started a round of laughter, and he was not a bit embarrassed. He seemed to glory in it. "And I inherited all the Blarney, they say." Again they all laughed aloud, and the dinner conversation was animated and enjoyable.

Burrell studied his guest with a twinkle of merriment in his eye for he liked a person with a lively spirit. "Tell us about your trip over from North Carolina, Jeff."

"Well, there is not much to tell. No rivers to ford; no damsels to rescue. But I am really happy to be here. Georgia must have the prettiest damsels in the whole south," he said, grinning at Ella Anne. She blushed instantly and looked down at her plate. Again Burrell's eyebrow twitched, but this time there was caution on his face instead of a smile.

After dinner the men went out on the porch to smoke – Jeff Dodd had brought Havana cigars.

"So, we have ordered the lumber to start building on a house for Robert and his bride. We figure with four of us working on it, we can have it built pretty fast," John William was saying.

Robert looked up, "Oh, I'm not planning to build a grand house right now; that will come later. I just don't want to be living with my parents."

"I can swing a hammer, and I'm not in any hurry. This is just a scouting trip for me to see if I can expand my freight hauling this far. If you want another hand, just let me know."

"Thanks," Robert said.

"Oh, John William," Burrell interjected. "I talked to Judge Tully while I was in town today. He said you have a big choice to make. If you want to stay near your family and do wills and deeds, he would be happy to see you stay. But if you want to handle case law and make a name for yourself, you should go to Atlanta. Something for you two to think about." He turned his head to include John Bailey in his vision.

John seemed extra quiet this evening. Burrell thought it could be that he would like to spend some time with Mary Elizabeth. "Well, I think it is time for me to turn in. Thanks for the smoke. I'll see you men in the morning."

"I should be heading back to town, too," Jeff said.

"No need for you to ride in the dark. All of our bedrooms are full at the present, but there is a pretty nice room in the stable, if you like."

Burrell stepped just inside the parlor to tell Minerva he was going up to bed.

"We will be up as soon as we finish this hand of cards," she answered. "Okay, folks, this is for the game. Whoever is ahead at the end of this hand wins the game."

Burrell had stepped back outside. "Jeff, I forgot to tell you, I don't usually allow colored stallions on the farm. So, you be sure you keep him locked up tight. I don't want any roan colts. John William, will you show Jeff to the stable?" He passed the parlor just in time to hear the girls squeal with glee, and young Garrett saying, "Aw, Mama, do we have to quit now?"

"Yes, you have to quit now," Burrell answered. "Young Garrett and Ella Anne come on upstairs. Mary Elizabeth can put things away tonight. Coming, Mama?"

As they went up the stairs, you could hear, "I wish yall would stop calling me "young" Garrett. People keep asking me if my first name is 'Young'."

****

As John William was coming back from the stable, he saw John and Mary Elizabeth walking out by the flower garden, so he went on up to bed.

In a little while, when John came in the room, he cleared his throat and quietly asked, "John William are you asleep yet?"

"No, not yet. What is on your mind?"

"It's that Jeff Dodd. He's trouble."

"What do you mean? What kind of trouble?"

"Well, I'm not even from the same county as him, but I've heard of the Dodds. Seems like they don't think rules apply to them. They have a big horse farm and raise very good horses, so no one says too much. But they just have a way of always getting what they want, if you understand what I mean."

"Well, he is a big man; that is true. But he has no idea the kind of trouble he will be in, if he lets that red stud get out of hand. I'll tell Dad tomorrow before the party."

****

Next morning after breakfast, everyone was busy with last minute chores before guests began to arrive. Ella Anne was about half way up the stairs as Minerva was coming down. "Where are you going, honey?" Minerva asked.

"To lay out my dress and slippers for the party."

"But I asked you to clean the inside of the windows on the bottom floor. Have you finished already?"

Ella Anne's long, reddish-blond hair was pulled up on each side like a dog's ears. She was twirling it with one finger as she said, "Aw, Mama, let Jenny do that. It's her job to do the cleaning," and she started on up the stairs.

Minerva made a half smile as she grabbed one dog ear, swinging Ella Anne around and they started down the stairs together. They stopped in front of a large row of window panes. Ella Anne could see Jenny on the outside washing windows. "Would you rather change jobs with Jenny?" Minerva asked; then she pointed toward the cleaning supplies she had laid out for Ella Anne.

Jenny was wearing a shawl around her shoulders against the chill of the early spring morning; soapy water was dripping from her hands and elbows as she cleaned. Ella Anne could just visualize how red her own hands would look after being in that water and cold air. Tears welled up in her eyes as she regretted her insolence and glanced at Mama for forgiveness.

She smiled an understanding smile. "Mary Elizabeth, if you have finished folding napkins, I want you to start carrying out plates and silverware. Set it on those planks Robert set across the saw horses, and be sure to cover them and find a way to anchor the cover down."

****

Somehow everything was done before guests began arriving, and the girls were dressed in their new dresses made from the fabric John William had brought them. Mary Elizabeth was in pink; Ella Anne was in mint green, and Sue Ellen Masters, Robert's intended, was wearing a yellow dress that looked absolutely lovely with her dark hair and eyes. John Bailey was positively beaming as he walked by and commented, "Why, standing there together, you ladies look just like a flower garden."

Before long it was so crowded that it seemed the whole county was there. Well, that was nearly correct because everyone really liked John William. The boys were thrilled to play baseball with young Garrett's new Louisville Slugger. The older women sat on the porch talking. The older men stood in the shade of the trees. The young girls kept the toddlers corralled in the front of the house. Couples walked together out near the flower garden. And somehow Ella Anne couldn't find anything to do, so she walked down to the stable to get a good look at that red horse.

She was just about to open the latch to his stall, when she was startled by Jeff's voice. "I got the impression your papa would hang my hide on the side of the barn to dry if he gets loose. Maybe you should let me bring him out for you."

"Papa worked for a lot of years to find the right bloodlines that beget grays. If we get a foal that is colored, Papa looks around for answers."

Ella Anne stood back and surveyed the red horse from the side. She rubbed his soft muzzle to let him smell of her hand. She studied his head, the set of his eyes and ears. She checked his teeth. She checked his throatlatch and the crest of his neck. She drew out the angle from withers to shoulder; she studied the set of the forelegs and the chest muscling.

She felt his knees and slid her hand down each cannon to the pastern. She measured the length of his loin. She studied the set of his hips to his tail head. She ran her hand over the stifle and gaskin muscling and held his tail aside to check the inside gaskin. She looked at him from the front, the back, and both sides; but never once did she touch the stallion's chest. Jeff could tell she knew horses.

"I wish you were that interested in me," Jeff teased.

She tilted her head slightly and lifted her eyebrows. "There is only one thing I can see wrong with him."

"His color," they said at the same time. Then they started to laugh. "Your papa already told me. Hey, since there is no one around to accuse me of babysitting, would you like to go for a ride?"

A quick, easy smile covered his face at his joke. But Ella Anne was at a stage in her life when being called a 'baby' cut like a knife and she hardly shared his mirth. She stomped off into the barn to get her black mare from the stall.

Ella Anne brushed the animal's back hard and fast with all her hurt and anger spilling out. She threw the saddle blanket on the horse carelessly and had to rearrange it. As she reached for the saddle, Jeff walked up behind her and took it.

"I'm sorry that I hurt your feelings. It was meant to be a harmless joke, but I didn't realize how much it was at your expense."

She said nothing, just watched him saddle the horse.

"I realize that you are a young lady; it's just that you are so small. You make me feel like Goliath looking down on little David."

She laughed then at the comparison and thinking how they must look together, she looked up at him as they led the mare out of the barn and into the sunlight.

"Such a majestic, powerful man," she thought and smiled.

As he lifted her onto her horse, Jeff really did realize for the first time that Ella Anne was indeed a young woman.

From amid the party guests, Burrell noticed them as they rode past the end of the stable and headed for the lane. He pulled old Mose away from what he was doing. "Saddle up quickly and follow them. Stay out of sight if you can."

*****

"Say, I thought you said there were no horses of color on this farm. Why are you riding a black?"

"Didn't you notice the mixture of white and black hair in her flanks? Satin has just enough gray on her that Papa says she can legally be called a gray. Besides, she throws a gray foal every time."

"My family has a horse farm in North Carolina. We breed for style and confirmation. Color doesn't matter. But I can see yall breed for all three."

She nodded, and they rode in silence for a while. "What are you doing here in Georgia, Jeff Dodd? Why did you leave North Carolina?"

"I really don't consider that I have left North Carolina. I own some freight wagons, and I buy goods from all over the world off the ships that dock around Pamlico Sound; then I freight it inland. I am sort of searching for new customers. Need to see if it would be profitable to come this far."

"I thought Pamlico Sound was too shallow for the big ships to enter."

"It is. They offload onto smaller ships at Morehead City. The smaller ships don't pull as much water so they can come through the Sound. Those are the Captains I know."

About that time, Ella Anne caught sight of old Mose behind them. "I'll race you to the creek!" she said, and cracked Satin with the end of the reigns. She had two horse lengths head start before Jeff realized they were racing. Now, Jeff knew his horse was faster than the mare, but he was going to play along. When they rounded a big bend in the road so that Mose could not see them, Jeff could see she was going to jump the fence.

"But, you can't jump that fence riding side saddle!"

She did jump the fence, and two more in short order with Jeff right behind her, and the race was on. They were out of sight before Mose rounded the bend, but he kept going down the lane thinking he was going to get a glimpse of them just any time.

With Ella Anne ahead of him, he began to observe how lovely she looked as she rode through patches of shade then into the sunlight again. Ella Anne's pale green dress flowed across the back of the satiny black mare. Her hair, long and silky, reddish gold in the sun, danced to the rhythm of the horse's hooves. How stately she sat a horse!

"Race you across the stream," she called over her shoulder, and instantly the mare was in full stride again. Jeff watched her make a smooth jump across the narrow stream and pull up to wait for him. As soon as he cleared the stream, she broke into laughter.

"Help me down, Goliath, and we'll let the horses graze in this meadow."

"Now I know why your father calls you 'Spitfire.' You are an uncommon young woman, Ella Anne Barnett."

Like a gentleman, Jeff helped her down from the sidesaddle. He lowered her down ever so slowly, and their eyes met. For a long while they looked into each other's eyes. Then slowly, ever so slowly, he brought her toward him for a long warm kiss. He set her feet on the ground and touched her under the chin, looking into her face all the while. Then he took her by the hand and led her into a patch of very tall grass that was growing by the creek bank. He pressed down the grass making a little room for them.

****

They were back on the lane headed for home within the hour. Hundreds of thoughts and questions raced through Ella Ann's mind, but they rode in silence. As they neared the gate, Jeff pulled up and motioned for her to stop. Picking a straw from her hair, he said "When we get back to the party, you act like you don't even like me anymore and go talk to some other people....or else they will know."

Back at the party, all the eligible young women were eyeing Jeff, vying for his attention. They had all heard about Jeff. "Martha Ector said that he has a thousand hands," Ella Anne heard one of them say.

Another one commented, "She said that it sure is fun when he chases you around the haystack."

One by one they all managed to have a cup of punch with Jeff, and two of them were gone from sight for a while when they had Jeff's undivided attention.

"Oh, here you are," Jeff said as he rounded the corner of the gazebo. "I've been looking for you."

"You haven't had time to miss me, and you are going to slosh," Ella Anne had been leaning on the railing watching birds play in the shade of the big trees. She looked up as he spoke then turned back to the birds.

"The race starts at 2 o'clock, and already this morning you have had seven cups of punch. I'm really surprised no one has spiked it. That would be one way to put you out of the race. You know the men are talking about your horse as much as the young women are talking about you."

"You are a little bit jealous, aren't you, Muffin? ...Aren't you, Muffin? Would you really like it if I win the race? ....Hey, this is becoming a rather one-sided conversation; come help me brush Dandy and get him ready for the race. I need to exercise him a bit to loosen him up, you know. Come on now." He held out his hand and she took it; together they ran laughing to the barn.

*****

Jim Dandy knew something was afoot as he saw the crowd and felt the exited hush fall when they saw him prancing and hopping around in a dainty step that barely seemed to touch the ground. It was as if he were asking, "Now? Can we go now?"

The odds on the big red horse just tumbled from double digits to flat even!

There were nine horses entered in the race today, and soon they were all exercising up and down the road. Everyone had their favorite to win, and all eyed the big red stallion with breathless suspicion. Garrett had poured lime from a sack to draw a white line across the lane. At 1:55 PM, Burrell called the riders to gather at the white line.

"Since nine horses cannot line up abreast, we will draw numbers for starting positions. One through five will line up on the line from left to right; six through nine will form a second line. Gentlemen, draw your number from Judge Tully's hat and take your places, please."

Ella Anne sat on her black mare away from the crowd and had a very good view of the proceedings. Her heart sank when she saw Jeff take his place in the second line. With that many horses in the race there would be a lot of jockeying for position, and Jeff might not be able to get through the first line of horses.

Then the gun was fired into the air and, with a tremendous yell from the crowd to urge them on, the horses were off. Some of the horses on the first line were fast starters, and they began to string out before they were completely out of sight. Perhaps Jeff could get through them, after all.

The young boys all ran a ways down the road by which the riders would return. They sat on the rail fences, hoping to be the first to sight the riders and alert the crowd that they were coming. With nothing to do now, Ella Anne rode over to the buggy placed at the start and finish line, which served as a podium for her father and Judge Tully.

"Good afternoon, Judge Tully, Papa."

"Ella Anne, my child, how good to see you," Judge Tully was saying before he really surveyed the young woman in question. "My God, Burrell, she's not a child anymore! You must look lively, Burrell, and keep a close eye on this young woman. She's going to be the most beautiful of all your daughters. How could this happen right before our eyes?" he asked Burrell shaking his head and shrugging his shoulders.

"You always say things like that to make me blush, Judge. Now, how are you betting this race?"

"Are you out of your mind? I'm betting on your brother, Robert, and your father's horse; there's no surer thing to put your money on."

Smiling mischievously at her father, Ella Anne said, "I'll wager one of Jessie's cakes against a bolt of cloth that he doesn't win this year."

"Done!" the Judge exclaimed. "Who do you think will beat him?"

"The big red stud from North Carolina! Papa, have you seen Mary Elizabeth?"

"No, not since all the guests arrived. She is supposed to present the roses though. There is your mother, ask her."

She moved off slowly toward Minerva who was surrounded by women. As she passed some of the eligible young women, she overheard one say, "You can't really believe that he is interested in her. Why, she is just a child!"

Before she could get her mother's attention, someone yelled, "Here they come!" and all eyes darted toward the road. Ella Anne rode closer to the finish line, yet away from the crowd. She had to see if she was just a child like they thought.

When they came in sight, there were two horses neck and neck, the rest were being outdistanced more with every stride. At first Ella Anne could see only her father's gray stud and occasionally Dandy's head could be seen a little in front. Then with a slow steady motion, Dandy was pulling ahead of the gray. First just his head, then his neck, then as they crossed the finish line, Ella Anne could see his full shoulder ahead of the gray. She wanted to yell and jump up and down, but she dared not call attention to herself. Then as a shout went up from the crowd, she allowed herself to shout, too, and clap her hands together. Jeff had won! Jeff had won!

Jeff turned his horse and came back to the buggy for his winner's handshake from Burrell and the roses from Mary Elizabeth. And all the marriageable young women gathered close around him. All but one!

After all the congratulations, the handshaking, and the back-slapping, Jeff waded through the crowd, leading his horse, and walked straight to Ella Anne. He handed the twelve red roses up to her and said, "I have to cool him down, you know. Will you ride along with me?"

As they rode back through the crowd toward the road, Ella Anne buried her nose deep in the roses and drew a long breath. As she looked up, she saw Martha Ector and the others staring; and her chin lifted just a little as she turned her head toward the road. "Just a child, indeed!" she thought.

Burrell Barnett, too, had been staring. "You're quite right, Judge; I'm going to have to look to my little spitfire a little closer."

Chapter Four
The Weddings

Robert was elated. With five men working on his new house, they had a small two-storied house ready in less than two months. Papa had helped him design it so that as their family grows, they can build another section on each end, making it look as if it were all built at one time. Papa had drawn out a picture of what it will look like in years to come, and Sue Ellen was delighted.

They had set the wedding date for Saturday, June 29th. The wedding was to be at the Barnett house since they had a beautifully curved staircase and lots of room. Sue Ellen and her mother had made her a gorgeous wedding dress of white satin and lace ordered from Atlanta. Robert bought her a wide gold wedding band to pledge his love.

Friends and neighbors brought over their parlor chairs and potted plants for Minerva to decorate the staircase and the parlor. Big Jessie proved she was the best cook in Floyd County when she brought out the huge three-tiered wedding cake and set it on the dining table. And Jenny followed her with a large crystal bowl of pink lemonade. Reverend Cook from Rome Methodist Church presided.

It was a beautiful wedding. From start to finish everything was perfect for the bride and groom. People were eating cake and drinking pink lemonade and congratulating the new Mr. and Mrs. Barnett. It was a joyous occasion.

John Bailey got Burrell's attention and they slipped into Burrell's study. After about half an hour, Burrell sent for Minerva to come to the study. Minutes later, with a great big smile on his face, John came out, almost running to find Mary Elizabeth.

Burrell held up a crystal glass and tapped it with a spoon. When everyone was quiet, he took Minerva's hand and said, "My friends, it seems there is no end to our joy. Mary Elizabeth and John Bailey have asked to be married next Saturday. Will you all be our guests once again and share our happiness?" Squeals of joy and an excited buzz filled the room.

Burrell again tapped on the glass, asking for silence. "Ladies, if you don't mind and if you will trust us….would you please leave your plants and chairs with us until next weekend?" Laughter filled the room of already joyous guests.

****

After everyone left, the exhausted Barnett family sat on the porch to relax and relive the wonderful moments of the day.

"Now tell me, you two, what are your plans? Robert has known exactly what he planned to do for several months, giving us time to adapt. Where will you live?"

Looking at John William as much as at Burrell, John Bailey said, "We have decided to take the high road and go to Atlanta to practice law. We have talked to Judge Tully. He is contacting friends of his to help us get acquainted and settled in Atlanta.

"I have found a small house in Rome to rent for a month or two while we are getting things set up in Atlanta. I took Mary Elizabeth to see it yesterday." He looked at her and took her hand, "I guess I can go tomorrow and give them the rent money." She just smiled.

"By George, John, I believe that is more than I have heard you say at one time since I've known you!" Burrell was pretty sure he liked this new son-in-law.

****

Things were in high gear early the next morning. There was not time to send away for material for a fine wedding gown. John said he thought Mary Elizabeth was so pretty in her soft pink dress from John William's party. He asked if she would consider wearing it to be married. He rented the house in Rome, which had to be cleaned thoroughly. After all, who knows who might have lived in it last! Jessie shared her smaller pans. Minerva shared her linens and a set of dishes with Mary Elizabeth, and they got the house set up for the newlyweds just in time.

Since John did not have the expense of building a house, he bought a ring with a pretty big diamond for Mary Elizabeth. He was going to be showing her off in Atlanta society!

Big Jessie outdid herself making another big wedding cake and punch. Jessie had made this cake with pink frosting to match the bride's dress. The parlor pretty much remained the same with borrowed chairs and plants. A thorough cleaning and they were set for another wedding.

The wedding, though not as elaborate as last week's, was beautiful and exciting. The house was filled with happy friends and relatives wishing them well.

While cake and punch were being served, Big Jessie called Minerva to the kitchen for her advice. Once there, she ran everyone out of the kitchen and shut the door. "Miss Minerva, I know this is not a good time to tell you this, but I have been so busy with these weddings. Only today did I notice that for two months Miss Ella Anne has not used up the clean little rags that I put in the drawer by her bedside." Then she broke down and cried.

Minerva was stunned, but not without a plan. "Now you dry your eyes, Jessie, and go to Mr. Burrell's study. Wait for me there. I'll go and find him."

Minerva gracefully walked up to the group of men who held Burrell's attention. Very charmingly she smiled and said, "May I borrow my husband for a few minutes, gentlemen?" She took his arm and led him to the study as if she needed his suggestion about more food or such. Burrell was concerned when he saw Jessie there; she was crying again.

"Now, Jessie, we'll get through this. Don't worry. Please tell Mr. Burrell what you told me." It was hard, but between sobs she finally got it all said.

Without much noticeable change of expression, Burrell began to think of recent events. "Jessie will you go get Mose for me. Now he is not going to get in trouble. I just need to ask him some questions."

Of course, Mose was worried when he entered Mr. Burrell's study. Yes, he had followed them, could see them now and again, until they went around that big bend in the lane. He never did actually see them again. But when he gave up and came back they were already here at the party.

"Thank you, Mose. Don't be upset. There is only so much we can do, right?"

Minerva left the study as Mose did. She located the group of young men with whom Jeff was talking, and ever so charmingly interrupted their conversation. "Gentlemen, I have a special need of this young man's help. Please forgive me for stealing him away." Jeff was puzzled, but when she gently put her hand through his arm and began to walk, he felt at ease. She walked him up to the door of Burrell's study; he opened the door and waited for her to go in. She said, "No. This is man talk. I'll wait out here."

The study was dim when he entered. Burrell's chair, behind the desk, was facing the wall. For a few moments there was a heavy silence. "You wanted to see me, Mr. Barnett?" Jeff ventured. Burrell slowly swiveled his chair around and took a deep breath before he began. "Yes, we have a situation. I have just been told we are having a roan foal."

"A roan? How can that be? I've kept him locked up the whole time I've been here!"

Burrell said very lowly, "I did what I could to prevent it. But it wasn't enough." He paused, looking straight into Jeff's eyes. "You cannot see it, Jeff, but under the desk I'm holding a Colt Dragoon. Now, if you are not man enough to hold up your end of the deal, I am about to castrate the bastard who sired that roan, right now. Am I making myself clear, Jeff?"

Jeff's face paled, and he began to nod his head up and down. "I didn't hear that, Jeff," Burrell said. Jeff finally found his voice, "Yes sir, Mr. Barnett. I believe I understand the situation. I'll marry your daughter."

Burrell's eyes narrowed, "That didn't come out sounding just right....did it Jeff?"

Jeff was shaking his head 'no'. "Try it again, Jeff."

"Mr. Barnett, sir, I would be honored if you would allow me to marry your daughter, Ella Anne."

With a nod of his head, Burrell raised the volume of his voice, "You can bring her in, now, Minerva."

The door opened and in walked Ella Anne and Minerva. By this time Jeff had learned the script for the role he was to play. He dropped to one knee, and took Ella Anne's hand. "Ella Anne, will you do me the honor of becoming my wife?"

Knowing nothing about the previous scenario, Ella Anne was stunned. The surprise made her eyes open wide, and her mouth was open slightly, as she nodded her head slowly up and down.

"I did not hear that, Ella Anne," her father said. "Yes. Yes, I will," she stammered out softly.

Jeff heard the click when Burrell released the tension on the hammer and put the pistol in his top desk drawer. "He wasn't bluffing one bit," Jeff thought.

"Has Jessie calmed down enough now?" Minerva nodded 'Yes'.

"Well, let's go announce another wedding to our guests."

Jessie found Burrell an empty crystal glass and a spoon. Minerva stood by his side as he tapped the glass for attention. Ella Anne and Jeff stood slightly to their side, but they were not touching. "Once again, my good friends, I have the honor to announce that another of my children will be married. Ella Anne and Jeff Dodd will be marrying. This is working out so well, we will have another wedding next Saturday. After that I believe we will be able to return your chairs and plants."

There was uproarious laughter.

"The only other offspring I have of marriageable age is John William, and he has not confided his intentions to me. If we do not put a stop to this, people will begin to think there is a party at the Barnett house every Saturday!"

Everybody laughed again and the happy chatter grew louder. Minerva smiled lovingly at her husband. "He is just masterful," she thought. "Who would dream that fifteen minutes ago he threatened to kill a man? Who would guess that inside his heart is breaking? He always knows how to handle things with finesse."

As people were leaving, the phrase, "See yall again Saturday," kept coming up.

*****

Again, a tired Barnett family sat on the front porch and watched the sun go down. This time there was an air of sadness.

Burrell broke the silence, "Well, Mama, our family is shrinking fast, isn't it?" She nodded sadly.

He looked straight at Jeff and Ella Anne. "Have you had time to make any plans yet? Where you'll live, anything like that?"

By now Jeff had learned that this old teddy bear was not to be toyed with. He looked at Ella Anne and began to stumble, "Well, my wagons are in North Carolina. We could go back there and live with my folks, I guess."

"No, by God!" Burrell sat up so straight and so fast, he nearly came off his seat. "You will not take my daughter away in her condition! I am not losing a daughter; I am gaining a son-in-law! In a month or two you will go back to North Carolina and get your wagons. You will meet the ships at the docks and buy as you have done before. And," he emphasized, "You will be back here within two months!

"Are we understanding each other, son-in-law? Because if you are not back within two months, there is not a hole small enough for you to hide in. I will finish the discussion we had in my study. Is that plain enough?

"Now, Garrett," his voice was gentle again. "Will you get the things you will need for the night? I want you to bunk with John William for a few days.

"Jeff, you can get your things from the stable room and move into Garrett's room, for now."

He slapped his hands on his knees as if all his business was put in order and he started to rise. "Minerva, I am going to bed, now. Come along Garrett, my man, let's go up."

"Papa, I think that is the first time you haven't called me 'young' Garrett!"

"That is because you are the now the oldest son I have left at home. That means you are going to have to start working like a man. I'll need your help. Okay?"

****

Burrell took John William to catch the train to Atlanta just about daylight. He was going to look around for an office while John Bailey honeymooned, so there was no big sendoff. Jessie packed him enough food to last about two days. "Jessie, a person would think I was going off to starve! Thank you." He hugged her. He hugged his mother, "I'll be back in a few days, Mama. It shouldn't take more than a week to locate a small office. That is all we can afford right now." He climbed into the buggy and in two minutes they were out of sight.

When Burrell returned, he found Minerva waiting for him in the porch swing. "I told him to look for a small office space for right now. The main thing is location – above a pretty busy street, in a good business neighborhood….so they can have the name of their firm painted in gold letters on the windows.

"Minerva, I told him to be looking for a building to buy sometime in the future; then he would have offices to rent and bring in money that way.

"We helped Robert buy his land. A young attorney who owns a nice building would gain prestige, and that is important in his profession. I look at it as helping him get started in his trade. Different trade – different type of help."

Minerva smiled at this man she had loved for over 25 years. "He just gives and gives," she thought. "Somehow you always know the right way to handle a situation, Burrell Barnett," she said as she saw Jessie coming to get them for breakfast.

*****

After breakfast that morning, the men, Burrell, Garrett and Jeff, walked out to look at things. "Let's go check the water in the central pastures," Burrell pointed the general direction they would be walking. "Garrett, this will be one of your jobs – your responsibility," he emphasized. "If those horses go without water, I will look to you for an explanation. Understand?"

He continued as they walked, "Now, there are several things you need to be alert for. Snakes! Rattlers can be lying right in the middle of a pile of dry leaves and you won't see them. Most of the time they will rattle at you, though, and warn you.

Copperheads are the worst. They are silent, and they can look just like a dry limb until they move. They blend in with the colors of the ground. If you get snake bit while you are off out here, you might not be able to get back to the house in time."

He handed Garrett a small cake of chewing tobacco. "Always keep this in your shirt pocket, son. Don't misunderstand, I don't want you to get to chewing this all the time, but if you get snake bit, you chew a little piece of this until it gets juicy. Make a small cut in the skin, right through the fang marks, and spit the juice on the bite. Put the tobacco over it and tie your handkerchief around it. That will begin to draw out the poison. And you need to keep your pocket knife sharp!

"I bought this for you when I took John William to the train." He handed Garrett a narrow box about three inches long and stood waiting to see the look on Garrett's face when he opened it.

Garrett was taken by surprise! His eyes got big and his mouth opened a bit, and for a moment no sound came out.

"Oh, Papa! This is so nice. Thank you!"

He took the pocket knife out of the box and held it in his hand, moving it around a bit to see where it fit his hand best. "Papa, this handle is made of polished antler!"

"Check the imprint on the blade…up close to the handle. It is Sheffield Steel, son. Finest on the market. Guaranteed to hold an edge. Those brass caps on each end of the handle are useful too. They make it stronger in case you try to use it as a hammer!" A sheepish grin stole across Burrell's face and he shook his head at a memory.

"A man needs a good pocket knife for all sorts of things. Now, you keep it sharp and keep the edge free of nicks. A dull knife is almost like not having one at all. That pen knife you have been using was okay for keeping a point on a pencil and cutting string and other things a boy needs. You are about to start shouldering a man's load and you should be prepared for whatever comes along. As you're working with the livestock and farming, there is probably not a day goes by you don't need a knife for something. You need to be ready for whatever is thrown at you, son. I got you a new whet rock, too. I'll give it to you when we get back to the house." He slapped Garrett on the shoulder lightly, smiled a quick smile, and pointed the direction he wanted them to walk

"Another thing to watch out for is loose rocks. Make sure big rocks in these washouts are secure before you put your full weight on them. In these hills and valleys – over here where the land is not cultivated – a

man can easily fall and break a leg before he tumbles to the bottom of a gully. Could even be morning before we could come out looking for you.

"These are just parts of everyday living, son. I just want you to be alert to everything around you.

"Now predators are a different thing altogether. We are not bothered by wolves and mountain lions much anymore; but you see, son, they hunt for a living. Unless they get to killing too much, I believe they have a right to find food. Most of the time, they will pick on deer, goats, lambs; usually something pretty defenseless. Sometimes you might even come across an old carcass of a full grown, wooly sheep, but not often."

He stopped talking while they crossed a gully that was washed out pretty deep. "When you find these gullies, you know they are pointing you toward water. Let's head that direction," pointing the direction the gully flowed.

"The thing is, when a mare lays down give birth, she is defenseless. The pain in her body is so intense, her muscles are too weak for her to stand, let alone fight off predators. And all predators have a keen sense of smell. They can smell blood for miles.

"Garrett, if you should come across this kind of a situation, where a mare is down and a predator is already on the scene, you shoot once, maybe twice. You notice I always bring a rifle when we walk the pastures," he said, holding up his rifle. "You should, too. Son, if that doesn't kill him or scare him off, do not under any circumstances get between him and his food!

"You see, a predator most likely won't stalk you, but if you get between him and his food, he will attack you just because you are there. And, son, you are worth more to me than all the mares on this farm – the whole farm."

He choked up and his chin quivered as he remembered those war years and coming home to his Minerva. And young Garrett was the celebration of their happy reunion. He slipped his arm across Garrett's shoulders as they walked.

"Well, here I've talked all the way over here. This is the main creek that runs through this pasture. Take note of how high it is right now. This is pretty typical for this time of year. When it starts getting pretty low in the heat of the summer, there will be dry spots between pools of water. The horses can drink from those pools for just a few days, but you have to start moving them to where there is water. Understand?

"And while you are walking, you can observe how close they have eaten the grass. That is important, too.

"Let's look around a little while we are here and take a look at the mares. Did you notice, Garrett, the grass where we have been walking has been about ankle high. I'll bet that over that rise to the east the grass is almost knee high. That's where we will find them, where the grass has not been grazed down."

They stood on the ridge and counted ten big-bellied mares and two standing off to the edge had lost their big belly. "We may have a couple of foals hidden out around here. Let's walk around and look for them. We can separate and cover more area. Now, Garrett, if you find one, don't get too close and don't yell out or she will have to hide him again."

Sure enough, Jeff found one and Garrett found the other not far away. Both black as the ace of spades. "That is the way we want them!" Burrell said. "When they lose their baby hair they will be gray.

"Now, Garrett, those two mares are not going to get very far from their babies right now. But when the colts can walk good and run around, the mares will take turns baby-sitting for each other."

"Wow," was Garrett's summation of the whole thing.

"Are you going to breed these mares right back, Mr. Barnett?" Jeff asked.

"No. I had rather let them concentrate on raising this foal. We'll breed them in about six months. No need to be greedy. Keep your stock in better shape that way."

"Jeff, you can call me Burrell. I figure as long as you are good to my little girl, there is no need for "Mr. Barnett" or "Mr. Dodd.""

"You know, Burrell, it has been real nice listening to you explain things and life to Garrett. It makes me feel comfortable and at ease."

"Well, men, this is what I call the East-Central pasture. If we go back northwest, I can show you a good place to check water in the Central pasture before lunch, Garrett. What do you suppose Jessie is cooking up for lunch?"

Garrett lifted his nose up to sniff the air, "From here I can't tell, Papa. The wind is from the wrong direction."

They all laughed and headed for the next pasture.

****

"Mary Elizabeth wore her pink that John William brought her and made a beautiful bride. What would you think about wearing your mint green? It's still very new, and it really compliments your hair and your coloring. You look positively radiant in it. Minerva was looking through Ella Anne's wardrobe to find a wedding dress.

Ella Anne sat slump shouldered on the bed with her feet crossed at the ankles, swinging them back and forth. "Oh, I don't know, Mama. That's the dress I had on when we…" Her voice trailed off.

Minerva sat down beside her, staring into the distance for a few minutes. "Well, didn't you feel loved and beautiful at that time?"

There was a visible change in Ella Anne's demeanor. A little smile drifted across her face. She held her head up and straightened her shoulders. She took a deep breath and smiled at her mother. "You are right; that is the perfect dress, Mama."

"Good girl. Now let's try some hair styles. Those dog ears are definitely out! If you wore it up, would it seem as if you were trying to look too old? Personally, I like it when you wear it pulled back with long curls."

They spent the rest of the morning trying hair styles, trying jewelry, making Ella Anne feel happy. "Oh, do you know what?' Minerva said, "Those pink azaleas are blooming! You could carry a bouquet of azaleas with a light pink ribbon and put the same ribbon in your hair.

"What if we pull your hair up in back, like this, put a wide, flat bow here, and make finger curls below the ribbon?"

"Oh, Mama, that will look elegant! Let's go ask Jessie if she will make pink frosting for my cake like she did for Mary Elizabeth."

They hurried downstairs, explained the plans to Jessie, and asked if she would make pink frosting. "I think I can do better than that for you, honey. If I press a lot of those spearmint leaves, I think that will color the frosting just about the same as your dress. What do you think?"

She hurried to give Jessie a big hug. She looked back at her mother. "I have been feeling ashamed, and you both are making me feel very special."

****

And so the week passed quickly. Burrell and Minerva, Jeff and Ella Anne drove to town. Jeff and Ella Anne got their marriage license; Burrell had to sign for her. While the ladies looked for ribbon and other odds and ends that are absolutely necessary for a wedding, Burrell took Jeff around town to get acquainted with some of the townspeople and let them know that he would be hauling products from the ships docking in North Carolina. Maybe drum up a little business that way.

Jessie and her crew had this wedding cleaning down to a fine art! Everybody knew their part of the chores, and setting up for the wedding went very smoothly.

****

A crowd had already gathered downstairs as Ella Anne stood in front of her looking glass, her hair fixed just right, dressed in her mint green dress, stockings and pretty slippers. Minerva slipped up behind and put her string of pearls around Ella Anne's neck. "I think these will look very good with that neckline, don't you?"

"Oh, Mama, your pearls!" her hand automatically reached up to touch them. She whirled around and hugged her mother for a long time. Finally, Minerva said, "It's time to go, now, darling."

Jenny stood outside her door beaming with love and handed her the bouquet. "Now, when your mama gets seated, I'll wave at you to start down the stairs."

Burrell waited for her at the foot of the stairs, took her arm and escorted her to the front of the parlor where the minister stood in his black robe. As they neared the front, Jeff stepped up, took his place beside her and they finally were standing before the minister.

As Reverend Cook performed the ceremony, Minerva was lost in thought – transfixed. Looking at this couple from the back, no one would guess that her daughter was 5 foot 8 inches tall. His 6 foot 4 inches made her look diminutive. Suddenly looking months ahead, she thought, "Oh, we may be in for trouble."

The minister said, "You may kiss your bride," and Jeff picked her up to kiss her. He held her there for a long kiss while her feet dangled slightly, her toes not even reaching the floor. After his experience with her father, he had been afraid to even kiss her this whole week.

The guests began to clap and cheer. This brought them out of their moment and brought a little blush to their cheeks. Men were shaking hands with Jeff; women happily wished Ella Anne the best and told her what a beautiful bride she was. Ella Anne suddenly turned around and threw her bouquet over her shoulder. She threw it high and far. Jenny, standing at the parlor door, caught it.

*****

This wedding ended rather differently than the others. After cake, punch and conversation, the guests gathered up their plants and chairs and loaded up to leave. When, almost all of the guests were gone and Jeff was pretty sure no one was looking, he picked Ella Anne up in his arms and bounded up the stairs, two at a time.

Burrell and Minerva sat in the porch swing and Garrett sat on the edge of the porch, swinging his feet and pitching some little pebbles he had picked up. They sat there until well after dark. Finally, Burrell said, "Well, Garrett tomorrow is just another day for you and me. Even on Sunday livestock has to be tended. I think you had better head up to bed."

"Yes, sir," Garrett said as he stood up and started for the screen door. Funny how you don't mind going to bed when you know you have something important depending on you tomorrow.

Burrell and Minerva just sat there swinging for a long time.

*****

For the next few days Jenny took up a breakfast tray and left it outside the newlywed's door. Really, the only time the family saw them was at dinner. They took long buggy rides. They sat in the porch swing talking. They whispered and laughed. Though Ella Anne was not allowed on a horse, they parked the buggy at the fence, Jeff lifted her across, and they walked to the creek. They were enjoying being in love.

They took a picnic lunch to their spot on the creek and enjoyed the quietness of nature, lost in that special connection between two people, of being together alone, belonging. Jeff was lying on his side by the creek, propped up on one elbow. He smiled as he surveyed his bride: her strawberry blond hair was soft and shiny as corn silk; her bright blue-green eyes just seemed to dance. Her skin was like porcelain except for a few freckles across her nose. "The result of being out with the horses," he thought.

He thought of her enthusiasm for life, her impetuous nature. Sometimes it seems she was filled with a lightning bolt. "Who would expect her to jump a fence, riding sidesaddle, and race him to this spot on the creek?" Those eyes sparkled like gems when she had an impulsive thought, and the smile that spread across her face was so big that it made her cheeks round and rosy. Yet there was a soft and gentle side to her, too. He had seen her playing with the baby chicks, so gently. He once saw her grab up one of Big Jessie's grandchildren who had fallen and cuddle the baby as if it were her own. And the love she had for the horses was a strong love; she adored their beauty and appreciated every ounce of their strength.

He suddenly made a statement that truly shocked her. "I really have a hard time saying Ella and Anne together. I think I'll call you my Ella Jane." And ever after that, to him she was 'Ella Jane'.

After a week of this, Burrell mentioned to Jeff that he could use his help with the horses tomorrow. And so their honeymoon was ended. Jeff worked hard on the farm, and he came in all sweaty and dirty in the evening. But to Ella Anne it was fun washing him down every night before bed.

Before long Ella Anne's dresses wouldn't close at the waist. She had a few dresses with a band just below the bust and no waistline. She was fine in those for another month; then it became apparent that she soon would need real maternity dresses. She was getting big really fast.

Nearing the end of July, Jeff stopped work and said he needed to talk. Burrell backed up against the barn and stood in the shade, wiping the sweat from his hat band with his handkerchief. "Burrell, this is the time of year that I need to leave to meet the ships." They stood there looking at each other.

"Well, I was kind of hoping you might like working around here."

"I do. But I make really good money freighting the way I do. It's like having a store, but without the overhead. And if I don't go now, the winter seas are so rough not many ships come into the Sound. I have five wagons and regular customers for almost everything I can bring back. If I buy another wagon, I can leave the other five wagons and drivers in North Carolina and drive the new one here myself.

"I think I can do it in two months, sir. I'm pretty sure I can be back here in two months. If I do that regularly, Ella Jane and I can have our own place."

Sadness crept into Burrell's expression and he narrowed his eyes, "Well, I wish you wouldn't, but you have to live your own life. Does your family know that you are married?"

"No. Not yet. I figured it would be easier to tell them when I get there."

"You might as well put up your tools and go tell Ella Anne. And you be gentle about it!"

Chapter Five
Long Haul to the Sound

Dinner was somber that evening. Everybody seemed to know this was a bad move except Jeff. Most of the meal was eaten in silence, and Jeff left next morning about sunup.

By riding all day, he made it to his brother's house in four days. He rode in just before dark, barely in time for supper.

"Boy, does it feel good to be off of that horse," he said, as he pulled his chair up to the table. Your place is looking good, John. You really have been working hard to get all this done since I was here.

"Sarah, this is a fine meal, ma'am. Big Jessie packed me a saddlebag full of hardtack and jerky. That's what I have been eating for four days to save time.

"I'm on my way to pick up my wagons and make another run to the coast, and I need to hurry."

He finally stopped talking long enough for John to ask," What's your hurry, Jeff?"

"I got married. Got a baby on the way. I've got to make my run and get back as soon I can."

"Does Ma know?"

"No. I figured it would be easier to tell them face to face." It was hard for Jeff to slow down eating long enough to talk. "Sure good food, ma'am," he said, smiling at Sarah.

He finally pushed back his plate, pushed his chair back a little and slouched down in it a little to rest his back. "You know, John, I really do like her family. I like being around them, being part of them.

"Her father is a big man, almost as big as me. But he is a big man in other ways. He talks easy, always gives you his reasoning for what he

says....always teaching, you might say. Not just how to do things, but why."

He was quiet for a minute as he thought of the Dragoon and the click of the hammer being released, "And if he tells you something, that is the way it is, no turning back."

"And her mother is the picture of grace, but you kind of get the feeling she could handle any situation in her own gentle way." His voice trailed off.

He blinked once, twice, and then it seemed he was going to sleep in his chair.

"Jeff, I know you must be wiped out from that long ride. I've got a little bunk house built now. You are welcome to sleep there, sleep as late as you need to and get some rest before you go on. We won't wake you. I'll grain your horse for you."

Jeff picked up the napkin and wiped his mouth once more, thanked them again, and headed for the bunkhouse. "Man, this feels like heaven," he thought as he stretched out, boots and all. And he was asleep.

"Sarah, did you notice the difference in Jeff?" John remarked as they started to bed. "He seems to have more concern and respect for people than he used to. A person might almost say that he is becoming a solid person!" Sarah had noticed it too.

"I just wonder what it will do to him being around Ma."

Early next morning, Jeff was gone. "He took those left-over biscuits. They must have been hard as a rock. I wish him well when he gets home."

*****

Four days later, he rode up at the home place. He was happy to see that his wagons were still where he left them, tall grass grown up around them. You never know what to expect! He dismounted and slowly walked to the door. "Ma, its Jeff. I'm home." There was no one in the house, so he put his horse away, and fed him. He found some hard biscuits above the stove and ate them as he was walking toward his bed.

*****

"Ma, Jeff is home! Come see! He is in his room – in bed with his boots still on!" The excitement in Wilma's voice could be heard all over the house.

"Well, it's about time!" Lou shouted back. "He has been gone so long, I was about to take over that corner room!"

Ma was coming up the stairs. "Will you girls quiet down? If your brother is that tired, let him be. Don't try to wake him." She stood at the open door to his room, "Yes, he is covered in dust from head to foot. He must have rode hard to get here.

"Wilma, go out and see to his horse. He probably fed him, but I'll bet he didn't take time to curry him," she said as she closed the bedroom door.

As she walked back down the stairs, her mind was busy. "Let's have a big dinner tonight to celebrate his coming home.

"Lou, go over and tell Dora that Jeff is home. Ask her to dinner tonight.

"Nora, you go out to where your pa and the boys are working and tell them. Tell them to come in a little early tonight.

"Selma!" she said in a loud voice. "Selma, we will need a big dinner tonight; Jeff is home. And I've invited Dora, too. Get someone in here to shine up the downstairs rooms; I want it to look nice.

"And I guess everybody will want a bath tonight. Start some water to heating; the girls and I will get our baths early and the men will be in a little earlier than usual. We are going to let Jeff sleep as long as he wants to; so he can bathe last.

"Now, tell Wilma to get ready for her bath as soon as she comes back from tending Jeff's horse.

"I'll go see what kind of shape his good jacket is in; it probably needs a good brushing, too."

With that she hurried back upstairs to find the jacket.

****

When everybody else had bathed and more water was heated, Pa went upstairs to wake Jeff. "Get up, boy," he called from the door. "We're having a party. You need to get cleaned up!"

Jeff roused himself and turned over, but he did not get up immediately. "Hi, Pa," he said sleepily as his father had already turned to leave.

Wilma hurried by and saw Jeff was sitting up, "Wake up, sleepy head. Ma's having a big dinner in your honor, and everyone has bathed except you. Better get cleaned up, now. Dora is coming for dinner."

Instantly Jeff was awake and at the door. "No!" he yelled down the hall after her.

"No, what, silly?"

"No, don't invite Dora!"

"Well, why not, silly? She wants to see you."

"You can't invite her over! I'm married!"

"You're what?" she asked as she turned and ran down the stairs. "Ma, come here quick!"

"He's what?" Ma shrieked in a very loud voice. "Probably some cheap little hussy got him drunk and got them married. Well, I'll take care of that! Jeff, get yourself down here right now and explain this to me!" she shouted up the stairway.

Jeff had already taken off his boots and was gathering up clean clothes. He needed a bath, anyway, no matter what the situation with Ma. He came downstairs barefoot, with his shirttail out. He knew this was coming, had been rehearsing it in his mind most of the way back. But he had hoped to tell them a little more on his terms.

He could tell by her quick, jerky movements that she had her war paint on. Now, how do you ease into a situation like this?

"What did you do, son? Let some little saloon floozy get you liquored up and lead you to a preacher? Well, she probably knows by now that you ain't coming back. Probably didn't even have a license either.

"I've told you for years you were going to mess around long enough and get caught up in some kind of trouble. Hell, I'm amazed you haven't been shot by a jealous husband!"

She turned and stomped off a few steps, then whirled back around and said, "Well, what do you have to say for yourself?"

"I've been married going on three months, Ma. We have a baby on the way."

"Lord, God! A baby!" She threw up her hands and stomped out the front door to walk it off.

Jeff knew it would take her a long time to cool down, so he went ahead with his bath.

****

At dinner Ma had seated Dora next to Jeff. Nothing was mentioned about his being married. Every time Jeff's wine glass was low, Ma nodded to the serving girl to fill it. After dinner, when all the men – Jeff had four brothers – went out to smoke, no one asked about his being married. They already knew, and Ma had forbidden any talk of it.

After a while Dora came out with two glasses of wine and sat down beside Jeff in the porch swing, handing one glass to him. One by one all the others got up and drifted away.

"I'm so glad you finally came home, Jeff. You have been gone so long, this time," She said.

"Yeah," Jeff was trying to figure some way out of this situation.

"Remember how much fun we used to have in this old porch swing, Jeff?" She reached over to touch his hand.

"You know, Dora, I'm still awfully tired, and I have to get out and find drivers for my wagons tomorrow. I think I had better head on up to bed." He stood up and handed his still full wineglass back to her.

****

Jeff didn't wait around for breakfast next morning. He was out lining up drivers for the trip to the Sound. He found three the first day and heard of two others who might be interested, but he couldn't find them. "Yall tell them I want to leave day after tomorrow if we can," he said as he mounted. "Maybe spread the word around. I'll be at the saloon for a little while. Anyone interested can leave word with Charlie. I'll check with him first."

He stopped in to see his banker, to let him know he would be making some large withdrawals. He made the rounds of his usual customers. "This will be my last trip to the Sound this season. By October the seas will be so rough, not many ships will try it. I'll be around in a day or two to see if you want anything. Thanks, now."

Last, he headed for the saloon. It was always hot and still in this part of North Carolina in August, and he had been talking all day. Jeff thought he would relax for a while. "Beer, Charlie," he said as he walked in. "I need to wet my whistle." He walked over to a table and sat down.

"How you been doing, Jeff?" Charlie asked as he sat down the beer. "I haven't seen you for a while."

"I've been in Georgia."

"Oh, visiting your brother?"

"Yeah. Hey Charlie, I'm looking for drivers for a trip to the Sound real soon. I found three, but I need two more. I spread the word that if anyone else was interested, to leave word with you. That okay?"

"Sure, Jeff."

"I want men that are experienced. I can't take a chance on losing a wagon and its load because of carelessness or inexperience. You know what I'm looking for, Charlie."

"Three teams?"

"That's right."

By this time, Sadie had spotted Jeff. "Buy me a beer, Jeff?' she asked. He could hear the swish of her knee length skirt as she sacheted up to the table. Jeff looked at her for a moment and thought, "Sadie or Ma?"

"Charlie, bring a beer for Sadie, will you?"

As Charlie set down the beer, Jeff finished his, flipped a coin for Charlie to catch, and said, "I'll check with you tomorrow, Charlie."

"I may as well go home and face Ma," he thought as he mounted up.

****

Instead of going home, Jeff turned and went up the lane to where his pa and the boys were replacing fence rails. Hot, sweaty, dirty work. His pa was happy to shade up and talk for a minute.

Pa took off his hat and wiped the sweat from the band with his handkerchief. They squatted for a minute in silence. Pa was waiting for his son to say what was on his mind. Finally Jeff said, "Pa, if she likes Dora so well, why won't she let one of the other boys marry her? Frank has been crazy about her for years. He is just scared of Ma. She won't let any of them get married! John just had to run off to get married."

"Well, you are the oldest. I don't know. I don't have an answer for you. Just get your hands together and leave on your haul as quick as you can. That's the best I can tell you.

"Hey, I'll bet a couple of the boys would like to help you bring in your mules just to get away from this fencing.

"Tom, Frank, you want to go help Jeff bring in his mules and get them ready to pull?" he called out in a louder voice. "I'll bet it takes you most of a day just to trim all them hooves!"

"Pa, I'm going to buy another wagon while I am down there. Where would you suggest I look?"

"Edward DeMoss in Greenville, NC, seems to be a pretty honest fellow. If he doesn't have what you want, I'd try whoever he refers. If it were me, son, I'd take six extra mules from here. Lead them behind the wagons like you always take along a couple of extras. That way you know they are sound. Where do you plan to go? New Bern?"

"Yes, sir. I know most of the Captains who dock there. Easier that way."

"Son, I'll go into town tomorrow and send a wire to Ed DeMoss, if you want."

"That would be great, Pa. Same type of wagon as my others. If he can have one located when I get there, it will sure make my trip go faster."

Tom and Frank were dusting off their clothes as they walked up. "What do you want us to do, Jeff?" they asked.

"Yall can show me what pasture my mules are in and help me bring them in. I guess tomorrow, we will need to trim hooves and check harness." He looked at his dad, "I guess it's all hanging where I left it."

"So far as I know." Pa put his hat back on and walked back to where the fencing was going on. Tom and Frank tightened their cinches, and the three of them headed toward the house.

****

Jeff owned a large herd of mules, and it did take all day to trim hooves. The two other drivers Jeff needed came out; they had talked to Charlie and wanted Jeff to know they were on board. They stayed to help. "I'll tell you what, men; we pretty well have this trimming going. If you would start oiling harness and looking for needed repairs, I certainly would appreciate it. Oh, and the wagon wheels need to be greased and the spokes watered down."

*****

All was done just before sundown. "Come on in for a quick supper, if you'd like," he told the two drivers. "Yall can come out in the morning and start harnessing. I'll go to town and see what orders I have; and we might be able to leave around noon. Do you think that could work?"

The other four men thought a minute, calculating how long each operation would take, and agreed they might be ready by noon. "We'll tell the other three drivers when we get back to town tonight."

Jeff laid out his plan, "On the way down, while the wagons are empty, we will use two teams to each wagon. Each wagon will lead four mules and carry the harness in the wagon. About half-way through the day we will rotate the mules. I think that way they will still be pretty fresh when we start back loaded.

"Tom, you remember which mules to pair up, don't you? Men, I really appreciate your help."

That night Jeff was so tired, he needed rest bad; but he couldn't stop going over things that needed to be done tomorrow morning. Bedroll, nice clothes to wear when he met the ship Captains. His money belt! Did I remember to ask Selma to pack food? He finally fell asleep about half-way down his list of things to do.

The smell of coffee woke him early, still tired, but he rolled out of bed and immediately started planning his day. He dressed and hurried downstairs for coffee and a biscuit, but Selma was taking eggs out of the skillet, so he took time to eat. "Yes, he had remembered to tell her he needed food to take with him.

"I put enough hardtack and jerky to hold six men between towns, and a few good things to eat, too. Mr. Jeff, its sure good to have you home again."

"Thanks, Selma, but it won't be for long this time."

On the way to town, he met the five drivers on their way to the farm. Things seemed to be going good. He found several of his customers with larger than usual orders already, and he did not have to wait long for the others to put together a list.

Last stop was to see Charlie. "Four bottles of whiskey, Charlie, and can you put them in a cloth bag? And wrap them so they won't clank together? Men working hard all day need a little comfort to look forward to in the evening."

"Only four, Jeff? You have six men, counting you."

"They are no good to me if they are hung over in the morning, Charlie. They will have to make this last!"

He handed Jeff the sack and a list of what he wanted from the coast. "Have a good trip, Jeff," he called as Jeff walked out the door. Jeff waved over his shoulder without looking back.

Everybody was waiting for him when he got home. Jeff inspected everything, just for his own satisfaction. Wagons were all hitched with extra mules secured behind. Extra harness and feed for the mules in the wagons. Food for the men and bedrolls loaded. And, yes, he did have his money belt on.

He shook hands with his pa and the boys and thanked them for their help.

"Everybody set?" he asked. "Well, let's move 'em out."

He turned to wave to his family. Pa and the boys were there. His sisters waved. But Ma was nowhere to be seen.

****

Jeff rode alongside the first wagon, lost in thought. "Unloaded and mostly down grade as the land sloped to the sea, we should be able to make 25 miles a day easy, especially changing teams like I planned. On the way back we will get only 20 miles a day. You can't ask any more than that out of your livestock.

"If that DeMoss fellow... What was his first name? If he has a wagon waiting for me, that transaction will go pretty fast. I'll allow five to seven days to buy goods and then start back. I told Mr. Barnett.... Burrell, I could do it in two months. It will be close, but I just might make it.

****

He hit it just right to catch the ships docking. China dishes, crystal glassware, several small side-buffets and lamp tables from China with pearl inlay, small chests of various sizes with inlay, fancy glass powder boxes with fur puffs, glass perfume bottles. And he got a good buy on several nice smelling kinds of perfume. Linen table cloths and napkins from England. Dresses and ladies hats from England. Frock coats and beaver hats for the men.

But the thing that always goes fastest is citrus fruit. He got a whole wagon load of oranges and lemons. The bananas were pretty green, and he bought a few stalks to see how far they would make it. "We'll see," he thought.

He bought tea from the East Indies, lots of coffee from a ship from Columbia. Funny thing, the further inland you go, people drink less tea and more coffee! He bought cigars from Cuba, and rum from the islands. Yes, Jeff did know some of the ship Captains quite well, indeed.

From the local merchants he bought medicinal supplies and machinery repair parts. You can't fix American machinery with foreign parts! He bought bolts of silk and linen cloth from the ships, but he bought more fabric from the local merchants. Most people won't pay for imported fabrics.

When, he finally had his wagons all loaded, he took his men to a tavern for a steak and ale. Three ate while three men with rifles watched the wagons. Then they switched places. "I think we still have about four hours of daylight left. Let's get out of town and as far up the road as we can."

****

The trip home was long and pretty uneventful. Only one mule came up lame, but Jeff had brought extras. They were using three teams, now, with the wagons loaded, but he still had three sound mules to switch around and rest them some.

They stopped in several towns along the way to deliver merchandise. But the day they unloaded all the orders in Hendersonville was a joyous day. All the men were home, except Jeff. He still had one wagonload to take to Rome.

He took the men to the saloon and told Charlie to set them up. Before they got too snockered, he reminded them they still had to drive his wagons out to the farm; then they could come back and finish the job if they wanted to.

At the farm, when the mules were put away and cared for, he paid the men and they headed back to town at a high lope. They wanted to get there before their buzz wore off! Jeff turned to his Pa and brothers, "Can I buy you men a drink?" They sat on the porch drinking and hearing all the details of the trip until everyone was a little fuzzy. Jeff staggered up the stairs and was out like a light.

He woke up next morning, hung over. He closed his eyes again because of the pain in his head and dozed off. When he woke up the next time he realized he had his arm around a woman. It was Dora, and they were both naked! "Oh, my God! Ma, what have you done?!?"

He carefully slid out of bed and dressed. He tip toed down the stairs. "Thank you, Selma, for having coffee ready. I need about a gallon in a hurry!"

While she fixed him some eggs, he fed his livestock, harnessed and hitched the mules to the new wagon and saddled his horse. He wanted everything ready for a quick getaway.

Saddle horse tied to the back of the wagon, he slapped the reins on the mules and said, "Get up, there." They slowly moved off toward Georgia. The only person he could see standing outside as he drove off was Ma, clutching her shawl around her shoulders.

In five days he made it to John's house. He was grateful for supper and a bed. Early next morning, Jeff said, "Yall come out to the wagon and see what you can find that you would like to have. You have been good to me. I want to do something nice in return." Sarah found a set of china that made her eyes shine; so he unloaded it for her. John was realizing how hard it was to keep farm machinery running; he chose an assortment of machinery parts. Jeff was happy to give, and they seemed very happy to receive.

As Jeff drove out their gate he waved over his shoulder, and thought, "Six more days to home."

****

With Jeff gone, Ella Anne seemed to get sadder by the day. She didn't want to eat much, even when Jenny took a tray up for her, she just picked at it. After a couple of weeks she wouldn't even come out of her room.

"She just sits there, looking out the window, wearing one of his shirts," Jenny was telling Jessie. "I can't even get her to talk to me much."

"Miss Minerva," Jessie relayed the news, "we have to do something about that girl. It ain't good for her to just sit up there and mope. You have such a way of making people find the good in things, even when things ain't so good."

Minerva was considering what might help as she climbed the stairs. She had thought at first that this would only last a few days, "But, I guess that is out." When Minerva knocked on the door, she could hear the sadness in her daughter's voice, "Come in, Mama."

"How did you know it was me?"

"There is a certain way that you knock. I just knew."

"We haven't seen much of you for several days. I thought it would be nice to have your company. I asked Jessie to heat some water. You can take a long, relaxing bath with something spicy in it to perk up your spirits." She started looking through Ella Anne's wardrobe for a pretty dress for her to put on.

"No need to look in there, Mama. I can't wear anything but Jeff's shirts and my nightgowns. Nothing else will reach around my belly."

"Then a nightgown, it is. Let's go down and get this day started." As they walked down the stairs together, Minerva was surveying her daughter's tummy. "She is awfully big for just four months," she thought.

When the bath was ready, Minerva held Ella Anne's hand as she stepped into the high backed copper tub, just right for soaking and relaxing. Jessie had crushed spearmint leaves in the water, and it smelled dreamy. Minerva pulled Ella Anne's hair up and pinned it, then put a little pillow behind her head. "Now you just soak a little while. Wiggle your toes in that warm water. I'll go see if Jessie has your towel and clean nightgown."

Minerva looked a bit panicked as she walked into the kitchen. "Jessie, have you seen her without her clothes? She is way too big for four months! She may be carrying twins! We must take her to see Dr. Wilson tomorrow and make sure everything is all right.

"Will you send one of the boys to fetch Garrett? I think he and Mr. Burrell are out in the West Central pasture.

"And, Jessie, make some of that mint tea for us, please. I think we will sit out on the porch for a while."

With a plan in mind, Minerva was in control again and calmly took the towel and nightgown in to Ella Anne. She pulled a cane-bottomed chair up near the tub and sat down. Touching her daughter lightly on the shoulder, she asked, "Have you given any thought to names for the baby, yet, dear?"

****

They had Ella Anne dried off and getting into her nightgown when Garrett got to the house.

"Did Mama need me, Jessie?"

"She'll be out real soon. Would you like a glass of lemonade while you wait?"

Walking out of the bath room, Minerva was saying, "Now, put this shawl around you, honey, and don't worry. There is no one here who will stare or be offended that you are in your night clothes."

She saw Garrett then. "Go sit in the porch swing and wait for me, will you, Ella Anne? Jessie is going to bring us some tea."

She put her arm across Garrett's shoulders and walked him a little farther from the door. "I need you to ride into town for me, please. Make sure that Dr. Wilson will be in his office tomorrow right after noon. I think Ella Anne needs to see him. And stop by the Emporium for some peppermint sticks, will you."

"Mama, I'm getting too old for that peppermint stuff. I'm a working man now."

This brought a smile to her face. "Well, get just a few for Ella Anne and me, will you, darling?"

Minerva waited for the swing to rock just right, touching the backs of her knees, and she sat down without breaking the motion. Jessie brought them two glasses of spearmint tea on a tray, and asked, "Is there anything else you think of Miss Minerva?"

"That's all I need. Are you comfortable, Ella Anne? I guess not, Jessie. Thank you."

"Mama, where is Garrett going? He just rode out of here like Yankees were chasing him."

"Oh, I had a hankering for some peppermint sticks, and I thought he might like a break from his work. I guess he was just glad to be going somewhere."

They swung for a while in silence, sipping their tea.

"I think tomorrow you and I should go into town and buy fabric to make you some new dresses that flare out big just under the bust. We can't have you wearing your night clothes all the time until this baby gets here. Do you think you will feel up to it? It might be good to stop in to see Dr. Wilson while we are in town, too. Let him see how you are progressing. Do you think of anything else you would like to do while we are there?"

****

Minerva and Ella Anne stood in the doctor's examination room, while Burrell waited in the outer room.

"Now, Ella Anne, I need you to lie down on the examination table so I can try to feel what you have growing in there. You have gotten pretty large for this soon."

He gently pressed on her tummy. His experienced fingers knew exactly where to press to measure the baby's progress without too much pressure: one hand on each side then one hand at the top and one at the bottom of the baby to measure length. He talked while he worked, "Have you been out to look at the mares lately, Ella Anne? Maybe find one that is due about the same time as you. Yall could keep each other company." They all had a little laugh at that.

He stood beside Ella Anne with his hand resting on her tummy. Looking at Minerva, he said, "I don't think it is twins, just one big baby. Have you felt any movement, yet?" he asked Ella Anne. She squenched her face; "Just a little," she said.

"Well, for the baby to be this big at just four months, I think we may be in for a bit of trouble." He looked directly at Ella Anne, "Ella Anne, I believe you may have a hard delivery. And I believe we need to start preparing for it now so we won't be caught off guard when it is too late to do anything about it.

So, with your permission, I would like to do a pelvic examination on you. Your mother can stand right there and hold your hand. I'll put a sheet across your knees so you don't have to look at me. And remember, this is just part of my job of delivering a healthy baby and keeping the mother healthy."

She slightly nodded her head 'yes' and focused her eyes on her mother. As Dr. Wilson put the sheet across her knees and positioned her feet on the table, Minerva said, "Honey, I did not realize you were getting so big so fast until yesterday when I helped you into the bath. I thought you might be having twins; that would make you get big faster than usual. That is why I sent Garrett to town yesterday, to make sure Dr. Wilson would be in his office today. You are my precious baby girl, and I have to do everything I can to take care of you."

Ella Anne smiled at that. She understood that Minerva was talking so much to try to keep her mind off the examination. "Mama, don't be upset. I have helped deliver foals. I know that is where the baby has to come out." Then they heard the clanking of some metal tools, and they both looked up.

"I've been measuring the width of her pelvis and the set of her hips," Dr. Wilson explained.

He straightened out her legs, shook his head and said, "That is one big baby. And the best thing I can tell you, young lady, is that we might just pull this off because you have perfect 'child bearing' hips."

They both looked at him with a questioning look. "Ella Anne, you are going to spread just like a cow!" he said with a big grin.

It took a minute to absorb his meaning; then they both laughed hilariously. Burrell couldn't stand the waiting any longer, and he poked his head in the door. "You can come in now," Dr. Wilson said with a big smile still on his face. "I guess this should be a family thing anyway.

"Burrell, she is having a very big baby. It is not going to be an easy delivery by any means. But the good news is that she has what we call 'child bearing' hips. Her bones will move a little more than some women's do, to give the baby more room. I just finished telling them that she was going to spread like a cow!" And they all laughed again.

Before Ella Anne sat up, Burrell noticed the large swell in her belly, and he understood what the doctor was talking about. As Ella Anne sat on the table, the doctor pulled up a straight backed chair and motioned for them to do the same.

He looked at Ella Anne, "To try to keep this baby from getting too fat, we need you to be on a very strict diet. Understand we do not want to starve you or the baby. It is just that the baby gets its nutrition from you, and anything sweet that you eat is going to make fat. Some of it goes on you, and part of it goes to the baby. In this situation that is bad.

"So I want you to eat moderate portions. You need one good serving of meat a day, preferably at breakfast or noon. The rest of the time you need to eat lots of vegetables, uncooked, if you like them that way."

He looked at Minerva, "A bedding of chopped onions, carrots and celery under a roast or a hen gives the meat a marvelous taste, and she can have the vegetables from that. They will have the flavor of the meat, and they are delicious themselves. I think the French call it 'Mire Poix'."

He looked back at Ella Anne, "Now, don't load up on potatoes, either. I want you to have one or two servings of potatoes a day, but don't go overboard on them. They are very good for you and the baby, but too much of a good thing… You know. Try to eat a couple of fruits every day.

"You need to walk a lot as long as you are able. I'd say to the barn and back, then rest. Do that several times a day.

"Ella Anne, I'm telling this mostly to you, because your parents will help all they can, but in the end it is up to you to keep yourself and your baby healthy. And stay away from those horses for the most part. I think it would already hurt you too much to try to ride, but be careful when you are petting them. If you got penned between a horse and the stable wall, it could start your labor early."

He looked back at Minerva and Burrell. "Don't expect this baby to go to term. As fast as it is growing, it is going to run out of room and want out of there. I would guess sometime in the first two weeks of October.

"Don't bring her back to town. Even a buggy ride is going to be hard on her. I'll stop in to check on her every time I am out that direction."

As Burrell held the door for the ladies, Dr. Wilson caught him by the shoulder and asked, "Her husband is a very big man, isn't he? Sometimes big babies run in a family line. I'll be ready for it."

Burrell helped his ladies into the buggy. "If you ladies have all the piece goods you need, we might as well head back home.

****

Ella Anne was very careful to follow Dr. Wilson's orders; it was easy as long as there were fresh tomatoes and peaches. She certainly felt better now that she had some dresses that were big enough. And Mama made sure they were pretty colors, with lace and ribbons. 'Things that make a woman feel pretty,' Mama said.

She walked to the barn and back three or four times a day, but by mid-September it was getting harder to walk. One evening she said, "Mama, have you noticed that when I walk, my feet are at least a foot apart? And my knees won't straighten out when I walk either.

"And my back hurts all the time right down here." She was actually pointing to a spot directly between her hip bones. She took a couple of more steps. "Mama! I think I wet myself!!"

Minerva and Jessie threw down what they were doing and rushed to her. Minerva called out in a loud voice, "Garrett, go get Dr. Wilson in a hurry!"

Burrell came running and helped get her up the stairs and into bed. He and Minerva looked at each other across the bed with frozen faces. This was not good. If the baby were born right now, it might not live.

Burrell's mind was working fast "Jessie, will you send one of the boys to get Robert for me. Tell him to bring a lantern and a shovel. Tell him to come quick.

"Minerva, I can't take time to explain right now. I know of something that might help." And he dashed off to gather a lantern and shovel and a toe sack for himself.

He was pacing on the front porch when Robert rode up. "Let Garrett take care of your horse. You come with me." He broke out in a run. "We have to find a weed that grows down by the creek. It has small yellow flowers and fern-like leaves. It grows in a clump and about twelve inches high, kind of bucket-shaped. I know I saw some during summer; there should still be some there. The weather has not turned; it should still have the yellow flowers. That is the only way we will know it."

It seemed as if his papa were talking to himself all this time, making no sense to Robert. "Papa, why are we looking for this weed?"

"Ella Anne is going into labor too early. If I can just find that weed I may be able to help her."

"Help her what, Papa?"

"Slow down her labor.

"When my father first came to this part of the country, it all belonged to the Cherokee. We just flat took it away from them, son! That is what we did! God forgive us. We just kept moving in closer and closer until we squeezed them out. That is what we did!

"Then when Andrew Jackson and the federal government took the land away from the Cherokees and moved them to the Indian Territory, the government had a lottery for veterans. Names of men who had survived the war with England were drawn to give them the Cherokee land. Sort of as a way to repay men for fighting for their country. My pa's name was drawn for the lottery and he picked this piece of land near the

headwaters of the Coosa River. He was already well established, so he divided it between me and my two brothers.

"When I was a boy, if we had a mare that had trouble foaling, this old Cherokee woman would come and help with it. She brought a pouch full of powder that she mixed with cooking grease. Then she would rub it all over the mare from the bottom of the ribs down to her hocks. Somehow it slowed down the labor until things could get right for the foal to come out.

"Once I went with her to find the weeds, so I know what it looks like. Now you look on that other side of the creek. I know there is some here someplace."

They must have walked a quarter of a mile up the creek before Robert sang out, "Pa, come look at this. Is this it?"

Burrell recognized the weed as he was running. "That's it, son. Now dig back from it a little ways so we don't cut off the roots. It has a long, white tap root, like a carrot. There are several here; we will need this whole patch. Tomorrow, in the light of day, we can come back and find some more. Oh, thank God!"

****

When they got back to the house, Dr. Wilson's buggy was there. Burrell handed the sack to Robert and said, "Take these to Jessie. Tell her to wash them; then grind just the root as fine as she possible can." And Burrell bounded up the stairs.

Ella Anne was in quite a bit of pain now. Her moans were growing louder. Dr. Wilson turned as Burrell walked into the room, and he shook his head. "I don't know, Burrell. I was in hopes she could carry it at least a month longer. I'm thinking about giving her small doses of laudanum to ease her pain. But if that baby comes too fast, even laudanum won't help enough."

"Dr. Wilson, I've got some stuff working downstairs, an old Cherokee remedy, that I've seen work on horses. Now, I'd rather try that than take a chance on losing both of them. Would you be okay with that?"

"I've got nothing better."

Burrell hurried downstairs to help Jessie. "I know I haven't been making myself clear, and I'm sorry for that. Jessie this is really good. What is that you are using?"

"This is called a cinnamon grater. It's like a little file; it takes off very small bits at a time, but it's very slow, Mr. Burrell."

"Do we have another one so I can help?"

"Jenny has the other one over at the table." Burrell looked over and saw Jenny for the first time. He saw the small pile of shavings she had.

"That's good. Let's put those two piles together, and I'll start mixing. It takes a while to smooth this on the skin, so we can mix it in small batches, and Minerva can begin applying it."

Robert was looking over everyone's shoulders, "I am sure Sue Ellen has one of those. I'll go get it, and let her know what's going on. I know she is frantic about the way I lit out."

As soon as Burrell got a little batch mixed, he took it to Minerva and explained, "Smooth this all over her lower torso, front and back, from the ribs down. It will slow her labor down without hurting her or the baby. I know this is not much, but as soon as they get more grated, I'll mix it and bring it to you."

He took time to caress Ella Anne's foot between his two hands and pat Minerva on the shoulder, and he and Dr. Wilson stepped out the door. As they hurried down the stairs, Dr. Wilson asked, "You said this is Cherokee? And you have seen it work?"

"I know it works on horses. I don't see why it won't work on people."

"Let me see one of those roots." Dr. Wilson sniffed it, tasted it and looked thoughtful for a few minutes. "I didn't get any sensation on my tongue. I don't believe it to be a narcotic that might interact with laudanum. If this stuff works like you say, we can give her just enough laudanum to dull the pain, and maybe we can get another two weeks' time for that baby."

Jessie and Jenny had another small pile of ground root for him to mix. Burrell hurriedly took it to Minerva. He knew this was a gamble. He knew only the Lord's Will could help them. At this rate, this could take all night, but he was grateful for something to do.

Robert and Sue Ellen came running in. Sue Ellen also had two cinnamon graters; so now they had four people grating. By the time Burrell took up the fourth batch, Minerva said she seemed to be a little easier, and they only had the root to the top of her hips. By morning Ella Anne seemed to be sleeping and only moaned in her sleep once in a while. One crisis was past!

Dr. Wilson had instructed Minerva about the laudanum. A lot of women used small doses to help with menstrual pain. He said he knew he was leaving her in good hands as he left for town.

At daylight, Burrell, Robert and Garrett were at the creek searching for more of the weeds. It seems they grow in small clumps a little bigger than a bucket top, and in the daylight they were much easier to find. They each came home with a toe sack full in time for breakfast.

The food and especially the coffee were welcomed, but Burrell was eager to get more of the root mixed up. He wasn't sure how often it needed to be applied.

****

Ella Anne lay in a state of semi-consciousness for about two weeks. Someone was by her side at all times. Minerva and Jessie took turns. When she was awake enough Minerva spoon fed her chicken broth, held her head up enough that she could sip water, and bathed her face, arms and legs in cool water. This was a hot and still September, hardly any breeze.

While Ella Anne slept, Minerva sat looking out an open window. The slight breeze lazily waved the lace curtain at her. "Sometimes I think this is the hottest month of the year," Minerva thought, as she gazed at nothing in particular.

Her thoughts drifted back to when she was Ella Anne's age. How she loved being out of doors. Oh the fun she had working with Burrell as they cleared this land and built their first house, the house where Jessie lives now. She was filled with energy and ready to tackle almost any job.

Then soon after the house was built, she realized she was expecting a baby, John William. Her life had suddenly changed! She could no longer go gallivanting around on horseback or lift heavy things to help Burrell. So she changed the direction of her energy. She became a homemaker! If this was to be her domain, it would be the very best, most gracious, most comfortable home that she could make it.

She and Jessie were both young and exploring new ideas of food and decorating and entertaining guests. "We have come a long way since then. I believe we have become very proficient!" she said out loud, thinking of the three weddings.

Ella Anne moaned slightly, and Minerva went to her. "Oh, how I thank God that I did not have this kind of trouble having my babies. An ordinary delivery is hard enough. Oh, I pray, God be with her in this!"

****

It was a hard fought battle, but as promised, Jeff showed up very late on the evening of September 28th. He was so thrilled that he had kept his promise to Burrell. But he wasn't sure if he had kept his promise to Ella Anne or not.

He was astonished to see so many lights on at this hour. He bounded up the steps and across the porch. Just as he reached for the door, it opened from the inside and a somber-faced Burrell stepped outside. "Glad to see you, Son. You made it home in time. The baby is trying to be born too early. We have held it off for two weeks, and I don't know how much longer Dr. Wilson will wait to let her have it.

"He kind of thinks the baby is old enough that it is fully formed now, and will have a good chance of survival. But it is a very big baby, and it looks like it is breech.

"Come sit in the swing with me a minute, son." He hesitated. "Having this baby could kill her, Jeff. There is a chance that the baby might not live either. I'm sorry to hit you with such sad news right away. But you know what? We are to a point now, that if it were one of my mares in this condition, I would do what I had to do to save the mare. But that is talking horses, not children.

"You can go up and see her now. She might not be asleep yet. But understand she is only semi-conscious. She may not even know you are there. Are you okay?"

Jeff sat there staring at the boards of the porch floor. Finally, he stood up. "Yes, sir. I'll go up and see her now."

Jeff climbed the stairs slowly and quietly. When he reached the bedroom door and Minerva saw him, she smiled a sad, weary smile, and waved him inside. She stepped aside and let him have her chair by the bedside.

Jeff took her hand in his and covered it with the other. "Ella Jane, I'm home," he said softly. After a few seconds, her eyes blinked slowly and a little smile crossed her face. Then she lay so still Jeff was afraid she was gone. He looked up at Minerva with panic in his eyes.

"I think she went to sleep, Jeff."

****

Jeff hung around the house the next morning. He stayed in Ella Anne's room, but she seemed to be always asleep.

He felt in the way, and he knew he had merchandise in the wagon that needed to be delivered. He asked Burrell if he thought it would be all right for him to go into town and take care of business. That seemed the logical thing to do, so he went to town.

At the Emporium, Mr. Goldman shook his hand and said, "Hey, I hear you are going to be a papa just any day now. The whole town is talking about that stuff Burrell came up with."

All the other store owners also knew that he was about to be a new father. His last stop for the day was the saloon where he delivered rum and cigars. While he was there, he was having a beer at the bar. Someone he didn't know walked up and slapped him on the back. "Barkeep, let me buy a drink for the new father." The bartender started to draw another beer. "No, no. Not that weak stuff. Whiskey for the new papa!" and he slapped Jeff on the shoulder again. He said it loud enough that everybody heard and got interested that Jeff was about to become a new father.

In a little while Jeff was beginning to get woozy. Over their protests, he strongly refused any more drinks, thanked them all, and wobbled out the door. He climbed into his wagon and slapped the reins on the rumps of his mules. About halfway there, Jeff was wishing that these mules knew the way to their new home.

Late in the afternoon, Jeff reached home. As the wagon neared the house, Burrell could tell by the slouched back, that Jeff was either sick or drunk. He almost hoped he was sick. "Then I wouldn't be so mad at him," he thought.

Burrell met him at the wagon and said, "Go on up to John William's room and sleep it off. I'll take care of your stock for you."

*****

Jeff finally was able to get up late the next morning. He didn't feel very good, but he went in to see Ella Jane. She was asleep.

He cleaned up and ate the biscuits and bacon left over from breakfast. When she handed him the food, Jessie just looked at him with no expression. Every time he went in to see Ella Jane, she was asleep, and no one seemed very pleased to see him when he walked into a room. So he wandered out, saddled his horse and went to town.

****

By keeping Ella Anne coated in the root mixture, the contractions were very light and far apart; but she was semi-conscious except when she actually went to sleep. This had bought them two weeks' time for the baby, and Dr. Wilson came out every day to check on them. The baby's heartbeat was strong and regular. Ella Anne's heartbeat was strong and steady. However, by this time he was absolutely certain that it was a breech presentation.

Today when Dr. Wilson came out his face was somber. "The baby was just too big to turn when it should have. We have given the baby all the time we can. I'm afraid to keep Ella Anne in this condition any longer. Minerva, use soap and warm water and wash off all of the root mixture that you can. Let's let her go ahead and have that baby. Lighten up on the laudanum, too. She is going to have to help me with this.

He rolled up his sleeves and put on an apron, like a butcher's apron. "Jessie, keep water heating for me. This may take a long time. Right now I need a basin to wash my hands.

"Minerva, will you be able to assist me, or would you rather Jessie helped me?"

"She is my baby, Doctor. I'll do it."

"Okay, we need to get washed up."

Jessie led him downstairs to the wash room, where there was strong soap for the men to wash up before they entered the rest of the house. And he walked back up to the bedroom with his hands held up to air dry.

"Minerva, open my bag and get out that jar of salve." She did. "Open it please." She did. "Now, ladies, please prop her legs up so I will have some room to work."

Dr. Wilson cocked his head a little to the side and raised one eyebrow. He said, "Minerva, hold the jar of salve for me." He scooped out a handful and said, "Ladies, this is a new product invented by a chemist in Pennsylvania; Cheseborough is his name. He calls it Vaseline. I just got it by mail order, and it may just be what saves both of their lives." While he was talking he had coated the inside of the birth canal with the slippery jell. "Now, Jessie will you stay with her while Minerva and I get washed up?"

When they came back into the bedroom, Ella Anne was conscious enough to feel some pain and she moaned. "Ah, good timing. In just a little bit she will begin to push and we will be in business.

****

Burrell found Jeff sitting at a table in the saloon. As he walked in, he watched Jeff eyeing the saloon girl at the bar. She was twisting her hips just enough to make her knee length skirt swish back and forth; a sultry little smile was on her face.

Anger rose in Burrell as he walked up slightly back of Jeff's right side and said, "You are needed at home, you son of a bitch! Don't you have any more self-control than that?"

Jeff had had enough to drink that he had a smart mouth. "You can't talk to me that way," he said as he started to get up. Before Jeff was completely out of his chair, Burrell had his right arm bent behind him and the more Jeff struggled, the higher he lifted. Burrell steered him toward the door. "Well, where are we going?" Jeff asked belligerently.

"You are going home to listen while your wife has your baby. No man can call himself a father until he has heard the screams while his wife is giving birth to his baby. Get in the buggy!"

"But I rode my horse."

"He is tied to the back of the buggy," Burrell said as he slapped the reins.

They didn't talk on the way home, but they could hear Ella Anne when they pulled up in front of the house. Jeff started to go in, but Burrell stopped him.

"But what am I supposed to do?" he asked.

"You are supposed to sit right here on the porch and suffer through the birth of your child."

As they sat in the porch swing, Jeff had a lot of time to think. He thought about that lovely afternoon by the creek with Ella Jane; then he remembered the chilling click of the Dragoon when Burrell released the tension on the hammer. He thought how nice it was having Ella Jane for his wife, and how he had enjoyed working with Burrell.

He could just see the look on his mother's face when she yelled, "Lord, God! A baby!" Then he remembered waking up with Dora in his bed. "I would have been a lot better off if I had just stayed here," he thought.

Then Dr. Wilson walked out with his coat on and his bag in hand. "It is a girl," he said and a smile spread across his face as if he were satisfied with himself. "A very big baby girl, with a spirit to match her mother, I think. "On my fishing scale she weighed a flat ten pounds! She has good strong lungs and a voice to match. Mother and daughter are doing fine, I believe."

He was still talking as he started down the steps, "Minerva and Jessie can handle it from here, I think. I am going home for a couple hours rest before my day starts."

From inside the house, Minerva called, "Burrell, would you like to see your new granddaughter?"

Burrell looked at Jeff and smiled. He held out his hand and they shook hands. They walked up the stairs together, but Jeff was careful to let Burrell go first. His right shoulder was still hurting a little. Ella Anne was awake enough to recognize each one of them. To her papa she proudly said, "Did you see her? Isn't she beautiful?" To Jeff she said, "You're home," and she smiled.

"What have you named her," Jeff asked.

"Rachael Minerva." And she gave her mama a tired little smile. At that Minerva put her face against Burrell's shoulder and sobbed. It was all over, now. Her babies were both fine. "Thank you," she whispered silently.

Chapter Six
The Wagons

Winter passed by peacefully, beautifully. Rachel was crawling, exploring things that were on her level of the world. She was a healthy baby and very happy. She was the darling of the family. It had taken almost two months for Ella Anne to recuperate enough to really enjoy life again. She did not even want to try sitting a saddle yet, but she could be around the horses and groom them. She helped Jessie in the kitchen when she had sit-down work to do; she did a little gardening. She spent a lot of time in the porch swing watching Rachael.

Jeff enjoyed working with Burrell and Garrett. Most of all Jeff was learning some of Burrell's ways....his definition of what was right and what was wrong...and that there was no gray area in between. There was an easy peace between Jeff and Ella Jane; it was so comfortable being with her.

Yet in the back of his mind, he knew the coming of spring meant it would soon be time for him to head back to the coast. He worried about it. How would Ella Jane feel about his leaving again? It was his job, yet he felt guilty about leaving her. How would Burrell feel about it?

Jeff made a lot of money on the last haul, but he sure caused a lot of problems here at home. And 'here' was home now.

Yet, if he and Ella Jane were to have their own place, he had to make these hauls. While he was pondering all this, his decision was suddenly made for him.

A man rode out from town one day with a telegram from Charlie at the saloon in Hendersonville. The message was short and to the point:

Jeff Dodd
Rome, Georgia

Hurry home. Your ma has put your wagons and mules up for sale.

Charlie

When he showed the telegram to Burrell, he was asking for advice. Jeff told him, "My ma is like this. If she can't get what she wants one way, she will keep trying other ways. And believe me; if I don't get back there quick, she will sell them!

"It is time for me to make another run to the Sound anyway; the ships will be coming in soon, and my customers will be needing merchandise too.

"How does this sound? I could make a run to the coast and bring all the wagons back here with me when it is finished. That way she would not have any leverage over me." Burrell suddenly began to see some cause and effect in Jeff's actions.

"I have been looking at that 80 acre piece of land on the other side of Robert. It is so small, no one seems to want it, and it would be just right for Ella Jane and me. I don't really plan to raise stock. I just need pasture for my mules. With one more haul I could buy it.

Several minutes of stony silence passed while Burrell thought this over.

"Burrell, I am kind of caught between a rock and a hard place. If I leave again, I will disappoint Ella Jane; but if I don't go, I will lose a pretty big investment that it took me several years to build."

"Well, son," Burrell said slowly as he thought. "If this is the way you make your living, your being gone for a couple of months at a time is part of it. Ella Anne will understand after a while. She is a sensible girl. Give her some time to adjust to the situation, and she will come over to your side. I'll try to help her understand.

"As for that other, I'd say you should be on the road right now! You stand to lose a lot if you don't get back there in time."

Jeff went directly to the house to start packing and explaining to Ella Jane. "Honey, if I don't get back there before she finds a buyer, she will sell them, even though they are not hers. That is just the way she is.

"Now, it should be just about like the last trip. I'll be gone about two months. And with the money I make on this trip, we should be able to buy that 80 acres next to Robert and Sue Ellen. We could build our own house. Not a big one, though, but it would be ours."

Ella Anne listened quietly; then began handing him things to pack. As he took them from her hand he could see the tears welling up in her eyes. "Aw, Honey." He put his big arms around her and hugged her long and hard. This would have to last for a long time.

Suddenly, he swung her full circle, her feet swinging out all the way around. "While I am gone, you and your mama can plan how our house should be. Maybe get Burrell to draw it out like he did for Robert and Sue Ellen. How does that sound?" She gave him a sad little smile and said, "Okay."

"Now, will you ask Jessie to throw some food in a sack for me while I go hitch my mules? Tell her anything edible that won't take any time. I can't wait for her to cook anything."

In town Jeff made a quick stop at the telegraph office.

Charlie Nixon
Silver Dollar Saloon
Hendersonville, North Carolina

On my way! Line up drivers. Spread the word – NOT FOR SALE. Do not tell Ma.

Thanks, Jeff

Another quick stop at the bank to set up an account, and he was on his way.

*****

"She did what?" John almost shouted as Jeff and his mules watered up. "I've seen her pull some really rough maneuvers on Pa and bully neighbors and townspeople. But, I believe that is the worst yet.

"Jeff do you need to sleep here tonight, or do you need to keep driving? Your call. Sarah will have dinner ready soon. You could have a good meal and a place to sleep."

"I can't take that chance, John. "Tell Sarah I would appreciate anything she has that doesn't need to be cooked. But there is still about three hours of daylight. I'd better use it."

****

When Jeff drove into Hendersonville about sundown, both he and his mules were bone weary. He had been moving from sunup to sundown for several days. He headed straight for Charlie's to find out the news.

"No, I don't want anything to drink, Charlie" Jeff waved his hand flat across. Have you heard anything about my wagons and mules?"

"She still hasn't found a buyer. I spread it around town that you were coming back, and you did not want to sell. Got you the same drivers lined up as your last haul."

"Charlie, I sure owe you for letting me know about this. Will you get word to the drivers that I want to start trimming hooves early tomorrow morning? Tell them to meet me here. I'll buy them breakfast to make up for such short notice. If we can get it done before it gets too late, I'd like to leave tomorrow.

"I am going to take my rig to the livery, and I need a room for the night, Charlie. I'd like to come up the back stairway, and tell those girls, if any of them knock on my door, I'll shoot them!"

Jeff was so tired he was asleep as soon as he got his boots off. He did not even remember his head hitting the pillow. When daylight broke, he felt better, bone weary, but better. He splashed his face with water and wiped at his neck and underarms. "That will have to do," he thought. "Maybe we can stop where the road crosses a creek and I'll do better."

He found the drivers waiting at the front of the saloon, and they headed down the street to the café. "Ham and eggs for everyone, Joe. A bowl of grits, biscuits, gravy, the works. We have a long way to go before dark. I need to feed these men good. And coffee, lots of coffee," he added.

As they ate, Jeff laid out his plan. "I want you men to ride out to Pa's place, round up my mules and start trimming hooves. They will be surprised because they didn't know I was coming, but I think Tom and Frank will help. Someone oil and check the harness. Better grease the axels and water down the wheels, too. I didn't take time to grease them when we brought them home in September.

"I'll see my banker and my customers and be out there as soon as I can. If we get this all done and there is any daylight left, I want to leave today. Does that sound like it will work?"

The others were heading out of town while Jeff paid the bill. "Joe, can you fix me up with some traveling food that won't spoil or need cooking for us to eat between towns?" Joe nodded his head. "I'll stop by on my way out. Oh, and pack it for bouncing around in a wagon, would you?"

He made the rounds of his customers and went to the bank. He went by the livery and hitched his mules then drove back to the café. As he left, he saw Charlie on the porch waving him to the saloon. In his hand was a cloth sack with a drawstring. "Good old Charlie," he thought.

****

It was about 10:00 AM when Jeff rode up to his Pa's place. "Funny how good that feels to call it 'Pa's place' instead of Ma's," Jeff thought with a grin. He purposely drove past the house and straight to the pens where the men were working.

"Sure knocked the props out from under Ma when those men rode up and said they were to round up your mules and trim them!" Tom was grinning from ear to ear. We have about half of them done. With you here, it will go faster." He nodded his head slightly toward the house, "The boys told me you wanted to leave today if possible. I understand. I think it would just make things worse if you tried to talk to her." With that, he picked up the foreleg of the mule he was working on. "Well, find yourself a place and jump right in!" he laughed.

Pa and the girls wandered out one at a time to say 'hello'. Lou looked at him with questioning eyes and said, "I took your room, Jeff. We didn't figure you would ever be using it now that you are married. Was the baby a boy or a girl? Oh, a girl? What did you name her? Rachael? Rachael Dodd! Oh, how pretty. Well, I'd better get back in the house before I'm missed. Bye, Jeff."

****

All was done, hitched and loaded by 4:00 in the afternoon. Jeff shook hands with his brothers, thanked them gratefully for all of their help and told them goodbye. Pa walked him all the way out to the wagons. "You are taking along a lot of spare mules, aren't you, boy? Are you buying another wagon?"

"This is all of them, Pa, I am not going to stop on my way back through. I sure thank you for taking care of my mules all this time. If you need to get in touch with me, talk to Charlie at the saloon. Okay?"

He nodded to his pa and motioned to the lead driver to move out.

As they rode along, Jeff smiled to himself and nodded. "I believe that worked out pretty smooth. No confrontation with Ma. Got all of my belongings that are really valuable. That was a good plan, too, telling the men to tie their saddle horses behind the wagons. On the way back I'll explain that the haul ends in Rome, and they will need their horses to get home. If I pay them extra, I don't think they will mind too much."

****

While Jeff was gone this time, Ella Anne had plenty to keep her busy. Rachael was energetic and adventurous. She had a lot of Ella Anne's spirit. She had blond hair and her face looked more like Ella Anne.

Ella Anne and her mother had fun working on house plans. They tried several designs and finally decided on the one that seemed to be most workable. It had to have at least two bedrooms, kitchen, dining room and parlor, and a little bathroom off the kitchen; that was the absolute minimum. And a nice big porch, of course. While they were working on the layout of the rooms and the size of each room, Minerva said, "Have you given any thought to the help you will need running this new house?"

A startled look crossed Ella Anne's face, "Oh, Mama! No, I hadn't thought."

"I talked to your papa about it. If Jenny and Bob want to go work for you and Jeff, it will be okay."

Delight spread over Ella Anne's face, "Oh, Mama, that would be wonderful," she said as she started pushing back her chair to get up.

"Now, don't you go running in there, and in your excitement, just throw it at her. We need to talk about what pay to offer them, and living quarters. You must be prepared to offer them security, or it will not be appealing to them. Take out another page of paper. Let's work on a sketch for a house for them."

After dinner that evening, Minerva and Ella Anne joined Burrell in his study. He could tell by their faces that they had something exciting to discuss. "What are you two cooking up?"

"Oh, Papa, Mama said that if Jenny and Bob wanted to come work for Jeff and me, it would be all right. I want your advice, Papa. Do you think they would?"

"I think they might. I know by the way she acts that Jenny adores you. Yall are just about the same age. With Jeff gone on these long hauls, you certainly need a dependable man to take care of things. And Bob is very dependable, a good thinker.

"I haven't seen anything to make me think he wouldn't like working for Jeff. What would you do about housing for them?"

"Well, Mama and I have been working on plans for a one story house. Maybe Jeff will be able to build a house for them too. Here, look at these diagrams Mama and I drew up."

"I like the plans for your house, but you must remember that Jenny and Bob are working on a family of their own. They will need a little more room, don't you think?

"Oh, you are right, Papa; we will work on that some more," she looked at her mother and nodded.

"What should we pay them, Papa?"

"Well, for the past few years I've given Big Jessie, house, food, and $10 a month for every one of her family who puts in a good day's work. The children run errands for free, you know. But this is 1889. The South is beginning to get on its feet, so to speak. I believe you should consider offering them $25.00 a month for the two of them. They are both hard workers."

"Okay, I'll talk to Jeff as soon as he gets home. And we can have the plans all drawn up. Now, don't let on that we are planning this until he says it is all right."

****

After breakfast one morning, Burrell offered, "I have no particular plans today. If you ladies are not busy this morning, maybe you would accompany me."

"Where are we going, Papa?"

"I think a little target practice is in order."

"Jenny, do you have time to watch Rachael for us this morning?" Ella Anne asked.

It was fun to be outside in the cool of the morning. "There is no livestock in this pasture so we will face this direction." Burrell set up a few bottles and cans he had brought. Now, I know both of you ladies are good with a rifle; I thought we might practice with my pistol. The country is getting so crowded now, new people coming in all the time; it's hard to tell who you can trust.

"Minerva would you like to try first?"

"Oh, Burrell, you know you taught me to shoot a pistol years ago," She protested.

"I know, but this one is heavier and you have to thumb the hammer back each time. If your wrist is not strong enough, you will shoot high every time because of the kick. Here, try it."

Bang, bang, bang. Three misses.

"Do you see they are going high? I really don't expect you ladies to have that kind of strength in your wrist; so you need to aim a little low to allow for the kick. Understand?"

Bang, bang, bang. Three hits and Burrell took the pistol to reload. "Oh, Mama. You did good! You always were a good shot." Memories of little Toby flooded Minerva's mind.

"Here, Ella Anne, see what you can do," he handed the pistol to her.

Bang… bang…bang. She had a little more trouble thumbing the hammer than her mother. "All high," Burrell said, taking the pistol and reloading the three shells. "Try aiming about an inch lower. See what that does."

Bang…bang…bang. "All right you hit that last one. Try about two inches lower than the target, this time. And remember as you practice, your wrist is getting stronger every time that pistol kicks. It will be sore tomorrow, but it will be getting stronger."

"Papa, why are we really doing this?"

He took a deep breath and looked thoughtful for a moment.

"Sweetheart, I'm not really sure I did you any favors in letting you marry Jeff." He stopped for a few seconds to see her reaction.

"But, Papa?" Her furrowed brow showed her disbelief at what she was hearing.

"Honey, he is a womanizer; I saw that with my own eyes when I pulled him out of the saloon the night Rachael was born. And once a man gets started at that, it is hard for him to change. Understand, I believe he is trying to change, but you need to keep that in the back of your mind.

"He is also a heavy drinker at times. When he is here, he doesn't seem to want to drink.

"That brings up the worst of all, his mother. Did you know she was going to sell his wagons and all his mules if he did not get back there fast when he made this spring run?"

She shook her head slowly. "I didn't understand, but I got the impression that he had to go."

Burrell nodded, "And when he gets back here this time, I suspect he might be all messed up in his thinking again.

"When she gets her claws into him, he seems to need to spend a lot of time in the saloon. And when he is drinking he just doesn't seem to have much self-control.

"Well, that is the long and the short of it. I'm sorry to have to tell you all of this, but you are a married woman, now. And I think you should know that you have these things to deal with. Most of the time, he is a decent man. But at those times he seems to lose control."

He hesitated a moment to let her digest some of this information. "You know there is a way out. There is such a thing as divorce."

She took a deep breath and looked very somberly at her father. "No, Papa, I bought this horse; I'll ride him!"

Burrell nodded in admiration of her resolve. "Now, it wouldn't be smart to jump on him for these things. That would put you into the same category as his mother. Just keep it in the back of your mind and be prepared. Maybe it will help you avoid some issues later on."

She turned back to the cans. Bang, Bang, Bang. She hit three in a row. "Excellent," Burrell and Minerva knew she would master this.

"Now, daughter, I want you to practice until you can hit within a three inch square every time you shoot."

"Why, Papa?"

"In Jeff's line of work, I think you are going to be spending a lot of time alone.

"Honey, if a man is coming after you when you are alone, almost anywhere else you hit him he can still keep coming. But if you can hit that little three inch square, his legs will be paralyzed on the spot and he will bleed to death where he falls. Am I making myself clear for you?"

She nodded, remembering how stiff-legged the new geldings walked.

"And, honey, don't ever point a gun at a man thinking you can scare him. As you point it, you cock it! And if you point a gun, know in your mind that you plan to use it. That moment's hesitation gives him the edge he needs. Do you understand?"

"I think so, Papa."

****

By the time Jeff got home from this run, Rachael was pulling up to things and trying to walk around them while she held on. She couldn't take very many steps before she would fall, but if she landed on her rear end, things were fine. Sometimes she stepped on her other foot while she was stepping sideways. That usually caused her to hit the floor, splat! Then she needed some tender cuddling to recover; then up and try the same thing again. Ella Anne kept her dressed in really pretty little dresses with her hair in finger curls.

Jeff's trip had been much more pleasant this time, hard, but not distressing like before.

Things were right between him and Ella Jane, now. Dr. Wilson said that having such a big baby had messed her up quite a bit inside, and she probably would not be able to have any more children. But things between her and him were okay.

****

Burrell had had a hard time finding out who owned that 80 acres, so he wrote to John William. It had passed through several owners and then to some heirs, but he finally tracked down the current owner. There were taxes owed on it. Burrell had talked him down to a pretty good price, if Jeff paid the taxes. So the legal work was quickly done and it belonged to Jeff and Ella Anne.

Jeff liked the house plans she had made. It was one storied, and it seemed small by comparison to the Barnett house. But the rooms were large enough to be very comfortable. They ordered the lumber and got started building as soon as possible. Burrell, Robert and Garrett were planning to help.

"And, do you know what, Jeff? Mama and Papa said if Jenny and Bob wanted to come to work for us they could. Mama and I have made a diagram of a house for them to live in and all. What do you think?"

"I hadn't thought about that," Jeff said. "Let me talk it over with Burrell in the morning. That just may be a very good idea."

****

Burrell pointed out all the plusses of having Jenny and Bob work for them, especially Bob. "You are going to be away for long stretches and you need someone you can trust to take care of the place and your stock.

You also need someone who will be respectful and take care of Ella Anne and Rachael while you are gone.

"You know what a hard worker Bob is; he is strong and healthy. Why, Jeff, they are just like family.

"You would need to talk to him yourself and see if he is willing to make the change, but it is my guess that he will."

Burrell and Jeff went out to where Bob was working and the three of them sat in the shade of a tree to talk. "There will be a lot of work for both of us right at first, Bob. We will have to build two houses, a barn and working pens just as fast as we can get it done. After that, it would be feeding and taking care of the place. Burrell said I couldn't find a better or more dependable hand than you, if you are willing to make the change. I know you have worked for Mr. Burrell for a long time."

"I think I would like that, Mr. Jeff. And I know my Jenny would like to be close to Miss Ella Anne. Have you talked to her yet?"

"No, Ella Jane is busting at the seams waiting to ask her. But, I thought I should ask you first. What do you say? Are we good?"

****

When Jeff and Burrell got back to the house, they talked to Ella Anne and Minerva for a minute; then went back outside.

Ella Anne and Minerva smiled at each other. Minerva took Rachael outside to the porch swing, and Ella Anne went to the kitchen. "Jenny, will you bring four glasses of that spearmint tea that I like out to the porch, please?"

"Yes, ma'am, Miss Ella Anne."

When she brought the four glasses of tea to the porch, she looked around for the men. "Why, there are only two of you. I thought you needed four glasses of tea?"

They each took a glass. "Thank you, Jenny," said Ella Anne. "Please sit down and have a glass of tea with us," she gestured toward a chair nearest the swing.

Minerva called out, "Jessie, can you come out here a moment?"

Ella Anne continued, "Jenny, now that Jeff is home from his haul, we are going to start building a house on that 80 acres next to Robert. We were wondering if you and Bob would like to come to work for us."

Jenny was so stunned that she seemed frozen with her glass of tea suspended just above the table. She looked from Ella Anne to Minerva, then back again with a questioning look on her face.

Minerva nodded her head and said, "Yes, Jenny, we have been planning this for some time. We have just been waiting for Jeff to get home to be sure it was going to work."

Ella Anne could hold her excitement no longer. "And Bob is going to take care of Jeff's mules and all. And we are going to build you a new house, too. .And we will be just down the road from our mamas!" She was so elated that she clapped her hands three times before she realized it

Jenny had sat down the glass of tea and sat with her hands folded in her lap and a blank look on her face; then tears began to roll down her cheeks.

"Oh, Jenny, don't be upset. I thought you would be happy," Ella Anne said with compassion, thinking Jenny did not want to come with her.

"Jessie, will you help us out here?" Minerva asked. "We had planned for this to be sort of a party; but it seems we have made Jenny cry."

When they finished explaining the situation to Jessie, she smiled at her daughter and said, "I think she is just a little overwhelmed, aren't you, honey?

"You see, Jenny can do everything that I do, but she has never had the responsibility for it by herself. But I think you can do it, baby. And just think of the fun you and Miss Ella Anne will have running a house by yourselves!

"I will be just down the road, right here, if you think you need help on something."

Ella Anne could be quiet no longer. "Jeff has already asked Bob, and he said 'yes', and you are going to have a nice new house. Look, Mama and I drew up these plans. Do you think you would like this? And we can have our own furniture and pick out curtains, and everything." In her uncertainty, Ella Anne's mouth was running away with her.

Jenny sat there for a long time rubbing her hand on the drawing of the house for her and Bob. She looked at her mother and said, "Oh, Mama," and began to cry big sobs.

"I think that means 'yes'," Big Jessie said as she cuddled her daughter.

Ella Anne jumped out of the swing and hugged Jenny and said, "Don't cry, Jenny. It will be all right. We will have fun."

The glimmer of a smile crept across Jenny's face, slowly at first as thoughts of the adventure marched through her mind. When she broke into a big, toothy grin, they all began to laugh. They sat there in the heat of the afternoon, drinking their mint tea and chattering like little birds. There were so many plans to make.

****

They built the cook house first so that Jenny could keep them fed good while the men worked. They built Ella Ann and Jeff's house next and got all settled in with borrowed pieces of furniture that the family could spare. They immediately began to build the house for Jenny and Bob, who had been driving a small wagon from the Barnett farm every day until their house was finished.

Sitting on the porch one evening, Jeff remarked, "I really like the plans your dad drew up for this house. When we get everything else done, we can build a very high-pitched roof on this house and make two, maybe three bedrooms upstairs. The reinforcements are already built into the house to support that added weight. Won't that make it a pretty house?"

After a short break, Jeff ordered the lumber for a barn.

"Jeff, that barn is so big it makes our house look little!" Ella Anne said with a pouty face.

Jeff laughed that she felt indignant. "Honey, do you realize that we have nearly 30 mules and only 80 acres. I am going to have to put up hay and feed for them. We have over 20 sets of harness that we need wall space to hang. It will all be used, besides there will be a row of stalls across that side for horses.

"Oh, that reminds me, I need to ask your father who around here will have hay and feed to sell."

Burrell knew some people who usually raised extra feed to sell. Jeff reserved the feed and hay, and Burrell was going to pay for it and see that it was delivered and stored well if Jeff was away.

"Bob, I know that you can handle this. I want Mr. Burrell to go along to make sure other people know you are the one they will be dealing with in the future if I am away. Probably next time, people will know to deal with you proper and there will be no problem."

By the time the barn was finished, it was time for Jeff to make his August run to the Sound. This time he hired local men to drive his wagons; men that Burrell knew were dependable men and could handle three teams of mules.

Jeff sent a telegram to Charlie,

Charlie Nixon
Silver Dollar Saloon
Hendersonville, North Carolina

Headed your way. I already have drivers. Please gather orders for me. Do not tell Ma.

Jeff

****

When Jeff returned this time he brought home new furniture for their new house: a beautiful bed with four tall, carved bedposts, two bureaus, a dining room suit with china cabinet and sideboard, a set of china, silver and crystal, and a high-backed copper bathtub. As a surprise for Bob and Jenny he brought a pretty bed and bureau for their new house "Next trip I will get new furniture for the parlor," he promised Ella Anne.

Rachael was walking a little, now. She grew so fast while he was gone. He was absolutely amazed at the changes in her.

This trip had gone rather smoothly, and Jeff was happy to be home with his family. He seemed comfortable and easy.

****

Bob took Jeff out to show him the work he had done on the fences. The fence between them and Robert had been in good shape, but the rest needed a lot of repairs. Bob had fixed them good enough to hold the mules for right now, while they were tired, but he needed Jeff to buy some more posts and rails so he could really fix it right.

They spent most of the morning in the barn looking at what all Bob had done to make the space usable. Jeff showed him how he would like the pens laid out and they figured how much material that would take.

Jeff would make the order this week, and he would be rested by the time the fencing was ready to pick up. "Bob, have you ever driven a wagon with three teams?" Jeff asked.

"No, sir. Mr. Burrell never needed to haul anything that heavy."

"Well, you can practice on that. We may be using those wagons more often. You never know what might turn up. Mr. Burrows at the lumber mill said he was glad to know that I had these heavy wagons if he gets any really big orders. Like when we were building."

Chapter Seven
Charlie

Life rocked along at an even pace for a couple of years. One time when Jeff came home from a trip Rachael was toddling; the next time she was walking; the next time she was running.

When he came home this time she was three years old and swinging on the front yard gate. Ella Anne had asked for some paint for the shutters Bob was building for the new houses. Well, it wasn't really new anymore, but they still spoke of it as the 'new house'. She wanted moss green and a little bit of peach for trim for her house and red for Jenny's.... Jenny liked red.

Life was really getting easy for Jeff. He made his runs to the coast twice a year, and did a little hauling for Burrows at the mill. Bob had the place looking really nice, everything clean, neat and organized. Jeff felt he was riding the crest of a wave.

He was sitting on the front porch swing watching Rachael play in the yard, when a lone horseman, coming from the direction of town, turned off the lane. Jeff stood to receive his guest and puzzled over who it could be as the man rode closer.

"Charlie!" Jeff ran across the yard to meet him. "What are you doing way out here? How did you find me? Who is running your saloon?"

Charlie dismounted and tied his horse. "Well, Jeff, after you left Hendersonville this last time, I thought about how you come and go, always doing something different, always have interesting stories to tell. I was not real enthused about spending another winter there with not much to keep me entertained. I decided I needed some excitement in my life.

"While I was standing behind the bar, polishing glasses, feeling really down, some fool walked in and offered me twice what my saloon was worth! Cash money! And I took it! Handed him my apron and walked out!

"I'm headed for Oklahoma. They are going to open up the Indian Territory in a few months. I thought I'd ride on out there and scout the area. Find out where I want to head for when they fire the starting pistol.

"Why don't you come with me? Tom and Frank are coming. I think they are a day or two behind me. I told them I'd meet them at your place. Do you have room for me, or do I need to go back into town?"

"We have a pretty nice room in the barn; we can fix you a place to sleep. "Ella Jane," he yelled over his shoulder, "Come look who is here! My friend, Charlie, from Hendersonville!

"Charlie, how in the world did you find me?"

"I knew you were near Rome, Georgia. I just stopped at the saloon and asked, and here I am. Lots of people in town know you, Jeff."

****

Two days later, Tom and Frank rode in all excited about the Oklahoma Land Run....going to get them some land of their own. "We are going to the Territory!" they said in blustery and slightly louder than usual voices.

"Did you boys run away from home?" Jeff teased with a grin.

Tom nodded his head and lifted his eyebrows, "When everyone went to bed one night, we slipped out the back and saddled up. Didn't tell anyone we were going or where!"

Ella Anne borrowed more covers from her mother to make them beds in the hay.

****

They spent days looking over the maps that Jeff had for his freighting. He had maps of Arkansas, Louisiana, Oklahoma and Texas; just what they needed. The more they looked and speculated, the more their excitement rose. And as the thrill of adventure rose, the more Jeff was dragged in.

Jeff had ridden over into Arkansas and Southeastern Oklahoma once to check the possibility of business there, but there were not enough people at that time to make it a paying haul. He had ridden through Texas down to Galveston. There were good possibilities for hauling from Galveston. Now that Oklahoma was opening up he could see definite possibilities for his business.

The soil in most of Georgia was wearing out from planting the same crop year after year. Of course, Robert kept telling people to plant something different in each field and rotate them to help replenish the soil, but no one listened to him. They just kept doing what they had always done, and the crops kept getting poorer and poorer. And there seemed to be less rainfall every year lately.

Times were getting hard everywhere it seemed. There were more people living hand to mouth than those who weren't. Jeff's business had begun to slow down some, too; merchants can't sell if people do not make a good crop. "I'll bet a lot of people from these parts are thinking of going someplace better, too," Jeff thought.

"Might be a good move to go along with these men and scout out this Oklahoma Territory and the people who are going to live there," he told Ella Jane.

It was hard to talk to Ella Jane about his going; she didn't like the idea one bit. "It will work out okay, Ella Jane."

"But Jeff, you just got home!"

"I know. It is several months until time to make my run to the Sound, and I'll be back in plenty of time, honey." He completely missed her point. In his mind he was already off on another adventure.

****

Next morning he asked Jenny to start making up some traveling food for four men. He didn't even want to talk to Burrell about this. He dreaded that narrow-eyed look Burrell always gets while he is thinking about something he is suspicious of.

Right after breakfast Ella Anne went out to the barn and started gathering up her mother's covers and shaking the hay out of them. "I guess we had better wash all of these before we return them," she told Jenny, "If they are going, they are going! But they are not taking any of Mama's covers! They can use what they brought with them."

Jeff saw them carrying in all of the covers and hurried over. "Honey?" he said questioningly and waited for her to explain.

She never looked his way; she just kept walking toward the house.

****

While the men poured over the maps at the dining table, Ella Anne appeared from the kitchen. "Jenny has some hardtack, jerky and some of those canned beans you brought. Are you using saddlebags or a pack horse?"

They all looked at her, then at each other. "Pack horse, I guess," Jeff said, and realizing they were being asked to leave, they started folding up the maps.

"Don't you dare take one of my mares," she said as she started back to check on Rachael.

Bob put the pack saddle on one of the geldings and helped them pack it so that each side weighed about the same. After they mounted, he walked along behind them as far as the house; then he stood in the shade and watched them go. It was a silent bunch that rode off. Jeff looked back, but Ella Jane was not there.

****

The four men and a pack horse made their way across the tops of Alabama and Mississippi, angling up to cross the Mississippi River at Memphis. They watched the terrain change as they traveled west. In Mississippi the land was low alluvial soil, right for farming. As they went farther into Arkansas it became more mountainous.

"Let's head for Little Rock, than go on up to Ft. Smith," Jeff suggested. "If I remember right, at Little Rock we either have to go North or South. Mountains start just west of there, and we sure don't need that."

They gathered some information at Little Rock. The court at Ft. Smith was to have jurisdiction over this whole area until the law caught up with the Boomers. The land had already been surveyed into counties and townships.

The land included in the run was right in the center of the Indian Territory: Canadian, Cleveland and Kingfisher, Logan, Oklahoma and Payne counties. Guthrie and Oklahoma City were the two favored town sites of the area. Everyone could file on 160 acres with title to it after they had improved it.

From the north the Boomers would line up along the Kansas state line. From the south they were lining up at Purcell, Indian Territory on the south side of the Canadian River. From the east, Ft. Smith was the starting point. The starting date was April 22, 1889, high noon.

At Ft. Smith they found people were already gathering. The town was overcrowded with families camped out in every level spot.

"This is going to be such a riotous place when they start the Run. Why did you bring your family into such a dangerous place?" Jeff asked one man. "They could be hurt or killed if your wagon hits a bump or a hole and wrecks."

"I am going to make the race on horseback. Ma will bring the wagon and kids along, after it settles down."

Charlie was interested in the two cities named. He wanted to locate where there would be a bustling business for a saloon. Tom and Frank were interested in finding good grazing for livestock. Jeff was more interested in the people.

He looked at the number of people already gathered at Ft. Smith and thought, "There has got to be at least this many coming from the north, west and south. They are opening up a lot of land, but not enough for every one of these people to get a good homestead.

"The ones who stay are going to have a hard year because it will be too late to break the land and raise a crop this first year, let alone build a house.

"They will need supplies, but if I freight up supplies, will they have money enough to buy them? The people I have seen here don't look as if they have much more than what it takes just to get by."

*****

It was impossible to get a room in Ft. Smith, so they slept with their horses at the livery. Early next morning Jeff said, "Well, the horses are rested; let's see if we can get some coffee and ride on over and see what this land looks like."

West of Ft. Smith, the country seemed to be settling out into open prairie for a while, flat, dusty and windy. The natural grass kept down the dust until the horses' hooves hit it and stirred it up. It got dryer, the further west they went.

As they passed creeks where there were tall trees, they began to notice people had already settled on these good areas, leaving just the open prairie for the Boomers who were waiting for the legal time to start. They soon learned these people were called Sooners. They were people with enough piss and vinegar to think they could withstand the legal racers and the law as well.

At Oklahoma City they found that United States deputy marshals had already laid out the town and were camping on the best locations. It was not legal for surveyors or federal employees to be there early, much less to make claims; but they were doing it and just daring anyone who challenged them on it.

Charlie found two lots that seemed to suit him and put his name on the stakes, just in case that might be enough to hold them. "We will just have to see," he said.

Jeff had seen enough to make his evaluation, "Guthrie is sure to be just about like this, too. Let's ride down to McAlister's Station on the way back. Mr. McAlister has been living out here long before they ever thought about opening up the Territory. Maybe he has some information for us."

They dropped down a little ways southeast to McAlister's Station and stayed a couple of days to rest up. McAlister did have some advice to share with the men.

"There are so many people who have just about lost everything because there hasn't been enough rainfall for the last few years; they are willing to try anything to make a new start. They are going to come in here with plows and a lot of kids to feed.

"This old country ain't going to like the plow. It is the roots of the natural grass that is holding down the sand when the wind gets to blowing. Once they break up the natural sod, they are going to find that we don't get enough rainfall to grow a good crop, and that sand is going to blow."

He looked at Jeff, "You might find enough of these Sooners and Boomers with enough money to buy your merchandise if you freight it up here, but I'd be sure I had a man riding shotgun on each wagon. There will be more people wanting to steal than to buy."

He studied Tom and Frank a few minutes and said, "The best grazing is further west and near the Texas border. The land just north of the Red River seems to be good grassland. Only problem there is, I hear tales that the Federal Government is going to keep that for the Indians. Don't intend to open it up to white people. You would be taking your chances there, too.

"Well, I don't envy you boys. There are a lot of possibilities here; your big decision is...is it worth the chance you take?"

The other men had wandered off to bed to think all of this over, and only Jeff and McAlister still sat on the porch in the dark.

"You said your wife raises a few horses. And you need to stay away from the areas that already have railroads for your freighting to make a living. There is a little valley in the southeast corner of the Territory that I think all of these people are going to overlook. It is nice grassland, if it is not overgrazed, right up next to the Lower Quichita Mountains and just north of the Red River. That might be a real nice spot for you. There's no towns around close, but you will be freighting up from Galveston. You will pass through a lot of Texas towns on the way. Something to think about." He touched the brim of his hat to say goodnight and went inside.

****

Next morning with a cup of coffee in his hand Jeff sat down and asked, "Well, you boys got any ideas?"

Everyone looked at one another to see who would speak up first. Finally, Tom said, "Frank and me thought we might ride on west and see that grassland McAlister was talking about."

Everyone looked at Charlie. "Well, I still like the idea of a saloon in Oklahoma City. There is bound to be plenty of trade. I might ride back up there and see if I can pay one of those deputy marshals to hold that spot for me. Might work and it might not. Just depends on whether I find an honest one or not. What are you going to do Jeff?"

"Well, if you are going to have a saloon out here, I had better go get you a load of lumber and a load of whiskey. Don't you think?" That got a laugh out of all of them. Besides, I told Ella Jane I would be back before Christmas. I still have time to see what the shipping at the Gulf Coast has to offer.

"Charlie, how am I going to get in touch with you? I'll need to know where you end up and how much lumber you want."

"After I make some kind of arrangements for some lots in Oklahoma City, I guess I'll go back to Ft. Smith and wait for the starting gun. You can send me a wire there. I'll check with the telegraph agent regularly. Jeff, mind you, I'll want as good lumber as you can get, but as cheap as you can get it. Okay?"

They all said goodbye and rode out in different directions. Jeff was the last to leave and he headed southeast to check on the valley McAllister told him about.

****

Jeff liked this little valley, nestled up next to a nice little mountain on the east, the Red River to the south, close enough you could almost smell it. Funny how running water changes the smell of the air. Grass as tall as a man's knee; but you could see that the top soil was sand. "Those farmers coming in here with plows are going to tear up the natural grass roots that hold this old country in place just like McAlister said, and it seems like there is always a good breeze." He found a rock to sit on at the foot of the mountain and let his horses graze while he thought.

He usually made his runs to the coast in April and August. "I got home around the first of October, and here it is starting November." He shivered and untied his heavy coat from behind the saddle. "If there were any moisture in the air, it might begin to snow soon. It would be foolish to try to make a freight trip in winter weather. There would be no ships at the docks anyway."

"How am I going to get lumber and whiskey to Charlie in April and be there to meet the ships in April too?"

The smell of pine made him aware of the trees on the mountain behind him. Just south of him was the East Texas Piney Woods! Instantly a plan formed in his mind.

"I believe there is a saw mill at Mt. Pleasant, Texas. If I put in the order now, they can have the lumber for Charlie's saloon ready when I come through in mid-April. The Gulf of Mexico shouldn't be as hard to navigate in late winter as the Atlantic. Reckon I can get a load of goods in Galveston in mid-March?

"First things first," he thought. "Where do I get across this Red River? I hear there are beds of quicksand in it." He thought a moment. "Well, I believe the first white people went into Texas at a buffalo crossing at Jonesboro not far south of here, but a big flood wiped out that whole town. I wonder what it did to the crossing? Well, Jeff, you will never know unless you ride down and see."

****

He could tell there had been no recent travelers where he thought Jonesboro used to be, so he swung west on the north side of the river. "I heard about Colbert's Ferry crossing; I wonder how far it is? That way I won't have to take a chance with my mules and wagons in the mud."

It turned out Colbert's Ferry was over three days ride west. Jeff could still see the effects of the high water when the Red gets on the rampage. There had been a railroad bridge across the river near where the ferry ran. It connected Colbert, Oklahoma and Dennison, Texas. Then Mr. Colbert got a grant from the United States government to build a bridge right beside it for horses and wagons.

Not long after the new bridge was finished, heavy rains to the northwest caused the Red to get up. Although the water did not quite reach the top of either of the bridges, the uprooted trees washing down the river tangled up against the pilings. They held for a while, but eventually the strength of the rushing water broke the braces of the railroad bridge, which was on the westward side. A section of the railroad bridge hung against the bracing for the wagon bridge and soon took it out. They rebuilt the railroad bridge, but Mr. Colbert went back to his ferry for wagons and horses.

Jeff talked to the ferry operator about his wagons and the weight he would probably be hauling. They decided the ferry could accommodate his wagons…if Jeff's mules would stand while the ferry was on water.

After crossing the river, he had three days ride back east to the lumber mill to find out how much notice they would need to get Charlie's lumber ready. "Twenty five cents for horse and rider to cross the river. Two dollars for each three-team wagon! But," he thought, "that is just an expense you have to figure in, like mule feed. And their ferry seemed sturdy enough for the load we will be hauling."

****

He hit Mt. Pleasant nearing sundown. The mill had already shut down for the day, but the owner was still in his office. Jeff laid out his plan, approximately how many board feet he would need and about when he would be back through to pick it up. "If this thing works!" Jeff emphasized. The man gave him a workable figure compared to the lumber he bought for the new house.

"Where can a man get a good meal and a bath here? Is there a telegraph office in town?"

"I might as well start taking orders on my way down to Galveston," he thought as he rode on into town.

****

Ella Anne Dodd
Rome, Georgia

On my way to Galveston to learn ship schedules. Be home before Christmas.

Jeff

****

Mt. Pleasant wasn't a very big town, and Jeff hit all the stores to see what types of things they carried. Turned out they had a real need for someone who would deliver to them. They had to go to Longview or Tyler for their supplies. He explained to them that he would make the trip twice a year regularly, so he took some pretty big orders from the local merchants, and the doctor was especially pleased.

Sulphur Springs was out of his way, but it was a town about the same size as Mt. Pleasant. It might be too close to Dallas to need his goods, but he planned to make this a leisurely trip anyway. He thought he would try his luck there. He hit Tyler, Longview, Kilgore, Henderson, Jacksonville, Nacogdoches, Lufkin, Livingston, Liberty, and then on to Baytown. He wanted to stay away from big towns like Houston.

He got some information from the harbor-masters at Baytown and La Porte, but he thought he would go on down and check out Texas City and Galveston to see what was available there. He was also calculating the difference in the price. If he could buy directly from the larger ocean ships, it might be worth his time and effort to meet them at Galveston.

When he found the office of the harbor-master at Galveston Bay, he splashed water from the water trough on his face, fore arms and armpits and took a clean shirt from his saddlebag. As he shook the wrinkles out of his shirt, he was reviewing questions he should ask.

The harbor-master was a cheerful fellow in spite of the responsibility of managing such a large port. He was as round as a barrel and really seemed to enjoy life and everything going on around him. He put out a big paw and said, "You can call me Steve." Jeff had caught him at a slack time, and they had coffee and whatever. He really gave Jeff the lowdown on the ships that usually docked here.

"Yes, most of the time ships can come in from South America and the Caribbean Islands year around. Citrus fruit from Florida sometimes finds its way over here. If not, there is usually citrus and coffee from South America most of the year. Of course, things from Europe and Asia can only get here in summer. You will need to go into Houston to get medical supplies and machine parts."

"What about liquor?" Jeff asked.

"Oh, that!" the harbor-master hooted and slapped his leg. "You will need to talk to Captain Jack Parrott! He is the best rum-runner around here."

"Do they still call them rum-runners?" Jeff asked. "I thought the Federal Agents met them at the docks nowadays. You can't get around paying taxes on liquor, can you?"

"Oh, he just likes the label! Captain Jack has been running between here and the islands for most of his life. He would like for his life to still have some adventure. Wait until you meet him. He sure is a character; you'll like him."

"Jack Parrott. Is that his real name? I don't think I ever heard that name before."

"Nope, but he has been calling himself that for so long, he probably doesn't remember what his real name is. He calls himself Jack Parrott because he carries a big parrot on his left shoulder all the time. He says, 'If the parrot ain't welcome, I ain't welcome!'"

"When will he be back?"

"Oh, you never know with him. Depends on the seas, the weather, and whatever is interesting to him in the islands. But, he makes pretty regular runs. I'll tell him you will be here in March. He'll probably make it."

Jeff really liked this man, and he had been a lot of help, too. Jeff stood up to go and held out his hand. He wanted to be sure he got this man's name.

"Well, my real name is William Adore, but folks started calling me 'Steve' when I first came to work on the docks as a young man." He smiled and looked deeply into Jeff's eyes as they shook hands. He was waiting for it to soak in.

"You had better get in the habit of calling me Steve. Unless you call me Steve Adore, people around here don't know who you are talking about."

Jeff had been meeting the ships at the docks for several years, but it still took him a couple of steps to catch the hilarity of the name. Stevedores load and unload the ships! He got the name when he was a young man loading and unloading ships! Jeff had to turn around and shake the man's hand once again while they laughed.

Jeff felt as if he had made a good friend today. He enjoyed Steve's company. But as he rode toward Houston, his mind was on business matters. How to find a good machine shop to buy parts, and who would carry medical supplies. Oh, well, a good saloon is usually the best source of information in town.

****

Jeff located a telegraph office first.

Charlie Nixon
Ft. Smith, Arkansas

Haul from Galveston may work out well. Lumber ordered. Where will you be? I'll stay in Houston a few days, hoping you get this.

Jeff

****

Jeff was proud of himself! He didn't over indulge at the saloon. Just stayed long enough to get a lot of information over a few beers and he was on his way again. He located a reputable machine shop and a medical supply company in one afternoon.

Now, while I'm here I had better do some Christmas shopping. Let that pack horse I have been pulling around earn his keep. He got a room for a week at a boarding house which had been recommended to him. "Oh, will you send out my laundry for me?"

After all this traveling, it would be good to sleep in a bed and eat real food again. "Of course, it probably won't hold a candle to Jenny's cooking." He was really starting to miss home and his family.

Jeff used his resting and waiting time to figure distance and time. He sent another telegram to Charlie with more information.

Charlie Nixon
Ft. Smith, Arkansas

Have figured time. Cannot have lumber there before 1st of June. Had you rather deal with RR? I am at Miller's Boarding House, Houston.

Jeff

****

This time he got a quick answer.

Jeff Dodd
Miller's Boarding House
Houston, Texas

Had rather trust you than RR. Will use tent until you get here.

Charlie

****

Charlie got the lots he had put his name on. Jeff did not even ask how much it cost him to get the marshal who had the adjoining lots to save them for him. But whatever it was, it worked, and Charlie's claim was legal. He was a Boomer not a Sooner!

****

Jeff made it home just a few days before Christmas, as promised. He was sure glad that Ella Jane was not still mad. Ma would have been! They had a very happy holiday with all of the Barnetts. Even John William, Mary Elizabeth and John made it home for a week.

After the holiday and all of the visiting, Jeff and Bob went to work trimming mules' feet, oiling harness and greasing wagon wheels. Robert came over and helped some when he had a free day.

Jeff put out word at the saloon that he needed six to ten drivers with experience handling three teams. They needed to understand this would not be a fast run and he wanted to leave mid-January.

It was pretty cold, but Rachael wanted to go outside to play. They had her bundled up in a warm coat and the stocking cap and gloves which Minerva had knitted for her. Jeff and Ella Jane sat in the porch swing with a quilt across their laps, watching Rachael play.

"Two families moved out while you were gone, Jeff," Ella Jane said sadly. "One bought a place in Texas and the other is going to try the Oklahoma Land Run. They both said their land was just worn out and wouldn't grow 'nothing' anymore." She was quiet for a minute, "But, nobody will listen to Robert when he tries to tell them how he makes his farming work so well. Except for the lack of rainfall, and he can't do anything about that."

This was his perfect opening to tell her about all of his big plans. He told her about the little valley he had found, protected on the east by a small mountain. One hundred and sixty acres would be enough for her to run her horses on and for his mules, and he would buy more land. He promised to build her another house… just like this one, if she wanted. It took a lot of talking to explain all of his plans to Ella Jane.

"Honey, the main thing is, you can see how things here are slowing down. If I keep hauling here, my orders are getting smaller all of the time. Oklahoma is booming and Texas has a lot of towns that the railroads have passed by. They need my service. I got some very big orders between Mt. Pleasant and Galveston. At Mt. Pleasant my wagons will be empty, and I can pick up Charlie's lumber and take it to Oklahoma.

"Then I can leave half my wagons and mules at McAlister's and come home to get you and Rachael. Bob and Jenny, too if they will go with us."

"But, Jeff, we would be leaving the security of my family. That is a big gamble moving to a new location where you don't know any customers."

"But actually, I do. I took time to meet people and take orders on my way down to Galveston. I met the harbor-master at Galveston, and he promised to help me line up good ship's captains to do business with. I already have a source for machine parts and medical supplies. I have a lumber mill lined up for Charlie's lumber. It is all falling into place.

"It will take us about a year to get all set up to build a house. That is the only down side that I can see. I have figured everything a dozen times on the way home."

"But what will we live in before we get the house built?"

"I'll buy a big tent. I've seen some real nice ones with rooms partitioned off and everything. Ones like really rich people use when they go on safari in Africa. It will work, Babe. I know it will."

"I've talked to Robert. He is willing to buy this place and give us a pretty good price for it."

"Have you talked to Papa about it?"

"No. I wanted you on my side before I mentioned it to him."

"Well, let's talk to him tomorrow. I want to hear how he reasons it out."

****

They sat around the fireplace, Burrell and Minerva, Jeff and Ella Anne. Jessie brought them hot tea to drink. "You may as well sit down and hear this, too, Jessie, since you may be losing your daughter if it works out."

Jeff laid out all of his plans, hoping Burrell could see his reasoning, knowing it was going to tear his guts out if Burrell disagreed. Burrell stared at the fire and listened quietly with his eyes narrowed as he processed all of this information. Minerva watched her daughter's face to see how she reacted. This was a big, big step; and it wasn't like they could run back home if things didn't work out as they planned.

After he covered the basics, the things he had explained to Ella Anne, Jeff began telling Burrell how he figured his time and why it would take so long before he could come back to get Ella Anne and Rachael. He ended the whole story by saying, "And I owe Charlie for keeping Ma off my back these last several years."

Burrell knew that Jeff was a good businessman. He could follow the plan Jeff had laid out and he seemed to have things covered pretty well. It was true that if they stayed here, Jeff would not be making as much money. And it sure looked as if there was money to be made in the west, for a man with a good head and not afraid of hard work.

This all sounded so good that if he were a younger man, Burrell might have been tempted to go himself. He looked at Ella Anne, half scared, half thrilled. He looked at Jessie, holding Rachael, but with little expression on her face. Then he looked at Minerva. He knew she had a good head on her shoulders. They stared into each other's eyes for a minute; then she pressed her lips together and half nodded. Burrell agreed.

"It seems like you have a good plan. It will mean a lot of hard work. It will need the good Lord's blessing for things to come together the way you planned, but it seems as if it just might work."

Jeff drew his first full breath since they started talking and slowly let it out. Ella Anne's eyes got even bigger than before as she thought about the immensity of this venture. Jeff would be gone for over six months before he would be back to get her and Rachael. Then they would load up all of their belongings in Jeff's wagons and head west…to the Territory! A shiver ran down her spine! Suddenly, her apprehension was gone, and her enthusiasm for the adventure soared. She began to see that valley in her mind and picture their new house nestled up close to the mountain. Yup, she was onboard for this adventure, all right.

Looking at Jessie, Burrell said, "Would you ride with us up to their house to talk to Jenny and Bob? I know Jenny will want to talk this over with you before she makes a decision.

"Minerva, Garrett, get your hats and coats! Let's make it a family outing. Something this big requires the approval of the whole family. We will stop by to see if Robert and Sue Ellen want to go."

****

"Now, Bob, Jenny, you know that you don't have to go if you don't want to. You will have a job with me or Robert if you want to stay here," Burrell said. He didn't want them to feel this was their only option, but he could tell by the look in Bob's eyes he was eager for the adventure. Jenny, however, looked sadly at her mother.

"Mama, Indian Territory is a long way off, and I might never see you again," and tears started to flow.

Jessie put her big arms around her daughter. "Now, honey, there's all kinds of things in this life that might make you never see me again. But you are going to feel my love in your heart all the way to Oklahoma. You are not going to be alone.

"You have never been more than five miles away from the place where you were born and raised. And if you want to go and see some more of the world, this is your chance, honey."

There was silence in the room. Everyone looked at each other, searching from one face to another. Ella Anne was especially looking at Jenny; she knew that she needed Jenny to make this work. Rachael ran passed just as Ella Anne saw the gleam begin in Jenny's eyes and a half-smile creep across her lips. Ella Anne grabbed Rachael up in her arms and swung her around. "Rachael, honey, it looks as if we are going to Oklahoma!"

****

Within days Jeff had found drivers. Their plans were laid; they were harnessed up and ready to leave. From his horse, Jeff looked over what they had loaded in the almost empty wagons; extra harness and mule feed, road grub and bedding for the men.

He looked down as Ella Jane laid her hand on his leg and held it there. They smiled for a minute; then Jeff motioned the drivers to move out. When he looked back she was waving.

****

Rachael wanted her mama to swing with her in the porch swing, so they made it go high. They held their legs out straight and pointed their toes each time it went forward. "Whee!" squealed Rachael as the wind they made blew her fine blond hair into her face, then all the way backward.

"What do you do to fill up the time when your husband is going to be gone for six months?" Ella Anne thought.

"You know, Rachael, I think it is time you started really learning to ride. By the time we get to Oklahoma you will be past three. You will want your own horse soon, won't you? Let's go saddle the old gray mare and let you practice some."

The mare was old and gentle. She was not prone to sudden jumps if something new came into sight. She had seen it all; no need to worry now. Ella Anne put the saddle on so that Rachael could hold onto the saddle horn. "Now, I'm really glad Jeff bought us these western saddles," she thought. "I never figured I would need a saddle horn, but who knows? I may even learn to rope!"

Rachael had ridden with her mother many times, but this was the first time she had been on a moving horse by herself. Ella Anne held the reins in her left hand to lead the mare; with her right hand she gathered up the material of the back of Rachael's dress. Ella Anne held it tightly to help her learn to balance. She led the mare around the lot slowly, but the uncertainty of a horse moving underneath you is a little unsettling. Rachael's eyes widened and she took a quick, deep breath.

Ella Anne held tighter and reassured her. In just a few steps Rachael began to rely more on her own balance than on her mother holding her. She was going to be a natural.

When they tired of this and went into the house, Ella Anne said, "Jenny, I know what we can be doing to get ready for this big move. We can plant a big garden and can vegetables for next winter. When we get to Oklahoma it will be too late to plant anything. But if we pack the jars real good, maybe we can make it all the way with most of them."

"I'll get some broccoli seeds from Mama, too, Miss Ella Anne. We can plant that after we get there; it grows real good in the fall. And asparagus should have time to root."

"Come on, let's ask Bob to help us plan a good spot."

****

"Right here is going to be the best spot for a big garden, Miss Ella Anne. I didn't mention it before because of the mules, but if there is rain this place always holds the moisture in the ground best. In February I'll spade it up and fertilize it from the pens. Then we can begin planting in middle March. We can have you ladies busy until Mr. Jeff gets back here in July or August."

"In the next day or two, I'll go to town and buy all the canning jars I can find before anyone else thinks about it. I guess I need to buy a big canning pot, too. It has been so easy to use Mama's, I didn't think about buying my own."

From this they drifted to what furniture needed to go with them and what they could do without. "Jeff is going to buy us big tents to live in, but they won't hold all of our furniture," Ella Anne explained. "And we need to be thinking about how to pack things. What we will need to use on the trip west, and what can stay packed until we get there. You know, it would be foolish to load and unload the dining table every time we stop. We can hold our plates on our laps.

"Oh, Jenny we will be cooking on a campfire! We need to plan for that, too. Plenty of time for that, but we will keep it in our minds, okay?"

****

Slowly January turned into February, and Jeff and his wagon train rolled into Ft. Smith. "There are so many people camping out, it doesn't look as if there is any space left for us to bed down," Jeff told the drivers. "Just hold them here for now. Let me find Charlie."

Jeff found him quick enough. Charlie was thrilled to see him. "How did you find me in this crowd?" Charlie asked.

"Where do you look for an out-of-work saloon keeper? In a saloon! You weren't hard to find at all. Do you have suggestions where we can park our wagons and camp for the night?

"Right now we are on our way to Galveston to load. We will be unloaded when we get back to Mt. Pleasant....except for your whiskey. Have you figured out what size saloon you want and how many board feet you need, things like that?"

****

The trip down to Galveston seemed long since they had already come so far from Georgia, but without a load, they made good time considering the distance.

Loading at Galveston Bay was exciting for Jeff. He had stopped in Houston and loaded machinery parts and medical supplies while the wagons were easier to handle in the city. Steve had told several of the ship captains, whom he liked, about Jeff, and when he would be back to load, so they were looking forward to meeting him.

And Captain Jack Parrott! You knew who he was as far away as you could see him. He wore the black tri-cornered pirate's hat, an eye patch, and the most striking parrot on his left shoulder. The parrot was large and colored red, yellow, green and blue....most astonishing bird Jeff had ever seen.

When Jeff was introduced to Captain Jack, they shook hands; then Captain Jack introduced him to the parrot, "Parrot, this is Jeff Dodd." The bird put out his right foot. "He wants to shake your hand," Captain Jack said. So Jeff shook the bird's foot. "The next time he sees you he will know your name," Captain Jack said with a nod and a raised eyebrow. "Now, I've got a boat load of rum and such; how much liquor can you haul?"

Jeff was able to get liquor, citrus, coffee. One ship from England had made it to the Caribbean Islands before the winter seas got too rough; so he was able to get some linens, clothing, crystal and English china that he hadn't expected.

The trip back up to Mt. Pleasant was also exciting because the merchants were so happy to see him. It was always fun seeing a store fill up with new merchandise. People started coming into the stores almost as soon as they saw the wagons stop. It made it a little harder to get unloaded and make sure each order was right, but the enjoyment they brought to so many people was worth it.

At Mt. Pleasant, the lumber was cut and waiting for them to load. Jeff told the mill owner he could pay him with a check on a bank in Hendersonville, NC or a bank in Rome, GA. The man's expression didn't change. "Or, if you want to make the deal a little sweeter, I might be able to pay you cash." That got a response from the man.

It was also helpful to Jeff because going home with a pocket full of money just invited robbers, and it tempted some drivers to become robbers.

He was almost robbed once; three men thought that because he was big, he would be slow and clumsy. Jeff just grabbed an axe handle from under the wagon seat that evened the odds. Two of them limped away dragging the third man by both arms. No, he wasn't afraid of a fight.

****

It was a slow trip from there to Colbert's Ferry. The wagons were loaded heavy, and Jeff would only ask his mules to go ten miles a day. Some of the drivers wanted to go on till sundown as usual, but Jeff explained that he wanted to get there with the lumber…and his mules!

When they reached Colbert's Ferry, the man in charge of the ferry took one look at the load his wagons were carrying and said it would cost three dollars per wagon. He was pretty sure his ferry would support such a load, but Jeff would have to wait for him to find more men to row a load that heavy. Jeff looked at his drivers; some of them were muscular young men. "What do you pay your rowers?" Jeff asked.

"Fifty cents a load, but if there is no traffic across the river they don't get paid at all. You can see I don't have anyone extra sitting around waiting for a heavy load."

Jeff walked back to where the wagons had stopped atop the river bank. "Any of you young men want to earn some extra money today." That got their attention.

"Doing what?" one of them asked.

"The ferry man pays fifty cents a load for extra rowers, and we get across quicker."

Four men walked down to the edge of the river for instructions. Two would be the extra rowers as each wagon crossed; then row the ferry back, and switch. "Does that suit everybody?"

Just for safety's sake, Jeff had a man holding the bridle of each mule while they crossed. Jeff winked at the ferry man, "It's their first trip by water."

****

With the river crossing behind them, they traveled east again along the river road headed towards McAllister's. Everybody knew McAllister's was out of the way, but no one wanted to tackle the Arbuckle Mountains. Besides McAllister knew where they could safely cross the Canadian River. The trip was slow and fairly uneventful until they got to Oklahoma City. And Oklahoma City was a rip, roaring boom town!

Most of the streets were lined with tents. Every lot was taken. Buildings made of new lumber shone like gems in the sunlight between the rows of white tents.

Every street was alive with horses and wagons. Brave people on foot darted between the traffic. Everyone seemed to be in a hurry to get somewhere. Excitement and expectation filled the air.

Charlie was plenty happy to see them. He had been looking forward to this for months now. He set up drinks for all of the drivers. "Three of you get your rifles and stay with the load. I'll bring you each a beer. In 30 minutes we will change, and you can go inside. Okay?" Jeff instructed.

"Do you have hands lined up to help build the place, Charlie?" "Yeah, some. Why?"

"If you have a real carpenter to boss the job, I brought four hands that might be willing to stay and help build your building. Plus you might need two guards each night to watch all this lumber so it doesn't walk away."

"Are you headed straight back to Georgia?"

"After a good night's sleep, we'll be headed back to get my family. I'm going to leave three wagons at McAllister's. I think three wagons will haul all of our furniture, don't you?"

Chapter Eight
Oklahoma

Jeff and Bob worked hard setting up the tents and building some stout pens to hold the stud horses apart. Then they started fencing. Jeff had brought enough barbed wire to put one strand around about 60 acres and cross fence it to keep the mules and horses separate. He figured the mares and geldings would want to stay close to the studs and would not really try the fence, but you couldn't have them grazing off very far. Someone else might try to claim them.

Then spring was coming on, and Jeff made another run to Galveston. At the Bay, Jeff looked first for Captain Jack Parrott's ship. Captain Jack was seated at a table with several other men when Jeff walked up. When the parrot said, "Jeff Dodd, Jeff Dodd," and started pacing back and forth, Captain Jack folded his cards and stood up to shake hands. "I told you he would remember your name. You had better shake hands with him, too. Don't want to hurt the parrot's feelings, you know."

****

This time Jeff brought back enough wire to finish building a good fence and lumber for a barn. They had almost finished putting up the third strand of wire when a herd of 50 or 60 horses appeared over the ridge. One of the herders rode straight toward Jeff as if he knew what he was doing in this part of the country.

Jeff stood up and stretched his back as he watched the rider coming. "I know that hat," he thought. "I know that horse!"

"That is my brother, Tom!" he said to Bob.

"What in the world are you doing here?" Jeff held out his hand as he walked toward the rider.

"There was no way Frank and I could get our string of horses away without Ma knowing it," he said as he dismounted. "When we told her about the grassland we found on west of here, she packed up the whole family and came with us. They will be along in the wagons in a little bit.

"Be all right if we camp here a couple of days and rest? I see you have a pretty good fence built to keep the horses separated. I guess we can keep our studs tied on the other side of the wagons so there shouldn't be any trouble there."

"Yeah, there is plenty of grazing for them, if you don't stay too long. I don't think my grass would support this many head for very long. Settle them down right out here. I'll go tell Ella Jane that we have company."

He ran to the house to give the news. "Ella Jane, we have company coming. My brothers are heading west with all their horses. We will have nine extra for dinner tonight! Can you swing that?"

"Since we have that fresh killed deer, we can. Oh, Jenny, we will have nine extra for dinner tonight. Let's cook both hind quarters off that deer Jeff shot yesterday and lots of vegetables. That should make it go far enough, don't you think?

"Now, I'll go and greet them; then come back and help." She smoothed her hair, brushed at the front of her skirt, took a deep breath, and hurried outside.

The wagons pulled up near the tent while the men were settling the horses. Jeff's pa was driving the first wagon. He climbed down and introduced himself, shaking her hand pleasantly. When the second wagon pulled up, his ma was driving. She sat there for several minutes staring coldly at Ella Anne. "So you are Ella Jane!" she said sharply.

"I am, and you must be Mrs. Dodd. Welcome," Ella Anne said with all the charm of a southern lady, completely ignoring her mother-in-law's curtness. "Do come in. Wash up and get comfortable. You must be very tired after such a long journey."

The girls climbed down from the wagons and began introducing themselves while their mother sat sulking on the wagon seat. "I'm Wilma; I'm the youngest. This is Nora; this is Lou; and this is Dora." As they started walking toward the tent, Mrs. Dodd climbed down from the wagon and stood there as if trying to make up her mind. Since she was being completely ignored, she finally condescended to follow.

"Oh, this is lovely," Wilma said as they walked into the tent. Just like you were on safari!"

"Jenny has a wash basin and towel set up for you. I know you will feel more refreshed when you get the trail dust off of you, and I will help her get tea ready to serve."

From the kitchen area, Ella Anne could hear Wilma commenting on how nice her furnishings were. "Jeff pampers her!" Mrs. Dodd said.

Ella Anne brought Rachael in from where she stood watching so many horses. She washed Rachael's hands and face to freshen her up; then they walked into the living area of the tent. "Rachael, I'd like you to meet your father's family. These are your aunts, Wilma, Nora, Lou and Dora. And this is your grandmother, Mrs. Dodd."

In her exuberance, Wilma swept Rachael up and swung her around, which Rachael always liked. Wilma stood holding her as she explained. "Dora is not actually our sister. She is a friend of the family, and she stays with us a lot."

Nora and Lou were happy to meet their niece and patted her back and spoke sweetly to her. From across the room Mrs. Dodd finally said, "How do you do, Rachael." and never moved closer.

The men were straggling in now. Another basin of water and more clean towels. Then tea was ready. "We could take a table and chairs outside if you like; it is so nice outside under the trees this time of year," Ella Anne said, as she picked up a chair and started for the door. Jeff and one brother carried the table; everyone else carried chairs except Mrs. Dodd. She immediately sat down in the chair Ella Anne had carried.

"Jenny, do we have some cookies or biscuits we can offer our company?"

When Jenny arrived with a tray of cookies and biscuits with jam in the center of the tray, she held the tray before Mrs. Dodd first, as protocol requires. You always serve the eldest female first! Mrs. Dodd took a long time surveying the tray. She finally selected two, and said, "That will be all," summarily dismissing Jenny with a wave of her hand.

"Thank you, Jenny, those look lovely," Ella Anne spoke up immediately.

****

The evening went smoothly with everyone visiting and chattering merrily, completely ignoring Mrs. Dodd except to ask occasionally if she needed anything. At bedtime, Jeff's family went back to their accustomed quarters in the wagons.

After breakfast next morning, Mrs. Dodd sat in a chair outside while everyone else visited. Ella Anne heard her say, "Rachael, stop that swinging. You are kicking dust on me."

Ella Anne stepped outside and said, "Rachael, would you like to catch your mare and get Bob to saddle her for you? You can ride around on this other side of the tent. That will be okay. But do not go near their wagons. They have stud horses over there." Rachael already understood about horses.

Later, when everyone was outside sitting under the trees, Mrs. Dodd said, "Those are lovely red chickens, Ella Jane. Have your boy kill some so your girl can fix me some fried chicken for dinner tonight."

Jeff could see the fighting spirit of a redhead overpowering Ella Anne's training as a southern lady. "Mrs. Dodd! Their names are Bob and Jenny! And those are my laying hens you are talking about. We will be serving back strap and shoulder steak for dinner tonight."

By now she was standing up, with her chin thrust out in defiance. Not accustomed to having someone tell her 'no', Mrs. Dodd began moving as if she intended to stand up also. Ella Anne's fists clinched and her eyes narrowed in preparation for combat.

"I'm sure you boys will find a lot of deer where you are heading," Jeff spoke up, trying to defuse an awkward situation. And it worked! As the men took over the conversation, their mother settled back down in her chair.

Early next morning, the Dodds loaded up and moved on to the west. "Well, I narrowly escaped that one," Jeff thought as he watched them go. Ella Anne had seen a considerable change in Jeff's demeanor while they were around. She was also happy to see them go.

Ella Anne picked up Jeff's arm and placed it across her shoulders, as they watched the Dodds move off toward the horizon. "Exactly where are they going, Jeff?" she asked.

"They are headed to probably some of the best grassland in the Indian Territory. Grass clear up to a horse's belly. McAllister told us he had heard that the government was saving it for the Indians. Did not intend to open it up to white people. They are calling it 'The Big Pasture'.

"But the boys said Ma insisted that, if they got there and got settled in, the government would let them stay like they did McAlister." Jeff thought about it a minute; then shook his head and said, "I don't know…"

****

"Well, Jenny, most everything in the garden is blooming. It looks as if all that canning we did may just last us till our garden starts producing.

She and Jenny had plenty of time to work out of doors. There was only so much housekeeping you could do in a tent; but these tents had really worked well for make shift. The winter had not seemed as cold as Ella Anne expected, maybe because of the valley and the mountain. Ella Anne loved that mountain; she stepped outside to admire its beauty.

From the front of the tent she could see a man letting his horse graze in the field that was planted with peas.

"Bob, would you go ask that man to please move his horse out of our pea field?"

With a nod Bob jogged up the road to speak with the stranger. Suddenly shots rang out, and Ella Anne could see Bob jumping from one foot to the other; then he began to run home.

Anger rose in Ella Anne like the righteous anger of the Lord! She glanced around for the oldest of Bob and Jenny's sons. "Willie, please go catch that big gray gelding and bring him up to the barn as quickly as you can.

"Jenny, I will need that split riding skirt that Wilma gave me. I have never worn it. I guess it is time to try."

Bob reached the front door by this time, out of breath from running so hard.

"Bob, will you quickly saddle that big gelding? Willie is bringing him up to the barn. I don't want a sidesaddle. This time I need a man's saddle. Not Jeff's, though; his stirrups are too long. Use the one I ride."

By the time all of this had taken place, the foolish man was still letting his horse graze on the peas. "Now, if that don't beat all I ever saw," he sneered as she rode up. "A woman riding a man's saddle!" He was sneering at her for riding like a man.

"Sir, why is your horse grazing on my peas?" She ignored his insult.

"I needed to take a ...nature break....and I guess he was hungry. I decided to have a smoke while he ate."

"Did my hired man not ask you to remove your horse from the peas?"

"Yeah, he did; and I gave him my answer."

"Then I will ask you once again to remove your horse from my peas."

"And if I am not so inclined?" The man was wagging his head cockily.

"Then which one do you want me to shoot first, your horse or you?"

His face showed the astonishment he felt when he realized she was holding a pistol on him... his was still holstered. Then she could see his face change as defiance rose inside him.

No anger or indecision showed on her face, though her eyes narrowed just the slightest.

"Sir, I can see by your expression that it will be you I shoot first if you reach for that gun. My papa taught me to aim for the tenderest part of a man. Said it paralyzes his legs and he will bleed to death on the spot. Have you ever heard that, sir?"

The man was holding his hands up high and backing toward his horse. "Don't hold no grudge now, ma'am. I didn't mean no real harm," he was saying over his shoulder as he mounted and rode off as fast as he could.

"Yes, Wilma," she thought, "I do like this divided skirt. It serves a real purpose!

"Maybe Jeff will bring enough of that barbed wire to fence the peas too."

****

The Dodd sisters caused quite a stir when Duncan, Oklahoma, held its first ever celebration and parade. Most everybody rode two abreast for a parade, but the Dodd sisters rode three abreast. People were so admiring the outstanding build of the three Morgans that they didn't notice until the women were right in front of them. The ladies were wearing split riding skirts and riding men's saddles! A thing that was unheard of!

A sharp thinking photographer, who was there covering the 'first ever celebration and parade', snapped a shot of the three women and it was published in several newspapers!

****

Time seemed to pass slowly while Jeff was gone on his freighting trips. As Rachael grew older, she and Ella Anne rode together a lot. Jeff had bought her a child's saddle, and she and Mollie had become constant companions. There really was not much for a little girl to do out here with no close neighbors.

It did not take long to run out of things one little girl can do to occupy her time. She helped Jenny in the kitchen some; she played with her baby doll some. She swung and she rode Mollie.

When she could find their funnel-shaped holes in the powdery dust, she played with the doodle bugs. She would find a thin twig and stir around in the hole, saying, "Doodle bug, doodle bug, come out of your hole. Your house is on fire and your children will burn." Sometimes the harmless little bugs would be stirred to the top of the sand; but they were gruesome to look at, so then she left them alone.

Occasionally, she could catch a big iridescent green June bug and tie a piece of sewing thread to its leg. Those big beetles, almost the size of a quarter, were strong enough to fly around in circles with Rachael holding the string. But she really didn't like it if one of them landed on her. They didn't bite, but their feet pinched when they tried to crawl up her arm! Oh, and if one happened to land in her hair!!!

One summer day when Rachael was underfoot and looking for something to do, Jenny handed her a syrup bucket. "Rachael, will you take this sorghum bucket out to the water trough and rinse all the syrup out of it? It has developed a hole and is calling ants into the house. The horses will like the sweet taste in their water.

"Once it is clean, you can take it out to where your mother practices her shooting. Would you do that for me?"

Another time when Rachael could find nothing to do, Jenny said, "Rachael go run through those geese over there, and let's see if they shed any of their down feathers."

Wow! This was great fun to actually be allowed to chase the geese and make them flap their wings and honk as they waddled. Rachael chased them around in a big circle, and small down feathers went flying everywhere.

"Okay, Rachael, do you want to help me gather some down to stuff our pillows and mattresses?"

Rachael began to look at the little feathers on the ground and wonder how to gather them.

"Let them settle down a little, now, and we will go to the barn and get the goose hook."

"What is a goose hook, Jenny?"

"It is a long skinny board that Bob whittled to make a hook on one end, kinda like a crochet hook. I can walk up behind the goose, but not close enough to scare him, and slip that hook around his leg before he tries to run away from me."

With the goose hook in one hand and Rachael's hand in the other, Jenny strolled around the yard for a little while. They talked quietly to each other. "We have to pretend we are not looking at the geese," Jenny said. One goose let them get close enough so that Jenny hooked his leg. Quickly Jenny grabbed both his legs and carried him swinging upside down over to a bench under a tree. He honked and flapped his wings violently, and tried to peck her hand. But Jenny had done this before; she was quick.

As she was sitting down, she grabbed those big strong wings and pinned them back behind her knees, leaving his broad, white breast exposed. "Now, you hold his head for me so he don't peck me. Be careful that he don't peck you!"

The angry goose honked and squawked and Rachael had to use two hands to hold his head still. Once he twisted around and almost pecked Jenny's leg.

With the big goose now under control Jenny explained the process. "See, honey, with one hand you rub his feathers backwards so that it raises up the longer ones. Underneath he has a winter coat of tiny, soft down feathers that keep him warm in winter. But it's summertime now, and he needs to shed those little down feathers, and they sure do make a fine feather bed or pillow.

"This time of year you don't have to pull hard; they just slide right out, so it doesn't hurt him at all. He is just mad 'cause he doesn't like to be held still. You can help me a lot today by holding their heads still. When you get a little older and a lot stronger, I will teach you how to do this by yourself. Would you like that?"

Back inside the tent, Rachael proudly told her mother, "Today I helped Jenny pluck those damn feathers off the geese!"

****

They discovered that they had neighbors in the valley when a man driving a buckboard came over one day. He had with him a little girl just about Rachael's size. He and his family were living on the north side of the valley in a lean-to. His wife, Maggie, was expecting another baby and was to the stage that she didn't get out much.

He had a young mare that was due to come in season soon. "I heard that you have a very fine string of horses. Would you consider letting me use your stud, ma'am?"

Ella Anne quickly surveyed the situation: the man's manners, his care for his appearance, pregnant wife; and he brought his little girl with him.

He seemed like a good risk. "Would you like to have a cup of tea, sir? We will talk business.

"Jenny, will you make a pot of tea, please? And do you have some fresh cookies for the girls?"

Rachael was most thrilled to have a playmate. The girl was actually just a few months younger than Rachael, but she seemed frail and quiet compared to robust, always-on-the-go Rachael. Rachael pushed her in the swing, but she was afraid to go very high; so Rachael showed her how high she could make it go. "You will learn," Rachael assured her. Next they looked for Rachael's doodle bugs.

Jenny and Bob had brought a table and chairs outside so they could watch the girls play while they had tea. "How far along is your wife?" Ella Anne asked.

"Seven and a half months. We didn't know she was pregnant when we left Tennessee, but she made the trip okay. She is feeling awfully heavy and a little bit blue right now. I thought she might enjoy some time just to rest, so I brought Sarah with me."

"Have you found a doctor in these parts yet? We don't go to a town often, and thank God we haven't needed a doctor. My Jenny is pretty good at doctoring small things."

"We found a mid-wife at Hugo, but there is not a doctor there, yet. I don't know if a doctor would come much farther than that."

"I'll come to visit her soon. It would be good to have a woman's company, and the girls seem to be getting along very well.

"Now about your mare, Jeff and Bob have built some pretty stout pens, and we keep the stud up all the time. I had rather you bring your mare on over here, before my stud gets wind of her and takes off on his own. Does that make sense to you, Mr.....I'm sorry, I didn't get your name, sir."

"I'm Dan Thomas, ma'am," he said and he held out his hand. "I'd be much obliged about the mare. That seems to be the surest way to handle the situation."

"What color is your mare, sir...Dan?"

"She is a bright sorrel. Why do you ask?"

"Our bloodlines are straight grays for several generations. This should be interesting. I'd almost bet you can count on a roan foal," she chuckled, remembering her Papa's words.

She purposely did not mention that Jeff had a splendid sorrel stud. She did not want a lot of people knowing that he was gone so much of the time. "If Jeff happens to be home at the right time, we can offer him his choice," she thought.

*****

June 12, 1890
Dear Mama and Papa,

It has been a while since I have written. Much has happened.

Rachael has enjoyed the letter you sent her for her birthday so much. It was waiting for us at the Hugo Post Office when we first went to tell them we would be receiving mail there. She carries it in the pocket of her pinafore much of the time. She has memorized most of the words and she pretends she is reading it.

She has become quite a little horsewoman. She and Mollie are best buddies and spend a lot of time together. I guess Mollie is the best baby sitter I could have.

We have neighbors now, in the north part of the valley. They are from eastern Tennessee. They have a daughter Rachael's age, though smaller and quite timid, but Rachael is changing that. They also have a new baby boy, which I adore and enjoy very much.

Jeff is gone a lot. Since the weather is different here, he can make three freight runs a year, and his business is growing. People keep asking him to go farther north into Oklahoma and also into western Oklahoma. The little towns that the railroads have passed over need his service.

We had a visit from Jeff's family. They have moved into southwestern Oklahoma. They stayed with us for two days to rest up before going on. Jeff was very tense while they were here, and I completely understand why. His mother does not like me or Rachael at all, and resents him because of us. It was strained, but we managed without incident. His pa seems nice, but doesn't get to say much.

We have 60 acres fenced and cross fenced and a barn built. Next Jeff has planned to drill a water-well and build a windmill and water tank. Then we can think about a new house. Until then, these tents are surprisingly not uncomfortable.

I do enjoy it here, with the mountain at our backs. The scenery is so varied that there is always something interesting. It is very peaceful and quiet. I do enjoy Jenny's company; I can't think how I could make it without her. Bob takes care of the place just as if it were his own; he is a hard worker.

Oh, the canned goods Jenny and I worked on so hard lasted us through the winter. Now our garden is producing very well, and we have plenty of fresh vegetables. We have begun to can a little along to prepare for this winter. We have venison quite often and occasionally prairie chicken.

Rachael, Jenny and I went to the little village, called Idabel, near here recently. There was a man with a toe sack full of cabbages he was trying to sell. Rachael was playing on the boardwalk, and he said to her "I'm selling cabbages. Reckon your mother would like to buy a head, little girl?" Rachael screamed and ran and hid behind my skirt. "Mama, that man has a sack full of heads!" she said.

The horses are doing really well. We have four new foals this spring and several more due in early summer. Oh, how I do love them. Thank you, Mama and Papa. We will have to think about a stud from another bloodline soon, Papa.

Well, I guess that just about covers it from here. Give my love to Jessie and her family, and Robert and Sue. What do you hear from John William and Mary Elizabeth and John? Are they rich and famous lawyers, yet?

Looking forward to a letter from you. Much love.

Your loving daughter,
Ella Anne

*****

Jeff's latest haul had been a trip to take whisky and kegs of beer to Charlie in Oklahoma City. Several wagons were loaded with fancy, engraved door facings, a specially built bar with a brass foot rail, an elegant big mirror and engraved tin ceiling panels. Charlie had been doing a booming business and was preparing to beautify the inside of his saloon. He said he wanted to give it some class. Raise the standards and demeanor of the clientele he attracted. There was still a pretty rough element in Oklahoma City that Charlie wanted to discourage from coming to his establishment.

"Sorry, I couldn't bring Ella Jane along. She is making a name for herself in our part of the state. She is such a perfect lady and hostess, but she's got every man's respect. I'm amazed you haven't heard of her all the way up here."

It was fun watching Charlie's face as he listened to Jeff's tales about Ella Jane. "She was fixing to tangle with Ma when Ma was rude, but I got the subject changed. I guess Ma decided it was not worth it." He shook his head, "But Ella Jane sure did!"

"That must be some woman you married, Jeff."

****

When Jeff came home this time it was late in the evening, but he noticed immediately that the floor of the main living area of the tent was bare. "What happened here? Where is the carpet that was here?"

"I burned it," Ella Anne said, flatly.

"But, why? That was an expensive, imported carpet. I wanted you to have it to make this tent seem more like a house."

"It was covered with blood."

She was looking down and stood silent for a long minute before she began to explain. "That dowser from Arkansas, that you sent to drill the water well and build the windmill and water tank? Well, he brought another man to help him, and they did a real fine job on the well. It is a very good well, Jeff.

"They were so elated when the job was finished and the well had come in so strong. They started drinking to celebrate. While they were liquored up, the dowser got to looking at Jenny. Said he had never seen such a fine looking black woman. Then after dark I guess they could see shadows through the tent.

"Well, Bob tried to stop them, and they dislocated his left arm. He yelled for Jenny to run to me; then they clubbed him over the head with a pistol.

"The man caught Jenny right about here, just inside our tent. I told him to leave her alone and move away, but he didn't listen. When I told him that my Papa told me to shoot for the tender part of a man and he would bleed to death, he started coming for me. I told him that I don't make idle threats, Jeff, but he kept coming."

She was silent for a moment, and her eyes began to mist.

"I pulled it to the right just at the last minute, Jeff. I just couldn't kill a man. I just couldn't. Not when Jenny was not really hurt."

Now, big tears overflowed and ran down her cheeks and she began to sob. "I sent Willie in to Hugo for that new doctor on my best gelding; told Willie to run him all the way or the man would die.

"The doctor got here in time. He didn't bleed to death, but it shattered the bone in his left thigh. The man will walk with a heavy limp for the rest of his life."

She completely broke down, sobs racking her body as she ran to his arms for comfort. That was the first time she had let her emotions out since the incident.

"You may see it different, Jeff," she sobbed and sniffed when she had control again. "But I told the man that whatever we owed him, I would pay to the doctor for saving his life.

"The Sheriff was here; he came out with the doctor when he heard there had been a bad shooting. I don't think that man will ever come back to this part of the country."

****

The weather just seemed to be getting dryer every year. Since they had the water-well, they irrigated the garden during the heat of the summer and it produced very well. Their neighbors, the Thomas's, however, did not fare so well. They were still struggling with provisions like housing and fencing. They had not been able to drill a well yet, so their garden quit producing when the weather turned hot.

Ella Anne, Rachael and Jenny went over to visit and took a basket full of vegetables. Maggie's eyes lit up when she saw the fresh vegetables. And Jenny had baked fresh cookies, too.

The girls enjoyed playing. Sarah's father had made her a swing, and she was thrilled to show Rachael how high she had learned to swing.

Ella Anne and Maggie were about the same age, and even though they came from different backgrounds, they were living in the same world now. They really enjoyed each other's company. It was good for Jenny to get away for a little while, too. She especially enjoyed the baby; he was crawling now and was so much fun to hold and play with. "Sure makes me want another one, Miss Ella Anne," she said. Ella Anne nodded and smiled sadly.

"Now, what are yall doing for drinking water… and water for your stock?" Ella Anne asked.

"Well, this little creek we are on is okay right now, but we can see it is getting lower all the time."

"Now, don't let your stock go without water. If you need to, bring some barrels and fill them from our well. I guess we are close enough to the Red; our well is still very strong," Ella Anne was saying as they drove away.

****

When Jeff got home this time, he was having fun teasing Ella Jane. "I hear we may have to furnish water for the whole county!" He stopped long enough for that to soak in. When he saw the puzzled look on her face he added, "Seems several other people would like to try to sink a water-well, but they can't get a dowser to come up here, since you shot the one who drilled ours." He grinned real big and pulled her into his lap so she would know that he was teasing.

"I don't think I need to worry anymore about leaving you home alone; what with the man in the pea patch and the dowser, you have quite a stand-up reputation, ma'am. I believe a man would think awful hard before he challenged you."

****

It seemed Jeff's trips took him closer and closer to his family all the time. It just seemed a shame not to stop in and see them, so he gave in.

They were so surprised and happy to see him. Ma was even very friendly this time. That made it feel good…until Jeff realized she had seated Dora next to him at the dinner table. "Well, we are back to the same old games," he thought.

Right after dinner, when the men stepped outside to smoke, Jeff told Tom and his pa that he had promised to catch up with his men and the wagons. He saddled up and left without saying goodbye to the women.

****

He was home for three months this time. It was such fun having him here; he always came home with wonderful tales to tell.

He and Ella Anne were sketching floor plans for their new house. That was the next thing on their list.

Jeff just could not get used to how Rachael changed every time he came home. She was coming on five now and had such a sharp mind. She was getting very good with her horse, too. He could tell they were going to have to move her to a more active horse pretty soon.

****

After Jeff's next trip, he noticed that Ella Anne was upset. She didn't say anything, but he could tell something was eating at her.

After Rachael was in bed for the night, they walked out under the trees to look at the stars through the leaves. It was like looking through lace. "Something is bothering you, honey. What is it?"

"I had some visitors while you were gone."

"I thought everyone knew to give you space," he teased.

"It was your mother...and your girlfriend!"

Jeff's countenance fell. "Oh, not again!" he said quietly and shook his head. "What did she do this time?"

He thought about it a minute and asked, "Just the two of them, rode all that way...alone?"

She pressed her lips together and nodded her head. "They had some very unsettling stories to tell about you, Jeff."

"I knew...I just had a feeling I should not have gone to Ma's house on that last trip. It seemed so nice because she was friendly this time, until I realized she had me and Dora sitting next to each other at dinner.

"I left right after dinner, honey; didn't even tell Ma 'goodbye'. I rode on out and caught up with the wagons. I swear. What did she say?"

"That you were in love with Dora, always have been. And that you only married me because you had to. She has a very vile mind, Jeff, and a filthy mouth."

"What did you do? What did you say?"

"Not much. I tried to reason with her, calm her down. But that was just like throwing coal oil on a fire. When she called Jenny a 'black girl' to her face, I walked to the cabinet, strapped on my pistol, and asked her if she had heard about the man I shot for trying to attack Jenny."

"What did they do then?"

"Not much. I suggested that they get on their horses and ride like the devil himself was after them. It was late in the afternoon, too. I don't think there is any way they could have made it home before dark."

"I'm sorry, honey. That is just the way my ma is. She just doesn't give up! If she doesn't get her way, she will keep trying until she does. Like when I had to go get my wagons soon after Rachael was born. If I had not gone when I did, she would have sold them. She didn't get her way then, so she is trying another way."

"She thinks she did."

"Did what?"

"Get her way! She said you slept with Dora while you were there."

"Honey, they got me drunk. I know I went to bed alone, but when I woke up Dora was in the bed with me. I can't tell you if I did or didn't sleep with her.

"Don't you see, honey, she twists things all around to get her way. It's like she has a knife in my back and every time she gets a chance she twists it again.

"Frank has been crazy about Dora for years, but Ma won't let him even court her. I don't know what it is in her mind that makes her keep trying to put me and Dora together. She has done things like this for a lot of years. Well, not this bad. This is the worst."

"Well, Jeff, I don't want to be disrespectful to you, but I'm saying it straight to your face. That woman will never be welcome in my home again. Do we understand each other?"

He pressed his lips together and nodded in agreement. "I don't care if it is just a tent, it is my home!"

"I'll figure out a way to get word to Pa or Tom. I promise, honey, she won't ever come to our house again."

****

"Honey, I'm so sorry that Ma treated you that way. I can't change things, and I don't know how to make it up to you. Can we just put this behind us and not let bad memories come between us?

"I was hoping we could draw up the plans for our new house while I'm home this time. Do you feel like doing that? It could be something we do together.

"I liked the saw mill man at Mt. Pleasant. I think he gave Charlie a good price on quality lumber. I could bring a load back on my next trip. I couldn't bring enough for a whole house in one haul, but we can get started on it. Then a second load should be enough.

"Do you still like the idea of the house in Georgia? We were going to build a high sloping roof to make bedrooms upstairs. I thought that would be pretty."

She sat very still and silent, showing no expression.

"I could ask around in Hugo to see if there is a good carpenter there. One who really knows how to design and build a house. What do you think?"

All this time she had been thinking. "I can't hold him responsible for what his mother does. She is hurting him as much as she hurt me. He just tries to avoid her. I guess after all this time he knows staying away from her is the best way to handle it. I guess now I know why his father is so quiet."

"All right, we will put this all behind us," she finally said very softly. "Let's get pencil and paper and start designing. Jeff, do you think we can work in a curved staircase like Mama and Papa have?"

"I think it would mean giving up a little space in the upstairs bedrooms, but we can try, if you like."

"And can we have a little room built along the side of each bedroom? I believe they call it a clothes-ette or closet. I think the wardrobes we have are beautiful as a piece of furniture, but this would hold so much more. What do you think?"

He smiled and nodded.

"And glass doorknobs? And, Jeff, instead of a cook house, I would like the cook stove inside the kitchen. And a little room just for the bath tub? Can we do that?"

At this point, if she wanted the house painted gold, he would have agreed.

Chapter Nine
The New House

Jeff found a carpenter in Hugo, Mr. Lawrence, who seemed to know his business. And, Jeff assured him that if his women folk were all treated like ladies, there would be no trouble. "That means you and anybody you get to help you.

"Ella Jane is a perfect lady and very gracious, but she will take care of any problem that comes her way."

The carpenter said that he had heard the stories the doctor and sheriff told, and he understood why she shot the man. "I only hope my wife might have the courage to defend herself if such a thing happened."

"Hey, that is an idea. My wife has a lot of time on her hands since all our children are married and gone. Maybe I could take her with me and the two ladies could visit while I work. Let us see if that might work."

****

The man did very good work on the house, and his wife became a good friend to Ella Anne. When the house was finished, Ella Anne made them promise to come back just to visit.

"Jeff, when we get all moved in, will it be all right if I ask the Thomas's if they want our tent. I think it would be better than that drafty little house they are living in. I've been comfortable living in it."

He was happy to hear her say that. He had worried about how she might feel....moving from her parents' beautiful home, to their new house that never got finished, then into a tent. She had never complained; but she wouldn't. If there were something that could be done about a situation, she would do it. But if nothing else could be done, she would live with it.

"Jeff, we should have a house-warming party when we get moved in! Wouldn't that be fun? Not a big one, just Bob and Jenny, the Thomas's, Mr. Lawrence and Frances. I don't know; we might invite the doctor and the sheriff. I would like to thank them for being so kind to us."

****

When Jeff left this time, Ella Anne said she had a request. That was unlike her; she seldom asked for anything. He had to listen closely to what she said to know what she would like to have. He liked bringing her things.

Her request, "Jeff, let's not spend a lot of money on furniture for our new house right now. Let's let that wait until we can build a house for Bob and Jenny."

And so it was, when he came home he was loaded with East Texas Piney Woods lumber again, and Mr. Lawrence built a nice house for Bob and Jenny.

****

October 20, 1892
Dear Mama and Papa,

We have our new house finished, and we have moved into it. I love it. From our front door it seems you can see for miles, and from our bedroom window I can sit and look at the mountain. We made a curved staircase like yall have, and it looks so pretty when you step inside the front door. Rachael will feel so beautiful walking down it when she gets married!

Jeff had a real pretty house built for Bob and Jenny. My how their family has grown! Tell Jessie she would be so proud of these children.

We had a little house-warming party on Rachael's birthday. Nothing pretentious; but people that we care about and who care about us came to share our happiness.

I made an elegant new dress out of the white satin Jeff had brought me. It has a fitted bodice, gorgeous deep sculpturing across each shoulder, with a billowing skirt. I felt positively regal coming down the curved staircase to greet our guests.

Then just at dusk Jeff's family arrived unexpectedly. We didn't even know they knew about our new house. I was furious to have Mrs. Dodd in my house, but I wasn't about to make a scene in front of our guests.

Fortunately, we had enough wine on hand and Jenny had baked all day, so there were enough hors d'oeuvres.

As Mrs. Dodd and Dora walked between guests, Dora bumped into me and spilled red wine down the front of my dress. I really think Mrs. Dodd pushed her! I had to go upstairs and change. I was so happy that I had a pretty blue dress ready to wear because I already had blue ribbons in my hair.

I think they spilled the wine on me on purpose, but no matter. Jenny and I have embroidered several large clusters of grapes with profuse greenery at a slant down the skirt, and you would never dream the stain was there. It makes the dress look as if it were made for a queen. This year I think we will go to their Christmas party! Won't they be surprised when I wear the same dress?

We gave our tent to the Thomas's. I think they were pleased. They had worked so hard on their little house, but it still was very drafty. Now they can concentrate on other things that are important, too.

Rachael said be sure to tell you that she has started to school. She is so happy. She and her friend, Sarah, were not quite six years old in time, but there were not many first graders. The teacher said she would try them.

She rides Mollie to a one room schoolhouse about two miles down the road. Actually, Mr. Thomas drives Sarah over here in the buckboard every morning, and Rachael and Sarah ride double on to school.

Rachael has learned to chase lizards to fill up her spare time. She has learned to tell which ones are harmless and which ones to leave alone, but she sure has fun when she catches one.

That seems to be all of the news at this time. When Rachael learns her letters a little better, I will help her write to you.

Love to all of you. Your loving daughter,
Ella Anne

****

"Mr. Jeff, on your next trip would you bring some White Clover salve for the cow's teats? My Jenny, she's…"

"Man, you don't shoot many blanks, do you?" Jeff laughed and slapped Bob on the back.

"What are blanks, Papa?" asked Rachael, who was trailing along behind them. She had seen her mama shooting bottles and cans, but she didn't understand 'blanks'.

"Oh, just man talk, honey. No bother."

****

Rachael loved school. She loved learning new things. She had always been very inquisitive about why the animals acted as they did, what made the windmill turn, what made the windmill pump up and down, how birds fly and grasshoppers jump. These weren't just idle questions; she wanted a reasonable explanation to help her figure it out. The teacher recognized that Rachael was very eager to learn and quick to understand, so she let Rachael move on a little faster than the other children.

She got to be monitor when the teacher had to be out of the room, because Rachael was a very responsible child…and because when she told everyone to be quiet, they knew she meant it. She loved reading aloud, and often the teacher gave Rachael a book to read to the class while she worked with the older students.

School was wonderful for several years. Rachael loved Miss Black, her teacher. Miss Black had an easy way about her; she made the children feel comfortable. She made learning interesting. But when Rachael was nine, Miss Black became Mrs. White. Not too much later, there was a little White on the way, and the school got a replacement teacher.

The replacement teacher had a sharp voice, and instead of asking the children to do something, the new teacher barked orders. Rachael said she didn't seem to want to help them learn, she just demanded that they follow orders. She would not give Rachael another book to read when she finished ahead of the other children, like Miss Black had done. She had to just sit there, and "Sit still, Rachael!!" Rachael spent a lot of time facing the corner with a dunce hat on, reading books she had brought from home.

This was a very proper school district; they had a two-hole outhouse for the girls in one direction from the school house and a two-holer for boys in the opposite direction.

July 4th was not too far off and Jeff had brought Rachael some small firecrackers. At recess, Rachael and some of the girls sneaked behind the boy's outhouse while it was being used and set off a string of firecrackers. The terrified boys came running out, trying to pull up their pants; the girls were running away and laughing. Everyone on the school yard was laughing, except the teacher!

No one had to guess who had brought the firecrackers. Rachael was the only one whose father could afford to buy such amusements. She and Sarah left school early that day!

****

One day at recess, Rachael found some baby toads that had just hatched and were learning to hop. She caught them and put them all in the pocket of her pinafore. Back in class, Rachael had forgotten about the baby toads, but they found their way out of her pocket.

Suddenly, the students realized there were baby toads hopping everywhere. Girls screamed; boys laughed; toads hopped. Boys tried to catch them. Girls stood up in their seats and screamed. The toads just hop, hop, hopped in all directions. The new teacher stood up in her chair and screamed until Rachael and the boys had caught every one of them and took them outside.

Then the new teacher made a terrible mistake. She caught Rachael by the top of her ear and pinched it hard. She tried to lift Rachael up to her tiptoes, but the teacher was short and Rachael was tall for nine years old. Rachael kicked her in the shins and said, "Come on Sarah, we have to go home!"

****

Jeff had a meeting with the school board. He mentioned that instead of helping Rachael learn at her own pace, this new teacher was holding her back. He mentioned that if he had to teach his daughter at home in order for her to get a good education, he would no longer be paying part of the teacher's salary, and the cost per child would be greater. They already knew about the toads!

He suggested that they find a better teacher who would help the children to learn; and he mentioned that he would like to find a brass bell for the school yard on his next trip to Galveston. That would be a nice addition to the school, don't you think?

After a short search for another teacher, the school board decided to ask Mrs. White to come back to teach. She had a sister who kept the baby, and brought him to school each time he needed to nurse. Her sister took over the class while Mrs. White went to the corner of the room with her new baby.

****

When Rachael was 15 years old, she had finished all the studies through the 11th grade. She became Mrs. White's unpaid assistant. She really enjoyed helping the younger students, while Mrs. White taught the older classes. Rachael made sure to praise the ones who caught on quickly and see that they had something else to read. And she was gentle and helped the others with things they did not understand.

By the time Rachael was 16, their little community, Idabel, was growing. New businesses were moving in and Idabel was becoming a town.

After her 16th birthday, Jeff started recruiting young gentlemen callers for Rachael. He only picked the ones that he could see were sharp enough to give her a good living. He picked a young lawyer, just starting up his practice. A new young doctor, who was unmarried, moved into town; Jeff invited him for dinner.

His little Rachael had become quite a looker, but she wanted nothing to do with the young men that Jeff chose for her.

While Jeff was focused on Rachael, he failed to notice the other lady in his life was gaining weight!

****

"Telegram for Mr. Burrell Barnett," the young man said, when Jessie opened the door.

"Yes, sir. I'll get him right away."

Personal telegrams were only used when there was an emergency. Burrell hurriedly opened it.

Burrell Barnett
Rome, Georgia

I am too young to start the change of life. Please tell Dr. Wilson that I need him.

Ella Anne Dodd

Chapter Ten
A Baby Boy!

The news could not have come at a better time for Dr. Wilson. Ever since his wife died last winter, he had had no energy, no care for life. The thought that Ella Anne needed him, needed him badly, gave new meaning to his life. And Indian Territory sounded exciting.

"Since that new young doctor has come to work with me, he has been seeing most of my patients anyway," he told Burrell. In his intensity he took too big a sip from his fresh cup of coffee and almost strangled trying to swallow it. "Burrell, you and I together pulled off nothing short of a miracle last time. Are you up to trying again? I am!"

"I don't think Minerva would let her go through this alone. There is too big a chance the same thing could happen. I will send Ella Anne a telegram and find out how far along she is. We can make our plans from there."

Life for these two older gentlemen suddenly took on a new flavor. Burrell began hunting for his weeds and Jessie began grinding. He wanted to have a lot of powder made up in case they needed it. He didn't know if these weeds even grew in Oklahoma.

Dr. Wilson changed all his patients to the new doctor as smoothly as possible. And he immediately sent away for a large jar of Vaseline. He wanted to be sure it came directly from the manufacturer as before.

****

Leaving Robert and Big Jessie in charge, Burrell felt secure in leaving the farm for a few months. Minerva was so thrilled about seeing her daughter and granddaughter that she was in a tizzy of excitement. They would take the train to Ft. Smith; then hire a buckboard from there. People in Indian Territory did not seem to use carriages.

By the time they arrived Ella Anne was five and a half months along. "Rachael came at six months," Dr. Wilson said. "From the shape of your tummy, I don't believe this one will be born breech, but you were right, it is going to be another big baby. Have you been using the diet I prescribed before? Eating mostly vegetables? And walking a lot?"

Jeff was away, not on a trip, just in town. He seemed to stay in town a lot lately. Mostly in the saloon, talking.

Ella Anne explained, "Somehow his mother found out about the baby. Probably through the telegrams we sent, but she has been sending him messages by everyone who comes this direction.

"He stays so upset...like he just can't think straight when she is on him like this. She won't dare show up here, but she catches him through people he sells to and such as that."

****

A few days later Burrell and Dr. Wilson went into town to meet the young doctor in Idabel. Dr. Wilson wanted to make him comfortable about a different doctor being called in.

Ella Anne began to experience some discomfort late that afternoon.

"Rachael," Minerva called loudly. "Rachael, go catch your fastest gelding and go to town. We need Dr. Wilson and Grandpa right away. And your father, if you can find him."

Grandpa and Dr. Wilson were easy to find, and they would hurry on home. Rachael was to stay and try to find her father.

She ran down the boardwalks looking in all of the stores where he delivered merchandise. She tried the bank and the barber shop. The barber suggested she try the saloon.

Rachael had never been in a saloon before, so she cautiously pushed the swinging doors open and held them open while she stared inside. When her eyes became accustomed to the dim light, she saw her father sitting at a table....with a saloon girl on his lap.

Someone said, "Hey, Jeff, isn't that your daughter?"

He quickly looked toward the door and saw his 16 year old daughter, still holding the swinging doors open wide. Her steely, narrowed eyes sent him more shame than a tongue lashing.

"Mama needs you." She called out coldly. She shook her head slightly and turned, letting the doors flap behind her as she left.

****

Everyone remembered their assigned jobs from years before, except the new young doctor, whom Dr. Wilson invited to consult on this delivery. "It will be like nothing you have experienced," he promised.

He watched as Burrell and Jenny mixed the powder and grease. Minerva smoothed it on Ella Anne, and Dr. Wilson administered the laudanum. "This powder is an old Cherokee remedy that Burrell knew about. He used it on horses that were having a hard time delivering. It lightens the contractions.

"We held her off for two weeks with Rachael. That gave the baby that crucial time to develop. This is the critical stage that determines if the baby is going to make it.

The last one was breech before we realized it; but I don't think this one is. God be with us once more."

This young doctor was getting the kind of education no medical school could prepare him for. It might be very useful to him if Mr. Barnett can find that weed here in the Territory.

****

When Rachael got home with news about her father, Burrell went back to town to get him.

"This time at least I know why he does this. I'll keep a better eye on him."

Burrell and Bob kept Jeff busy around the farm for the next two weeks. As long as his hands stayed busy and Burrell kept his mind off his mother, Jeff did good.

It seemed like a lifetime, but finally Dr. Wilson said he could keep her on laudanum no longer. It was time to let her have the baby.

****

"It's a boy!" Dr. Wilson exclaimed with a shout that could be heard throughout the house.

Jeff heard it from the porch. He clapped his hands and jumped up. "Now, Ma can't hold that over my head anymore! My Ella Jane has done it. I have a son." He felt Rachael's cold stare and turned around to see no expression whatsoever on her face.

After quite a while Dr. Wilson came down the stairs and onto the porch. His face was solemn, and he didn't begin to speak right away. "The baby seems fine, but we nearly lost Ella Anne. Such a big baby, and she is older now. I never even thought she would get pregnant again after the damage done to her insides. She is liable to be very fragile after this."

He looked at Jeff, "She is asleep now. You can go up and hold her hand, but she is not going to know you are there."

After Jeff went up, he turned to Burrell, "You had better keep a close eye on that one, Burrell. You seem to have a real good effect on him." Dr. Wilson had caught on to the problem here.

He sat down beside Rachael and picked up her hand. He just held it for a while between his two hands. "Well, young lady, you have a fine baby brother. What do you think about that?"

Rachael did not know what to think. Her world had turned so many corners in the last two weeks that she was still trying to catch up. She sat very still with a blank look on her face.

"I'm sure your Grandma will be with you for a while yet, but I'm afraid the brunt of this will fall on you and Jenny. I don't think your mama will ever be strong again. A whole lot of raising this baby is going to fall to you."

He studied her for a while. "Your mama needs your strength to get through this. You can do it, Rachael. I believe in you."

She looked at him with tears in her eyes and slowly nodded her head. She thought about her mama for a little bit and smiled. "I can keep the horses out of the pea patch, Dr. Wilson!"

****

Ella Anne was still bedfast when the baby was a month old, but she was feeling a little better all the time. Dr. Wilson was becoming optimistic about her recovery. He thought he liked it here in the Territory, and he was going to stay. But Burrell and Minerva were preparing to go back to Georgia.

Jeff, thinking things were going to be okay, had gone to town. As he rode down the street of Idabel, he recognized Tom's horse tied in front of the saloon. He swaggered in to tell him the good news.

Tom raised his eyebrows and nodded. "Ma got the news just about as soon as that young doctor got back to town. He was so excited that he told everyone in town how that old doctor saved your baby... and your wife.

"Ma is on the warpath, Jeff. No telling what she is planning."

"Barkeep, hand me a bottle," Jeff said softly.

****

"Jeff bet the farm! And he lost it! I was there; I saw it!" Burrell couldn't believe the words that were coming out of his own mouth.

"When I went to find him he was drunk and playing poker. He had a good hand, a full house. But he bet the farm! The other man had a straight flush! It was a legal bet; I tried to stop him, but he was out of control, and wouldn't listen.

"Jeff is passed out in the saloon, but I heard the man who won telling the sheriff that he wanted to serve papers as soon as possible." He calmed his voice down and looked directly at Ella Anne, "You have a sweet little spread here, and he wants it."

He looked at Minerva; with downcast eyes they took hands and walked out to the porch to sit in the swing. They sat in silence for a few minutes, finally Burrell said, "It would make no sense to move Ella Anne back to Georgia with the way things are slowing down there."

They continued to swing. "My papa bought a half a league of land in central Texas through his nephew who was settling an estate in Big Spring, Texas. As far as I know, he has no plans for it; just bought it for an investment.

"Wouldn't it make more sense to move her and the kids and livestock down there where they have a chance of making a living?"

"It kind of looks as if it is all up to her, doesn't it?" Minerva agreed.

"As far as I can see, we have enough lawyers in the family who can justify us taking Jeff's wagons to move her to Texas. If he wants them after that he can come get them. But we had better do this fast or we may lose the livestock too."

They went upstairs and told Ella Anne their plan. "We have to move fast, honey, or you may lose your stock along with the farm. It was all legal; I saw it.

Minerva gently touched her daughter's shoulder. "Do you think if we make you a bed of hay in a wagon, you can tough it out for ten days or so? That is how long your papa thinks it will take us to get there.

"I think Dr. Wilson may go with us, too. After all, you are the reason he came out here."

****

So it was a done deal. That night Bob, Burrell and Dr. Wilson began loading furniture while Jenny and Rachael crated chickens and geese and packed everything they could. By morning light six loaded wagons with extra mules and one milk cow behind pulled out for Colbert's Ferry. Burrell, Bob and Minerva drove wagons; Burrell had been able to find three extra drivers on short notice. Jenny and Rachael were on horseback, each leading a string of horses. These were desperate measures for desperate times.

It took several days for the sheriff to get the paperwork done. It took Jeff several days to sober up. When the sheriff went out with an eviction notice, he was the first to find the place deserted. He high tailed it back to town to confront Jeff. But he found that Jeff had such a fuzzy head, he could not even realize what was being said. "Well, anyway here is the eviction notice. You have been served. The place is legally his now."

When Jeff sobered up enough to realize what this paper meant, and with a throbbing head, he slowly rode out to his farm. But he found that everything but the house was gone. He sat down on the porch steps to try to think. The tracks were getting dim, but still readable. They took mules, wagons, furniture, horses, all the sacked feed, everything. There was nothing left but goose feathers!

They were headed west. Where could they go that is west of here? "I guess I'll follow the tracks as far as I can, then start asking questions. A caravan that size will attract attention, wherever it goes."

****

The man at Colbert's Ferry recognized the rigs, and Burrell saw his glances and hesitation. "These are my son-in-law's wagons and family. He will be along in a few days."

That seemed to make it all right, and they went straight across. The ferry man stopped to look at the baby. "We'll meet him in Mt. Pleasant," Ella Anne said. The man nodded and Minerva slapped the reins on the rumps of the mules.

"Mama, that was a lie," Rachael said as she rode up alongside of the wagon.

"I know, darling, but that is the route your father usually takes. It was what the man was expecting to hear. It may buy us a little time. You doing okay, honey?"

"I haven't ridden this far in one stretch before, but I'll be okay. It's Jenny that I'm concerned about. She is not all that familiar with riding horseback."

"I guess she will be by the time we get there," Ella Anne chuckled.

****

When Ella Anne felt like sitting up for a while, she enjoyed watching the scenery change. North of the Red the soil was mostly red sand. But south of the river in north Texas the soil was growing darker, even black, more like clay. Look how tall the trees are; this land must be very fertile. And for sure they get more rainfall here.

The deeper they went into Texas, the greener the landscape became. Now they were seeing Black Jacks and oak thickets....seemed like literally a forest of oak trees, tall with broad spreading branches. Many varieties of low shrubs and wild flowers filled in the landscape. Now and then they passed a meadow…just fields of red, yellow, blue, violet and white wild flowers that looked like they had been painted by a painters brush! A stroke of red to the right, then a swath of purple back to the left. "Central Texas is beautiful," she thought, and she looked forward to a new life here.

****

"I think we are finally in Bell County," Burrell said. "Now to locate the land Papa bought. We will stop in the first big town and ask directions."

In Killeen, Burrell located a law office. "My name is Burrell Barnett. My father, Wm. J. Barnett, bought half a league of land, the William Tandy League. Can you help me locate it? I am here to settle my daughter and her family on it.

"Might be helpful if you contacted my cousin, Wm. Carroll Barnett, Jr. in Big Spring, Texas. He was the attorney who settled the estate in question."

He was back to the wagons within half an hour with directions. "It's not much farther. That lawyer is going to check with Wm. Carroll in Big Spring, just to make sure everything is legal, but he gave me directions. We can go on out there."

They were all relieved when they saw that the land had a pretty nice house on it. It just needed a good cleaning from sitting empty. Next day they had Ella Anne in her own bed in her new home.

****

As soon as they were settled good, Burrell and Minerva had to go back to Georgia, leaving Rachael more or less in charge. Of course she would have the wisdom of her mother's advice. And they knew Bob and Jenny would take good care of things.

But it didn't take too long for Jeff to track them down. As soon as he saw his wagons, he knew he was at the right place. He didn't even bother to knock; he just walked in. Everybody knew he rode up, but they expected him to knock! Ella Anne was sitting up in bed when he came into her room.

He was mad! Mad that they had left him, mad that he had to track them down. Most of all he was mad that he had lost their farm, but he was transferring his anger onto Ella Anne for leaving him.

He ranted and raved for half an hour and didn't show any signs of letting up. "I know where he gets this!" Ella Anne thought. Calmly, she said, "Jeff, you cannot see it, but under these covers I have a pistol. It's cocked. And this time I won't pull my shot! Do we understand each other?"

He did understand all too well because he could see the shape of the barrel pressing up against the covers.

"Jeff, this is not your land. You have no say around here, and you are not welcome here. Take your mules and wagons and go.

"Rachael, make sure none of our horses go with him, darling."

"Well, I can't drive all six wagons at one time!"

"Then I suggest you drive one wagon out into the lane, then come back and get another one and do the same. If you are halfway decent to Bob, maybe he will help you get them hitched. If not, you are on your own.

"And Jeff, anything you leave behind is mine! Don't leave yourself any reason to come back!"

Chapter Eleven
Ma Wins

Jeff didn't seem to know what to do with himself. The railroad had a major station in Temple. There was no need for his freighting business here....even if he had wanted to work. He really felt no interest in hauling freight to the smaller towns that the railroad missed. He did not want to go back to Oklahoma. He became very depressed and sullen.

Living in the Territory, life had been one continuous adventure. He had been happy as a lark. Delivering to small towns that the railroad bypassed had made him a hero every time he arrived in a town.

Meeting the ships at Galveston was always exciting; the docks were bustling with people and merchandise. He was pursued by the ships' captains when they heard he was in town because he always spent a lot of money. There was inspecting merchandise and haggling over prices. It made him feel good to hear someone call after him, "Mr. Dodd!"

It made him feel good to have drivers working for him who respected him, knew how he wanted things done and did their best to please him.

Then there was always the trip home to his Ella Jane. He loved bringing her new things for the house and little personal gifts. She always seemed so pleased with everything he brought her. It made him feel like a hero.

But all of that was gone now. He had been playing "Mr. Big Shot" in the Territory when he bet the farm. Not only did he lose the farm, but he lost Ella Jane's trust and respect. "She won't even let me on the place to talk to her now." These thoughts tumbled through his mind. "She threatened me with a pistol! And she'll use it too! Her papa taught her well! I don't dare go out there and try to talk to her."

Life had not gone as Jeff had planned it. He sat in the saloon, nursing a glass of bourbon, and thinking.... Regrets! Lots of regrets!

"Everywhere I go Ma finds me, trying to run my life. Bringing Dora along; throwing her at me. I can't have a life with Ella Jane because Ma gets mad, and when she gets mad, she gets even! Seems like the only peace I get is when I'm on a haul or in a saloon!

"Seems as if we had a pretty good life as long as we lived near Burrell. But every haul I made to the Sound took me right by Ma and Pa's place. Didn't seem right not stopping to see them. But every time she would get her hooks into me, she'd get me all twisted up inside.

"Seems like, once I got home, it would take me several months to get my thinking straight. Burrell sure helped me with that. I made good money, but was it really worth it?"

He drained the last of a bottle into his glass and tossed it back. He sat the bottle down on the bar loudly, "Barkeep, bring me another bottle."

Mostly he just hung out in the saloon, getting drunker and meaner all the time, often in fights and too drunk to win despite his size.

Tom rode in one day during one of those fights when Jeff was taking a licking from two men. He joined in and soon had the fight stopped. He drug Jeff outside and soused his head in the water trough to sober him up.

"What's going on, Jeff?" he asked while Jeff sputtered and coughed to get his breath.

"Ella Jane left me. I followed her here, but she won't let me come to her house."

"What about that sweet little spread you had in Oklahoma?"

"I was drunk and I lost it in a poker game. When I sobered up and went out there, Ella Jane, Rachael, the baby, everything was gone. The only thing that showed she had been there was goose feathers."

Jeff finally quit feeling sorry for himself long enough to ask, "What are you doing here, Tom?"

"Well, Ma found out from the man at Colbert's Ferry that you were down this direction. We are still following you, big brother."

"But, why did you leave that good grassland in Oklahoma?"

"The government finally got around to settling the Indians on it. They called it the Big Pasture. Ma tried to buffalo the Colonel they sent to run off any white people who were squatting on it.

"He listened to her for just so long; then he raised his hand and ordered his men to begin shooting horses when he dropped his hand. While his hand was raised to give the signal, Ma gave in. We only got out of there with our horses. They didn't give us time to load up anything. She is mad enough to bite a ten-penny nail in two.

"She will be glad to see you, though; have you back in the family, as it were."

****

Ma was glad to see Jeff...very happy to hear about his situation with Ella Anne! "Jeff, sit down here next to Dora.

"Dora, honey, pour him a glass of that good wine.

"Frank, set another place at the table... for yourself. Over there by Tom will be good."

Her interest turned back to Jeff, "What do you plan to do around here, Jeff?

"Since you can't fight the railroad, why don't you join them? Looks to me like they could put your freighting experience to good use on the railroad. There is a man I know," she glanced up at her husband. "I have gotten acquainted with the railroad agent because we have been shipping some of our horses back East. Several people are interested in introducing some new blood lines in their Morgan herds up there, especially the people who breed them for running.

"Well, anyway, I'll talk to him about you possibly working for the railroad next time I see him."

****

Turned out the railroad agent did have an opening for a man with Jeff's experience of buying and selling, and moving freight. Having a job to go to every day was very good for Jeff. It kept his mind busy on pleasant things so that he couldn't think of all of his mess ups. As long as he did what Ma wanted, things were peaceful at Ma's house, and he had a nice

place to live. Since things with Ella Jane were so messed up, Dora turned out to be a comfort to him.

Once in a while he would see Ella Jane and Rachael in town. Rachael drove her mother in for monthly meetings of the Society for Women's Right to Own Land; SWROL they called it. "Wouldn't you just know that would be the cause she chose to champion?" Jeff thought.

For two years Mrs. Ella Anne Dodd was president, and with all the lawyers in her family, she had some pull in the legislature.

Ella Anne could look straight at him and straight through him at the same time! She never seemed to notice his being present and quickly avoided any possibility of being at the same gathering of people.

Still, Jeff made it his business to know of Rachael's comings and goings. With his position as Purchasing Agent for the Texas & Pacific Railroad, he still had a little pull in the area. When he located a promising young professional man, he never failed to mention his pretty young daughter was unmarried. "She is a pretty good horsewoman, if you want to take along a horse with a sidesaddle."

The years slowly slipped by without any particular incidents. Until one day a young man appeared in town, dressed in the latest fashion and driving a fancy buggy with fringe on top. Showy little sorrel buggy horse, too. Jeff felt an instant dislike for this young man, with his black hair combed very smoothly and very smartly across his head.

Without ever meeting the young man, Jeff discovered that his name was Epsy Hale. He was from a very big family out in the Westphalia area, lots of brothers, uncles and cousins, and all owning land. Epsy, it seems had been away playing baseball in the minor leagues. He must have been a pretty good second baseman, too. People were saying he had a shot at the majors coming up pretty soon, until he got hurt.

He tagged Ty Cobb out at second base, but Cobb cleated him in the ankle. The story was out that Cobb sharpened his cleats with a file for just such a purpose. It left Epsy with a very slight limp, but he would never play baseball again on that ankle.

Jeff saw him a time or two around town, but never paid any attention to him…until one day there was Rachael riding with him in the buggy with the fringe on top!!

Jeff's mind began to race. He wanted this stopped! He knew well enough that he could not go out to the house to talk to Rachael. He could send someone else out there to give her a message; but then Ella Jane would hear as well, so that was out.

Maybe he could ask one of Rachael's friends to ask her to meet him in town. They could have lunch together in town; he could buy her an elegant meal at the hotel dining room. That would be the way to talk to her.

It took more than a week before Rachael would agree to meet with him; but it was worth the wait. Jeff sat nervously at a table for two in the center of the hotel dining room. As she pushed open the door and stood in the light, a hush suddenly fell over the diners, and every man in the room turned to look.

She wore white! White slippers, white stockings, a smooth ankle-length white skirt that flared slightly. Her blouse seemed to be made of white gossamer, with full sleeves and high fitted cuffs. Her fitted bodice showed slightly through the gossamer and punctuated her tall, slender figure.

Her golden blond hair was pulled up, as was the fashion of the times, topped with a small white hat with a slender white feather encircling one side of her face. And she carried a white ruffled parasol, which she crisply snapped shut as she stepped inside the stunned, silent dining room.

Jeff was as amazed as the others in the room. He was filled with pride at the sight of his lovely daughter. He stood up and pulled out a chair for her. She stood, looking at him as if she were deciding whether to accept. Then she slowly walked toward the table and nodded, as she took her seat.

Jeff tried several ways to start a conversation with her, but all she gave was short answers, very to the point. "Would you like to order?" he asked finally. "Anything on the menu. Nothing is too expensive for my little girl."

She narrowed her eyes for a minute, but did not pick up the menu. Jeff had seen that look on her mother's face many times, and he braced himself. "What did you want?" she asked.

"Why, I wanted to spend some time with my little girl," Jeff began.

"No, you didn't. You want something. What is it?"

"Well, I saw you buggy riding with that new young man in town."

"And?"

"Well, I don't know him and I don't want you seeing him," he tried to keep his voice as low as possible. He could see that people around them were listening, but the look in her eyes grew colder.

"I forbid you to see him!" Jeff finally said louder than he intended. Her right eyebrow went up in defiance.

"I am very careful not to see anyone whom I do not believe will treat me like a lady. I don't see that you have much say in the matter of whomever I choose to see."

"Young lady, that is no way for you to talk to your father. You are not showing respect!"

"That's right! Not since the day Bun was born, and I found you in a saloon with a woman on your lap! You are absolutely right; I have no respect for you at all!" Her voice was getting louder.

"Shhh," he said, looking around. By now people were turning to stare at them and he frowned as he looked at their faces then back to her.

Rachael raised that eyebrow. "You are the one who picked the place!" she said as she stood up, turned and walked very slowly and stately toward the door. Without looking back, she snapped open her parasol and stepped outside.

****

Rachael had a date planned with Epsy for Saturday of that week. They were going to a church picnic and fund-raiser. Every woman was to bring a basket lunch, and the men bid to see who got to have lunch with the best cook or their favorite girl.

Epsy helped her into the buggy; then handed her the basket lunch she had brought. It was fried chicken, he could smell it! She smoothed her skirt while he went around and climbed into the driver's seat. She laid her hand on his arm. "I've got to tell you something very serious," she said.

"What is it?" he asked with a startled look.

"My father has forbidden me to see you anymore. So if you want me to go with you today, you will have to marry me," she said softly and looked straight into his eyes for his reaction.

"That sounds good to me," he said with a growing smile. "Where can we get married?"

"Not around here because everyone is afraid of my father. My mother has an uncle in Weatherford who is a judge. We can be a long ways toward there before the picnic is over."

"Okay!" He leaned over and kissed her on the cheek. "We're engaged!"

She smiled, and called over her shoulder, "Bun, will you bring that valise I have hidden behind the Crepe Myrtle? Put it into the back of the buggy, will you, please?"

When Bun brought it, Rachael said, "Please tell Mama that we are running off to get married. Will you do that for me?"

Bun had been sitting on the porch steps taking all of this in. He ran into the house and Epsy slapped the reins on the horse's rump. They were off to Weatherford! "I brought fried chicken for our supper," she said.

It was a little more than a two day drive to Weatherford. With such a light buggy and a fresh horse, they should be there before word got out that far. However, Judge Barnett had heard tells about Jeff Dodd, too. He was not about to marry them.

Epsy had a twin brother in Coahoma who had gotten married two years earlier, so they struck out west. "Mind you, Epsy, as we travel, you may kiss me good-night, but until we are legally married, nothing more."

Arriving in Coahoma three days later, they found that everyone there already knew that Jeff Dodd was a hard one to deal with. He often made stops at the Big Spring railroad station. After asking all over Coahoma and Big Spring, they found a Methodist lay-minister in Stanton who said, "I work for the Lord. I'm not afraid of Jeff Dodd or anybody else, for that matter!"

They were married in the minister's parlor. His wife cut roses from her garden, which were cherished items in the dry West Texas soil, so that Rachael could have a bouquet to carry. Epsy's twin brother, Earnest and his wife, Ethel, stood up with them. Epsy wore his good black coat and gray, herring bone weave trousers. His black hair was combed smooth and straight across his head.

Everyone stood in their designated places as they waited for Rachael to enter from the dining room. Suddenly she was there! They all gasped, for as she stepped into the doorway and paused, it seemed as if a ray of light had entered the room. The sunlight from a window behind her silhouetted her snow-white dress. The dainty white feather drew attention to her hair that glistened like spun gold.

Rachael's heart melted…this was just the effect she had been planning for. The tears of happiness that instantly formed gave her eyes a dewy shimmer.

Earnest and Ethel had invited a photographer to the wedding. Their wedding present to the newest Mr. and Mrs. Hale was a wedding picture. Epsy sat in a straight backed dining room chair, and Rachael stood to his left, with her hand on his shoulder. They were the most somber, most proper couple ever.

They honeymooned on the way back to Temple because Rachael had to hurry back and help take care of her mother and little brother.

Now that he had real responsibilities, Epsy began looking in earnest for a good investment. He bought the cotton gin in Rising Star, which seemed a long way from Temple. But, Rachael made the trip by rail often to see her mother and help when she could.

****

Ella Anne stood wearily in the middle of the parlor waiting for Jeff to dismount and come inside. Her health had steadily declined since Bun was born. The doctor said there was just nothing he could do to help. Having two big babies had weakened her too much. By now he was not even expecting her to get any better and each passing year left her weaker.

Rachael and Jenny were in the dining room hiding on each side of the door to the parlor. They knew trouble was brewing, and they knew better than to be part of it. Wide eyed, six year old Bun did not know why they were whispering, but he knew to be quiet by the way Jenny was holding onto his hand so tightly.

"When we were young, there was such a sparkle in her eyes," Jenny whispered. "She would ride across hell and just dare the devil to try to scorch her."

"What do you mean? She is still that way. I've seen her stand up to a man twice her size....with a reputation for hitting women....and she knew the odds were stacked against her." Rachael was remembering growing up in Oklahoma. So many people moved in so fast, it took quite a while for the law to catch up. People had to stand up for themselves or get run over by bullies. There were many times when her father was away on freighting runs, she had seen her mother stand her ground and not give an inch.

"You're right, she will. But do you see the sadness in her eyes? She does this now because that is just the way she is made. But this time she does it knowing she is going to get burned."

Jeff walked in with his head bent over, looking first to one side then the other, hardly looking at Ella Anne. He rubbed his hands together uneasily, rubbing the back of one hand out to the end of his fingers; then rubbing the other, as if the rubbing might ease his quandary. "Dora's pregnant, Ella Jane. Ma says I've got to marry her. She says you have to give me a divorce."

"Your ma always has been able to manipulate you, Jeff Dodd. She never stops trying!"

"You know she is not going to give me any peace until I marry Dora. That has always been what the tussle was about. Ma says you are too sick to be a wife to me anymore, so you might as well give me a divorce."

"Well, Jeff, you tell your mother that this old mare still has a little kick left in her!

She took a deep breath and let it out slowly. "You marry Dora, if that is what you want to do. You can be a bigamist! Because I will never give you a divorce! Never!"

By now she was leaning on the high-backed parlor chair nearest her. Jenny left little Bun standing alone as she ran to support Ella Anne.

Suddenly newly married Rachael was standing between her mother and father, eyes flashing. "Just go on….marry that tramp. But don't ever

come back here. You never have been much of a husband or father that I remember anyway! Just go, and don't ever come back!"

He turned hesitatingly, as if he could not make up his mind what he ought to do. He finally walked out quietly and got on his horse.

This was not a pleasant solution, but seemingly, one he would have to live with.

Chapter Twelve
Mama and Bun

Soon after that they received word that Ella Anne's grandfather, William J. Barnett, had passed away and the property on which she now lived was to be divided among his heirs. Probably Ella Anne could have negotiated and kept the land. But she was so weak that it just seemed better to move in with Rachael and Epsy.

"Jenny, Bob, we have been together for so long," Ella Anne said, "it just seems like we are blood kin," the sadness in her voice was clear. "I can't offer you a home and work anymore.

"Bob, you pick out two mares. Make sure you get bred ones. We will sell the rest. Yall can live here and take care of the place as long as it takes for John William to settle the estate.

"Maybe some of the family will get this place and you might want to stay on here. But by that time you may have a house of your own or find you a job with someone else."

She looked at the floor and shook her head sadly. "I don't know what else to do." She stood up and hugged each of them, then slowly sat back down.

"Now bring the children and let me say goodbye to them.

She reached out and took the oldest by the hand, "Willie, you know you always were my little man. You know that I love you all, and it is hard to say goodbye. Be good to your Mama and Papa."

She leaned back in the chair and sighed. All her strength was gone.

****

Rachael was happy to have her mother and little brother with her. She didn't mind the added responsibility in the least. It was just good to have their company.

"You and Bun can share this big bedroom for now, Mama. There is room enough for two beds in here. If Bun needs anything in the night, I will get up with him. I will move mine and Epsy's things into the little bedroom. There is plenty of room for the two of us."

Ella Anne would sit at the table and peel potatoes or chop vegetables while Rachael did the cooking. And they had the nicest conversations. Their conversations just streamed from one thing to another, like a small rivulet moving down the hillside changes its course when it hits a rock in the streambed. Things like peeling peaches for a cobbler, led to the way Jessie used to slice the peaches just the right size. The sweet peach-flavored juice filled the dish, but there were some pieces of peach that you could still bite into and savor a bit longer. And the delicious crust, that woman could make! Did you know she was renowned for her cooking in our corner of northern Georgia?

Then memories of Ella Anne's childhood came rushing back. "One day I was holding my pinafore skirt out for Jessie to drop peaches into. I was going to get to help her make a cobbler. Papa called from the porch, 'Ella Anne, I think it is time for you to learn to ride a horse by yourself. Would you like that?'

"I almost dropped the peaches in the dirt because I loved being with the horses. Jessie quickly made a pouch with her apron skirt and took the peaches, and I went running.

"Papa saddled a gentle old mare and put me in the saddle. He told me to hold on to the pommel of the saddle until I learned to balance. He gathered up a handful of the back of my dress to steady me and made the mare step her hind feet around a couple of steps. That way I would get use to the idea of her movements. Then John William led her slowly around in a circle with Papa holding on to me...much the same way I did with you. Remember?

"Papa was so caring and patient. He loved to teach you why something needed to be done, as well as how to do it.

"And John William seemed to have been grown up even when he was still a boy. He followed Papa's example and always wanted to know more about why things happen. He liked to compare what happened in one situation with what might happen in another situation. I guess he was really born to be a lawyer."

Ella Anne found something good to say about almost every topic they drifted onto.... everything except Yankees and Mrs. Dodd!

Rachael knew to try to steer the conversation away from those two subjects because her mother would get so intense and animated. By the time she wound down talking about either subject, she needed to go lie down because she had used up all of her energy.

It was wonderful having Bun around to look after, too. Rachael had taken much of the responsibility of raising him until she married and moved so far away. Now she was happy to have him around again...him and his antics.

When Bun started to school, the smallpox vaccine was becoming available in most areas. The government was trying to avoid smallpox epidemics, and they wanted every school child to be vaccinated.

Bun was very interested in the instruments laid out on the white cloth-covered tray in the doctor's office. Everything about the doctor's office held such wonder for him. He sat very still as he watched the doctor use a scalpel to scrape away the top layer of skin on his upper left arm. The spot was only about the size of a dime. The doctor put two drops of vaccine on the raw place with a dropper....one, two. Then, for being such a brave boy, he gave Bun a dime.

Rachael was proud of Bun for not being scared, so she took him to the drug store and let him spend his dime on an ice cream cone. Then she needed to hurry home to check on Mama.

After the retelling of his adventure and receiving Mama's acclaim for his good behavior, Rachael got busy on supper and Bun disappeared outside. When Rachael called him in to wash for supper, Bun proudly showed them what he had been doing.

With his pocket knife he had made four more small scraps on his left arm and two on his right arm. He had sharpened a twig and carefully touched the pointed twig to his vaccination and touched a scrapped place twice – just as he had seen the doctor do.

Rachael washed the new scraps with soap and water and had him put on a clean long-sleeved shirt to protect the open places.

Two days later Bun woke up with a fever and said that his arms hurt bad! Who would have thought that every one of those places would take? Rachael ran to the cotton gin to get Epsy to drive them to the doctor. The doctor explained, "This is just about like him having a real case of smallpox! We must find a way to keep his temperature down, or this could kill him."

"He would fit in that new galvanized watering trough we bought, and we can use my wash tub to water the team." Turning to Epsy, Rachael said, "Can we bring that into the house?"

Epsy brought a man from the cotton gin to help empty the trough and carry it into the kitchen. They laid a towel in the bottom and put about four inches of water in it. Ella Anne folded another towel to use as a pillow so water would not get into his ears, and Epsy laid a very limp little boy in the tub of water. For five days the three of them took turns bathing Bun with a wash cloth..... his arms and legs, his chest, but most of all, they bathed his face and head. When he began to moan a little, and told them that he was cold, they knew he would be all right. They took him out of the water, and that night he got to sleep in his bed with just a wet cloth across his forehead. But needless to say, when he completely recovered, he had seven smallpox scars on his arms.

As summer came on, Rachael and Ella Anne would sit on the back porch and drink spearmint tea in the late afternoon...just watching the garden grow. Rachael would pull a few weeds then come back up on the porch, but Ella Anne contented herself with shooing the flies away from the tea until Rachael retuned.

One afternoon they heard Bun yelling his lungs out, and Rachael ran around the corner to find him hanging upside down, arms and legs wrapped around a tree limb, holding on for dear life. Two Jay Birds were dive bombing him! He had tried to rob the eggs from their nest and got caught.

Jay Birds are fearless fighters, especially when someone gets near their nest! With the feathers of their topknot extended forward, the loud screeching sound that they make is frightening as they dart by your head! Then suddenly they hover in mid-air flapping your head with their bright blue wings. They are fearless all right!

Rachael stood beneath him. "Drop into her arms, Bun". She caught him in her arms, but with that added weight, her knees buckled, and they both hit the ground laughing like crazy....Jay Birds still diving about their heads. They had to run into the house, and it was a long time before the birds gave up and went away.

Bun reached into his pocket and said, "Aw, they got broke in my fall." He pulled out shells of two bird eggs, with slime dripping between his fingers.

*****

Mama was slowly but steadily losing weight. She was sleeping more and staying awake for shorter periods by this time, and it worried Rachael. One day Ella Anne said, "Rachael, I noticed a few ripe tomatoes this morning. I think I'll walk out to the garden and gather them before the bugs and the birds get them."

Soon Rachael realized her mother had been out by herself long enough and went to check on her. She found her lying by the tomato vines with a bright red tomato in each hand. She had gone peacefully all right.

Rachael sat on the ground holding her mother in her arms and rocking back and forth. The tears she shed were not so much grieving as they were tears of remembering. Ella Anne was only 41 years old, but she had packed a lot of living into those years. Her mama had always been enthusiastic about life, and she lived it to the fullest. Rachael knew she was just so tired that it was time for her to go.

Bun came around the corner to see what they were doing. Before he got too close, Rachael called, "Bun, will you run right over to the gin and get Epsy for me. Tell him I need him, now."

****

They had a simple burial for Ella Ann Barnett Dodd in Longbranch Cemetery not far down the lane. A lot of local people knew and loved Ella Anne, and there was quite a crowd at the cemetery. Even a few people from Bell County who owned automobiles showed up. Ella Anne had made some really good friends working for the Women's Rights Movement.

Epsy closed the cotton gin for the day, so several of his employees came. When the funeral was over, people were milling around and talking. One of Epsy's hands said, "Hey, Mr. Hale, isn't that big man over there your father-in-law? Standing outside the fence?"

Epsy looked and said, "Yes, but don't tell anybody else. Rachael doesn't need to know right now."

Jeff stood by the cemetery fence watching. He dared not go closer, not after the way things had been. He just stood there and remembered. Most of all he remembered those blue eyes that could stare sternly… seemingly reaching the depths of his soul; then suddenly melt into loving, smiling eyes. That is what he wanted to remember… those smiling eyes.

****

The house really seemed empty for a few weeks. Rachael and Bun comforted each other as much as they could, and Epsy tried to help.

"Bun," Rachael said one morning, "You know that Mama loved us very dearly. And that she would not have left us if she had had the strength.

"You know that she went to be with Jesus, and as long as we love her in our hearts and memories, she is still with us. You know that, don't you?"

He nodded his head slowly.

"Then, as much as we miss her, let's not be sad and feel as if she is gone. Let's remember all the fun we had with her and the good things she did. That way we will always be happy and have her still with us, in a very private way. Do you think we can help each other do that?"

He nodded again, but this time the sadness was leaving his face and they began to talk about the fun times they had with their mother, how much she loved porch swings, the cute way she had of doing things, and how strong and fearless she was.

Chapter Thirteen
The Trial

They soon discovered that Rachael was pregnant with their first child, and this helped take their minds off of their loss. "God takes a life, and He gives a life," Rachael thought.

They didn't have much time to adjust to the situation before, Rachael's aunts, Nora, Lou, and Wilma, showed up at their door. "Ma is demanding that since his mother is dead, Bun should come to live with us."

Rachael's blood came to an instant boil. "I have been responsible for raising Bun for most of his life. He can continue to live with me, thank you!" and she began pushing them out the door.

"Ma is not going to like this," Wilma warned quietly. Nora was not so quiet in saying, "We'll be back. You just wait!"

Three days later, Bun didn't come home from school at his usual time. Rachael walked over to the school house with a little concern. She found Mrs. Little, the teacher almost frantic. "They walked in here like they owned the place, picked him up out of his seat and took him away! I tried to stop them, tried to tell them I couldn't let him go with them. But they said they were his aunts, and his father wanted Bun with him. Then they slammed the door shut in my face. I didn't know what to do...I still had the other kids to look after. I'm so sorry."

Rachael's heart sank so that her chest felt empty. "What can I do?" she thought. "They are well on their way to Temple by now." She hurried to the cotton gin to talk to Epsy about it.

Rachael was upset and her mouth said everything that she thought. "If I get an attorney, would I have any chance of getting him back? He is Bun's father. Even if he doesn't care about him, does he have more right of custody than I do?

"I know it's not him that wants Bun, it is his mother. She just wants to stir up trouble like she always does!

"Every time he and Mama seemed to be happy together, his mother would find some way to get at him and make him do what she wanted."

She covered her face with her hands. "Oh, Epsy, what am I going to do?"

Epsy held her hands and let her talk out her emotion, while tears flowed down her cheeks like a dam had broken. When she finally fell silent, she looked deeply into his eyes searching for the strength that she did not have at this time.

Epsy had been thinking hard. "We will send a wire to John William. Since he is in another state, he will not be able to really help, but he can recommend a lawyer here who would be trustworthy. A request like this will carry more weight coming from another attorney.

"Stay right here. Let me make some arrangements to keep the men working, and we will go into town to the telegraph office."

So the telegram was sent, and there was nothing to do but wait. The ride back home in the twilight was long and silent.

****

Almost a week later, Epsy had a visitor at the gin, a young lawyer from Ft. Worth. "My name is Donald J. Crawford, sir," he said holding out his hand. "I am with the Law Firm of Solomon and Jacobs in Ft. Worth. I have been sent here to get details on this child custody case. Judge Barnett in Atlanta asked our law firm to represent your wife in her suit to retain legal custody of her younger brother."

"Let me make arrangements with my men so that I can leave the cotton gin, and I'll take you to the house. You need to talk to Rachael."

In just a few minutes, Epsy was back and they stepped outside. Epsy's eyes opened wide with admiration at the shiny, red Model-T Touring Car the young lawyer was driving. The black cloth top and black fenders gave it just the right balance of color. "Wow! That looks brand new. Brass headlights! All that shiny brass everywhere!"

"It is new," Mr. Crawford said. "It is one of the first off Mr. Ford's assembly line! We have had it only about three months. This is the first out of town trip it has made. Get in."

"Forgive me, sir. I didn't know an attorney as young as you could afford an automobile this nice. Wow! Do you mind my asking what it cost?"

"Oh, it's not mine. It belongs to the law firm, for just such occasions as this. Is this the house? It cost $950! That Henry Ford has hit upon an idea that will make him a lot of money! Build a product that the working man can afford and you will sell as many as you can make."

As they turned off the lane, Epsy could see Rachael peeking out the side of the lace curtains. He was not at all surprised. You just did not see automobiles like this in Rising Star!

Inside, Epsy introduced Mr. Crawford to Rachael. She invited them into the kitchen and immediately started a pot of coffee while they talked.

"Your uncle, Judge Barnett, is very upset about this turn of events, Mrs. Hale. I am here to get information from you, facts that will stand up in court. In particular, we would like to build a case around things that your father might not realize that we know. I am depending on your memory of your father's comings and goings. I understand he has quite a reputation."

Rachael sat there blinking and nodding her head slightly as she tried to comprehend. The coffee began to boil over on the wood stove. This brought her to her senses, and she jumped up to clean up the mess.

She sat cups of coffee in front of Mr. Crawford and Epsy, then the sugar bowl and creamer that matched the cups. Then she began to find her voice. "Mr. Crawford, I find myself in a rather awkward position. I want desperately to get my little brother back, but Epsy has only had this cotton gin for two years. We are not in a financial position to afford your services."

"Oh, that has already been arranged, Mrs. Hale. This is a professional courtesy for your uncle. If the situation were reversed, he would help us as much as a man in a judge's position can. Did you know there is talk of his running for the Georgia senate next year? We will be well repaid if that happens.

"Now, let's begin with some details about your father. Exactly where does he live and what is his occupation?"

"They live in the Temple area; I don't know much more than that. Last I heard he was a Purchasing Agent for the Texas & Pacific Railroad."

Mr. Crawford was thinking out loud, "Let's hope he is not so well liked that the railroad gets their lawyers in on this! You said 'they'; who exactly are you talking about?"

"I had in mind his mother and all of his brothers and sisters. They raise horses somewhere in the Temple area. My father may not still be living with his mother since he remarried, but it was his three sisters who stole Bun from the school house."

"Give me their names, and what is the teacher's name?" Mr. Crawford was writing as fast as he could, getting all the information down.

"His sisters are Nora, Lou, and Wilma... Dodd, I guess. I don't know if she has let any of them get married. The school teacher is Mrs. Little; I don't know her first name."

"Now, you said your father had remarried. I understood your mother has been deceased for only two months."

"That is correct. My father married again about two years ago."

Mr. Crawford's grip on his pencil went limp and he looked puzzled, "But, I found no record of a divorce."

"There was none."

Mr. Crawford stared straight at Rachael with sadness in his eyes and shook his head slightly. Then suddenly he began to write feverishly on his legal pad. "This should put a quick end to his petition for custody," Mr. Crawford was saying.

"It's not him who wants custody of Bun. It's his mother."

Again Mr. Crawford looked puzzled. "His mother would have to be nearing seventy years old. Why would she want custody of an eight year old boy?"

For the first time Epsy entered the conversation, "This man is obviously here to try to help us. Rachael, why don't you just lay out the whole story so he will know what he is dealing with?"

Slowly, Rachael recounted things from her childhood that would help Mr. Crawford understand what kind of a personality he would be dealing with. Dora... losing the farm in Oklahoma... Big Pasture... Dora... bigamy. All this, because she never quits. If one way doesn't work, she will try another direction, until she finally wins.

"They were about to start shooting horses?!?" Mr. Crawford exclaimed.

"That is the only time that I know of her not getting her way. Sometimes I wonder if that Colonel is still alive," Rachael said softly, looking off into the distance.

Mr. Crawford had been writing as fast as he could to get his thoughts onto the legal pad. "As soon as I get back to the firm, I will present this to the board. We have some very good legal minds there. I can see a good possibility we could win this for you."

They heard hoof beats approaching the house. You could tell the horse was tired by the sound of the hoof pattern. They all looked out the kitchen window in time to see Bun slide off a weary bay Morgan. He didn't stop to tie the horse, but ran up the back steps into the kitchen and grabbed Rachael around the waist burying his face in her midriff.

She held him, and they both sobbed. Finally when he loosened his grip a little, she sat down and took him on her lap. "Bunnie, how did you get here?"

"I waited until they were all asleep, and I ran away. I don't like those people, Rachael. They are not nice people."

"But, Bun you stole a horse!"

"No, I didn't. They said he was mine. I didn't take a saddle, though. I rode night and day." He looked at her while he took a breath. "Rachael, I'm so hungry."

She poured him a glass of milk; then started preparing something for him to eat. Epsy looked out the window at the horse; he didn't care if he was tied or not. He just hung his head low. "I'll go take care of the horse," he said.

Rachael was asking questions as she cooked. "Bun, are you okay? They didn't hurt you, did they?"

"No, they didn't hurt me. They bought me new clothes that I didn't like and made me wear them. I had to stay in the house and sit still all of the time.

"Mrs. Dodd talks mean to everybody. She doesn't ask, 'Will you do this for me?' like you and Mama. She just says, 'Do that!' in a mean sounding voice."

Mr. Crawford was getting an earful and writing as fast as he could. "Was your father there, son?" he asked in a kindly tone.

"He came in once. He was drunk. He said Dora was mad at him. Mrs. Dodd told him to go up to bed and sleep it off.

"She can't cook either. She has a black girl working for her to cook and clean, and she doesn't treat her nice like you and Mama treated Bob and Jenny. She is mean to her."

"Did she make you call her Mrs. Dodd, son?"

"No, she told me to call her Grandmother, but I wouldn't do it. I called her Mrs. Dodd."

Rachael sat a plate in front of Bun. "You can start on these fried potatoes, while the meat is browning."

"Can I get you something, Mr. Crawford?"

"That is very good coffee. I'd like another cup if you have it."

Bun could only stay awake for the milk and potatoes. He almost fell asleep at the table, so Rachael put him to bed right away.

Mr. Crawford was still writing when she came back into the kitchen. This time he was writing slower, and he would put the top of the pencil to his lip once in a while when he was thinking. "I'm planning strategy, now. Trying to figure what points to emphasize," he said. "I have a lot of information to present to the board. I may as well start back to Ft. Worth.

"Mrs. Hale, it has been a pleasure talking with you. You are a very kind and gentle lady. I certainly hope this goes well for you. At least you have him back for now.

"As soon as I get back to Ft. Worth... sometime tomorrow, I will prepare a petition for an injunction preventing them from taking him from you until this is settled legally. We will file the custody suit in 91st District Court in Eastland. It is the boy's legal place of residence, and Judge Barnett knows the judge personally.

"If I were you, I would not send him to school until this is settled."

****

Rachael was at the back of the house hanging clothes on the clothesline when she heard Bun yell her name. He was scared; she could tell by the sound of his voice, and she ran as fast as she could into the house to find him.

What she found was Nora, trying to hold on to Bun by both his arms, but he was fighting her every way he could. Lou was gathering up his clothes.

"Wilma, go get the horse he took and tie it to the back of the wagon," Nora said. "Be still, you little brat!" she said to Bun, who was trying to stomp her foot, and she jerked him around hard.

Rachael was trying to help Bun get away from Nora. When Nora let go of Bun with her right hand and made a fist, Wilma yelled, "Don't hit her! Can't you see that she is pregnant?"

Instead, Nora shoved Rachael down on the bed. "Wilma, if you don't go get that horse, we will leave you here and you can ride him home."

One of the hands at the gin stopped working on a cotton trailer and ran inside looking for his boss. "Were you expecting company, Mr. Hale? A team and carriage just pulled up at your house and three women got out."

Alarm spread over Epsy's face. "Send someone for the Marshall on a fast horse. Tell him it is an emergency!" Epsy shouted as he began to run toward his house.

Nora came out of the house, struggling to control Bun. Bun bit her hand, and she slapped the side of his head. Lou threw the drawstring bag with Bun's clothes into the buggy; then she tried to control Bun while Nora whipped the horses into a run. True to her word, Nora left Wilma to ride the horse bareback at least until they could get out of sight.

Epsy was near enough to see all this but not near enough to stop their getaway. He found Rachael sitting on Bun's bed. She was bent over with her arms across her stomach, crying. "Rachael, are you hurt? Is the baby hurt? What happened?"

When she could control her crying, she sobbed, "I think I am all right, just jostled. But if it had not been for Wilma, Nora would have hit me with her fist. Oh, Epsy, what can we do now?"

"I have sent for the Marshall. Judging from the way she was running those horses, they will be out of the county by the time he gets here. But he is a Federal Marshall; he can cross the county line…if he is in town, that is."

"If you think you are going to be all right, I'll go into town and wire your uncle. He will know who to contact to get something done, or do you want to go with me?"

"No, I am nearing six months; I don't think I should do any unnecessary traveling."

"You know, unless they tie that kid up, they are going to have one uncomfortable trip back to Temple!" Epsy chuckled as he walked out the door.

****

Two days later, a young man wearing a Western Union cap rode up to the cotton gin on a bicycle. "I have a telegram for Mr. Hale, he said.

Mr. Epsy Hale
Eastland, Texas

Understand the boy has been kidnapped a second time. Papers for custody hearing in 91st District Court in Eastland have been filed. Will notify you when hearing date is set. Federal Marshal will not be able to help get the boy back until things are settled legally.

Donald J. Crawford, Atty. at Law
Law Firm of Solomon & Jacobs
Ft. Worth, Texas

****

For the next month Mr. Crawford was a busy young lawyer. This was to be his first big case. Since he had personally witnessed the boy's initial return, Mr. Solomon and Mr. Jacobs were to be the attorneys of record on the proceeding. Mr. Crawford was doing the research and preparation, but still could be called as a witness if the occasion arose.

The court date was set for October 30, 1910, 91st District Court, Eastland, Texas. Because travel was limited in Rachael's condition, Mr. Crawford would personally fetch Rachael and Epsy in one of the firm's automobiles.

****

The smartly dressed attorney from Belton took off his hat as he entered the office of Appellate Judge Brown. He gave the secretary his brightest smile and set a small vase of flowers on her desk.

Now that he had her attention, he asked if the judge were in and handed her his calling card. He was carrying a large manila envelope and looked very important. She hurried inside the judge's chambers.

When she returned, she said that the judge had just a few minutes before another meeting was scheduled, and opened the door widely for Mr. Fred McIntosh, Atty. at Law.

After a quick handshake, Mr. McIntosh said, "Your Honor, since you have limited time, I will quickly get to the purpose of my visit."

The judge waved his hand to indicate a chair for Mr. McIntosh, and they both sat down.

"Your Honor, I am representing clients in Bell County on a child custody case. The case was filed in 91st District Court in Eastland because that is where the child's sister lives. The boy is with his father in Bell County, and we are asking that the trial be moved to 27th District Court in Belton."

The judge narrowed his eyes slightly as he thought over this information. "Filed in Eastland; so the sister is bringing the charge."

While the judge was thinking about who had precedence in the matter, Mr. McIntosh took the papers from the envelope he carried and laid them on the judge's desk. "And did I pick a good spot to leave the team and buggy you ordered?" Mr. McIntosh asked, vaguely pointing out the judge's window. The top sheet of paper read, "Two white Morgan geldings, harness and buggy. PAID IN FULL." It was signed Jim W. Smith, El Paso, Texas.

"Is this Mr. Smith your client?" the judge asked suspiciously.

"No, Sir. He is not," Mr. McIntosh stood up to leave. He held out his hand and the judge shook it. "Good day to you, Judge Brown."

****

Not far down the hall, Mr. McIntosh entered the office of Appellate Judge Caegen, took off his hat and smiled his brightest smile at...the man sitting behind the desk. McIntosh found a book shelf along the wall on which to set the small vase of flowers and walked toward the desk holding out his hand to shake hands with the secretary. He asked if the judge were in and handed the secretary his business card.

"Let me see if he has time, Mr. McIntosh."

Shortly, the secretary returned and ushered Mr. McIntosh into the judge's office.

He held out his hand to the judge and said, "Thank you for seeing me without an appointment, Sir. My name is Fred McIntosh, Attorney from Belton.

"I am representing clients in Bell County in a custody case, which was filed in 91st District Court in Eastland, Texas. The child is with his father in Bell County, Sir, and we would like the trial to be moved to 27th District Court in Belton, Texas."

"Why was this originally filed in 91st District?"

"I believe that is where the boy's sister lives, Your Honor," McIntosh said as he slid a stack of papers from the large manila envelope he carried and laid them on the judge's desk. "And," he vaguely waved at the window behind the judge's desk, "did I pick a good place to ground the horses and carriage you ordered?"

The judge glanced behind him at a pair of fine black Morgan horses and a handsome carriage. He looked back at McIntosh mistrustfully. McIntosh pointed to the top sheet of the papers on the judge's desk.

"Two black Morgan geldings, harness and carriage. PAID IN FULL" It was signed, William B. James, New Orleans, Louisiana.

"Is this James your client?"

No, Sir. He is not." McIntosh held out his hand and said, "Good day to you, Your Honor."

****

At the far end of the hall, Mr. McIntosh entered the office of Appellate Judge Blalock. As he entered, he took off his hat and gave his brightest smile to the cute little blond secretary. "Why, you are not old enough to be working here, are you?" he asked as he sat a small vase of flowers on her desk. She was obviously impressed and picked them up to smell. From his vest pocket he handed her his card, and asked if the judge were in.

"Why, I do believe he is. Just a minute, sir."

It always seemed so much easier when the secretary was a woman. He smiled and shook his head approvingly as he watched her go.

In a moment she returned smiling, "Judge Blalock will see you, sir." McIntosh walked through the open door and offered his hand, but the judge glanced up and pointed to a chair for him to sit. "This one might not be so easy after all," he thought. The judge did not look up from what he was reading for a long minute. McIntosh had played in this business for a long time; he knew better than to interrupt the judge's consentration.

Finally the old judge looked up and said, "Yes?"

"Your Honor, I represent clients in Bell County in a child custody case. The case was filed in 91st District Court in Eastland. The child is with his father in Bell County, and we would like to ask that trial be moved to the 27th District Court in Belton."

"Why was it not filed in 27th District to begin with?"

"The child's sister is petitioning for the boy to be placed in her custody, Your Honor. The sister lives in Eastland County."

He carefully placed a stack of papers on the judge's desk and walked to the window, "I hope I didn't take up too much space. This is the only place I could find to hitch the team and carriage you ordered."

The judge's head turned slowly, and he stared at McIntosh suspiciously. McIntosh nodded toward the stack of papers on the desk. The top sheet read, "Two sorrel Morgan geldings, harness and carriage. PAID IN FULL" It was signed Thomas W. Smith, Ft. Smith, Arkansas.

Mr. McIntosh said, "You have a good day, Your Honor." He held out his hand to the judge, who was still thinking through this deal.

"Is this Smith your client?"

"No, Sir. He is not." They shook hands and McIntosh walked out the door talking to the pretty young secretary.

****

October 15, 1910, The Western Union delivery boy arrived with another telegram.

Mr. Epsy Hale
Eastland, Texas

Dodd's have petitioned that the boy's legal residence is in Bell County. Appellate Court agreed. Trial has been moved to 27th District Court in Belton, December 15, 1910.

Donald J. Crawford, Atty. at Law
Law Firm of Solomon & Jacobs
Ft. Worth, Texas

****

Donald J. Crawford, Atty. at Law
Law Firm of Solomon & Jacobs
Ft. Worth, Texas

Baby is due around Christmas. Rachael cannot make the trip to testify.

Epsy Hale
Eastland, Texas

****

Mr. Epsy Hale Eastland, Texas

Will arrive November 15 with a court stenographer to take a deposition of her testimony.

Donald J. Crawford, Atty. at Law
Law Firm of Solomon & Jacobs
Ft. Worth, Texas

****

As promised, Mr. Crawford and a court stenographer showed up about 10:00 in the morning. "Mrs. Hale, I have been telling this man about your delicious coffee all the way down here. Is it asking too much of you?"

"Here, let me take your coats. I can do better than that. Yesterday I baked a chocolate cake. We will all ruin our dinner together.

"Epsy will be home for dinner about 12:00. I will set a place for each of you, if you will stay."

****

They were finished with the deposition by the time Epsy came home for lunch. Mr. Crawford had taken such good notes on his first visit that he knew just the right questions to ask her so that she could tell the whole story. Rachael felt much better about not being able to be at the hearing.

"I saw your automobile, Mr. Crawford. How are you?" Epsy said as he walked in the kitchen door.

"Very good, Mr. Hale. We have sampled your wife's fine coffee and chocolate cake while we took the deposition. Meet our court stenographer, Jack Wilson."

"Welcome, Mr. Wilson. It looks as if Rachael has us set to eat."

They were satisfied they had covered the testimony well. Everyone felt more comfortable and relaxed with the deposition over. Conversation was easy and jovial.

"How have you managed to hide this wonderful cook out here, Mr. Hale? She should have her own restaurant in Ft. Worth. The coffee alone would make it a hangout for businessmen."

"Most of my recipes came from Georgia with my mama and her hired woman. They were both good cooks. Most of the recipes go back at least two more generations in the Barnett family."

The kitchen door opened slowly and a very tired, very cold, eight year old boy dragged himself to Rachael's lap.

"Epsy, would you get him a glass of milk?

"What happened to you, Bun? Did you ride your horse all the way again?"

"No, they said I stole him, so they took him away from me. This time I walked. But I did take some left-over biscuits and bacon. I have been sleeping in barns and vacant houses so no one would tell them I had been there."

"Here, finish my plate, Honey, and let me put you to bed. You need a lot of rest. How long have you been traveling?"

"A week or more."

"Rachael, if he has been sleeping in barns and vacant houses, it would be smart to bath him in lye soap to get rid of any fleas and ticks he might have picked up," Epsy warned.

****

All the men joined in heating and carrying water to the galvanized tub. After Rachael gave him a thorough bath and shampoo, she put Bun to bed. She sang him just a short song, and he was sound asleep.

Mr. Wilson said, "That boy is very brave to strike out like that on foot."

"And he really has good timing," Mr. Crawford said. "Both times I've been here as a witness that the Hales did not even know he was coming, let alone go and steal him.

"My guess is that this time they will send the Federal Marshall for him since they have this custody hearing pending, and it's in their district. I think we will stay another night or two in Eastland just to see how this thing plays out.

"Does that sound right to you, Jack?" Jack was already nodding in agreement.

****

As Mr. Crawford predicted, two days later the Federal Marshall showed up at Rachael's door to serve papers on her. Was he surprised when, instead of a defenseless young woman, a man reached for the papers and began to read aloud the allegations!

"Sir, this is a false accusation. This gentleman, indicating Jack Wilson, and I are both officers of the court, and we were here, having diner here when the boy walked in.

"Mrs. Hale is in no condition to travel, as you can see. Why don't we accompany you into Eastland to see the judge? I'll bet with the proper handling, this can be fixed."

Mr. Crawford and Mr. Wilson had coats and hats in hand. Mr. Crawford put his hand on the Marshall's shoulder and helped him turn around. Together they walked back to their automobiles.

Later that evening, Mr. Crawford and Mr. Wilson were back with encouraging news. By the advantageous turn of events, they were able to get a friendly judge worked into the mixture. He gave permission for the boy to stay with Rachael until the trial, but he must appear in court for the hearing.

Rachael was satisfied with that and was grateful. She and Bun enjoyed their time together, even though it was short.

When December 15 was near, Mr. Crawford and Mr. Wilson showed up to take Bun to the court in Temple. Mrs. Little went along as a witness. She sat in the back seat with Bun. Even in Mr. Crawford's Model-T, the ride was a solemn one.

Solomon, Jacobs, and Crawford were ready with their presentation. The opposing attorneys sat very smugly waiting for the hearing to begin. Mr. McIntosh was not one of them.

When the judge approached his bench and called the court to order, it was with a very dry tone of voice. "Prosecution may call the first witness."

"Your Honor, our main witness could not be here today because she is expecting a baby in just a few days. However, we have a deposition of her testimony to present to the court."

"Approach the bench."

The judge glanced at the document for a few minutes. "This only demonstrates the sister's desire to have the boy live with her. I see no corroborating statements to back up her charges."

"Sir, I have documents showing that Mr. Dodd remarried two years before the boy's mother died, and there was no divorce. The boy's sister is the nearest thing to a mother the boy has known. The Dodds kidnapped him twice; I have the school teacher here to testify that they took the boy from her school room forcibly. I have two witnesses to the fact that the child found a way to travel from Temple to Eastland by himself twice. This shows who the boy wants to live with."

"You are out of order. Deposition is denied. Be seated."

"Your Honor, I would like to call Bunyon Douglas Dodd for the Prosecution."

"You are out of order, Mr. Solomon. I will not have a minor questioned in my Court. Please sit down or I will charge you with contempt of court."

"Defense may call your first witness."

"We call Mr. Jeff Dodd, the father of the boy."

He was sworn in by the bailiff and took the witness stand.

The judge did all of the questioning. "Are you this boy's father?"

"I am, your Honor."

"How long have you been denied access to the boy?"

"My wife left me when he was first born, Sir. I have not been allowed to be around him since birth."

"Where is the boy's mother?"

"She died several months ago. I have been trying to get custody of him since she died."

"And what prevented you from seeing your son?"

"My wife threatened me with a pistol if I tried to come back to her house, Sir."

Mr. Solomon stood up, "Point of Order, Your Honor. The wife has been dead for five months now. In that time Mr. Dodd has not attempted to visit his son at his daughter's house."

"Denied, Mr. Solomon."

"Can you provide for your son, Mr. Dodd?"

"Yes, Sir, I work as a Purchasing Agent for the Texas & Pacific Railroad."

"You are excused, Mr. Dodd."

Mr. Solomon stood up and said, "Cross examination, Your Honor."

"Denied! Next witness," the judge bellowed, giving Mr. Solomon a stern look.

"We call Mr. William Bates, Mayor of Belton, as a character witness, Your Honor."

"Mr. Bates, approach the stand and be sworn in."

"How are you acquainted with these people, Mr. Bates?"

"They are very generous people, your Honor. They donated a whole beef for the Fall Festival. Pillars of the community, Sir."

"Call your next witness."

"We call the Right Reverend Williams, Your Honor. Bishop of the Episcopalian church."

"Right Reverend Williams take the stand and be sworn in."

"Sir, are you acquainted with the Dodd family?"

"Yes, I am, Your Honor. They have been attending my church regularly ever since the boy has been with them. Quite an addition to the church. Very generous people."

"Any more witnesses for the defense?" "No, Sir, your Honor."

"My decision is for the father to have custody of the child. Court dismissed!" And he banged his gavel. "Bailiff, clear the court!"

With stiff neck and lifted eyebrows Mrs. Dodd walked proudly past the attorneys for the Plaintiff, tilted her head from side to side, took a short breath and snorted it out, as if to say, "Now you know who you are dealing with."

Walking out the courthouse door, Solomon, Jacobs, Crawford and Wilson were stunned by the scene outside, but it was not exactly out of character. Four nice carriages with matched Morgan teams awaited outside. Those horses were really eye-catchers.

As the others continued down the steps, Mr. Crawford pulled up suddenly and stood on the top step of the courthouse shaking his head slightly. When he finally joined the others, Mr. Wilson asked, "What was the hold up?"

"Oh, just thinking of something Rachael said. 'Sometimes I wonder if that Colonel is still alive.'"

****

This trial had attracted a lot of attention in central Texas. The Dallas Morning News reported that there was a strange occurrence at the Appellate Court. "All three judges suddenly acquired new carriages and beautifully matched teams at the same time."

A young reporter for the Ft. Worth Star Telegram became very interested and followed the proceedings to Belton. He covered the trial in detail from start to finish. He ended his article with a short paragraph.

"Strange shenanigans happened here. Watch for three pairs of matched Morgans arriving at the Appellate Court building each morning. District Court, City Hall and the Episcopal Church in Belton have also been blessed with fine teams of matched Morgans."

Chapter Fourteen
Rachael's Own Family

When Epsy came home for dinner three days before Christmas Rachael quietly told him she had started her labor. He immediately became intense. "What do we need to do? Will it be soon? What can I do to help?"

"Sit down and eat your dinner, first. Right now, I am only having dull pains in my lower back. After we eat, you or one of your hands can go tell Dr. Johnson. I don't know how long it will be before I need him, but he needs to know to expect someone to come for him at any time.

"And would you go tell Gladys down the road that I would really enjoy her company this afternoon, if she would not mind. Since I've never been through this, I'd feel better if she were here."

"Of course, of course," he said.

"This is a very busy time at the gin. Is it okay if I go back to work until you need me? I will make arrangements for someone else to run the gin when it is time."

"Of course you can go back to work, but send someone to tell Dr. Johnson and get Gladys to come. I don't want to be by myself. Okay?

"Mind you, we may have a very light supper tonight."

Epsy gobbled down his food and went to the gin to put someone in charge. He went first to tell Gladys. Yes, she would drop her work and come right over so Rachael wouldn't be alone. Next he went on into town to talk with Dr. Johnson.

"I have seen Rachael recently, Mr. Hale. I don't think you have to worry about her having all the trouble her mother did. She has eaten just as I asked her to and watched the weight she gained carefully. I expect it will be a normal delivery.

"The baby may be a little larger than some, but not as big as she or her brother were. If you do not come for me sooner, I will come out tomorrow to check on her progress. You said Gladys is with her? She will recognize the signs and tell you when to come to get me. Gladys has had a whole tribe of her own and helped her daughters and daughters-in-law.

"You can go back to work and we will come get you when things get serious. Sometimes a first baby can take even a couple of days."

Gladys had just arrived when Epsy got back to the house. "We are going to bundle up and walk around as long as she feels okay. It feels good to be out in this good crisp air. When she gets tired of that, we can play rummy. Rachael always beats me; that should make her feel good!" she laughed and smiled at Rachael.

"Now, Rachael, I would suggest that you put this heavy sweater on backwards, and then put your coat on over it. That way the baby won't be exposed to the cold."

They strolled leisurely down the lane enjoying the winter scenery. The huge Red Oaks were all decked out in their red leaves for winter. Some of the other trees had yellow leaves and some were brown. Many of the trees had already lost their leaves. But the Red Oaks were definitely red.

"Do you suppose that is why they named that tree a 'Red' Oak?" Rachael mused. "I love to see the contrast in the colors of the leaves this time of year. And just look at those Live Oaks over there. They keep their dark green leaves all year round." She thought a minute and laughed, "You never see them undressed!" She chuckled softly at her joke.

Crossing the little creek with its dense growth of trees and underbrush brought memories of all the mosquitoes that were here during summer.

Soon they were nearing a cotton field that still had field hands picking cotton. "Probably one of the last to be picked," Gladys said. "Honey, I think we have walked about a half mile, are you ready to turn around and go back? We don't want to bring this on too fast, you know. Just let nature take its course."

By the time they reached home, Rachael began to feel more than dull pain in her back. "Do you know what?" Gladys asked. "We probably have time to make one of your chocolate cakes that Dr. Johnson likes so well. Then we will just sit down and play Rummy."

Making the cake kept Rachael busy so that her mind was not on the pain, but by the time she finished frosting it, she was having sharp pains. They timed them about 20 minutes apart.

Gladys walked over to the gin and told Epsy of her progress; then the two women sat and played cards until twilight was coming. Rachael needed to go to the bathroom. She suddenly called out, "Gladys, I can't stop peeing!"

"Oh, honey, your water broke," Gladys told her. "We will start getting down to business pretty soon now. What time does Epsy usually get home?"

"Pretty soon. They won't be able to see inside the gin very much longer."

Gladys thought about it just a minute. "Maybe he needs to shut it down now. We don't want to push this too close. I'll walk over and get him started this way. If you feel like you need to, you just lie down, but you will notice the pain more. If you can stay up and keep moving, it will be easier for you.

"Now, don't worry. I'll hurry right back." Her normal, slow way of speaking never hinted that she was in any hurry, but short, round Gladys was out the door and headed to the gin at a double quick pace.

****

Epsy arrived on the run just as Rachael was having a hard pain. She was in the kitchen holding onto the back of a chair and slightly bent forward. She moaned loudly and sent Epsy into a tizzy. He had helped cows and horses deliver, but how do you help your wife?

"Let me help you sit down," he said taking her arm.

"No, Gladys said it would be easier on me if I can stay up and keep moving. Hold my hand. As soon as this one is past you can walk with me inside the house. Gladys says the pains are down to ten minutes apart. It will be time for you to go get Dr. Johnson soon."

They walked slowly and quietly for a short time. "Epsy, what kind of names do you have in mind? If it is a boy, we will name him after you, of course. But, I just really think this is a girl. All I can think of lately are girl's names."

Epsy thought as they walked. "I don't think of anything right off. What do you have in mind?"

"Mama had a sister named Mary Elizabeth. Mama said she was so pretty, with dark brown hair and brown eyes. When Mama talked about her, she sometimes called her Bessie. I think Mama loved her a lot.

"Epsy, do you like the name Bessie?

"Ohhh, Gladys, this is a really bad one. I don't think I can walk anymore."

With Epsy holding one arm and Gladys holding the other, she hobbled over to the bed that Gladys had prepared for the delivery.

Gladys had put layers and layers of paper over the end of a small bed and had stacked all the pillows in the house to support Rachael's back in a semi-sitting position.

Quietly and gently, Gladys said, "Now, Epsy, I think it is time for you to run like the wind to get Dr. Johnson. Her water broke a little over an hour ago, and this pain was only five minutes from the last one. They are getting very strong.

"Get him back here as soon as you can. I don't want to have to deliver this baby by myself."

He was putting on his coat as he was half-way out the door. Rachael called, "Epsy!" and he stopped. "Be sure to tell him to bring a new jar of Vaseline. Can't have a baby without Vaseline!"

****

While Epsy had been in the house, Gladys sat at the kitchen table playing Solitaire. Now she brought the cards to the bedroom and she and

Rachael played Rummy between Rachael's pains. It sure did help pass the time, and it kept Rachael's mind off when the next one would come, kept her more relaxed.

****

Epsy and Dr. Johnson arrived just as the pains were to the pushing stage. "My, what good timing," Dr. Johnson said as he slipped off his coat.

"What can I do?" Epsy asked.

"Well, according to Rachael's grandfather, a new father is supposed to sit in the porch swing and endure the screams of his wife as the baby is being born. But because of the weather, we will let you off on that one.

"I don't think this will take a long time, but do you know how Rachael makes that delicious coffee? "You need to stoke the fire in the kitchen stove so we will have plenty of warm water for this baby," Dr. Johnson said rolling up his sleeves. "And where can I wash up? What is this going to be? A boy or a girl?"

"Rachael says a girl," Epsy said as he motioned for the doctor to follow and disappeared around the door.

****

Gladys was experienced at this, she kept Epsy busy getting this and that. She let him bring warm water just to the door; then she took it from him and sent him after something else.

Dr. Johnson was also good at his job. He kept Rachael talking most of the time.

"What have you named this little one, Rachael?"

"If it is a boy, we will name him after Epsy, of course," she paused for another pain.

"And if it is a beautiful little girl, what name have you picked?"

"I would like to name her after Mama's sister, Mary Elizabeth. We will name her Bessie!" Rachael's voice had been getting louder with each word of that last sentence. This was a really hard pain, and she pushed with all she had.

Moments later Dr. Johnson said, "Well, hello, Bessie!"

Handing Dr. Johnson a soft cloth to dry the baby, Gladys said, "Oh, Rachael, your mama would have been so proud of you."

Tears of joy streamed down Rachael's face.

When Epsy was allowed into the room to see his wife holding their new baby, Rachael reached up for his hand. She was so full of emotion that a river of tears streamed down her cheeks.

"Epsy, I want to name her Bessie Mae. Mae is Gladys's middle name. and do you realize she was born on Bun's bed?"

****

Early next morning, Epsy made a quick stop at the gin, then came home and hitched the team to the buckboard.

"Rachael, I am going into Eastland for cigars. A man needs to give good cigars to his friends to celebrate his newborn baby.

"Would you like anything special while I am in town?"

"Oh, a Hershey chocolate bar would be so nice, Epsy. I love them so."

"And do you need me to do anything here for you before I go?"

"I believe you have put everything I will need within reach. Gladys will be here as soon as she has her home settled. I will be...we will be all right till then. Thank you for asking."

****

This was a special day and Epsy had dressed special to go to town. He wore his best khaki pants that Rachael had starched and ironed to make a sharp crease down the legs, a light blue chambray shirt with white collar, his wide, white galluses, newly shined shoes, and of course, his overcoat. Epsy didn't like to draw attention to himself. He had a suit, but that was for weddings and funerals!

Eastland was an up and coming little town in 1910, quite a bustling little community. Eastland even had a Ford dealership.

Epsy went to the emporium and bought two boxes of cigars, and he began to spread the word that he had a new baby girl born last night. It was not too long before the word spread ahead of him, and as he walked along the boardwalk, people began coming out of the stores to congratulate him.

Epsy was a pretty quiet man, didn't say anything that didn't really need to be said. But his big, toothy smile displayed his pride and how much he was enjoying all of this attention. While he walked around town, he wandered by the Ford dealership.

"Yes, sir! They have one on the showroom floor," he thought, so he walked in to have a look.

He was met by a very surprised salesman. Almost everyone in town had been in to look at the new Model-T Touring Car, but here was a man he had never met before.

He introduced himself and shook hands with Mr. Hale from Rising Star, the usual salesman stuff.

"I'm in town to buy cigars because my first baby was born last night," Epsy volunteered "I thought I would like to see one of these Model-T's that I heard about."

"Yes, sir. This is one of the first off the new assembly line."

"What is the assembly line?"

"Why, every part on this automobile," he put his hand on the fender, then quickly jerked out his handkerchief and rubbed off the fingerprints. "Every part on this car is interchangeable with every other Model-T Touring Car. They move them along on a conveyer belt and assemble them as they go." He motioned with his hand to demonstrate how smoothly the conveyer belt moved them.

"Really shiny. Does it run good?" Epsy asked.

"This little gasoline engine purrs like a kitten and has power to pull hills, too. You will not have to back up Ranger Hill like some of the older automobiles. No, sir! This one will pull it easily."

Epsy began to slowly walk around the automobile. He squatted down to look at one of the showy, wooden spoke wheels, painted white. He felt the solid rubber tire. He braced against the fender to see if there were any give to it. He pointed to the shiny brass headlights and gave an approving nod of his head. He stood looking at all the shiny brass.

The salesman was beginning to think this man was really interested, might even buy the automobile.

"Is this the only one you have?"

"Well, right at the time it is the only one. When we sell this one, we will order another one from the factory."

"Well, what does one of these cost?" Epsy asked.

"Even though it would leave us without one to show, I can let you have this automobile today for $1,100."

Epsy knit his brow and shook his head slightly. "I saw a red one the other day that I really thought was pretty." He continued to look at the Model-T as he walked the rest of the way around it; then he headed for the door.

The salesman was stunned. He really thought he had a sale working here. "But, Mr. Hale, although Ford makes these automobiles in six different colors, this beige with black fenders is really the most popular color."

Epsy had turned around to hear the man out. He thought a moment; then turned back toward the door.

"Mr. Hale, let me sweeten the deal a little. If you would be interested in this beige Model-T, I can let you have it for $1,050." He raised his eyebrows, smiled, and nodded once to show he was in earnest here. We can finance that for 3% interest.

"Is that the lowest you would go?" Epsy asked. "Bottom dollar," the man answered.

"A friend of mine bought a red one in Ft. Worth for $950. I guess a trip to Ft. Worth would be worth $100," and again he turned toward the door.

"But, I can't make any money at that price!"

"The dealer in Ft. Worth seems to."

Knowing he was found out, the salesman asked in earnest, "Would you be interested in buying this beige Model-T for $950 cash?"

"Fill her up," Epsy said. "While you make out the papers for $950, I'll go stable my horses at the livery for the night. Then you can give me a driving lesson. My name is Epsy W. Hale from Rising Star. Do you need more than that? Will an hour give you enough time?"

Epsy walked back to where he had left his team and wagon at the emporium. He stopped in the store one more time to buy the Hershey chocolate bar before he went home. He took the horses and wagon to the livery, went to the bank, greeted a few more people, then he went back to the Ford dealership.

It took a little over an hour. By the time Epsy returned, the salesman was pacing the floor. He was absolutely sure he had let a sale slip right through his fingers. "Why didn't I encourage him to wait? The paperwork could have been done in half an hour easily. What if I filled that tank up for nothing?" He took out his handkerchief and rubbed on the fenders again.

A real look of relief came over his face when he saw Epsy walking up to the door. "If you will step right this way, Mr. Hale, we have the papers waiting for you." He put his finger on the line for Epsy to sign and handed him a pen from his shirt pocket.

Epsy ignored the pen, picked up the papers and began to read. Not just the area around the blank lines, he read the whole thing. Then he reached for the pen the salesman was still holding, and signed.

Epsy reached into his left pants pocket and pulled out a wad of bills. He slowly and deliberately counted out ten $100 dollar bills, with the salesman's head nodding each time a bill hit the desk.

"That should take care of any taxes and license, and leave a little extra for you," he smiled at the salesman. Epsy knew he had given him a hard time.

"Thank you, Mr. Hale. It has been a pleasure doing business with you. By the way, I never did ask what kind of business you are in."

"I own the cotton gin in Rising Star. Here have a cigar."

"Why, Mr. Hale, if I had only known...I would not have demanded cash, sir. Your check would have been honored. I am ever so sorry."

"Just gave me a chance to see more people and brag about my baby," Epsy smiled.

The papers were signed, the car was gassed, and money changed hands. The salesman drove the car off the showroom floor and around the block, explaining to Epsy each maneuver that he made.

"Do you think you got it?" he asked. "Now you drive it around the block; I'll be the passenger." Epsy had watched Mr. Crawford carefully, so he did pretty good driving for the first time. "You'll get the feel of it driving back to Rising Star, Mr. Hale. Happy to have met you," the man said as he stepped out of the car. He was un-wrapping his cigar and smiling as Epsy drove away.

****

Epsy really did enjoy himself as he drove home to Rising Star. It was fun to have a new automobile. He made sure he drove through the little town of Rising Star on his way to the cotton gin, giving out cigars all over town. Then he gave cigars to all of his hands at the gin, "But, remember, you cannot smoke these anywhere around the gin!" he cautioned. At last he was ready to show his new prize to Rachael.

He parked it just outside the bedroom window where he thought she could see it best, and went inside. Of course, she had heard the noise. She thought it was Mr. Crawford returning. Epsy walked into the bedroom and handed her not a Hershey bar, but something new from

Hershey: a bag of Hershey's Kisses. About as big around as a nickel, this Hershey's Kiss was a perfect drop of solid chocolate that came to a point on top; each one was wrapped in shiny tin foil. And he gave her a big kiss on the cheek.

She was thrilled with the new kind of Hershey's chocolate and immediately began to pull down the little paper strip that stuck out the pointed top. She offered him one, and they sat there enjoying the chocolate together. "Look out the window and see what else I brought home," he said. He helped her out of bed and to the window.

She gasped at seeing the Model-T and covered her mouth with her hand. "Is it ours?" she finally asked.

"Rachael, I have been doing really well at the gin. I have been putting money away. We can afford it, and I thought we ought to celebrate having our new baby. You know I have never been as crazy about horses as you and your mama, and I really liked Mr. Crawford's new Model-T Touring Car. Rachael, it is so much fun!

"And look at the way those seat cushions are padded and tufted in that diamond shape. It won't bounce you around like a wagon does.

"As soon as you feel up to it, we will wrap Bessie up real good and take a drive to show people our new baby. What do you think?"

****

Oh, how Rachael loved that baby! It was like having her very own baby doll! Come to think of it, as a child, she never really learned to play babies. She had dolls, but it was more fun to play outside than to make up things to do with dolls. Mostly she just talked to them, teaching them about the horses and how to catch bugs. Now, with a baby of her own, she loved it!

Gladys came over every day for a week, but Rachael recovered her strength very quickly. When Gladys came over, Rachael just took care of the baby. Then when the baby slept, Rachael began to get bored and wandered into the kitchen to talk to Gladys while she cooked and cleaned. She was such a wonderful friend.

Soon Rachael was helping with the cooking. She would peel potatoes and chop vegetables, anything she could do sitting down. And they enjoyed conversation about little Bessie and tales about Gladys' children when they were young. Gladys gave her instructions of what to do if this happened or that happened.

One day Rachael wanted to bake a cake, so she was on her feet quite a while measuring and stirring. They played Rummy while the cake was baking. Then she needed to stand up to spread the icing properly. Rachael was shocked and heartsick when Gladys announced, "Rachael, do you realize you are doing almost all of the work, now?

"I don't think you really need me here, and my own house could use some extra attention. If there is a problem with the baby, or if you get to doing too much and feel like you need me, I'll come back over. Will that be okay, honey?"

She had seen the startled expression of uncertainty on Rachael's face. "I'm sure you can do everything by yourself. Just remember what your mama and Jenny did when Bun was little. You have it all stored in your head. When you need to use it, you'll remember."

So the next day, Rachael got up and cooked breakfast for Epsy instead of sleeping until the baby woke her up. They really enjoyed talking while they ate breakfast. "Rachael, I am so happy you are back in the kitchen. It was really good of Gladys to come over and help so much, but no one can make biscuits like you can!"

Oops, the baby woke up, and it was time for Epsy to go to the gin anyway. And thus a new phase of their life had begun.

****

Bessie was a very healthy baby. There were hardly any upsets as she was growing up. Rachael found plenty of time to enjoy her new baby and still keep her house work done.

It never really upset Rachael when something got spilled; she just wiped it up and replaced the glass of milk or whatever it was. Epsy always smiled when he remembered how Rachael put it, "My house is clean enough to be healthy, and cluttered enough to be comfortable."

As long as Bessie was crawling, of course the floors had to be mopped every day! But when she started walking good, Rachael could slack off the mopping a little and concentrate on other things.

When spring was coming on and they were working on their garden, Rachael had a little trouble figuring out how to divide her time with Bessie indoors and the garden outdoors. By summer Bessie was old enough to be outside, too.

One evening when Epsy came home, there was something new not far outside the kitchen door. Rachael had found a short piece of picket fencing that was not being used and she had made a circle out of it about four feet across. She had stuck sticks in the ground to hold it in place. And there was Bessie inside, playing with a small pot and a spoon while Rachael worked in the garden.

"Of course, I will need you to put some stronger posts in the ground to hold it in place because pretty soon she will be able to push it over, but it works for now!"

Chapter Fifteen
The Coon Hunt

During spring and summer, the demands on Epsy's time at the gin eased up. He kept a few hands on at the gin year around, and they made repairs to the gin and cotton trailers. Occasionally Epsy had an idea to make changes at the gin that would make the work easier during ginning season. Mostly they worked at a leisurely pace, and sometimes he came home in the middle of the afternoon and just spent his time with Rachael and Bessie.

This was the slow season for his cotton farmers, too. Once the seed was in the ground and all repairs were made, there was nothing else to do but go fishing. Sometimes Epsy went fishing with them. There was a catfish hole in a bend of the creek not too far from the gin, sometimes they pulled in some really big ones that had been just lazing around in the slow-moving deep pools.

One evening just about dark, barking dogs... lots of barking dogs... brought Epsy and Rachael to their feet to see what the ruckus was.

Rachael's geese added to the noise. Though the dogs were on leash, they thought the dogs were after them, and they went scurrying everywhere squawking and honking, with wings flapping and feathers flying.

It was several young farmers with their coon hounds; they came to see if Epsy wanted to go hunting with them tonight, "See if we can scare up a coon or two."

"Sure, that might be fun. Rachael, do you mind if I go? This would be great fun with the men."

She turned her head slightly to the right, cut her eyes back to the left and made a half smile. She flipped her hands up slightly several times, the way she did when she was shooing geese out of her way.

He grabbed his jacket and hat, kissed her on the cheek, and he was gone. Rachael and Bessie sat in the rocking chair on the porch and listened to the hounds baying. It surely was a pretty sound. Each of them had a different tone to his voice. One of them had such a deep voice that his name was 'Boomer'. Even from here Rachael could tell when Boomer struck a trail.

From this distance the baying kind of lulled you to sleep, so after a while Rachael and Bessie went inside and went to bed.

****

The barking of the dogs woke Rachael up in the middle of the night, though this time the excitement was gone out of their voices. They were tired now and on their way home.

Epsy came in the kitchen door as quietly as he could and began to build a fire in the wood stove. Rachael got up to see what was going on.

Epsy's jacket had several three cornered tears, his hat was gone, and there were several deep scratches down one side of his face.

"Good Lord, help us!" Rachael said, and she quickly flipped her eyes toward Heaven, as she hurried to see how deep the scratches were. Then she got bandages and iodine while Epsy put several pots of water on to heat.

"Epsy, are you hurt anywhere else? Tell me what happened."

Rachael had put water in a small pan to heat faster so she could clean the cuts on his face. One scratch just missed the corner of his eye. When she daubed the blood away, she could see his cheekbone in the two center scratches.

Epsy was silent for a short while, wincing slightly when she touched his face with the soft, wet cloth. Her puzzled look demanded an explanation. So, slowly he began to tell her how it all unfolded.

The dogs, well old Boomer, struck a trail and the pack of dogs went flying after him. It was hard to keep up with them in the dark. Since Epsy was the only one without a dog to handle, he was elected to carry the lantern.

When the coon treed, the dogs gathered around the tree, jumping as high as they could and barking. "I was holding the lantern as high as I could so maybe we could see his eyes shining and one of the men could shoot him.

"The coon ran out on a limb right over me and jumped on my head. The dogs turned and started jumping up on me trying to get to the coon.

"The coon jumped again as hard as he could to get away from the dogs, and his hind foot was on my cheek when he jumped. His claws dug in deep. He must have jumped quite a ways or maybe into the next tree, but the dogs never could find his scent again.

"The men said they might as well call it a night since I needed to have these scratches tended to. Rachael, would you put some more water on to heat? I have to take a bath. I think I have fleas on me from that coon."

Rachael put iodine on the scratches and went to put another bucket of water on the stove. She began to chuckle; she was thinking about the scene Epsy had described... about the coon on his head and the dogs jumping up. She began to giggle. By the time she turned around to look at Epsy again, she was racked with laughter.

She put her hands up to the top of her head indicating the coon; then she raised her hands up and down beside her body several times indicating the dogs jumping. She was laughing so hard, tears were rolling down her cheeks.

Finally, Epsy saw the fun in it. What a funny sight that must have been...had he been watching it, and he, too, began to laugh. They laughed while they were carrying water to the bath tub, spilling water with every step.

"You know, I'll bet those men were splitting a gut trying not to laugh when we were on the way home," Epsy said. And they began to laugh again.

She handed him a bar of lye soap. He handed her his clothes and she carried them outside, far, far away from the house. She would deal with those in the morning.

Rachael put a bandage on Epsy's cheek, and they went to bed still chuckling every once in a while.

****

And so the summer happily slid by. The garden was good this year, and Rachael was very busy canning all that she could.

One day when Epsy came home early, Rachael met him at the door with a basket of fresh vegetables from her garden and a warm loaf of bread wrapped in a tea towel. "Epsy, will you take this to Mrs. Jones, the one who cleans houses for people who need her help? I just heard that her husband has been laid up for a while and she has not been able to have a garden this summer. I will send her some of ours as often as I can."

So Epsy cranked the Model-T again and drove off. At Mrs. Jones' house, Epsy knocked quietly out of politeness, and she quickly answered the door. "Yes?" she said in a questioning tone of voice.

"My wife, Rachael, sent me to give you this," he said, handing her the basket. "She just heard that you had not been able to have a garden this summer. She said she will be sending more over regularly, ma'am. Our garden has really done well this year, and I believe she has about worn herself out canning. She just can't stand for things to go to waste."

Gratitude showed all over Mrs. Jones' face as she took the basket. She quickly started to un-wrap the bread.

"No, ma'am," Epsy said. "I believe she wanted you to keep the tea towel, too."

He quickly tipped his hat and turned to go. He called back over his shoulder, "I expect I'll be seeing you soon, Mrs. Jones."

****

At the supper table that night, Epsy was very quiet.

"What's on your mind this evening? You've hardly said a word since you came back from Mrs. Jones' house."

"Rachael, what do you suppose is wrong with him? Her husband. I didn't see him, but that house needs some upkeep. Humph, it looks like it needs rebuilding! Why, I'll bet when it rains, the water hardly slows down when it hits that roof."

"I don't know, but I'll bet I can find out at the ladies' church social tomorrow afternoon."

****

"Well, it turns out that Mr. Jones was hurt on a job he was doing and his legs are almost paralyzed. He cannot work because he can hardly walk. He can do nothing but sit down all the time. Now, where can he ever find a job where he sits all the time? At a bank or something like that? I don't think the man has much education."

"At my gin! We can teach him to do the paperwork as the cotton trailers come in. That will free up one of the other men...or me. I'll go talk to him tomorrow."

It took a little bit of convincing, but Mr. Jones agreed to give the paperwork a try. Although he had never done such work before, Epsy assured him that it really was not complicated. He probably already knew most of the cotton farmers. He just had to get to know their trailers and mark them on that farmer's sheet.

"But ginning season won't start for a few more months. You won't need me until they start picking," Mr. Jones protested out of consideration for Epsy.

"Oh, I have plenty of things that need to be counted and weighed. I think I can keep you as busy as you want to be." Epsy hooked his thumbs in his galluses, "Now, will you need a ride to the gin tomorrow morning?"

****

Within a week, a load of new shingles were delivered to the gin. "Where do you want me to put these, Mr. Hale?" the driver asked.

"Fred, will you go with this man and show him the way to your house? Tomorrow, Tom and Pete are going to start re-roofing your house. Sort of a way to get our business deal off the ground, you see."

Fred could hardly believe his ears, but he hobbled to the wagon and climbed up in the seat. As they drove off, he never took his eyes off Epsy. They were soft, thankful eyes. Enough said. Epsy touched two fingers to the side of his forehead in a half-salute and smiled.

The next day, Tom and Pete showed up early to begin the new roof. They brought hammers and roofing nails and ladders. While Tom began tearing off the old shingles, Pete re-hung the screen door. "Mr. Hale said to do this first, ma'am."

In a little while, Epsy and Rachael and Bessie showed up with another big basket of vegetables and a ham. "You will need to feed hands well when they are working hard like this out in the sun," Rachael said. "And I put in some spearmint for the tea. That always seems to take the edge off the hot afternoon."

****

After a short while of working at the gin, Fred Jones knew all the customers, knew their trailers, knew the paperwork and was happy at his job. He was making enough money to take care of his wife and his responsibilities. He had his dignity back.

He tried to thank Epsy one day, but while he was stumbling for the right words to say, Epsy slapped him on the back and winked. "You are doing a good job, Fred," and he strolled on over to look at another part of the gin.

****

About the middle of December Rachael began planning a party for Bessie's first birthday. Epsy would be very busy at the gin, so it could not be a family party. But there were several children in the area who were around five and under. She counted up: the Bostons have two, the Densons have one, the Johnsons have one, and the Smiths have two. "That is all the little children within walking distance, and most of the mothers do not handle a team. I have six kitchen chairs, and Bessie can sit in her highchair."

The weather most likely would be cold, so it had to be held entirely inside. She would not want the children running from room to room. There were too many things of interest to little hands. Bessie had been taught what things she could play with and what things were not to be touched, but other children would not know.

Rachael would plan the party around her kitchen table. Her shopping list included: a new oil-cloth, table cloth, one with many bright colors, a package of white paper and crayons for the children to draw pictures, and a package of different colors of paper to make paper hats for everyone.

All children seem to love chocolate, so she would make that chocolate cake everyone seemes to like so well. "I can buy some of those Hershey's Kisses and put two or three on each child's plate," she thought. "And I'll make some sweet lemonade. That sounds like a party to me."

On the day of the party, however, it snowed! Rachael was concerned that the mothers might not want to get their children out in the cold and snow, but everyone showed up.

And what a wonderful party it turned out to be. When it began to snow, Rachael had set out several large pans and bowls to catch enough snow to make snow ice cream.

The children were delighted with the party. For that many small children to be cooped up in one room for so long, they did very good. They were delighted with the funny hats, and they sat, or stood on their knees, in the chairs and drew funny pictures. Sometimes they just looked at each other and giggled. It was very seldom that they saw so many children their own age.

When it was about time for the party to be over, Rachael indicated to the mothers that she had a stack of wash cloths and a pan of warm water on the cabinet to clean up the sticky children.

It had been a fun party. The mothers had a chance to visit while the children entertained themselves around the table. Just watching the reactions of the children was fantastic. The party was a huge success!

When everyone had gone, Rachael cleaned up the mess; then she took Bessie to the bedroom for her nap. It was later than Bessie usually took her nap, so she was rubbing her eyes and beginning to whine. Rachael was tired, too, so they took Bessie's nap together!

****

Rachael sat a pan of biscuits in Epsy's plate and handed him the butter. "I think you will have to spade up the garden by yourself this spring,

Epsy. I'm sure, now, that I am pregnant. I think that is the reason I have been so tired all the time lately."

Epsy cut open a hot biscuit. He shook his hand and blew on his fingers as he smiled up at her. He put his arm around her waist and squeezed a little; that was the best hug he could manage while he was sitting at the table. Epsy loved having babies and seeing his family grow.

****

The baby should be here in October, so Rachael planned to use most of the same baby clothes she had used for Bessie, unless this one was a boy, of course. She would have her hands full this summer, that's for sure. "I can use the same dresses I wore with Bessie; maybe I could use a couple of new ones. Yes, that would be a good idea; this time I won't have the time to wash as often. But Bessie will need all new summer dresses, and I had better get some yarn and start knitting sweaters while I rest in the evening," she thought.

So when Epsy had time away from the gin, he took her into Rising Star to buy material at the mercantile store. While she looked at patterns, material and buttons, he browsed the hardware and seeds. He picked a new shovel and hoe. He thought he remembered cracking the shovel handle late last year, and if he was going to get one of the hands to help with the garden, they would need two hoes.

He carried them to the counter and saw that Rachael was still looking at patterns. He returned to look at seeds. There were so many different varieties of each thing; he had to read the back of each seed packet. After what seemed to him a long time, he returned to the counter pushing a garden plow. "Rachael, what do you think about getting a garden plow instead of making the rows with a hoe?"

He stopped for a minute and looked at the stack of piece goods she had sitting on the counter. "You're getting all of that?"

"Oh, Epsy, am I getting too much? I only got material for me two maternity dresses, but Bessie will need all new dresses for the summer."

"No, that is fine. I'm just wondering how long it will take you to make all of the dresses, sewing by hand. And you are planning to knit sweaters, too?" He cocked his head a little to the side and raised his eyebrows while he thought.

"Well, what do you think about this garden plow?" he asked and started pulling seed packets from his shirt pockets, then he searched for the packets he had stuffed in his pants pockets. He was really getting the gardening fever. "I think I would like to get it. I can make the furrows for the seeds better and quicker; then I can use this tiller implement to get rid of the weeds that grow between the rows." He nodded his head once and said, "Yup, I just decided; I'm getting it."

"Will this be all you need today, Mr. Hale?" Mr. Clark, the mercantile owner, asked.

Epsy looked at Rachael, "You got everything you need? Did you order the hazel nuts?" She nodded. "Okay, we're good."

He noticed Bessie standing in front of the candy counter, quietly admiring the many colors of candy canes behind the glass, her hands neatly clasped behind her. "Do you want a candy cane, Bessie?" Her eyes lit up, and she nodded her head. "Better give Bessie a candy cane, too."

"What color do you want, Bessie?" Mr. Clark asked.

She pointed to the brown and white striped ones and said, "Woot bee-ah."

"Put this on your bill, Mr. Hale?"

"No, we are starting to sell some of last year's cotton. I'll pay cash for this."

****

On the way home, Epsy thought back to the mercantile store. Bessie was such a well behaved child that he had almost forgotten she was with them. She did not meddle or pick up things. She probably would never have asked for the candy she was staring at. She was a very quiet child and didn't say anything that didn't need to be said.

His heart swelled up with pride as he thought of what a good teacher Rachael was. When Bessie first began to reach for bright colored or shiny things, Rachael taught her to always ask first. Then when she asked, Rachael took the time to hand it to her and explained what it was.

She let her hold it for a little while, then said, "This is not something you can play with, honey, but you may hold it and look at it when you ask. Understand?" Then she thoughtfully drew Bessie's attention away by pointing to something else and saying, "This is something you can play with, and I won't mind."

He reached over and tussled Bessie's blond hair as she sat in Rachael's lap and smiled at her. She smiled back...Papa's smile meant a lot.

They drove along home in silence, listening to the "chupa, chupa, chupa" sound of the engine.

****

The next day Epsy drove the Model-T to the gin instead of walking. Then about mid-morning, he slipped away and drove to Eastland. Rachael had been so interested in starting on the new dresses, she didn't even notice until he drove up close to the kitchen door just as she was about to call him home for dinner.

He hopped up on the kitchen steps and said, "Come see what I got for you!"

Rachael set the skillet of gravy she was stirring to the back of the wood stove. She wiped her hands on her apron as she turned around and there was a puzzled look on her face He had taken her to buy material yesterday. What else could she need?

She picked up Bessie and stepped out the door. Epsy proudly escorted her to the touring car. A beautiful wooden cabinet stood in the floorboard of the back seat. The legs were black iron designed in a beautiful scroll pattern.

A new Singer treadle sewing machine! She gasped when she saw it and put her hand to her mouth. That was exactly the reaction Epsy had planned for.

"Here, let me get it out of the 'hoopy' and into the house for you. Where would you like me to put it?"

"Oh, Epsy, it's beautiful! But I don't even know how to sew with a machine."

"There is an instruction booklet with it. And I watched a demonstration on it. I'll bet together we can figure it out."

****

Epsy showed her how the top layer of the cabinet lifts up and folds out to the left, making a larger table surface and exposing a large cavity. He lifted the small wooden strip at the front and reached into the cavity to pull up the machine. He replaced the wooden strip of the front and let the machine settle into the groove designed to hold it. The rest was pretty much her department!

Rachael read the instruction booklet and practiced putting the circular leather belt into the grooves of the treadle pulley and the flywheel of the machine. She learned how to run the thread through each hook and lever on the top of the machine and through the eye of the needle, just as the booklet showed.

She learned how to make the thread wind onto the narrow rod of the bobbin, slip the bobbin into the shuttle case and pull the thread up through the little keeper at the top, leaving about two inches of thread pulled outside. "Hmm, that looks like a cocoon," she thought as she placed it into its cradle just underneath the needle.

"Now, hold onto the end of the needle thread; then turn the wheel with my right hand. As the needle goes down, the thread goes around the bobbin. When the needle comes back up, I pull the thread and it should bring the bobbin thread up to the top," she said to herself as she did each step.

"Whee!" she said out loud when she pulled the thread and the bobbin thread actually came up like it was supposed to! She clasped her hands together, holding them close to her chest, and sat there smiling to herself. Then she slid the shiny cover back across the bobbin area and sat with her fingertips patting the edge of the wooden machine cabinet.

This was such a beautiful machine, black with delicate golden scroll painted on the arm across the top and down the right side. She touched the red spot with the Singer "S" emblem and traced the gold scroll around its edge with her finger.

Then she admired the wooden cabined with its black iron legs designed in a beautiful curvy pattern, reminding her of the golden scroll painted on the machine itself. Each side of the cabinet had two small drawers to keep her supplies handy. She pulled out each drawer and wondered what all she would keep in them.

"Maybe my pin cushion," she thought. "It should not be too hard to teach Bessie that pins will stick her fingers. But I'll have to keep my scissors up higher than this.

"These drawers will be the perfect place to keep spools of thread. Bessie will enjoy the different colors, and it won't hurt too much if she gets them tangled."

She began to wonder how it actually sewed the material. So, on to the next step; she picked up the booklet and read some more.

She cut two narrow strips of cloth, placing them together with the printed sides facing each other. She placed the cloth under the needle and lowered the... 'presser foot?'. "Snap!"

"Well, I guess that lever lowers the presser foot!"

Following each instruction carefully, she placed her feet on the rectangular foot treadle and turned the shiny wheel at the top with her right hand. She felt her feet rock forward with her toes down, then backward with her heels down. After a few times she realized that she didn't need to turn the wheel with her hand. Her feet made the wheel turn and the needle go up and down.

"NEVER!" the booklet said, "Never, pump the foot treadle without material under the presser foot or the thread will become tangled and knotted." Something that would be hard to fix!

"And look at the stitches coming out behind the presser foot!" she thought. Again she clasped her hands, took a satisfied breath and sat there a moment enjoying her accomplishment. She practiced sewing on the narrow strips until she was satisfied that she could make it sew a straight line and turn corners only when she actually wanted to turn.

Next her mind flew to the new material. She already had a dress for Bessie cut out. As she reached for the material, she heard Bessie stirring.

Picking up the booklet again, she double checked to make sure she knew how to disengage the leather band running between the flywheel and the treadle. "Attached to the inside of the right leg of the machine cabinet is a small, spring-loaded lever. When the lever is pressed, it hooks the circular leather belt. Pump the foot treadle while pressing the lever. The leather belt will become disengaged."

"To close the machine: The machine is hinged in the back. Lift the sewing machine by the arm across the top; then lift the small, hinged wooden strip on the front surface of the cabinet. Lower the machine slowly into the opening beneath the surface; this loosens the leather band. Pull it up into the area concealing the machine. Fold the hinged table area on the left across the top. The booklet said to always disconnect the leather band when not sewing for safety! Then she hurried in to see Bessie and help her wake up happy.

*****

For the next few weeks Rachael happily sewed every spare moment. When all the dresses were made, she began to look around the house. "I could make new curtains for our bedroom and make it look brighter," she thought, "and in the kitchen! Ohhh!"

Within a month Epsy realized his gift had not only made her a very happy woman, he was reaping the benefits as well.

Chapter Sixteen
Jewel & James

When ginning was finally done, Epsy found he had time on his hands and started looking around for something to do. Rachael kept busy all the time. The weather was starting to get hot and she was getting pretty big with the new baby. She kept her house spotless and all of her work done up, plus she was canning vegetables from the garden at least one day a week. She was a busy, happy homemaker.

She never complained. There was no need. This was all just part of a very happy life. But once in a while Epsy saw her stand up straight and rub the small of her back while she stretched.

One day Epsy came home for lunch with news…a surprise! "Why don't you take your bath early and get dressed like you would for church? I would like to take you out this afternoon. Gladys is going to keep Bessie for us. Is that okay?"

****

He washed up and put on a clean white shirt and his black coat. He dressed Bessie in one of her new dresses and took her over to Gladys' house while Rachael dressed.

Rachael put on her nicest maternity dress, white stockings and white shoes. She fixed her hair up in the back. She seldom wore it up, and Epsy thought it really did flatter her face.

"Where are we going, Epsy?" she asked when they were in the car.

"You'll see when we get there."

They drove into Rising Star, to the drug store. Epsy helped her out of the Model-T and supported her while she stepped up onto the boardwalk. Inside the drugstore, they picked a table toward the far end of the soda fountain, a little secluded.

The soda jerk came over and asked for their order. Epsy smiled at Rachael and said, "Two Dr. Peppers, please. With ice," and he held up one finger for emphasis.

"Oh, Epsy, this is just like our first date!" she exclaimed, and her face beamed.

They sipped their Dr. Peppers through two straws and smiled at each other. These soda fountain glasses were such fun just to look at, with the small bottom; then they flared up and out at the top like an upside down bell. With ice in them, it was not long before they began to sweat on the outside, and soon you could easily spin them in place in the puddle of water.

They remembered funny things from their dating time and enjoyed their quiet laughter. Soon they were talking about the new baby and the changes it would make in their lives.

A young couple about their age sat down at the table next to theirs. They must be new in the area; neither Epsy nor Rachael knew them.

Too soon their magic time was up, and as they passed the newcomers on the way out, Epsy introduced himself and Rachael to them. James and Jewel Logan were very happy to meet a couple their age. They had just leased the Brown farm a couple of miles south of the gin and didn't know many people yet.

"I own the gin and we live in the house just east of it," Epsy said. He glanced at Rachael for a quick assessment of her reaction to meeting the new couple. "We would be pleased to have you over for supper and dominoes as soon as you are settled in."

"Do you need any help?" Rachel asked Jewel.

"Oh, I couldn't let you, in your condition. It looks as if you have all you can take care of there," nodding her head toward Rachael's tummy. "When is your baby due?"

"About late October, I think. We already have a daughter, one year old. But we could have coffee at least."

Epsy put his hand on the small of Rachael's back to guide her ahead of him. "Well, I hope we will see you soon."

They were not in a particular hurry, so they drove the long way home, just enjoying each other's company. When they picked up Bessie she was thrilled with the Hershey's chocolate bar she found hidden in Papa's coat pocket.

****

Two days later Rachael was pleased to see Jewel drive up in a buckboard. "She handles that team pretty well," Rachael thought as she made her way to the front door to invite her in. "She just may be my kind of a girl."

Jewel was dressed in a nice, fresh house dress, stockings and her good shoes; but her face looked tired…so tired. "Do come in," Rachael said, holding open the screen door for her guest. "You are the perfect reason to sit down for a cup of coffee and a cookie. I am so happy to see you."

They went immediately to the kitchen and Rachael started a fresh pot of coffee and set out plates and the cookie jar.

"How is your moving coming along? Are you just about settled in?

"Well, as much as can be done at this time. I have worked hard, but the house on that place leaves a lot to be desired.

James says the land is good, and as part of the deal, Mr. Brown is letting us have half the cotton it makes this year. You know his health got so bad, he said he just could not stay here long enough to pick the cotton. James says we will just have to be patient with the house until we sell next year's crop.

"Mr. Brown really made us a good deal, you know?"

Rachael set two of her fancy cups filled with steaming hot coffee on the table, with creamer and sugar bowl to match. She placed two cookies for her guest and one for herself on the matching bread plates.

"Oh, these are delicious tea cakes!" exclaimed Jewel after her first bite. "And is that just a hint of cinnamon?"

Rachael nodded. But she did not begin eating her cookie yet.

Her guest suddenly looked confused. "Is something wrong?" she asked looking at Rachael's cookie lying on the plate.

"No, it's just that I am pregnant. I work hard at keeping my weight down. This is one way that I restrain myself from gaining too much weight.

"I can enjoy watching you eat while we talk; then I can eat my cookie slowly. I will be happy that I had something sweet, but I will not be tempted to eat another."

Jewel still looked confused.

"I was a very large baby, and carrying me messed up my mother's insides. I could carry that same tendency to have large babies, so I follow the diet that Mama's doctor recommended for her. Lots of vegetables, just two fruits a day, lots of water and no sweets."

She smiled a beaming smile at her new friend, "This is the first cookie I have had since I knew I was pregnant." She quickly raised and lowered her eyebrows to emphasize her happiness at the occasion. "So, eat. And we will get acquainted.

"You don't have any children, yet?" Rachael asked.

"No. We have been married for three years, and no baby yet," Jewel said softly with a sad tone in her voice. "But, you said you have a one year old?"

"Yes, Bessie is napping. She should be waking up soon. She will be happy to meet you.

"Well, I don't remember seeing either of you around here. Where did you move from?"

"We are from the other side of Comanche. Both of our families farm, but James just couldn't find any land to lease around there for us to get started. And he said he didn't want to just stay there working as a hand for his father.

"When he heard about Mr. Brown, he came out to see what kind of deal it really was. Of course, James was interested in the land and how it produced...and that Mr. Brown would let us have half of this year's crop. He didn't pay much attention to the house.

"I'm sorry that I am so down in the dumps. I am not very good company." She hung her head and stirred her coffee.

Rachael patted her arm and said, "Why this is the way it's supposed to be. You start off with little or nothing, and you work together to build your life. It would not be any fun at all if the house was perfect when you first moved in.

"When Bessie wakes up, let's go to your house and see what ideas we can come up with. Do you have a sewing machine?"

Jewel shook her head 'no'.

"Well, I do. Epsy bought it for me when he found out I was pregnant again. I have been having so much fun making dresses, and I have made new curtains for almost every room.

"Mr. Clark, who owns the mercantile store, usually will let people run a bill until the cotton is sold. Maybe you can buy some paint and material for curtains. That will make it feel like 'your' house!

"I can't help you paint, but I can make new curtains for you."

Just then she heard Bessie stirring. "Now, you wait right here. Let me take her to the potty; then we will be right back."

****

When necessary things were done, Rachael appeared carrying a beautiful little blond-haired girl with a sleepy look on her face. Rachael poured a small glass of milk for her and sat down holding Bessie on her lap. "Would you like to share my cookie?" Rachael asked as she broke the cookie in half.

Jewel was enthralled with Bessie and couldn't wait to get well enough acquainted for the child to allow Jewel to hold her.

"Bessie, we have a new friend. Her name is Jewel." Bessie blinked and looked this stranger over while she ate her cookie, and Rachael took her first bite of cookie.

"After we finish our cookie we thought we would ride in Jewel's buckboard over to see her house."

At the thought of getting to go somewhere, Bessie began to wake up from her drowsiness, and soon they were leaving.

Jewel asked if Bessie would like to pet the horses' soft noses. Bessie nodded her head, so Jewel lifted her up and held her close enough for her small hand to reach the horse's nose. "First hold your hand close enough for him to smell of it and he will see what a sweet little girl you are. Then he will like you and let you pet his nose," Jewel told her.

The horse took two deep breaths, smelling her hand; then Jewel indicated she could rub his nose. "Thoft," Bessie said and smiled at Jewel.

****

Jewel let the horses plod along so the wagon ride would not be too bumpy for Rachael. They stopped at the gin to tell Epsy where they were going. The rest of the way they talked about their childhoods.

Jewel had grown up on the farm near Comanche; she had several brothers and sisters. When she was old enough to have a boyfriend, she had already known James most of her life, and she knew he was the one for her. He would come over and push her in the swing underneath a big oak tree just to spend time with her.

Rachael told her about growing up in Oklahoma, how lonely she was until Sarah moved into the valley and what good friends they had become. She told about some of the fun parts of her childhood. She skipped over all of the bumpy parts.

Soon they were at Jewel's new house, and she was right; there was a lot to be done. There were a lot of tall weeds all around the house; the house needed paint badly. The front screen door had drug for so long that it had worn a groove in the porch floor.

James, of course, was more concerned with seeing that the weeds were kept out of the cotton. He spent little time in the house, so it had not really bothered him.

Inside, their furniture was nice enough to be very comfortable. Long ago the living room had been wallpapered, but now, that walpaper was sagging and peeling. Rachael could see why Jewel was so depressed.

"Let's look at the kitchen," Rachael said. "That is where I spend most of my time, and if that room is happy, I am happy."

Well, there was ample cabinet space, and at one time, the cabinets had been painted an off shade of light green. The room was large enough to be comfortable and had several windows, so there was lots of light.

"See what I mean?" Jewel said sadly. The two women just looked at each other for a moment.

"Well, I like white cabinets. Do you?" Jewel nodded her head. "And what color would you like best for your curtains?"

Jewel hesitated. "Well, what color makes you happy?" Rachael asked. Again, Jewel hesitated.

"Maybe it would be best to see what they have to offer at the mercantile store and make a decision from that."

James opened the back door and smiled as he walked over to the water bucket. He drew up the long-handled dipper full of water and drank deeply.

"Hi, Rachael. It's nice to see you, and who is this pretty little girl?" He reached out to pat Bessie's arm.

"This is Bessie," Rachael said. Jewel swooped Bessie up in her arms and carried her over to where James stood.

"Bessie, this is my husband, James. He likes little girls, too."

James took her little hand in his and shook hands. "You are a very sweet little girl," he said, putting his hat back on. He was ready to go back to work the cotton.

He turned to Jewel and said, "More blooms opening up all the time, honey. We may make a real good crop." And he was out the door.

"I guess we need to be started home, too," Rachael said.

As they slowly drove to the gin and turned east, Rachael had been planning. "Now, you talk to James and see if he wants to talk to Mr. Clark about running a bill. Some men don't like to do that.

"I'll talk to Epsy. Sometimes his permanent hands are just looking for something to do this time of year. We might be able to get you some help. We'll see."

They reached the driveway of Rachael's house and turned in. Rachael said, "Jewel, this has been a most pleasant afternoon. I'm so glad we met. It is wonderful to have a friend to visit with.

"Now, Friday evening yall come to supper about 7:00. I think we will have fried chicken. And you gotta know Epsy likes to play dominoes."

****

When Epsy came home that evening, Rachael was full of excitement. She had a new project to work on.

"Epsy, you should see the shape that house is in! There are weeds waist high and fallen tree limbs all around the house, just a breeding place for rattlers. The screen door drags. The inside hasn't been taken care of for some years.

"Poor Mr. Brown probably never did a thing to it after his wife died. Then his health got so bad that he couldn't. They don't even have a garden at all. James is only concerned with making a good crop of cotton, and poor Jewel is stuck inside constantly looking at the awful shape that house is in."

She drew a breath and looked at him. "What is your situation at the gin? Can you send a couple of men over to help with the yard work?

"Jewel is going to ask James about starting a bill at the mercantile store to buy paint and material for kitchen curtains. That poor woman has got to have something pretty to look at. She can ignore the rest of the house, but if her kitchen looks happy, she will feel better.

"Oh, and I want to send her some vegetables from our garden instead of canning this week."

****

Next morning while Rachael and Bessie picked vegetables, Epsy went to the gin and lined out two men to help the Logan's get settled in.

James came outside to meet his unexpected guests. Epsy pulled up in this Model-T, followed by a buckboard and two men. Epsy handed him the basket of vegetables and said, "Logan, can I talk to you man to man, with no holds barred?"

James gave him a very puzzled look; then nodded his head slowly.

"I know that you are working hard on your cotton... as you should. Your fields look very clean of weeds.

"But, Rachael tells me that your home life is apt to suffer a serious setback unless we give you a little help.

"Is it alright with you if these men cut the weeds and clean up around the outside of the house?"

James slowly looked around at the house and yard as if seeing it for the first time. Then he suddenly looked troubled and stern. "They are on my payroll year round and right now we are looking for constructive things for them to do to stay busy. Won't cost you a thing.

"If you will take a ride into town with me, I'll introduce you to Mr. Clark at the mercantile and tell him it looks as if you will make a good crop this year. He will let you set up a running bill that you will pay when I buy your cotton."

Epsy stopped talking and looked at James just to see how this was setting with him. "Rachael tells me that your wife's kitchen needs to be a happy place so that she can be happy. The girls will do the work. They just have to buy some paint and material for curtains, I believe."

All this information had blindsided James. He stood quietly, first looking puzzled, then tense, then questioning again.

"Is this making sense to you, Logan? Believe me, little surprises such as this reap unexpected rewards that you would not believe!"

James Logan had to think for a while to digest all of this information. As it began to soak in, he started slowly nodding his head. He turned slowly to go in and tell Jewel the plan, and that he was leaving for a while. "Will you feel safe with Mr. Hale's men working here while I am gone?"

"If Mr. Hale trusts them, I will too," she said.

James got his hat and started out the front door. As he was climbing into the Model-T, he heard Epsy say to one of his men, "Fix that screen door first."

****

The two men talked above the chupa-chupa noise of the engine as they drove into Rising Star. "You have a lot of blooms opening up already. Looks as if you could make a good crop this year," Epsy said as they drove along beside James' field.

"Yeah, right now it looks really good, but inside I'm tied up in knots, thinking, 'Will the rains we need come before the bowls open? What if it rains after they open and before we can get it picked.' I don't have much saved up to carry us if we don't make a good crop this year."

Epsy could tell this man was bearing his soul here, talking out his worst fears to a stranger. "Man, if you don't learn to lighten up, you are not going to live past 40 years old. Farming is not something you can control regardless how hard you work or how much you fret.

"You have to do the work you know needs to be done, when it needs to be done; then let the Lord handle it from there.

"Hey, do you like to fish? Things are slow at the gin this time of year, and I have found a nice deep pond on that creek that runs just east of my house."

He looked around to survey the land, "I imagine it runs somewhere near the back of your place, too. Maybe we could go fishing together sometime when we are both caught up…. Let your horses have a little rest."

****

At the mercantile, Epsy introduced James to Mr. Clark and laid out their plan. "It looks to me like he is going to make a pretty good crop," Epsy told him.

James hung his head slightly as he explained, "This hurts me deeply, Mr. Clark. I don't believe in owing people. I had just enough saved up to carry us through till the crop came in, but Mr. Hale's wife pointed out that my wife is pretty miserable living in that house, run down as it is. I…"

Mr. Clark smiled. Over the years, he had seen this situation so many times. "Don't be upset, Mr. Logan. If Epsy stands up for a fellow, he is all right with me, too." He slapped James on the back, "Now, you tell your wife to come in, and I'll be glad to help her with what she needs."

As they left the mercantile, Epsy said, "Let's take a Dr. Pepper home to the girls, since we are in town. What do you say?"

****

Epsy stopped in front of the house just long enough to let James out and survey how much work his men had done.

"So I'll tell Rachael yall will be over for supper tomorrow night?"

"We would be very pleased, Epsy. About 7:00?"

Chapter Seventeen
Coween

Rachael and Jewel were having as much fun as school girls looking at all the brightly colored material, trying to decide just which one was bright enough, but not so bright that Jewel would get tired of it. And she had to explore all of them before she could even decide on which color she liked best. Right now she liked all of them!

"Well, let's see what colors are available in oil cloth for the tablecloth. That may help you get started in one direction," Rachael suggested.

The oil cloth was hung against the wall in long rolls. An iron rod ran through each of them and hung on brackets at each end. There were several to choose from. At the top was the usual red and white checked and blue and white checked, which did not set off a spark in Jewel. The next one down and just below eyelevel was a very pretty one with flowers on a green background, sort of like flowers in a meadow.

Rachael could see Jewel's expression change from excitement to disappointment when she thought about it being green. She had looked at those green cabinets long enough; no more green.

Beneath it there was a solid white…which would get boring soon enough with white cabinets.

As they were turning away, Jewel noticed that the flap of the green oil cloth was long and was covering another roll. She lifted it and discovered the same pattern with a pale pink background. The smile on her face told Rachael this was the one. Pink was her color. And they had been looking for something bright!

Now they went back to the piece goods, and it didn't take long to find a material that blended with the oil cloth very nicely. Jewel had the measurements of her kitchen windows, and they began to figure yardage.

"Do you want them to hang all the way from the top in one piece? Or would you like to put a ruffle at the top and make the curtains hang from about shoulder high? That would leave an open space to let in more light," Rachael was thinking out loud as much as asking a question.

"Oh, yes! That last one!" Jewel exclaimed. "Oh, Rachael, this is so much fun. This is the first house I have been able to decorate on my own."

"Okay!" Rachael echoed her enthusiasm and smiled at her. "Those are tall windows, so you will need about 12 inches for the ruffle at the top. Let me measure from your shoulder down. How low do those windows go, about to your knees? And I think a 2 inch hem.

"Would you want pink or white rickrack to cover the seam of the hem, or would you like white lace better?"

While Jewel was looking at rickrack and lace, trying to decide, Rachael was figuring yardage. "Twelve, fourteen, sixteen inches for the ruffle. Thirty-eight, forty, forty-two inches for the curtain. That's fifty-eight inches times two; that's one hundred and sixteen inches, divided by thirty-six inches to the yard.

"Mr. Clark," Rachael called out, "I need help figuring this, please. Please put down one hundred and sixteen divided by thirty-six."

"That is about three and two-thirds yards, Rachael," he called back. "Jewel, just those two tall windows in your kitchen? And is there a short one over the cabinet?"

"Two tall ones and a short one over the cabinet. That's right."

"That's seven and a third plus another yard and a half for the short one. Mr. Clark, we will need nine yards of this fabric. Do you think there is that much on this bolt? I think it will be close."

"You ought to know, Rachael, as many new curtains as you have been making!"

"I know! Ever since Epsy bought me that new sewing machine, sewing is all I want to do!"

Mr. Clark was measuring fabric, "There is just over nine yards here, Rachael."

"Well, give us the whole thing just in case I mis-figured. We will have some for tie-backs. I might even make her some matching pot holders. That would be fun!"

Jewel had decided, if she could have these the way she wanted, she would like a small lace to break up the flower pattern.

"I think twelve yards of the lace, if you have it, Mr. Clark. Then we need five curtain rods with hangers and one gallon of white paint, the kind you can wash.

"Oh, Jewel, are you having as much fun as I am?"

Jewel looked up with a big smile on her face that said, "How can I ever thank you?" and nodded her head 'yes'.

****

It took Rachael a little over a week to make the curtains. Between doing her housework, gardening, canning, and taking care of Bessie, she was a busy woman. And beginning to get a bit tired.

On the evening they took the curtains over to Jewel and James' house, Rachael told Epsy that she thought she had enough food canned for the year. "Do you think it will be all right if I tell Jewel I will pick what we need for our meals, and she can have the rest to can?

"It is past the first of August. The garden won't produce very much longer, but she can get some vegetables put away.

"Epsy, they seem like such good friends. I hope that never changes."

****

James met them at the front of the house and said, "She wants yall to come in the back door. She is so proud of the way the kitchen looks." He smiled at Epsy, and nodded his head to say, "What a difference a gallon of paint can make in a woman!"

Epsy understood completely.

When they walked into the kitchen, it took their breath away. She had painted the cabinets, yes; but she had painted the window frames and the table and chairs, too. And the pale pink oil cloth fairly sparkled against the white paint. The table was round, and she had rounded the oil cloth to match. Everything looked so bright and new!

Jewel was so happy to see the astonishment and admiration on Rachael's face, she was thrilled beyond words. "Well, actually, it took two gallons of white paint to stop the green from showing through. But once I got started painting, I just couldn't stop!"

The men put up the curtain rod hangers while the women put the curtains on the rods. Then they stood back and looked at the new kitchen, turning first this direction then the other. It was perfect; just like a picture out of a magazine.

Soon they were having supper in Jewel's new kitchen. "Hurry with the dishes. Let's play a few hands of dominoes before it gets too late."

****

So it was that the back door became the front door at the Logan house. Each week the two couples had supper and dominoes at alternating houses. When Epsy, Rachael and Bessie went to the Logan's house they automatically went to the back door.

Until one evening James met them as they drove in and said, "We can go in the front door tonight."

They stepped into another astonishing sight! Jewel had torn off all of the old wallpaper, and filled the cracks between the boards. She had sanded it smooth and painted the walls light beige. Her couch was a little darker beige with deep red flowers. She had one dark red chair and one brown one. All her end tables were dark wood; and on a table between the couch and the brown chair was a beautiful deep red table lamp. On another table she had a bowl of red flowers, and she had white lace curtains on the windows.

It took Rachael's breath away. She had been in this room before, but it was so dark and the wallpaper was so droopy that she had not seen the beauty in the furnishings.

"Oh, Jewel, you have made this into a completely different room! How long have you been working on this?"

"About a month," James offered. "And she is building muscles from all the work she has been doing and losing weight in all the right spots." He nodded his head toward Jewel, "She is really looking good."

Of course, then they had to take a second look at Jewel, and she fairly beamed. "James said I can start on our bedroom next. I can't wait to get started. Having the house look nice just makes me feel so good.

"I am going to paint the bedroom light blue. You know, Rachael, I think I like the painted walls better than the ones with wallpaper anyway. And it sure is easier than trying to hang wallpaper. I could never do that by myself!"

****

One day Jewel drove the buckboard over to visit in the late afternoon when she knew Rachael would be resting. Sure enough, Rachael had brought a kitchen chair outside and was sitting in the shade of their big oak tree with a glass of spearmint tea. She was watching while Bessie played quietly.

While Jewel carried out another chair Rachael poured her a glass of tea. Bessie was stirring the cone-shaped doodle bug holes with a twig. There were several of them in the shade of the tree. Bessie would stir and mumble something, then move to another hole and stir and mumble.

"I have been teaching her how to say, 'Doodle bug, doodle bug, come out of your hole, your house is on fire and your children will burn,' " Rachael laughed. "I keep wondering what she will do if she ever gets one to come out." They both laughed at the thought of the ugly, but harmless little bugs.

They sat quietly for a while watching Bessie. "Rachael, you have such beautiful flowerbeds, yet, I haven't heard you speak much of the work they take."

"Oh, what I have in my flowerbeds here, doesn't really take any work at all. Those dark green plants with the purple blossoms are Mexican Petunias. Don't you think those blossoms look like little phonograph speakers? If you give them a little water they multiply from the root as well as the seed. "Once I got them started I just kept digging small clumps of them and spreading them around the house. They just take over if you don't dig along the edge where you want them to stop."

She pointed to the front of the house, "That shrub on this front corner with the puffy little red blossoms is Chinese Lantern, and on the other front corner I have a Salvia. It has a tiny red blossom on the tip of each limb. From a distance, it makes it look like the bush is on fire. So some folks call it Fire Bush.

"All of them bloom most of the summer. They are hardy in this Texas heat as long as you give them a little water.

She pointed toward the kitchen door, "Right there by the back door I have some of Mama's favorite...spearmint. I sprinkle a few coffee grounds on it once in a while because it wants an acid soil." Next to them there is a little patch of Bachelor Buttons. My mother loved them, too. She hesitated and took a sip of tea.

"Oh, and under our bedroom window, I have a Rosemary bush. I really like the clean smell of Rosemary.

"Those two gray-green bushes out in the front yard are Sage bushes that I brought back from Big Spring, when we ran away to get married They were so small, we carried them both in a syrup bucket." She had to stop awhile and smile at the memories that brought up. "After every rain, they are just covered with light purple flowers.

"And I just pour my dish water on a different area until I've worked my way around the house."

They sat in silence again watching several small white butterflies bobble up and down around the Mexican Petunias. The very edge of their wings seemed to be scripted in gray ink.

"I guess it will get cold before flowers could get started, even if you start them from root, like the petunias. But I'd be happy to give you a start in the spring.

"This fall you can start preparing your beds. You know, dig up where you want them and fertilize the soil. I think it is kind of fun to gather pretty rocks to outline the flowerbeds.

"But you know flowerbeds are a good place for snakes to hide. If you are going to have flowers close to the house, you are going to need to have geese. They kill snakes or chase them away.

"Hey, one of my geese is setting on some eggs right now. Would you like some geese when they are goslings?

"You will have to get James to build a small house and pen for them at night. But you have plenty of time to think about it before they will be ready to take away from their mama. They will keep snakes away from the house....and barn too, if you let them roam. You just train them to come to the pen at night to be fed and then close them up...away from coyotes.

"A goose can whip a fox with his wings and finally discourage him, but coyotes are stronger."

Rachael liked her geese.

"Rachael, have you decided on names for the baby?"

"Not really. If it is a boy, of course, we will name him after Epsy. But I seem to be carrying this one just like I did Bessie. I kinda think it will be another little girl."

"Well, what names are you considering if it is a girl?"

"I sort of like Corrine. You know like the song, 'Corrine, Corrina, Where you been so long?' But I don't know what Epsy thinks. We haven't talked about it much.

"We'll just have to see when it gets here."

****

It was Epsy and Rachael's turn to host supper and dominoes this evening. The season had turned and there was just a bit of a nip in the air. Cool enough to feel fresh, but not enough to be cold.

Supper was over, and the men went outside to smoke while the women did the dishes. Jewel opened the door a bit and asked, "Rachael wants to know if yall want cake and coffee now, or play dominoes first?"

"Let's play dominoes first; right now I'm stuffed."

The men finished their smokes and came into the kitchen....and found it empty. They could hear muffled voices but they were not sure where they were coming from.

Jewel finally came out of the bathroom, "Rachael will be a little while. Her water broke.

"Epsy, she wants you to bring Gladys over and go tell Dr. Johnson to be prepared. We thought Bessie can go home with James and me for the night. Is that okay with you?

"I will go get her dressed in her nightgown and she can sit in my lap while we play dominoes a little longer until Rachael gets too uncomfortable."

Rachael finally came out of the bathroom, looking a little weak and pale. She was willing to sit at the table and let others get coffee and cake to eat while they played three handed dominoes. "None for me, please," she said.

Gladys arrived and began to prepare the small, extra bed with heavy layers of paper. She filled all the large pots with water and stoked the fire in the stove. "We probably won't need this for a while, but the water can be warming."

Gladys was teaching Jewel a lot about a new subject tonight.

"I would suggest you take Bessie home with you when Epsy gets back. Last time it worked well for Rachael and me to play Rummy. She always beats me; but she won't get excited doing that like she would if yall keep playing dominoes."

When Epsy got back from Dr. Johnson's, Bessie got hugs and kisses from her mama and papa. "Be sure to tell Aunt Jewel when you need to go potty, okay, honey?" Rachael reminded as she caressed the side of Bessie's face. Then they wrapped Bessie in her favorite blanket and loaded up to leave.

"I am happy that she went with them so easy," Gladys said.

"She really likes Jewel, and James gets down on all fours and lets her ride his back like a horse. Not having any of their own yet, they really spoil her."

****

For a while they played three-handed Rummy, but Epsy got antsy and went for a walk. He came back in and put some wood on the fire; he sat at the other end of the table sharpening his knife.

Finally, Rachael began to hurt enough that she wanted to walk around some. "Epsy, have you thought of a name you like, yet?" she asked, taking his hand.

"Oh, I have been thinking ever since you suggested Corrine, and I like it better every time I think about it. I guess that would be okay with me."

"Well, then, would you like to go fetch Dr. Johnson? I think Corrine is going to be here pretty soon."

He grabbed her by the shoulders and kissed her cheek. Then he was out the door. Rachael did not know if he kissed her because he loved her, or because the baby was so near, or because she gave him permission to get out of the house. "Ha, ha, ha, ha," she laughed out loud.

Then Gladys thought about the funny way he took off, and they had a long laugh together. It was good to laugh; it took her mind off the pain in her lower back.

****

When Dr. Johnson arrived, they were ready for him. "She has been holding back as much as she can," Gladys said. "We have been doing everything we could think of to help her relax when the pains come."

Dr. Johnson had a knack for putting people at ease. He immediately began a steady stream of conversation to keep everyone's mind busy on something else. "Epsy, you go in the kitchen and keep the fire hot in the stove and lots of pans of water heating. I'll come along and wash up, now. Be right back, Rachael."

When he returned, he rummaged through his medical bag and pulled out a large jar of Vaseline. With a beaming smile he held it up for Rachael to see. Together, they said, "Can't have a baby without Vaseline, can we?"

"I put that in my bag several weeks ago to be sure I would have it with me when your time came." He applied the Vaseline and went to wash up again. He came back with a fresh-brewed cup of coffee. Rachael could smell it and her mouth watered.

He spent a little time laying out things that he thought he might need, "Gladys, can you find a couple more pillows to prop up Rachael's back?

"Well, Rachael, it looks as if you are ready any time another pain hits. Hey, have you seen what Jewel is doing to that house on the old Brown place? They asked me over for supper recently. She has turned the inside of that house into a very happy place. James says she has done it all by herself, too. And she fairly beamed when she was showing it off.

"She said that you made her kitchen curtains. I thought they were very nice."

"Yes, Jewel and I had so much fun choosing material. That was a fun day."

"Well, I hope I haven't scared the pains away," he said as he reached to feel Rachael's tummy. "No, the muscles are tensing again. Can you feel it yet, Rachael?'

She nodded, "But it hasn't gotten hard yet."

"Well, who was winning on the Rummy game that I interrupted?"

"Rachael was, as usual," Gladys said. "I don't just let her win because of her condition. She is just good at Rummy, or just plain lucky."

"Well, is this the only time you two play Rummy? Rachael, do you play a lot and just know which cards to hold?"

Rachael was nodding in answer to his questions, but she was beginning to push so she did not try to answer.

"Rachael, I think all of that relaxing you did trying to wait for me to get here must have helped. That baby is moving right on. It won't be long now. One more hard pain and one big push should do it.

"Oh, what are you going to name this one? Epsy, if it is a boy, I know. But if it is a girl?"

She started to answer, but she suddenly gave a big push and her voice came out very loud. "Cor-rine!"

"Well, Corrine, it is then. This looks like a fine baby girl."

He quickly cleaned out her mouth and nose and held her up by her feet so he could swat her lightly on the behind. And Corrine let out a loud squall. Gladys wrapped her in a soft little blanket and began cleaning her, but Corrine just continued to yell as loud as she could.

Epsy came running to see if something bad was happening. "It's okay," Dr. Johnson reassured him. "She had a comfortable place where she was, and she is just mad about leaving it.

"Pour me another cup of coffee, will you Epsy? I'll be in there in minute or two."

****

But they soon found that the only time Corrine did not yell was when she was nursing. "She looks real good," Dr. Johnson said. "I don't think anything is wrong with her except that she is mad, but I'll hang around a little while to make sure." About the time Dr. Johnson finished his coffee, Corrine finally fell asleep.

"You know, Epsy, I believe this one may be as feisty and loud as Bessie is quiet and mild. Congratulations on your new daughter," and he shook Epsy's hand.

After Gladys had things cleaned up and in place, she said, "I think, I'll just lie down in the spare bedroom and rest a little till morning, just in case the baby doesn't stay asleep. I think Rachael needs to rest as much as possible."

****

Dr. Johnson had been right with his assessment of the new baby's character. She was a handful! If she was awake, she made a lot of noise and needed a lot of Rachael's attention. Jewel brought Bessie to see her new sister, but decided to keep Bessie with her for about a week so that Rachael could rest a little during the day.

Corrine seemed to be as different from Bessie as daylight is from dark. Though not black like Epsy's hair, her hair was dark brown, and her eyes were brown. Every noise she made was louder than Bessie; her voice was just naturally strong. Her movements were quick, and she was very active, always out of one thing into another.

She crawled earlier, walked earlier, reached for things she was not supposed to have earlier and more often. She jabbered most of the time she was awake, and she was alert to everything that went on around her.

Rachael soon learned to encourage Bessie to, "Let's lie down and take a nap while Corrine is asleep."

Thankfully Jewel came over every two or three days to play with the baby, and let Rachael rest.

One day while Rachael was a bit overwhelmed with all the responsibility, Epsy showed up at the kitchen door at an off hour of the day. Holding his hands behind his back, he smiled at her a minute. Then he said, "Guess which hand!"

Rachael played along and chose his right hand. He brought around a bag of Hershey's Kisses and handed them to her. "Oh!" she was thrilled. But he still held the other hand behind his back.

"Guess again!" he said. She pointed to his left hand, and he brought around two Dr. Peppers. He knew what his Rachael liked! "Let's get some glasses and have a tea party to celebrate our new baby."

While Rachael got glasses and opened the Dr. Peppers, Epsy washed Bessie's hands and set her on her knees in a chair at the table.

Rachael placed three Kisses each in three small plates, and Epsy brought Corrine's rocking cradle into the kitchen and set it by Rachael.

Bessie loved the tea party. "Celebwate our baby, Coween?" she asked.

****

Bessie loved her baby sister. She was interested in everything that needed to be done for 'Baby Coween' and wanted to help. And she was quite a bit of help to Rachael, always willing to go get a diaper or a wet cloth. She fairly beamed when they called her the 'big sister'.

One day Rachael set aside time to make a stuffed baby doll for Bessie. Then they would sit together and rock their babies. Every time Corrine needed a clean diaper, Bessie's baby needed one too.

When Rachael changed a dirty diaper, Bessie squeenched up her nose and mouth and said, "Oow, Mama, Coween ith a thtinker."

As Corrine grew Bessie was her constant companion, helping when she could…telling when she couldn't.

When Corrine was toddling well enough to play outside with Big Sister, Rachael had a little time to get some work done because she trusted Bessie's mothering instinct.

Bessie brought Corrine in the kitchen door, holding her tightly by the hand. Bessie's face was squeenched up, and she said, "Mama, Coween ith a thtinker."

"Did she dirty in her diaper?"

"No, thyee thtepped in gooththyit!"

Rachael broke down in laughter and squatted down and hugged the two girls. Then the three of them laughed for a long time just because it was fun to laugh together.

When Epsy came home, Rachael said, "Sister, tell Papa what Corrine did today."

Again she squeenched up her face and said, "Coween ith a thtinker. Thyee thtepped in gooththyit."

****

It was hard for Epsy and James to find time to go fishing together. It was sometime close to Christmas when the cotton picking was finally finished. Then the gin was working from daylight to dark to get all those rows and rows of cotton trailers unloaded and the cotton ginned. When the ginning was finished, it was almost time for James to begin turning the soil to prepare for planting.

Epsy finally convinced James to plant his seed; then let himself and his horses rest until there was really a need to fight the weeds. So they squeezed in a few fishing trips here and there.

One day after they found a grassy spot where the underbrush was not crowding them in, they set their lines and were enjoying the shade of the trees overhead. James asked a question that had been on his mind ever since he met Epsy. "I knew some Hales who lived near Comanche. They said their family was from Bell County. Must have been a bunch of them, the way they talked.

"Epsy, are you part of that Hale family?"

There was a long silence while Epsy remembered back. Finally he decided how he was going to answer his friend.

"My great-grandpa and all his brothers grew up along the state line between eastern Tennessee and western North Carolina. You were right; there was a bunch of them, must have been twelve or more boys. They all moved to Mississippi for about forty years; then they decided to come to Texas. By that time, there was a whole wagon train of just Hales. One of them didn't move off by himself. They all went or they all stayed. They were from Scotland; I guess you would call it a clan.

"They must have reached Bell County in 1873 or 1875, just depending on who you listen to. Anyway, we had one sister and one brother born in Bell County before we were born; the older ones were born in Mississippi."

Epsy noticed James furrow his brow with a questioning look when he said, "we were born."

"I have a twin brother, Earnest.

"Well, time you figure twelve boys and their boys, there must have been fifty to seventy-five families; they settled just about the whole eastern part of Bell County. We lived around Pendleton.

"Of course they brought their slaves with them. Well, they weren't slaves by that time, but they didn't know any other life, so they just stayed on and kept working for their former masters. They were just called hands instead of slaves.

"The Hales were farmers and stockmen, and they expected their sons to work the land. When I was fifteen – sixteen, and we would play games after work, I discovered I was good at baseball. I mean real good.

"Ever after that I dreamed of playing for a professional team. I learned all I could about the game, the teams and the stats. Every time there was a holiday and a picnic in Belton, we would have a baseball game.

"When I was nineteen, there was a man at the picnic who told me I should try out for one of the teams. Told me when and where they would have try-outs.

"Oh, how I dreamed about going to those try-outs; dreamed it so much it twisted in my gut! But I knew better than to tell anyone I was going. It just wasn't allowed for anyone to leave the family.

"I knew better than to take a horse, too! So late one night after everyone was asleep, I got my best friend, Erney, to take me to the train station in

Temple. Erney was the son of one of my papa's hands; he was about my age, and my best friend. He took me to the station and got the team and wagon back home so that no one knew. Next morning, they just found my bed empty.

"Well, it turned out that I was good enough to make a semi-pro team. I played second base for several years, and there was talk of my going to the majors, until Ty Cobb cleated me in the ankle while he was trying to steal second. I tagged him out, but I got cleated in the process.

"They said he used to set in the clubhouse and sharpen his cleats with a file. Then instead of diving for the base with his hands, he slid in feet first.

"His cleats were sharp, all right. Cut through the leather top of my shoe and cut my ankle to the bone. Even when it healed, I couldn't play baseball any more. I still have a little bit of a limp from it."

He fell silent then, and nothing was said for a long while.

There was a deep sadness in his voice when he continued. "I heard my papa finally figured out that it was Erney who took me to the train. Said that he whipped Erney real bad with plow lines." Then he was silent with his memories for a while.

"After I got hurt and couldn't play anymore, I went back to Bell County, and they all just acted like they didn't even know me."

"Everybody?"

"Well, all of my family."

"Your own ma and pa?"

Epsy nodded his head and sat there in silence again. "I always heard 'A bitter root grows deep.' I finally understood the meaning of that saying.

"Well, after I left, I guess a few others got brave enough to move away from the family. Now, my papa and his family, my twin brother and several of my uncles and cousins live around Coahoma, near Big Spring.

"I don't have any idea who that might be at Comanche, but it most likely is some of them that moved away.

"Hey, we've been sitting here for quite a while and haven't caught a thing. I haven't even seen our corks bobble. Do you want to move to another spot?"

*****

True to her word, when Rachael's new goslings had a covering of their adult feathers, she and Epsy took six snowy white young geese over to James and Jewel. James had fixed up the old chicken house to pen them up at night as Rachael had instructed.

Jewel just happened to have some fresh cookies made, which thrilled the girls no end. "You may have one cookie each, and please don't ask Aunt Jewel for more," Rachael cautioned. So Jewel fixed them places at the table and they stood on their knees in a chair to eat.

When they had finished and started squirming in the chairs, wanting to go play, Rachael smiled and said, "Ask Aunt Jewel if you may be excused from the table."

They both looked at Jewel and said, "Be excused from the table?"

"Of course, you may," she said helping them down.

The men sat down at the kitchen table with their coffee and started talking business, so Jewel and Rachael took their coffee to the living room. The girls had more room to play and Bessie knew where Jewel kept a bucket of small toys just for them.

James gazed after the girls as they left the room. "Do they always do that?" he asked

"Ask to be excused from the table? Oh, yes. Rachael taught them to always ask before they leave the table. It gives her a chance to check their plates and see if they have eaten a good meal. That way, they won't come back asking to eat between meals."

From the kitchen, James heard the excitement in Jewel's voice, "Oh, you are?"

"Well, I'm not for sure yet," Rachael said quietly and she nodded her head, "but, probably. I haven't told Epsy yet, because I'm not really that sure."

When Epsy was ready to go, Rachael helped the girls pick up the toys from the living room floor. She would pick up a toy, place it in Corrine's hand and say, "Now, let's put it in the bucket."

"Oh, you don't have to do that," James said. "We can pick them up later."

Jewel gently laid her hand on his arm and said quietly, "Let's not interfere, James. This is the way she is teaching them." And she smiled, nodding her head to show that she approved.

As they waved goodbye and turned to go back into the house, James asked, "What were you so excited about a while ago?"

"Oh, Rachael thinks she may be pregnant again," she said with a slight sound of sadness in her voice.

She could see the love in his eyes as he reached for her and held her in his arms tenderly. "At least we get to love theirs. She will need your help more than ever now."

****

Epsy sat at the table sharpening his knife while Rachael finished the dishes. "Rachael, did you know that fellow, Coleman, planted peanuts this spring? Soon as his cotton was picked he began working his land getting ready to plant peanuts as soon as it warmed up.

"I stopped and talked to him the other day. He said he was just tired of worrying about whether it would rain at the right time so the cotton would grow, or whether it would rain at the wrong time and ruin his cotton. It looks like he has a good crop of peanuts coming up.

"I don't know what the market for peanuts is like, but if he makes a good crop, it could start others to planting peanuts and really hurt our business. We will just have to watch and see what happens."

He was quiet for a few minutes.

"My brother Robert came through the other day and stopped by the gin for a few minutes. He was going back to Pendleton.

"Rachael, my papa is dead."

"Oh, Epsy, what was the matter with him?"

"He was shot.

"Seems the whole family was sitting on the front porch on a Sunday evening, and Papa was watching a rabbit hop around near enough to shoot him. Papa told Robert to go in and get his .22 rifle. As Robert was coming through the screen door, the latch hook somehow hooked the trigger and shot Papa through the neck. He lived for a few days, but they knew he was not going to recover.

"Sure is messing Robert up in his mind, knowing that he shot his own papa. Knowing it was a freak accident doesn't help him any."

He slowly dragged the knife across the whit stone, and he was quiet with his memories for a while.

"He said my uncle B.T. is getting in pretty bad health now. He knows he won't be able to farm much longer. He has over a section of land in cultivation north of Coahoma, and he only had one boy. He is kinda looking for someone to lease about half of his farm."

"You didn't tell me Robert was here. Why didn't he stay to eat?"

"Oh, I don't know. I'm kinda surprised he stopped at all.

"Hey, there is still a little daylight left. Do you want to go over to see James and Jewel for a few minutes?"

****

When Epsy and Rachael arrived home after dark, with two sleepy little girls, they were shocked to see a carriage sitting by their front door and lights on inside their house.

Epsy motioned for Rachael and the girls to stay in the Model-T while he investigated. He found the three Dodd sisters, Nora, Lou and Wilma, making themselves at home inside.

"Where is Bun?" Nora demanded when he stepped in the door.

"I have no idea. Isn't he with you people?"

"No, he has run away again." She was looking out the window to see who was in the Model-T. "If he is not with you, we must have gotten here before he could make it on foot. So, we will wait."

Epsy noticed that beside the door were three valises. They really were prepared to stay! He picked up the bags and opened the front door. "If you will step right this way, ladies, I will load your valises for you. There is a very nice boarding house in Rising Star that I am sure will be happy to have your business."

"Well!" Nora said with a snort and astonishment in her voice.

"Oh, come now, ladies. I'm sure you have been asked to leave better establishments than this!" Epsy said as he ushered them to the carriage and helped each lady inside.

****

Only when he was sure they had turned toward Rising Star and were well on the road, did he go to help Rachael and the girls out of the Touring Car.

"What is that all about?" Rachael asked.

"Bun has run away again, and they were sure he would be here. They came prepared to stay the night, but I offered them the boarding house in Rising Star. I didn't want you to get upset."

"Upset? Whatever are you talking about? Of course, I am upset if Bun has run away again!"

"That is exactly what I am talking about. And there is no way I would allow them to stay in our house and upset you even more!

"Now, let's settle ourselves down so we can be calm while we get the girls to bed. We don't want to make them sleep fretfully.

"You and I can talk about this some more later. Okay?"

Epsy and Rachael sat up way late, expecting Bun to show up. When they finally gave up and decided to go to bed, Rachael left the kerosene lamp burning low on the kitchen table… just in case.

****

Nora, Lou and Wilma were back by mid-morning the next day and barged right in, again expecting to find Bun there. They all sat down in the living room.

Nora did not like the bed they gave her at the boarding house; she did not like the food they served for breakfast. She did not like Rachael's girls or anything they did. "No wonder she is not married," Rachael thought, "she is becoming more like her mother all the time. Abrasive personality and every word out of her mouth sounds of insolence."

"Girls, come into the kitchen with me for a while," Rachael said. She sat them at the table and gave them each a tea cake and a glass of milk. Nora walked into the kitchen and reached into the cookie jar in the center of the table. "I'll have one of those tea cakes."

Corrine was holding her glass carefully with both hands, but they were small hands. She was startled by Nora's reaching across her and the glass slipped. Milk spilled on the table and ran down the table cloth onto the floor.

"Now, just look at that! You little brat; you've splattered milk all over my skirt!"

Rachael stopped wiping up the milk. She reached behind her to the stove and picked up a large cast iron skillet. Holding it at an angle and about waist high, Rachael stared at her. The expression on Rachael's face did not change, except for the narrowing of the eyes. "Get out of my house! You are not welcome in my house! Do not ever come here again!"

Surprise of all surprises, Nora turned and walked out and the others followed her!

****

When Epsy came home for dinner, his first words were, "I'm sorry, Rachael. I was busy this morning, and I didn't see them until they were leaving."

That was all she needed to start crying. He held her while she sobbed; he knew her heart was breaking with the thought of Bun not being here. God only knows what the three wicked sisters had done. "I'm so sorry I was not here to help you," he whispered.

****

The Dodd sisters hung around for about a week, driving by the house and staring, looking for any evidence of Bun. But they did not stop.

"I guess they think we may have him hidden in the storm cellar," Rachael thought.

****

Two months later Rachael received a letter from Bun.

Rachael Hale
Rising Star, TX

Dearest Sister,

I arrived in California by freight train. I have a good family to stay with. I am doing fine. I miss you.

Love, Bun

There was no return address.

Of course, she told Epsy, but they planned to keep the news strictly between themselves, lest the Dodd's find out.

Every month or so Nora, Lou, and Wilma showed up for a visit. Their attitude had changed; this time they were trying to be polite and friendly. They never asked about Bun or his whereabouts. They were just hoping that Rachael would let something slip.

They did notice that Rachael was pregnant again, and they became interested in names for the baby. Nora said, "If it is a boy, you will have to name him Jeff O'Neal!" She said this with a smile on her face until Rachael slammed the iron skillet down on the stove. She never looked up, just began cooking.

"Well, if it is a girl, maybe you could name her after one of us," Wilma said. She always was the nicest one. Rachael kept her back turned and acted as if she did not hear.

With each visit their insistence that the baby be named after one of them became more demanding. Finally, Rachael had had enough of this hinting about the baby's name. "If it is a girl, I am going to name her Neva. I suppose Neva Lou would sound nice together."

****

Epsy was working long hours at the gin when it was near time for the baby to be born. While Rachael did the supper dishes, he sat at the table sharpening his knife. He always did that when he was thinking about something serious.

"Rachael, Coleman did real good with his peanuts this year. I found out that three more of my farmers are going to plant peanuts next year. It really looks to me like the ginning business is going to suffer."

"What will we do?" she asked.

"A city man came to the gin today and offered me more money for the gin than I knew they had printed at the mint.

"Rachael, I took it before he had a chance to look around and see what is happening here. We went into Eastland and signed the papers on it today, and he deposited the money in our bank account."

"But Epsy, the baby is due so soon! We can't move right now!"

"No, we don't have to. I told him I would stay and work the gin until the end of the year. He can work along with me and learn the ropes. I don't think he knows anything about ginning. And I am going to get one quarter of this year's profits.

"By the end of the year, the baby will be about three months old. It will be strong enough to move by then, don't you think?"

"Move where?"

"Coahoma. I leased uncle B.T's place. I think I'll farm for a while."

"But, Epsy, you always said you didn't like farming."

"Didn't like farming for someone else. I might like it if I can farm the way I want to.

"Rachael, I think I'm going to buy me a tractor to farm with!

"I am going to buy stocks with the rest of the money and let it be earning us money without even working for it."

Epsy had it all figured out, but Rachael's world was falling apart. She was having a new baby soon. Much more work to do. Moving…and

with a new baby. Leaving her friend, Jewel. It was just more than she could handle. She sat down at the table and began to cry.

Epsy reached over and patted her hand. "It won't be all that bad, Rachael. James and I have been considering this for a while. I am going to ask James if he would like to lease a quarter section of the land. Even with a tractor, I don't think I want to try to farm a half section.

"Moving wouldn't be so bad if James and Jewel go, too, would it?"

****

James liked the idea of moving to West Texas, and Rachael and Jewel soon started thinking about new houses. And suddenly it was time for the baby.

Rachael and Epsy, Gladys and Dr. Johnson, and Jewel and James had a system worked out. Everybody knew their parts and they took having this new baby in stride.

*****

Nora, Lou, and Wilma made their monthly visit and found a third little girl had joined the family. Lou proudly picked up the sleeping baby and said, "Well, hello, Neva Lou." Her voice showed that she was proud as punch.

"I named her Neva Louella," Rachael said, "so she could be named after my mother, too." That took all the wind out of their sails, and Lou quickly put the baby down.

"Well, have you heard anything from Bun?" Nora asked harshly.

"Haven't seen him," Rachael replied.

"No telling where, that no-account kid could be. We've had the Marshall looking for him, too. If he shows up, you had better tell us if you know what is good for you.

"As long as it has been, I really doubt he will show up here," Rachael said and she went back to her work…smiling ever so slightly.

Chapter Eighteen
West Texas

West Texas in January was a dismal looking place! The only trees were short, more like large bushes, except they had no leaves. They were just a big clump of small limbs with thorns. Of course in the draws, there would be one or two that actually were large enough to be called a tree, but still no leaves in January.

And the wind blew ceaselessly! Cold, strong wind that cut into you like a knife. "Earnest says the wind blows like this in West Texas because there is nothing between here and the North Pole but barbed wire fences!" Epsy said. That was supposed to make everybody laugh, but with their teeth chattering so bad they half believed it was true. This was an exceptionally cold winter.

Everyone in the Touring Car was bundled up in winter coats and caps, with blankets across their laps to keep warm. Epsy, Rachael and the baby, Neva, in the front seat, James and Jewel had Bessie and Corrine snuggled between them in the back seat. They were on their way from the boarding house in Coahoma to look at the land they had leased...and see what the houses looked like. B.T had said each quarter section had a house on it, but no one knew what kind of houses to expect.

"Let's see, James. I believe he put my name on the SE one quarter and yours on the SW one quarter; so the house on this corner should be ours. Let's go in and look at it; then we will go look at your house on the next corner."

It was a four room frame house with sand-blasted white paint. The shingles looked as if they had withstood the wind pretty well. There was a small room built on the back...probably the bath room.

"The screen door drags," Epsy said, toeing the groove it had worn in the porch floor. He opened the door for Rachael so she could get the baby out of the wind.

She gasped and her jaw dropped when she looked around inside. There were a few pieces of old furniture here and there, but everything...everything was covered in sand. It was just as cold inside as it was outside; there was just no wind inside. A pot-bellied stove stood next to the wall between the living room and one of the bedrooms; but right now, the iron stove was as cold as ice.

"B.T. said it had been setting empty for some time," Epsy said shaking his head. "I guess we have some work to do between now and planting time."

He had glanced into each of the other rooms. "I only see one broken window pane, that one by the front door."

Rachael had given the baby to Jewel while she looked around. She quickly found her way to the kitchen...her room. She made a quick survey and calculated how the furniture would fit. There was not a lot of cabinet space, but she had room for Mama's china cabinet and buffet. She could make it work.

"Look, Epsy, there is a drain board built right into the top of the cabinet!

Excitedly, she turned to look at Jewel, "Jewel, look at these grooves. No more using a cup towel to drain dishes!"

Next she checked the bedrooms. They were pretty large, but there were no built in closets. She had her mama's wardrobe; they could make that do until Epsy got some closets built.

Epsy knew it was going to be a strain for her to move into this house, especially with a new baby. So when she walked back into the kitchen, he was right behind her, wanting to reassure her that whatever was wrong, he could make it better.

Back in the kitchen, Rachael began planning how her furniture should be arranged to best advantage. She opened the upper cabinet doors. There was not very much sand in them at all. In fact, there was not too much sand in the kitchen or bedrooms. Maybe that broken window in the living room was the reason for all of the sand in there.

She squatted down and opened the lower cabinet

doors. And sitting there was a big, gray raccoon, with black around his eyes like a bandit's mask. He arched its back, hissed, and ran at her...just to the edge of the cabinet! Rachael let out a yell and tried to back up, but her legs could not move fast enough in a squatting position.

She threw herself backward into Epsy, who half caught her; then he fell, too!

James and Jewel and the girls hurried to the kitchen door to see what all the noise was about. From across the room the girls could only see that there was an animal in the cabinet. They were wide eyed. Bessie covered her mouth and backed up a step, but Corrine craned her neck and inched forward to get a better view. Holding the baby with one hand, Jewel grabbed Corrine's shoulder with the other.

Scrambling to get off the floor without hurting Rachael, who was lying across his legs, Epsy pushed the cabinet doors shut, and everybody began to recover their wits. Then, still sitting on the floor, Rachael began to giggle. Once she started everyone began to laugh uproariously. They suddenly went from so startled they couldn't move to laughing so hard, they couldn't catch their breath.

"Well, now that we know he is there, tomorrow I will bring some heavy gloves just in case I have to help him move out." And they started laughing again.

"Let's go see what is living in your house," Rachael said smiling at Jewel. So they loaded up and headed west. Half way there Rachael started giggling again about the coon in the cabinet, and everyone had to laugh again.

Soon they began to see James and Jewel's house in the distance. Everyone was leaning to one side then the other trying to get a better view. When they finally pulled up beside it, Rachael quietly said, "The last man to live here really loved his wife."

No one else commented on that; they were too much in awe of the excellent condition of the house. They sat in the Touring Car a few minutes to drink in the sight. The outside paint still looked new, the shingles were new and red. There were fir trees planted around the outside of the yard to help hold the sand away from the house.

When they went inside, the picture continued with fresh paint throughout. All Jewel could say was, "Ooh, Ooh, Ooh. It's perfect! Just perfect!"

"Did I tell you, this man loved his wife?" Rachael asked when they got back in the Touring Car.

"Or maybe his wife was particularly talented," James said under his breath, and he smiled appreciatively at Jewel and squeezed her hand.

As everyone was getting settled in the Model-T, Epsy said, "Well, Rachael, we can tell the lady at the boarding house that we will be there for a little while. I will fix that window and get started cleaning tomorrow. That will make it a lot better the next time you see it."

He looked back over his shoulder, "James, what do you say we let the ladies and babies stay at the boarding house tomorrow and come back to do some cleaning? We can go into Big Spring and check to see when they expect our furniture to arrive on the train. We might have some time to look over the land a little, too."

"I'm with you."

****

After the girls were all asleep that night, Rachael started giggling again. "You know, now I can better appreciate how you felt when that coon jumped on your head," she whispered. So they snickered quietly with their coon memories until they fell asleep.

****

For the next few days Epsy and James worked hard cleaning and working on the houses. Epsy replaced the broken window and built closets in each of the bedrooms. Then he began to look at the cabinets, wondering how best to add to them. "Better get Rachael out here to figure this out," he thought.

When the inside of the house was as good as he could get it without Rachael's approval, he began cleaning weeds from around the house…waist high weeds. He had to get rid of these weeds because they might hide snakes.

About one hundred yards from the house was a small run-down barn and what was left of a chicken house. Clearing around the barn, he found something strange.

Fifteen or twenty feet from the barn he found a six-inch pipe about hip high standing straight up. It had been hidden by the weeds and he hadn't seen it before. Inside the pipe he could see spider webs, but he thought he smelled water.

He found a pebble, dropped it down the pipe, and began to count. About twenty feet down he heard a tiny splash. "Water! This is a water well!" he shouted. There was no one there to hear him, but he shouted it again! "Water! This is a water well!"

Epsy ran to the Touring Car and drove to James' house to tell him the good news.

"Let's look around here and see if you have one too!"

The two of them began to work on the tall weeds energetically. They cleared about one hundred yards in all directions, but found nothing.

They sat dejectedly on the porch to rest. Finally Epsy said, "Well, let's look on the bright side of this. You got the nicer house, and I got the water well. It will be a lot easier for you to haul water from my house than having to haul it from town."

"You are right there. We were not expecting a water well anyway. It just would have been like opening a birthday present if we could have found one."

"Let's go into town and tell the girls. We can talk about this over supper tonight."

****

"Rachael, I can buy an Aero Motor windmill pump. I think I'd rather hire someone who really knows how to build a windmill tower. One I'd build might not withstand this strong wind and we would lose the motor, too. But with a big overhead water tank, you can have running water in the house! What do you think about that?"

Word spread like wildfire that Epsy had found a water well on the land he had leased. Most everyone was thrilled for him. But not Epsy's family. The most he got from them was a 'humph' and a snort.

A second-cousin of Epsy's was actually their closest neighbor, just across the road and East a short ways. "But, don't you see, Bitsy, these underground water veins run from NW to SE. If you would drill a well, yall may be sitting right over the same water vein. The dowser can help you find where it is."

"Humph," she snorted. "I don't want anything to do with a water-witch!" she said and curtly turned and walked away.

****

Before long the windmill and water tank were built; the windmill motor arrived just about the same time as the furniture.

"Did my geese make it okay?" Rachael asked. "The RR man at Temple assured me he would take good care of my geese. And the furniture? I do hope nothing was broken."

The inside of the house was repainted, and Epsy had extended her cabinets and built closets. He had repaired the chicken house and built a strong fence around it. He dug a trench nearly a foot deep and buried the fence wire to keep the critters out. He also put chicken wire across the top of the pen to keep the geese from flying out and hawks from flying in.

The windmill motor was installed and the well was pumping. Epsy was so relieved when he tasted the water. It was good enough to drink. Sometimes, out here you might drill a well and get water that was gypy…too much alkali in it for people or livestock to drink.

When they were all settled in….with running water in the house…Epsy began to toy with the idea of a tractor again. It was soon going to be time to turn the soil and begin preparing to plant.

Midland was the closest place with a Ford dealer who handled tractors, so he went in to talk about ordering a new Fordson tractor. The trip took him all day, but Epsy liked buying new things. He came home with cigars and was all filled with excitement.

He turned off the dirt road and stopped beside the house. He was startled to see Rachael up on a step ladder, reaching as high as she dared, to wrap the water pipe coming out of the water tank.

"What are you doing?" he asked as he walked up and steadied the ladder.

"Myrtle Cox said there must be another cold front coming. Her right knee is swelled almost twice its normal size, and she can hardly walk on it.

"I like having running water in the house. I don't want our water to freeze!" She had cut a blanket into strips which she was spiraling up the water pipe, using binder's twine to hold it in place.

"Well, if Myrtle Cox says it is going to get colder, I had better help you," he said. I'll climb up the windmill tower and see if I can reach the pipe. Maybe you can hand your strips off to me and I can wrap it up to the top."

And it worked! Epsy was hanging onto the windmill ladder with one leg and reaching as far as he could. Rachael was standing on her tiptoes higher than she liked to be on a step ladder; but they were able to reach each other.

Satisfied that her running water would not freeze, Rachael went back into the house; but Epsy went to the barn and began rummaging through things that had been left there.

Soon he showed up at the kitchen door. "Rachael, if you will help me, we will wrap these toe sacks over the blanket. Then I will grease them with this axel grease that I found. If there is rain or snow with that cold spell, this will keep them dry."

****

Supper was slim that night since Rachael had been working outside all afternoon. She had enough canned vegetables from her garden in Rising Star to put a good meal together, but not her usual fare.

"So tell me about your day in town," she said after they sat down to eat. So much had happened since he got home, Epsy had forgotten to tell her his exciting news. Now he was filled with excitement again. "I bought a tractor! Just wait till you see it!

"It is an experimental model Mr. Ford is making. He calls it an Automobile-Plow. Great big iron wheels," he held his hand up to show her they were as tall as his head and as wide as both arms could reach, "with cleats that will hold in this sandy soil. It has a two-cylinder engine that will out-pull sixteen horses, and a spring-seat shaped to fit your bottom!" He bounced up and down in his chair, demonstrating riding on the tractor.

"And I can just sit up there and ride instead of walking behind a team all day! I paid $750 for it. They had to order it; but it should be here in about two weeks. Then we will be farmers!"

Epsy was thrilled with this, and he expected her to share in his enthusiasm. Instead she sat looking at him with a quizzical look on her face, and asked, "Epsy, what is a cylinder?"

He reared back in his chair and slapped his leg. He was instantly racked with laughter, hard to breathe laughter, and it took several minutes for him to get control of it.

Finally he thought he could explain it to her. "Pretend the top of this table is the top of the engine," and he used his hands to measure out the approximate size. He placed two tea glasses a couple of inches apart.

"Pretend these are holes in the top of the engine. Now you have to understand that this engine is built out of a block of iron, with those holes cut through it." Again he used his hands to indicate the size of the block of iron.

"Those holes are called cylinders because they hold the pistons in place as they slide up and down. Now from underneath there are two pistons that push up through the cylinders, one at a time," and he used his fists to indicate the action of the pistons.

"Each time this piston comes up to the top, a little bit of gas is squirted in there and a spark ignites it. That forces the piston back down and the other one comes up.

"Then it squirts a little bit of gas and the spark ignites it and pushes that piston down so that the first one comes back up." He did it slowly several times; then he made the action continuous.

"The pistons pushing up and down are what make the wheels turn round and round.

"Can you kind of understand what I'm talking about?"

He had been doing such a good job with his demonstration that she actually did sort of understand. She nodded slowly as she thought about it. "And it can out-pull a sixteen horse hitch?" she asked quietly as she shook her head slowly and tried to imagine a sixteen horse hitch. She had seen her father's wagons with a six mule hitch, and once in a while eight. But sixteen?

****

Epsy soon ran out of work to do around the house and went over to help James mend harness, sharpen his plow and such, so Rachael and the girls went along to visit with Jewel.

On the way home Rachael said, "Epsy, you really should help James put chicken wire across the top of their chicken yard. Chicken hawks are bad enough, but when it gets warm enough for Jewel's young geese to want to come out of the chicken house, they will be able to fly over the fence. And it's too cold to trim their wings yet.

"This is their first experience with geese. I don't think they know these things. Yall could work on that tomorrow or the next day. I have some sewing to do."

*****

Epsy received a telegram that his tractor would be delivered February 20th. It was coming by rail, and the train would make an unscheduled stop in Coahoma at approximately 12:30PM to unload it.

Usually the train went straight through Coahoma and stopped at the Big Spring Station. However, there was the question of how to deliver the tractor back to Coahoma. Couldn't drive it down the road with those cleated wheels. Couldn't find anything large enough to haul a tractor. And after all Epsy had ordered the works: a two row plow with planter and harrow.

So the dealer had arranged for the train to make an unscheduled stop on the seldom-used Coahoma side railing just long enough to unload this one shipment.

Normally, this side railing was used only to safely move a freight train off the tracks for a faster moving passenger train to pass it.

Epsy and James had their heads together constantly for the next few days, planning how best to get the tractor and implements from the RR siding in Coahoma to Epsy's farm.

Best calculations called for two wagons. Epsy would drive the tractor down the bar-ditch, and James and John Cox would haul the implements in their wagons.

They left home about 9:30 that morning. The trip to town would take an hour at most, but this would be a Red-Letter Day! Everyone knew the tractor was being delivered around noon and many people had never seen the train stop in Coahoma. Few had even seen pictures of a tractor! The town would be full of people today, all right, even though it was in the middle of the week.

Yes siree! They would need time to talk to a lot of men this day!

Jewel rode with James to pick up Epsy, and she would spend the day with Rachael. Even though the women and children of other families would be there, they were sight-seers. Rachael and Jewel's husbands had work to do and did not need the distraction of looking out for their women.

Rachael and Jewel cooked a large meal and invited Myrtle Cox to join them around suppertime. They knew the men would be as excited as kids with a new toy. It would take a lot of figuring and conversation once they were home.

They enjoyed a leisurely day of discussing recipes and plans for their flower gardens, cooking and watching the children Rachael gave instructions on how to trim goose wings, but they couldn't help watching for the first glimpse of their husbands coming up the road.

At last they saw them coming. Epsy was in the lead...in the bar-ditch, but in the lead. The horses did not want to get too close to such a loud and strange noise. It made a continuing popping sound as it slowly crawled toward the house; about every third or fourth pop was quite a bit louder than the rest. They could see the hinged flap on the top of the exhaust pipe merrily flipping up and down, "With each stroke of the piston," Rachael thought to herself with a tiny smirk of satisfaction on her face.

Rachael and Jewel stood beside the house with the children lined up between them, just waiting for the new tractor to turn in the drive. The girls giggled and began to jump up and down, clapping their hands. Myrtle was smiling on the porch steps with her bad leg propped up.

Epsy stopped the tractor right beside the house for everyone to admire. James and John Cox pulled in from around the barn and kept the horses a little ways from the tractor. They soon joined the little group to admire the tractor and tell stories about the day in town.

Finally, Epsy moved the tractor out to where the field started and turned off the engine. With the sudden quiet everyone realized they were still shouting, and they began to laugh at themselves.

James brought his team up close to the house and shouted, "Epsy, where do you want this unloaded?"

"Just unload it here in the backyard for now. This will take some planning."

The three men began to unload a Maytag washing machine, with a wringer that could rotate to wring clothes between three rinse tubs. There was a framework to hold the three square galvanized tubs up next to the washer so that it made one big square. And there was a small kerosene engine mounted underneath the washer itself to make the dasher oscillate, so that it swished the clothes back and forth.

Rachael's eyes got big and her mouth dropped open a little. Then a sparkle ran through her eyes, and a big smile spread across her face.

Jewel started giggling and clapping her hands. She patted Rachael on the shoulder and said, "What do you think? And did you notice the square rinse tubs? One to rinse out the soapy water, a second rinse to see that all the soap is gone, and one for the bluing-water to keep the whites from getting dingy!" Jewel touched each tub as she gave their designation. She was so happy for her friend.

Suddenly Rachael realized this was for her. Evidently everyone had known but her. She covered her mouth in astonishment, and she began to tear up. "Oh, Epsy. Oh, Epsy," was all she could say.

"I can't believe you have done this for me," she said finally.

Epsy put his arms around her, gave her just a little squeeze, even in front of all these people, and said, "Rachael, I ain't no kind of man if I bought myself a new tractor, and you still washing clothes on a rub board."

Chapter Nineteen
Cotton Farmers

So Epsy and James enjoyed farming, enjoyed neighboring. When one of them had a particularly hard job to do, the other gladly pitched in to help. They planted at the same time, so both were free to fish awhile before it was time to plow between rows to keep down the weeds.

They enjoyed fishing in the occasional, deeper pools of the dry creeks that ran through West Texas. Not that they caught many fish; mostly relaxing and just talking, letting the conversation drift from one subject to another. Sometimes, just helping a friend see another way to look at a situation before it becomes a problem. There was plenty to talk about. But sometimes there were long periods of silence, just thinking.

It was fun, and really miraculous, watching the cotton grow. The plants break through the crust on the top of the soil as tiny sprouts, which begin to make leaves. Then slowly they grow to about knee high. Here and there they begin to bloom until every plant is covered in the ivory-colored blossoms. Then one by one the blossoms fall off, exposing little green balls that begin to grow fatter and fatter until they can stretch no more; but the cotton inside of them is still growing. When they pop open you can see the snow white cotton begin to bulge out of the bolls. Finally, what had once been a sea of green plants is now a sea of pure white cotton.

Now was the time for them to begin thinking about picking this year's crop, and would they be able to find good hands to pick for them.

One afternoon in late summer Epsy came home from such a day of fishing with James and found Rachael had fixed an unusually festive meal.

"Are we having company for supper tonight?" he asked as he washed up for supper.

"No, but I do have some news for you."

He had sat down at his place at the table, but instead of placing a pan of biscuits in front of him to begin buttering; she swung around him and pertly sat down in his lap. She just sat there with her arms around his neck and smiled at him.

"What is the surprise?" he asked.

"The cow has gone dry," she said with a little toggle of her head...still the cute little smile on her face.

"What cow has gone dry? Rachael, we don't have a cow."

"Well, we may need to buy one, with four kids drinking milk the way they do."

"Four?" Then he caught on to her joke, her surprise. "Are you sure? When will it be due?"

"Sometime in June, I think."

"I'm going to be a papa again! Can you beat that? This will be our first summer baby! Are you feeling all right?"

"Just fine. Maybe this time we will get our boy!" she said, smiling at him. She jumped up and took the biscuits from the oven; then began setting food on the table.

"Girls, Papa is buttering biscuits! Better get your hands and faces washed." She put Neva in the highchair then washed her face and hands with a wet cloth.

That night Epsy dried and put away the dishes for Rachael. There was a sweet feeling of peace and expectancy between them.

****

Miraculously, the pickers showed up just at the right time. They began their work in South Texas, where the cotton matured earliest and worked their way north. They began in whatever field was ready to pick first, then moved to the next field that was ready.

At this time of year, farmers talk to the Lord regularly about not letting it rain, or worse sleet, while the cotton is still in the bolls. This degrades the quality of the cotton, causing it to bring a lower price at the gin.

When they came to Epsy's field first, Epsy and James hung a cotton sack across their shoulders and picked right along with the rest of them. As soon as Epsy's field was finished, they picked together in James' field.

The weather held for both of them to get their cotton in, but it was beginning to get cold and a bit cloudy by the time the pickers got ready for John Cox's field. John was getting a little old to pick cotton all day, so Epsy and James picked for him, too.

It was hard work staying bent over all day long, pulling a long, white canvas sack with a strap across your chest and one shoulder. A full sack will weigh 100 lbs. to 110 lbs.

Just as bad is the fact that the cotton bolls are dry now, and have sharp ends where the boll split open. Your aim has to be good or you come home with cut and sore fingers that can easily get infected if you don't take care of them.

Pickers are paid ten cents a pound. If the cotton is good, a strong man who is a good picker can pick about four sacks a day. Maybe the wife can pick one sack a day. Each of the children that are big enough are also given a cotton sack. Little kids have their own cotton sack made out of a toe sack. The whole family works in the fields.

Good money for itinerate people who follow the harvest. As the pickers migrate north, the gins furnish houses for them...bare minimum, but a house, none the less. They live solemn lives with only the bare necessities while they are working a harvest. But the money has to last them through the rest of the year.

Sometimes around here the cotton harvest is not completely over until Christmas. Those farmers who wait too late to plant are the last to have their cotton in. Their cotton has endured wind and damp weather longer. They have missed the Fair to Midland price range that makes a profit for a farmer. Their crop comes in at the Poor price range, which means they just break even for the year.

Epsy's experience in ginning had taught him the importance of testing the soil often to know the first instant the ground is warm enough for the seed to germinate. That diligence made a big difference in the quality of the cotton when it was ready to be picked.

****

This winter came in just as autumn had hinted, wet and cold. There was more sleet and ice than last year. It even snowed once deep enough to have a snowball fight and make snow ice cream. But mostly it was bitter cold and damp.

At a lady's social at the community church, Rachael heard that Epsy's cousin, Bitsy, and all of her kids were down with the croup…Epsy's cousin, Bitsy, who lived within a stone's throw of them and had not once raised her hand to wave.

Rachael could imagine what it would be like if all her girls were sick with the croup, and she had it too. With little ones there was always the chance of them choking to death during the night. Rachael wondered if Bitsy knew to put a cool damp cloth across the throat to stop the choking.

Well, Rachael had her hands full taking care of her own little ones; she could not even offer to go over and stay so that Bitsy could get some rest. But she could make a big pot of chicken soup!

She kept a piece of strong wire hanging on the chicken yard fence; she pinched it again to make sure the hook in the end of it was tight enough to hold.

Inside the chicken house she surveyed the chicken population. That old red rooster was several years old already, but he still kept the hens serviced and kept the young roosters in line. These young roosters really were intended for fried chicken, but they were getting old enough they were chasing the hens, now. "We could pick out the best to save for a rooster," she thought. "Sorry, old guy, it's time to let the young ones take the lead." And she hooked the leg of the old rooster and drug him outside of the chicken house.

Her hands were quick. She had his neck wrung and was putting away the wire hook before the noise inside the chicken house began to quiet down. She went to the burning pit, had the feathers plucked, and the rooster dressed in record time.

She was back inside the house before the girls even missed her, and she busied herself making chicken soup. You have to put some garlic and basil in it. That just does something special to chicken soup.

Before it was time to start her own supper, she had the chicken soup ready. She put Sister in charge of the little ones. She tied on her head scarf and put on coat and gloves. With a pot holder in each hand, Rachael proceeded to walk the two hundred yards or so to Bitsy's house with the hot, heavy pot of soup.

She stepped up on the porch and set down the pot of hot soup so she could knock. Barely had she begun to knock when the door opened. Rachael had the feeling that she had been watched the whole time she was walking.

She picked up the pot of soup and extended her arms slightly, "I heard that you have sick children and..."

The screen door was opened quickly, the pot snatched from her hands and the door slammed in her face. It happened so fast it made Rachael blink. She really was not sure who the person was who took the soup!

She stood there a few minutes waiting for the person to empty her pot and hand it back to her. But it was cold and the wind was howling! Five minutes was as long as Rachael wanted to wait outside!

Her walk home was definitely faster without the heavy pot of soup! She fairly ran!

****

"And, Epsy, she kept my pot and pot holders!"

"It is not really out of character," he said, sadly shaking his head. "This is surely a new twist on the situation, though. If Bitsy can't say that it was her idea or that she was right all along, in her mind it never happened.

"Don't worry about the pot; I'll just buy you a new one next time we go to town."

He was quiet for a minute, staring at the floor. "Rachael, that was really a nice thing you did."

****

The next trip to town for groceries had the prospect of being a fun day. Besides refilling her cabinets, Rachael would allow herself to look for a new pot. She did not spend money frivolously.

While she was studying the pans that were on display, Epsy had taken the girls off to another part of the general store to keep them occupied.

She finally made her decision and carried the new pot up to the counter. There she found each girl was holding a roll of something in her hand.

They were giggling and seemed to be sucking on something that made their mouths juicy. Epsy had something in his mouth, too. They were smacking! And it smelled delicious! They were all smiling at her as she walked up.

Rachael was having fun just watching the expressions of delight on her children's faces, but she was puzzled. "What do yall have?" she finally asked.

Epsy handed her a roll of candy mints. One end had a tiny red thread packed among the folds of waxed paper which held the end sealed. She pulled the thread, and it quickly circled the end of the roll, cutting off the waxed paper.

Instantly, she knew! It was spearmint! She put one in her mouth and immediately her mouth began to water, slowly melting the sugary mint. She, too, had to smack as she moved it around in her mouth.

"What is the hole in the middle for?" she asked.

"Don't know," Epsy ventured, "but look on the package. They are called 'Life Savers', so I guess that is why the hole is in the middle. So they will look like life savers on a boat." He smacked again as he rolled his mint to a different part of his mouth.

"See they are rolled in tin foil to keep them fresh. The roll with the blue wrapper is peppermint, and the one with the green wrapper is spearmint."

Each of the girls held up their roll of Life Savers; each had chosen a different flavor. The orange colored wrapper was for orange flavor; red, for cherry; yellow for pineapple. They pointed to the candy display; there was also green, for lime flavor, brown, for root beer; white, for cocoanut, and one roll had a mixture of all the flavors!

"I knew you would want spearmint." He smiled at her, that lingering little smile that made her feel so special.

"Now, remember girls," he cautioned, "you can suck these down your throat if you are not careful. Then I would have to turn you upside down and shake it out."

The girls all giggled. They loved it when their papa played with them.

****

Winter seemed to pass very slowly because the weather was too bad to get outside and do anything that wasn't absolutely necessary. They didn't even see James and Jewel very often, but Epsy was pretty good at keeping the girls entertained when they were all cooped up in the house.

"I wish there were some way of keeping this baby entertained," Rachael thought.

"This is going to be another active child," she called to Epsy from the kitchen. "It wants to be on the move already."

Epsy was listening to a news cast on the radio. The only thing that broke the tedium was the news of German aggression in Europe. The United States, under President Wilson, was trying to stay neutral. Europe was so far away that it was not too hard to think this would not affect us.

But it did affect us! And everybody knew it when a German submarine sank the Lusitania, a British luxury liner, in 1915. There were 128 Americans aboard. By 1916 German submarines, called U-Boats, began sinking US merchant ships that were carrying supplies to Britain.

All the European countries seemed to be folding under the treachery of the German political machine and the severity of the German warfare. It seemed that only Great Britain was holding out against them. Americans began to consider, "If England falls, what is next? With that much power, would an ocean stop them? Would we be next?"

****

Slowly the overcast, bitter cold faded into cloudy and cold, then cloudy and cool, but the rain held off.

"Really, I think it is just as well," Epsy told James. "As much wet weather as we had this winter, if it came a big rain right now, we would just have to wait for the mud to dry up.

"That moisture we got during the winter was slow and had time to sink in. As soon as the soil warms up, I think we will be set for a bumper crop this year."

And James was ready to get out and busy. He hadn't even had children to play with all winter. "If we have to play cards or dominoes much longer, just the two of us, we are going to go crazy."

Finally, they decided that the soil was warm enough to plant, and the men could get outside and work. The girls could play outside with a sweater on; it really was a rest for Rachael just to have the house quiet.

When the weather warmed enough to be really pleasant outside, it seemed like the mosquitoes were swarming everywhere. Because of all the moisture they had during the winter, mosquitoes found stagnant water to lay their eggs everywhere…in an old tire leaning against the barn, the watering can for Rachael's flowers, inside the seed cans on the planter. They found jillions of places still holding moisture. Rachael made a mixture of olive oil, water and citronella, and she kept it by the back door. Whenever anyone was going outside, they were careful to put some on them.

Jewel came over to spend the afternoon, and her first question was, "How do you make that oil that Epsy uses to keep away mosquitoes? James is just covered in bites."

Rachael told her the general amounts to mix. She was looking for a bottle that was empty to mix some for Jewel to take home.

Jewel smiled shyly and pulled a small bottle from her pocket. "I was hoping you would mix some for me to take home today. In fact, I may just take it out to where James is working."

It was good to get to visit with Jewel again. Rachael had missed her very much during the winter.

*****

It seemed that the early part of the summer passed fast. They were back to their Friday night suppers and dominoes again. Rachael was again making baby clothes, and the girls were growing like weeds. Plus, this fall would be Bessie's first year in school. Rachael made her more dresses than usual. Starting school was a very special occasion.

Before the new baby was due in June, Rachael had found a doctor that she liked in Coahoma. The town was big enough now that you had a choice of two doctors, one old and one young.

Rachael chose the young one, Dr. Young. She liked his personality, and he seemed to listen to her closely when she tried to ask him about something. Besides he liked kids. That is very important when you have a growing family. Rachael had even invited him and his wife to supper once. It was good for the girls to get to know him, trust him; and it helped Rachael see what kind of man he really was.

Epsy's work was pretty light at this time of the year, so he hung around the house more than usual. Rachael and Jewel were experienced at this baby business; they had their plans laid out. Myrtle Cox volunteered to help Rachael and the doctor. It seemed as if everything was set.

While Epsy was outside building a cow lot onto the side of the barn, Rachael stepped to the back door and called, "Epsy, it's time!"

"Time for what?"

"Time for the doctor."

He came running. "Do you mean, time to go get him right now?"

"Yes, I think this one is coming fast. Now let's get the girls' night clothes and a clean dress ready. You can take them to Jewel's house, pick up Myrtle and bring her here. Then go get the doctor as quickly as you can."

As Epsy was helping Myrtle up the steps, Rachael called through the screen door, "Remind him about the Vaseline!"

****

Epsy knew his part well, he kept the fire going in the stove: water heating, and coffee made. When he heard the baby cry, he ran to the door of the bedroom. "Is it a boy or a girl?" he asked.

"Another little girl, and she has black hair just like yours," Dr. Young smiled. "Man, you know what you are doing, don't you?"

Myrtle had the baby wrapped in a soft blanket, and she handed her to Epsy. He smiled happily at the newest in his growing brood of girls.

"I think she is going to have my skin tone, too," he said. "Rachael, I was pretty sure you were carrying another girl, and I have been thinking of names. I know what I want to name her."

"Well, it's your turn, Epsy. Tell us her name," Rachael said.

"Jeta Lee!" he said smiling, and nodding. "I heard that name a few months ago and liked it because it was different. She sure looks like she could be a Jeta Lee, doesn't she?"

"She sure is different. All the rest of the girls look like me. She looks just like you, Epsy. Jeta Lee it is!"

Sister and Corrine were both a lot of help with this new baby, but when school started and Bessie was away at school, Corrine got to be the big sister! She took over the responsibility of keeping Neva safe and 'in line'.

Chapter Twenty
Good Bye, James & Jewel

On the first day of school for Bessie, Epsy drove the whole family to the school. They greeted the teacher, Mrs. Smith, whom Rachael and Bessie already knew through the community church. Bessie met the older kids from their area that would be walking past their house to school. Yes, they would stop by for Bessie to walk with them every morning.

And Bessie loved school! Rachael had already been teaching her the numbers and letters, so she found school to be easy. Besides several in her class were not the oldest in their family, and she got to mother them.

Bessie often read to her little sisters in the evening, pretending that she was the teacher and they were her class.

*****

Epsy was right when he predicted a bumper crop of cotton this year. The soil was just right, and he and James planted earlier than most everyone. Theirs was the first to bloom, first to open the bolls, and first to be picked. They made a Good grade of cotton in a bumper year.

*****

When James and Jewel came over for supper one night, James wanted to go outside and smoke. He really wanted to talk.

"Man, have you been listening to the news lately? We are headed for war just as sure as you are born. If we don't get in on this soon and help England while they are still standing, we are going to be fighting them by ourselves…over here! And at the rate they are going it won't be much longer, either.

"I've been thinking about this a lot. If the United States gets into it, I'm going to have to go fight, Epsy."

"I don't think we have anything to worry about, James. We are farmers. The government needs us to stay here and keep the nation fed and clothed."

"That will work for you. You have four dependents plus Rachael; I don't know if they count your wife as a dependent or not.

"There is talk about starting a Selective Service system, where they give you credit for how many dependents you have. If you don't have any dependents, you are at the top of the list to be drafted.

"I'm 31 years old, Epsy, and my only dependent is Jewel. I am at the top of that list!"

"Well, James..." Epsy started to say something, but there were just no holes in James' reasoning.

"You know my dad had a heart attack this past summer," James began again.. He seems to be all right for now, but if I go back and take over the family farm, as head of the household, that would give me two more dependents. Plus it just might keep Dad from having another heart attack." He fell silent for a moment.

"If I'm going to do this, I've got to make a quick decision. Dad is growing peanuts now; it will be time for planting soon after we get our crop in."

They sat in silence for a while, thinking about the seriousness of this war possibility, about Jewel and James leaving.

"If we leave yall, it will be just like losing family, Epsy. I feel closer to you than I do to my brothers. And I know Jewel feels the same about Rachael.

"I have been trying not to mention it to Jewel because I don't want her to worry. But I just had to talk this out with someone.

"Can you see the shape I'm in? I'm in a hole that I don't think I can climb out of... Epsy, think about this for a couple of days. See if you can come up with any suggestions."

****

Epsy thought hard about the possibility of losing James and Jewel. But he had to admit that James seemed to have thought this through to a logical conclusion. Epsy could see no other way around it. Going back to Comanche seemed to be his only choice. Plus if he left his dad farming in the summer heat, he probably would have another heart attack.

While the women did the dishes and the men smoked one evening, Epsy confessed, "James, I have been giving a lot of thought to this Selective Service thing. Bad as it will be to lose you and Jewel, I believe you have covered all the angles and thought it through to its logical conclusion. I think you are right about the war; it's coming! And I believe you are right about your dad; you can't just stand by and watch him have another heart attack."

James bit down on his bottom lip and nodded his head. Really his mind had been made up for several days; he was just hoping Epsy could see a different side of it.

****

On a quiet day, while the girls were down for naps, he and Rachael were playing Rummy in the kitchen. "We made one heck of a crop this year, Rachael; I have been thinking about buying a new Tin Lizzy."

She was looking at her cards, and didn't seem to have heard his statement.

"Would you like to go into Big Spring with me to shop for a new automobile? We could ask James and Jewel to go and make it an all-day affair."

"Rummy!" she said and started laying down her cards. "When do you want to go?"

"How about tomorrow? Do you have anything special to do tomorrow?"

"No, nothing that I can't do another day. And, Epsy, can we eat at that little café that has those good hot dogs?"

"That sounds good to me. I'll go over and see if James and Jewel can go tomorrow." He started to get up, but she was shuffling again and looked at him questioningly.

"Well, you have already beaten me, anyway. I'll concede the game."

****

The weather was cold, but not bitter cold and it was dry. The trip into Big Spring was an adventure. The back seat was getting fuller all the time; the two older girls were in the middle, Jewel held Neva on her lap and Rachael held the baby in the front seat. The girls were used to Coahoma, but they seldom got to go to Big Spring so they were excited about everything they saw.

The first place Epsy wanted to go was the Ford house. He drove around the block slowly. They strained to see the two Model-Ts that were on the showroom floor, but on the lot beside it there were two more.

"Which one do you like best, Rachael?" he asked.

"Well, I think that sort of jade green one with the green canvas top is very pretty. See how the canvas top wraps around the side of the back seat? That would help keep the girls warm. And I wouldn't have to worry about one of them falling out!"

On the next circle around the block, Epsy pulled into the two-pump gas station on the corner. The drive way sat across the corner, so that you drove in from Aylford St. and drove out on Third St. Epsy went inside to get a mechanic to come out and pump some gas for them.

The gas pump looked like a tall cylinder made of thin metal, with a big glass bubble on the top. On one side of the gas pump, about waist high, a long pump-handle stuck straight up. On the other side was a rubber hose with a nozzle on the end. The nozzle was hung on a hook on the side of the gas pump.

The man asked Epsy how much gas he wanted. Epsy said about two or three gallons, so the man began pumping the handle back and forth. "Ohhh," the girls drew in their breath in astonishment as they began to see the golden gasoline spurting up in the middle of the glass bubble. It was such fun to watch it spurt up each time the man pumped!

When the gas in the bubble reached a mark that said "3 Gals", the man stopped pumping. He lifted the nozzle from its hook, took the cap off the gas tank on the car and inserted the nozzle. The girls watched in amazement as the gasoline in the glass bubble slowly drained out and then was gone. The girls were seeing such amazing things. They stood with their heads leaning outside, so they would not miss a bit of this activity. And as the gasoline poured into the gas tank, they suddenly realized that the smell of the fumes was making them dizzy!

"That will be 27¢, sir," and the mechanic held out his hand.

Epsy fished in his pocket and brought out a handful of change. He picked out a quarter and two pennies, placed them in the man's hand, and touched the brim of his hat as he nodded his head in thanks.

They drove the rest of the way around to the Ford house. "Okay, we will go in now. When we get inside, Rachael, you and Jewel take the girls and look at all the automobiles they have. But only look at that green one very quickly, then move on. James and I will talk to the salesman about engines and gears.

As directed, Rachael and Jewel and the girls, inspected the two Model-Ts on the showroom floor from a woman's perspective; they ran their hands over the slick leather seats, pushed down on the tufted cushioning, stepped up on the running board and sat down. But not behind the steering wheel! Then they wandered outside to look at the two on the lot.

It didn't take long to look at the two outside because of the cold, so again they looked at the ones on the showroom floor. They even got inside and sat in the red and black one to talk while they waited.

While they were sitting there, the salesman could overhear Rachael say, "Yes, it is very pretty, but it is probably too expensive."

The salesman was thinking, "This is going to be a hard sell. His friend has asked some pretty detailed questions about the engine. Now the wife is talking expensive."

"Well, what is the difference in the price of this red and black one and the green one?" Epsy asked.

The salesman took a deep breath and sort of blew it out his nose fast. "About $100," he said, honestly thinking it would cost him a sale.

"Okay, I'll take the green one," Epsy said. "Will you take a check on the First State Bank here in Big Spring?"

The salesman looked at him for an instant as if it had not soaked in yet. "Well...did you want to talk about trading in the one you are driving?"

"No, that is the reason I brought along my friend. He will drive it home."

"Well, yes. Of course, we will have to check with the bank for a check that size."

"I understand, Epsy said.." We are going to go eat and look around town some. Do you think about 2:00 o'clock would be enough time?"

"That will be plenty of time, Mr. Hale."

"Remember, I want the gas tank full," Epsy said with a smile and a nod. Then James got the door, and Epsy helped escort the girls outside.

****

"Jewel, I hope yall like hot dogs. I just love them, and there is a little café just down the street from the bank that really makes good ones, lots of chili and onions!"

Once they were inside the café and seated, James had the opportunity to ask Epsy, "Why didn't you talk to him about trading in the one you are driving now?"

Epsy had been waiting for just such an opening. "Because I want you to have it," he said with a big smile, looking James right in the eyes.
The look on James' face changed from concern to dismay. "I..I don't understand."

"You are the reason this automobile is running, James. You can do things with it that I can't do. And I haven't found a way to repay you, so I want you to have it."

****

Driving home was an adventure for both couples. Rachael got the older girls settled in the back seat of the new jade green Model-T; Bessie on one side, Corrine on the other, and Neva in the middle. "See these windows here on the side? You can look out of them or out the front, but you must stay seated. Do not get up on your knees, and do not stand up.

Okay?" She had that stern motherly look in her eyes that warned them they had better not forget. "Yes, Mama," Bessie answered for everyone. Epsy handed her the baby when she was seated, and they were off.

James and Jewel were still in disbelief as they drove along behind the new 'Tin Lizzie' as Epsy liked to call it.

They would look at each other and smile a sheepish smile, then shake their heads, but it was hard to find words to say. Finally, Jewel said, "Where did God find friends like this for us?"

****

When Epsy pulled into his driveway, James stopped along the side of the road. Jewel found Rachael inside dealing with some very tired little girls. Jewel didn't say much; just hugged Rachael extra hard, shook her head, and said a heartfelt 'Thank you'. Then she went back to their new, used Model-T with tears in her eyes.

James walked up beside Epsy as he was walking around the new T-Model checking this, admiring that. "Epsy, I don't know how to begin to repay you."

"I consider it prepaid by all the times you have worked on it for me. It would have cost me a pretty penny, if I could have found someone to work on it." Epsy held out his hand to shake, and said, "Fair enough?"

"Fair enough." They shook hands; he slapped Epsy on the shoulder and walked slowly out to Jewel and their new Model-T.

*****

The next week supper was at James and Jewel's house, James had had time to talk to his dad and mom about his plan. His folks were overjoyed and relieved to have them come back to the family farm. But Rachael could tell that Jewel had been crying.

When they were alone in the kitchen, Rachael asked what was the matter, and could she help? Between sobs, it took a long time for Jewel to explain all about the war that was coming, the Selective Service system, no dependents, James' father's heart attack, the peanuts. But the bottom line was, "We have to move back to Comanche!" then she buried her face in her hands and wept.

And Rachael wept, too; her heart was breaking to lose such a dear and trusted friend. We will say we will visit, and they will say they will come back often. But she knew how lives change and you can't hold onto the past. Moving two hundred miles away was almost like putting an ocean between them.

Supper and dominoes were very somber that night. They put the girls to bed in Jewel's spare bedroom and played dominoes much later than they usually did. Neither couple wanted to let it end because they knew, in all likelihood this would be their last evening together.

****

For the next few days Epsy helped James get things sorted, what he needed to take and what he needed to sell. Would it be better to take his farming equipment, or sell it? With two men and two teams, he and his dad could have their plowing and planting done in record time.

His dad probably would not want to stop working altogether right off. He could work when he wanted to and take a break when the weather got hot. That might be the best way to handle James' moving in and taking over.

Since the Central Texas Railroad runs right through Comanche County, rail was by far the best way of moving. Should he bother with shipping the horses by rail or sell these here and buy more there?

"If you sell here just after cotton harvest, you will have to take a low price for good horses," Epsy offered. "If you buy there right at the beginning of peanut planting, you will pay a high price for whatever you can find. If you ship them by rail, there is a chance your stuff might get side-railed. You would need someone to ride in that car to see that the horses are fed and watered."

James sent a telegram to his brother, Bob, "Might his fifteen year old son ride up here on the train, and ride with the horses coming back to Comanche?" James would pay for the young man's train fare, and pay him for how many days it took to get the horses there.

It was agreed that the young man could help James with his horses, so James paid for the ticket in Big Spring. Bob would take the boy to board the train in Comanche and the ticket would be waiting for him. Telegraph lines work wonders, don't they?

Now the question was, how much space would it take to ship furniture, farm implements, two horses and two mules? A whole boxcar? Half a boxcar? What was the rate? Per item? Per square foot?

James and Epsy made several trips to the Big Spring station, trying to get an authoritative answer to these questions. They spent hours there trying to see the right man who could write a bill of lading.

When they finally did find the right man, Epsy found himself face to face with Rachael's father!

This was one of the better moments in Jeff Dodd's life. He thought he saw a chance to impress his daughter, and he did help James with his freight. Jeff said he would see that it was paired with something that would go straight through to Comanche, and he would have the conductor check on the boy from time to time to make sure he was safe.

Within the week, arrangements were made and the heavy things had been hauled to the freight yard. Rachael cooked supper for them and sent biscuits and boiled eggs home with them for breakfast. The last things loaded on the wagon were their bedding and her fragile things like dishes and lamps.

And suddenly they were gone!

****

Rachael was sad and heavy hearted for the next week or so, but she had no more tears to cry. This is the second time she had lost such a dear friend suddenly, and oh, what a hollow spot that left in her heart. At least she got to say 'good-bye' to Jewel.

Oh, how happy she was when she got the first letter from Jewel telling her about the trip to Comanche, and "true to his word, Mr. Dodd got our furniture and horses here in very good time".

"My father?" This was the first Rachael knew that her father had anything to do with their move! Oh, well, at least he did something good this time.

Rachael and Jewel wrote letters at least once a month. Jewel needed to hear about all that the girls were doing. They had filled such a lonely spot in her heart.

****

One evening late in January, Epsy got up from listening to the news on the radio and walked into the kitchen. "Did you hear that the British intercepted a message from Germany to Mexico trying to get them to enter the war against us if we side with England? They are calling it the Zimmerman Telegram. The Germans promised to give Texas, New Mexico, and Arizona back to Mexico. That is all the territory we won from Mexico in the Mexican-American War 70 years ago! That's how sure of themselves they are!

"You can sure see that James knew what he was talking about. It won't be long now before we are in this war. And that will make it world-wide. There's no two ways about it; James made a good move going back to his family farm!"

He was quiet for a moment, thinking about James and Jewel.

"We ought to get a good price for our crops this year because the government will be stock-piling supplies."

On April 6, 1917 the United States Congress declared war on Germany! And when they passed the Selective Service Act, all men under the age of 45 had to register for the draft. Epsy went to the Post Office in Big Spring and found the Draft Board office to register.

"Rachael, the man asked me my age, and I told him 32. He asked me how many dependents I had, and I told him, 'My wife and four daughters.' He asked, 'and how many sons?' I told him, 'None.' He smarted off, 'Well, you are not even producing any fighters!' I told him, 'Oh, I beg to differ with you. I don't think that a smart man would try to push my daughters around once they get grown!'

"He thought he was insulting me, Rachael, but I'm proud of my daughters!"

****

When the war news on the radio finally said that Germany had agreed to an armistice, people drove to town in whatever they had that would move. They drove up and down the streets cheering and yelling. It was a great celebration!

Epsy just shook his head slightly and clucked under his breath. He just did not believe the German political regime had given up on their goal of world domination. Just did not believe it!

Sure enough the fighting started up again! The German war machinery had to be completely broken beyond repair before they finally quit fighting. Then it was time to celebrate!

****

One evening when Epsy came home, Rachael was in an especially good mood, "Want to be a papa again?" She didn't let him answer that. "Well, you are!" she smiled at him. "This is going to be five, Epsy. Whatever will we do? Will it be another girl or a boy this time?"

"I've given up on having a boy. We might as well start picking out names for a girl. When is it due?"

"The middle of March. Epsy, I want to name her Jewel. What would go pretty with Jewel? Well, we have plenty of time to think about that. The biscuits are just about ready."

****

While Rachael cooked supper one evening, Jetty, who was toddling everywhere, plopped down at the sewing machine and began pushing with her hands to make the foot treadle go up and down. Rachael made sure the belt was out of the grooves; then she let Jetty entertain herself with the sewing machine.

Jetty giggled a few times and caught Neva's attention. Neva watched for a while then decided that she wanted to join the fun. She sat down beside Jetty, and for a while they pushed the treadle together. Slowly, Neva began to elbow Jetty aside, so she could have a turn all by herself. Jetty did not give in so easily and she began to cry. When Neva finally got control of the treadle, she really began to make it whir while Jetty cried.

Rachael stepped into the living room. "Neva, you must get up from there and let Jetty play."

Neva turned her head to ask, "But, why can she play with it and I can't?"

"Because your fingers are bigger than hers, and…" Rachael began. She heard the thump when Neva's fingers got caught underneath the treadle, and Neva began to scream.

Rachael ran to pick her up and love her. "Darling, that is exactly why you can't play with it." She kissed the throbbing fingers. "Your fingers are bigger than Jetty's. Hers won't get caught under the treadle, but yours will. When you were two years old, I let you play on the sewing machine, but you are going on four and getting to be a big girl."

Neva was still cradling her hurt fingers with her other hand and snubbing. "It makes a feller's fingers smart, doesn't it, darling? I'll chip a piece of ice for you to hold on them." And Mama kissed them again.

"Come into the kitchen and talk to me while I finish supper. Would you like to help me make a chocolate pudding for supper?"

Chapter Twenty One
The Golden Wedding Ring

Since it was planting time, the morning milking chores had fallen to Rachael. She was getting pretty big with the baby when she went out to milk this particular spring morning. The cow was very gentle and even acted like she liked being petted. She was easy to milk; it was just squatting down to sit on that three legged stool that bothered Rachael.

She had finished milking and set the bucket of milk up on the little shelf Epsy had built for her. She just had to set the milk bucket down before she turned the calf in with the cow. As she turned around, she saw something shining in the loose dirt and manure of the cow lot. She slowly bent over and reached for it. It was a golden wedding band...a wide, golden wedding band. And it just fit her finger! She quickly put it in her pocket and opened the gate to let the calf in.

She took the milk inside and strained it. She placed it in the ice box, right up next to the block of ice so it would cool quickly. She went back outside to separate the cow and calf and throw a small block of hay for each of them.

Back in the kitchen, she poured herself a cup of coffee and sat down at the table. She slowly, questioningly reached inside her pocket and felt for the ring as if it might not really be there. But it was! A beautiful, wide, golden wedding band. She had found it! And there was no way of knowing who might have lost it!

She washed it with soap and water and dried it carefully, polishing it a little with the towel. She found a small matchbox to put it in and set it on the back of the counter until Epsy got home that evening. She could hardly find enough things to fill up the day, for thinking of the ring.

When Epsy got home and had played with the girls for a few minutes, it was her turn for his attention. He walked up behind her while she stirred something at the stove and said, "Ummm. What are we having for supper tonight?"

"Epsy, sit down. I want to show you something." She set the pan to the back of the stove. She took the box from the cabinet and sat down at her place at the table. He sat down and waited...and waited...and waited.

She placed the little box on her table and rubbed her finger down the length of the box. She slowly outlined the diamond-design on the box top. Every time she thought she had the right words in her mind and started to speak, she decided against it and shook her head slightly. She turned the box around and bit the side of her bottom lip. She nodded her head; then shook it again. This was very hard!

Finally, Epsy said, "What is in the box, Rachael?"

She looked down at the small, red matchbox with the blue diamond on top. She pushed one end so that the box slid out of its covering and held it up for him to see.

"A golden wedding band," she said quietly, her voice hinting of awe.

He took the ring from the box and looked all around it. "Where did it come from?" he asked.

"The cow lot... I have no idea who lost it... But it fits me! Oh, Epsy, can I keep it?"

A wave of humiliation rushed over him. Seeing how shy she was about keeping something she had found made him realize how much she had wanted a wedding ring.

For a minute he stared at the floor. Since they had run away to get married, he had not had time to plan for a ring for her. He felt just as tightly married to her with or without a ring.

He had no reason to think she would act out of place and make a man think she was not married. Rachael, who was so shy about asking to keep the ring, was not at all slow to let a man know that she was a lady in every aspect of the word. She would put up with no insinuating talk or actions. He had seen times when fire fairly flew from her eyes.

When he finally looked up, he said, "Rachael, if you had it all to do over again, would you marry me?"

"Why, yes, Epsy," she said softly.

He reached across the table and took her left hand. "I would too," he said as he slipped the ring on her finger and smiled that lingering smile that just reached down into her very soul.

Her eyes filled with tears, and she leaned across the corner of the table and kissed him lightly.

****

When Epsy came in from milking, supper was ready so she sat an oblong cake pan of biscuits across his plate. Their family had grown so much that she had to use a bigger pan for biscuits.

"Now, you wash up and then butter; I'll strain the milk. When we finish supper, I think you had better take the girls to Mrs. Smith's house and bring Myrtle back with you. The timing should be about right," she said nodding her head.

Epsy ate in a hurry and gathered up the girl's night clothes. "Yall want to spend the night with Mrs. Smith tonight and play with her cat? Eat up and I'll take you over there."

****

Epsy got Myrtle and Dr. Young, built up the fire in the kitchen stove, heated water, and made coffee, while Rachael did her mothering job as quietly as possible. "She has always been like that," he thought, just will not complain."

Dr. Young stepped out of the bedroom door about the time Epsy heard the baby cry. "It's another little blond haired girl, Epsy. Five girls in a row!"

Epsy went to the bedroom to hold his new daughter.

"Epsy, what will we name her. I want to name her Jewel, but I haven't found the right name to go with it."

"Well, I really liked my mama's mama. She was a very gentle woman, soft spoken. Her name was Laura Bynum. Would it work for you to make Jewel her middle name?

"Why, yes! Laura Jewel is pretty. That is her name then, Laura Jewel. Oh, I can't wait to write and tell Jewel."

****

Come summer, Epsy was a busy man. Even with a tractor and two-row equipment, he really worked hard to farm a half section by himself.

Very little moisture had fallen during the winter. There was enough moisture in the soil to sprout the seed, but they would need an early rain if they were to make it through the summer. As usual, Epsy planted early, but the rains did not come. The cotton was stunted and produced about half per stalk what it did the year before.

"Seems like I'm working harder and producing less," Epsy said at the supper table one night. "And the heat just gets worse. It is really taking a toll on those poor men walking behind a team."

Rachael and the girls suffered in the heat of summer, too. True, they were under the roof or in the shade of the house or barn, but the heat seemed suffocating. There was no escaping it.

Rachael made sure that Epsy carried drinking water in a square syrup can on the tractor. She always squeezed a lemon or two into his water. Long ago she had learned the helpfulness of lemon to thwart the heat. Somehow it replaces what the heat takes from your body. Jenny often quoted her mother, big Jessie, "Lemonade is a fun way to take your medicine for the summer heat." Rachael believed in lemons!

In fact as it grew hotter, she purposely emptied another syrup can for him to have a can of water just to pour over his head and bath his face and neck with his handkerchief. She sure did not want him having a heat stroke. "I will use that syrup to make Jenny's sorghum cake tomorrow. It has been a long time since I thought of making that."

And weren't they pleased to have that water well! They were about the only ones in this area with a water well at their house. Everyone else was hauling water, sometimes for several miles. Most days the girls played in the shade under the water tank just so drops of water would occasionally fall on them.

In the extreme heat of the early afternoon Rachael heard the tractor nearing the house at an unusual time. Epsy had been plowing weeds between the rows.

He stepped up on the back steps and said, "Rachael, I'm going to walk over and check on Bitsy's husband, Frank. I've made two rounds and his

plow has not moved. I can only see one mule standing there. He might need some help.

As Epsy neared the mule standing in the field, he could see that the other mule was lying on the ground, still in harness. He was so wet with sweat; it looked as if someone had emptied a tub of water on him. And there was Frank, slumped over the crossbar between the plow handles.

He felt cold and clammy, yet he was sweating all over, a lot. Epsy checked to see if he was still alive. There was a weak pulse, but it was really hard to see him breathing.

Quickly, Epsy unhitched the mule that was still standing and hoisted Frank up on his back. Frank could not sit up, so Epsy sort of leaned him over with the mule's neck supporting Frank's head. Epsy walked beside, holding on to Frank's arm and leg.

When they reached the house, Epsy put Frank's arm across his shoulders and dragged him up the steps. He didn't bother to knock; he just opened the screen door and started toward what should be a bedroom. "Bitsy?" he hollered. "Come help me!"

He got Frank to the side of the bed and sort of directed his fall across it. "Bitsy, get his clothes off and bathe him all over with cool water. And start giving him spoons full of water. Be careful not to strangle him.

"I'm going to get this mule in the shade and get him some water before you lose him, too."

As he was watering the mule, making him drink very slowly, and slowly pouring water over his back, Epsy could see Rachael walk up to the kitchen door with a pitcher. She had watched as Epsy carried Frank to the house and guessed the cause. She had made a big pitcher of lemonade.

"Bitsy?" she called as she stepped inside. "I brought lemonade. It will help him recover from the heat faster than plain water."

She took a glass from the cupboard and poured some lemonade. "Here, spoon feed him this," and she went back to the kitchen.

Bitsy could hear her opening and closing cabinet doors. Curiosity made her leave her ailing husband to see what Rachael was doing.

"Where will I find something to pour this into? I want to take my pitcher home with me!"

Rachael found a crock jar just about the right size and poured the lemonade into it. She covered it with a cup towel that was hanging on the three bar towel rack above the sink. "If you want us to go for the doctor, just tell us," Rachael said as she walked out the door.

****

While it was cool the next morning, Epsy used his tractor to pull the dead mule out of the field and into the bar ditch. He cleared the weeds from around it with a hoe; then gathered all the dead tree limbs he could find and built a fire over the mule. He knew that was not going to be enough wood, so he went to Frank and Bitsy's wood pile and began loading a wheel barrow with wood.

Bitsy ran out the door and yelled, "Hey! What do you think you are doing?"

"Your mule; your wood," Epsy said and kept loading.

****

Rachael felt very somber for the next few days. She did not see anyone outside at Bitsy's house; but Bitsy didn't ask, and Rachael didn't offer.

A few days later, when Epsy wasn't busy outside, Rachael said, "Do you think your uncle would mind if we go pick mesquite beans in that quarter section that is still in pasture?"

"Whatever do you want mesquite beans for?"

"To make jelly. I found Mama's recipe for mesquite bean jelly. Since we have been here, I have really missed having fruit trees to make jelly. I think right now is a good time to start a big project. I've got to get out of this mood."

"Let's go tomorrow morning. I'll drive over and tell B.T. we will be out there. I'm sure he won't mind us taking the mesquite beans, but I want him to know who we are and what we are doing.

"Do you need extra sugar? While I am out, I can just go on in to Coahoma. What else do you need? Lids?"

*****

So while it was cool next morning they made it a family outing. This was something everyone could help with. It was also a teaching situation. Rachael was giving instructions. "Now, girls, most important thing is to watch for snakes. They could be curled up under a mesquite bush and blend in with the fallen beans, so look under every bush before you walk right up to it. Okay?

"Next thing is never pick up beans off the ground. They could have germs on them that will not wash off and would make us very, very sick.

"I'll tell you how to pick them. The ones that are ripe are a pinkish brown color and kind of dry looking. You know, tan with reddish streaks on them. Now it does no good to try to pull down on them. The limb just bends down and then it will spring back up. You could get a nasty scratch from the mesquite thorns.

"See, like this. Catch a few that look ripe and push up. If they are ripe, they will pop loose from the limb without your pulling at all."

She had given each girl a pan appropriate to her size to put the mesquite beans in. Sister had Jetty with her, and Corrine had Neva with her. Although Neva really did not think she needed any help until Rachael reminded her to watch for rattlesnakes. Epsy carried Laura and walked with them while Rachael filled her toe sack with beans.

"This afternoon I will start making jelly, and tonight we will have mesquite bean jelly for our biscuits."

All the girls cheered as if they seldom had any jelly at all on their biscuits. It is just that homemade jelly tastes so much better!

At supper that night, everyone was excited to try this new kind of jelly. They did not know people could eat mesquite beans.

"Well, hey! This sort of tastes like honey with something else mixed in with it," Epsy said.

"Yes, I always think it has a bit of a cinnamon flavor," Rachael added. Yes, I'd say that pretty much tastes like the jelly Mama and Jenny used to make."

****

When the weather changed and started cooling off a little, Rachael knew it was time to begin her winter sewing. This year Corrine would start to school; she had to make enough dresses for two girls in school, plus dresses for everyone to wear at home. It was important to Rachael for her girls to look nice when they went to school. The girls had their Sunday dresses; but there was definitely a difference in their school dresses and their play dresses.

On the next trip to town for groceries, Rachael got two Big Chief tablets that have larger spaces between the lines, a #2 pencil for Bessie and for Corrine, a fat pencil designed for small fingers to hold. She got two gray, soft-gum erasers, two boxes of crayons, "And two cigar boxes, if you have them."

On the first day of school, again Epsy drove the whole family to school to meet the teacher and visit with other families. This was Corrine's first day of school; she needed her family around for a while.

Bessie brought her friend, Imogene, over to meet her mama and papa. Imogene's mother followed; she also wanted to meet Rachael.

Actually Rachael recognized the woman from church; they had met briefly. She had only two children, a boy, who was Bessie's age, and Imogene. They were always clean and well behaved in church.

"I am happy to have a chance to visit with you, Mrs. Hale. My Imogene idolizes Bessie. They made friends at church last year. She is one year younger than Bessie, but Bessie is very nice to her."

"Oh, I'm sorry. My name is Jessie Wood," and she held out her hand to greet Rachael. She also shook hands with Mr. Hale. "You can call me Epsy," he said.

"Well, my husband is not with us this morning. He is working in the field while it is cool. The heat got to him this summer, and his health has suffered. He gets really sick if he tries to work in the bad heat. So he works early and late and he is at the house during the heat of the day."

"We can certainly understand that; we've seen it happen. It is very nice to meet you, Mrs. Wood."

A few days later, Bessie brought a tearful Imogene home with her from school.

"Her mama was not at home," Bessie explained. "She was afraid to stay at her house alone. Her brother was playing with some other boys, and he didn't care. But Imogene felt all alone and started to cry."

Rachael set all the girls down to milk and tea cakes while she thought over the possibilities. She stepped out back and saw Epsy close to the house. "I think the girls and I will walk back up the road to Mrs. Wood's house for a while. She was not at home, and Imogene was scared to stay alone. But Mrs. Wood doesn't need to come home and find her daughter not there.

"If we are not back by dark, will you come get us?"

****

Mrs. Wood was just helping her husband from the car to the house, when they arrived. When she had everything settled, Mrs. Wood came to her daughter, "I am so sorry that you were scared, darling. I'm glad that you went home with Bessie. That was a smart thing to do.

"Papa stayed out in the sun too long today and got sick again. I had to drive him to the doctor."

"You drive?!?" Rachael interrupted.

"Not too well, but I had to learn in a hurry when Ed got sick this summer."

"Oh, that possibility never crossed my mind," Rachael said quietly as if in thought. "Well, since you are home, now, we may as well walk on back home. I should get started on supper soon. I hope everything is okay."

"Lemonade!" Rachael said as she started to leave. "Lemons will help him with the heat. Do come to visit me, Jessie."

Chapter Twenty Two
Chickens, Geese and a Badger

Epsy's production was down a little from the year before, and his quality was not as good. This year's crop came in at Standard grade. When it was all said and done, Epsy made a little profit despite the heat and dry weather.

But there was no moisture to speak of when winter came again, just the cold wind and sand. That everlasting cold wind! Now his joke about there being nothing between West Texas and the North Pole except barbed wire fences didn't seem very funny at all.

And the tumbleweeds rolled! And Epsy spent a lot of time sharpening his knife and thinking. "Seems the only things that can survive these dry spells in West Texas are mesquite trees and tumbleweeds."

When no rain had fallen by early April, Epsy made a decision. "Rachael, the soil is too dry to even sprout the seed. And if it rained tomorrow, the crop it would make would be so late it would only be Poor grade. I have decided not to waste money buying seed this year.

"I have decided that I have to sell enough of our stocks to live on this year. Or maybe I can get a job with the railroad."

And it turned out that he did get a job with the railroad. The Texas & Pacific was building some spur lines in this area, and because of his bossing experience running the cotton gin, Epsy was hired to push a crew.

Every morning Epsy took his lunch pail and drove to Big Spring to work. He came home each evening singing, "I've been working on the railroad all the live long day," and it made the girls laugh.

****

Since their family was growing they needed more eggs. And since the weather had been so dry, coyotes were killing more of their hens. So Epsy brought home fifty baby chicks from the feed store; they partitioned off part of the chicken house to hold them for a while. The weather was still a little cold for baby chicks, and they were so small that with very little effort, they could go through the chicken wire fence.

The baby chicks were so cute that the girls spent a lot of time in the chicken house peeping over the half wall Epsy had built, watching the chicks running everywhere, cheep-cheeping. The girls were not aware that chicken poop was sticking to the bottom of their shoes.

After telling them time and time again to wipe their feet in the dirt before coming inside, and cleaning her kitchen floor dozens of times, Rachael made a rule. "If you go out to watch the baby chicks, you must take off your shoes before you come in the kitchen door. If I find chicken poop on my kitchen floor again, I will hunt down the one of you who has on shoes and you will get to clean up the floor!"

By late summer the pullets started laying those smaller-than-normal eggs. The girls would get tickled when they found a small egg. "I want this one for my breakfast tomorrow," they would say.

These were Barred Rock chickens, sort of black and white checkered, so the eggs they laid were brown. Rachael liked brown eggs; their yolks were bright orange. Now she had plenty of eggs to bake with, everybody had eggs for breakfast, and she even had some to sell to neighbors. Quite a few of the baby chicks grew up to be roosters, so they had a lot of fried chicken.

It was really strange that one little chick had started following Epsy when it was very small. Every time he saw Epsy he would run to him and follow him wherever he went. As time went on, it was a full grown rooster that ran to meet Epsy when the Model-T pulled in.

Epsy called him Biddy. He would squat down and talk to the rooster and stroke down his neck feathers. They glistened in the sun and felt like satin. Then Epsy went on about his chores and Biddy followed.

But Biddy did not like Rachael and the girls. Many a time Rachael looked out the window to see him chasing one of the girls, neck outstretched and his neck feathers ruffled, wings flapping, and the girls yelling at the top of their lungs.

Biddy had grown to three years old with spurs over an inch long. He was king of the chicken yard and he really strutted about.

One winter evening, Epsy came home and went straight to his chores outside. When he came in with the milk, he could tell by the aroma, they were having something special tonight. He strained the milk then sat down to butter biscuits.

Rachael set a large pot of chicken and dumplings in the center of the table, and Epsy dipped everyone's plate.

He was filling his plate a second time, "Rachael, this is delicious chicken and dumplings.

"Hey, Rachael, I haven't seen Biddy this evening. Have you seen...."

"Yes, you have."

"I have?"

"He's in the pot!" She pulled her skirt to the side and showed him a three inch gash above her ankle. She said nothing else. There was no expression on her face. She just stood there looking at him.

Epsy nodded once and pushed back his plate.

****

With Corrine in school the atmosphere of the one-room school was not as usual. She was a good student, too good, in fact. She was fast with her school work, and she thought ahead. She had an opinion on almost everything.

Mrs. Smith had noticed for the past year that Bessie was very advanced for her grade. Bessie was a good student...and a good teacher.

Mrs. Smith put a record on the wind-up Victrola for Corrine's second grade to practice their cursive writing while she was teaching the fourth grade. The students were to practice their penmanship in rhythm with the music. When Mrs. Smith asked the second grade a question, Corrine quietly answered it, without looking up.

Mrs. Smith began to watch Corrine each time she asked a question, and without missing a stroke with her pencil, Corrine mumbled the answer.

Mrs. Smith skipped ahead of the material she had been drilling the second graders on. She asked a question without first giving any background or explanation, and Corrine quietly answered.

Over two-week's time Mrs. Smith was convinced that Corrine could easily do second-grade work. At the end of school one day, she wrote a note, folded it, and pinned it to the front of Corrine's dress. "Now, I don't want you to take this off before you get home. Let your mother unpin it. Okay?"

On the way home, the boys walking with their group began to tease Corrine. A note pinned to their shirt is the way Mrs. Smith communicated with their mothers when they had misbehaved. And they assumed that Corrine was in trouble for something.

They began to dance in circles around Corrine as she walked, taunting her, "Corrine's getting in trouble!" "Corrine's getting in trouble!" they sang. Walking backwards, Imogene's older brother, Rabon, asked, "What did you do little Miss Smarty Pants?" He stuck out his chin and wagged his head back and forth.

Corrine shoved her book and lunch sack into Sister's hands and tackled him. Before he saw what was coming, he was on the ground and Corrine was sitting astraddle of him, hitting him in the face with both fists. She bloodied his nose and made a cut just under his left eye.

Bessie and Imogene pulled her off of him. "That's what you get, Rabon! If I wouldn't have to answer to Mama, I'd help her!" Imogene scolded. "You in the third grade and teasing a first grader!"

****

"Well, who did you fight with?" Mrs. Wood asked when Rabon walked in the door.

"Corrine!" he said with a quiet, down-cast tone of voice, his eyes on the floor.

"Mama, all the boys were teasing her, and Rabon got right up in her face," Imogene helped. "She just lit into him like a wampus cat!"

"You were fighting with a second-grade girl?" Mrs. Wood asked as she caught him by the top of his ear and lifted him to his tip-toes. She escorted him to the kitchen, "Now you get cleaned up! Maybe we need to find some more chores for you to do, young man."

Later, she came in with tincture of iodine and doctored the cut by his eye. "Are you sorry for teasing Corrine?"

"Yes, Ma'am." His tone of voice sounded more of embarrassment than repentance.

"Well, comb your hair and tuck in your shirttail. We are going over to let you tell Corrine and Mr. and Mrs. Hale how sorry you are."

"Mama, she beat up on me!"

"You hurt her feelings. And sometimes hurt feelings are worse than hurt faces."

Bessie, and Corrine were just getting home when Mrs. Wood, Rabon and Imogene drove up. They sort of all walked in the house together. Rachael could not figure out the situation. She greeted Mrs. Wood first, then the children all in one sweeping motion. She could tell something was wrong, but she could not understand what.

"Rabon has something he would like to say," Mrs. Wood began. The look she gave Rabon told him he had better not take too much time!

"Corrine, I'm sorry for teasing you. "Mrs. Hale, I'm sorry I teased Corrine."

"Well, looks to me like you came out on the short end of it, Rabon," she patted his shoulder. "She is tougher than she looks, isn't she?"

"Yes, Ma'am."

Mrs. Wood spoke up, "I'm afraid he is more embarrassed than sorry. But it is a start."

"Corrine, let's look at this note you are wearing on your dress." Rachael unpinned the note and read it silently. She narrowed her eyes as she thought back to her own school days.

"Well, looks as if Mrs. Smith wants to talk to me about putting Corrine into the second grade. Now, isn't that something? We will have to talk to Papa about that, won't we?"

All the girls breathed a sigh of relief. Like the boys, they actually thought she might be in trouble.

After the Woods left, Rachael took Corrine aside for a little private talk. "Always look for the good in others, honey, and love them for that. It will often out-weigh the bad."

****

It was all the talk at school the next day, how Corrine beat up on Rabon, a fourth-grade boy. "It would have been okay if she had fought like a girl," he told the boys. But she used her fists!"

*****

Corrine had established a reputation for having a quick temper, and the boys at school were quick to take advantage of it.

When Neva started first grade the boys found out they could make her cry if they untied the sash of her dress, or tugged at the back of her skirt or tugged at a wisp of her hair then ran. This always brought a lot of laughter. Sometimes just pointing at her, covering their mouth and laughing would make her start to cry.

Corrine was quick to take up for her little sister. She spent her recesses chasing boys and pounding any of them she could catch.

At quieter times, the girls would sit on a split rail fence around the school yard and talk. The boys made up a little saying to taunt her, "Corrine Hale, sitting on a rail, picking her teeth with the end of her tail." And then the chase was on!

****

When Neva started school, Jetty was just turning four years old and the oldest one not in school. Laura was about two years younger. They played good together, but when the older girls were at school, Jetty enjoyed getting to be the big sister.

She showed Laura all the fun things to do, things that the older girls had taught her. Things like walking around in the back yard until the geese got used to you being there. Then you could get up close behind them, stomp your feet and wave your arms and chase after them when they ran. It was fun to watch them waddle when they ran. They would flap their wings and squawk and honk.

That was fun until Mama came to the back door and scolded them.

She taught Laura how to stir the doodle bug holes in the shade of the water tank. Jetty could climb the first three rungs of the ladder on the windmill tower. Laura struggled to get on the first rung and then she got scared. She cried because she was afraid to step back down. Rachael had to come out and get her off the ladder.

And when Mama hoed weeds in the garden, it was fun to walk barefoot in the soft cool dirt behind her.

One day Rachael heard the old gander honking riotously, and Laura came to the back door crying. Rachael hurried outside to find out what was the matter.

The gander was at the door of the out-door toilet, angrily strutting back and forth and honking. His long neck was stretched out, feathers ruffled, moving his head from side to side menacingly. Every time he passed the door, he pecked it two or three times. Then he would hiss and honk some more. Over all the noise, Rachael could hear Jetty crying inside.

Rachael got the goose hook and scared the gander away from the outhouse. She opened the door to find Jetty sobbing and holding her thigh. She carefully moved Jetty's hand and saw a dark bruise the size of a silver dollar and growing larger. She knew immediately what had happened. Jetty had chased his geese as much as the old gander would stand for, and when he caught her off guard, he bit her.

A goose's bill is not sharp on the end. It doesn't really hurt if they peck you like a chicken. But when a goose bites, they actually bite with their mouth open, pinching a piece of skin and twisting. It hurts a lot worse than getting pecked by a chicken and it really makes a nasty bruise. Plus they have those big, strong wings flapping you from both sides. The bite hurts bad, but the whole experience is very traumatic!

When Epsy came home Jetty was walking only on the toe of her left foot and limping. She wasn't crying any longer, but it was easy to see that she was in pain.

He picked her up and sat her on his lap as Rachael replayed the whole event. "And, Papa, I was so scared I wet my panties, too. I'm sorry," she doubled up her fists and put them to her eyes and sobbed.

"It's all right, honey," he comforted. "We will just have to think of some other arrangement about the geese."

****

The next day when Epsy came home there was a delivery truck following him. Everybody ran outside and lined up beside the house to see what it was bringing.

"Bed springs? Coil bed springs! And cotton mattresses with blue and white striped ticking! We have seen them in the Sears and Roebuck catalog, but I didn't think we would get them." Rachael clapped her hands together and held them there.

"Well, times are changing, Rachael. We should stay up with the times. It's the latest thing, and it's supposed to be real comfortable sleeping.

"Got one set for each bed. So now we don't need to keep geese anymore." He reached down and patted Jetty on the head.

"It is going to cut down on your work a little too, Rachael. Plucking the goose down and trying to stuff those tiny feathers in the mattresses! I've seen how they fly back up!"

As soon as the men got the new mattresses set up on the beds, the older girls were happy to put clean sheets on them and lie down to try them out. This was exciting! When you bounced just a little, it kept springing back. "Oh, Daddy, we are really going to enjoy these!"

That night Epsy and Rachael were talking quietly while the girls were getting to sleep. "Rachael, unless you know of something better to do with those goose down mattresses, there are some fellows working in my crew who are out here without their families. They are sleeping on the bare floor right now. Would it be all right with you to give them the goose down mattresses?"

"That would be a fine thing to do."

"And you know Thanksgiving is just around the corner. Can we have roast goose for Thanksgiving dinner?"

She knew just which one he was talking about.

****

The geese hens were already three or four years old, and there were only three of them left. They continued to lay eggs for a few months. But in the spring, when it was time for them to hatch out goslings, they sat on infertile eggs long past time for them to hatch. Sadly one by one they gave up and abandoned their nests.

They no longer had the gaiety and arrogance of proud geese parading around the yard; their lives were much more somber and quiet. After a while they were all gone.

****

On the way home from school one Friday afternoon, one of the girls found a dead badger in the ditch.

"He probably was hit by a car and crawled into the ditch and died," Bessie said. "Are you sure he is dead?"

Corrine found a stick and poked him; she lifted up one of his paws. "Look at those claws!" She slowly slid the stick out to the claws and let them wrap around the stick. "Those are about an inch long! I've heard that their teeth are long and sharp, too. They are terrible fighters." She used the stick to lift the badger's lip.

"Oh! My!" someone said.

"What can we do with him?" their minds were already working. "We could scare Mama," Jetty said mischievously.

"Yeah, that's a good idea," Corrine was on board with this prank quickly. "You know where Mama crawls through the barb wire fence when she takes lemonade to Papa when he is plowing? We could prop him up right there so she won't see him until she is through the fence and still bent over!"

Everyone started giggling, thinking about how bad their mama was going to beat up on that old dead badger! On the way home they cut through the cotton field to set up their prank. They set his back feet down in a furrow so that it looked a little like he was rearing up on his hind feet, like badgers do when they fight. They propped one of his front paws up on a clod of dirt to make it look as if he were taking a swipe at something with those big claws.

Corrine had a hard time doing it, but she pried his mouth open and finally made his lip curl up like he was snarling. Then they made sure that the fence stave was leaned against the fence.

Mama always carried that fence stave when she went into the cotton field just in case she found a snake…or a snake found her. She always said that snakes were fond of the cool, fresh-plowed dirt in the hot summer weather.

The next day being Saturday, the girls could hardly wait for it to get hot enough to warrant Mama walking out to the field with a pitcher of lemonade. As she walked from the porch to the fence, the girls all found places at the kitchen windows to watch. They were holding a hand across their mouths to keep from giggling out loud.

They watched expectantly from the house as Mama carefully set the pitcher through the fence and gathered up her skirt. She held her skirt with one hand and lifted the top strand of wire with the other. She bent low as she eased between the wires, and just as she started to stand up and bring her other leg through the barb wire, she saw the badger.

"Badger!" she yelled. "Badger!" She grabbed her stick and began to beat the dead badger. With every whack, the badger seemed to jump up toward her. She hit him again and again, hopping around so the badger would not scratch or bite her feet and legs. She hit him across the head and across the back several times, but the badger seemed to keep jumping at her. When she finally got a good swing at him from the side, he went sailing across the cotton rows.

The girls could stand it no longer! They poured out of the kitchen door, and the sound of their uproarious laughter reached Rachael. She looked up to see all her daughters jumping up and down, clapping their hands and pointing at her.

She stood stock still for a moment looking at the girls as the full impact of the situation soaked in on her. She walked over to where the badger had landed and poked him with her stick. He was stiff as a board!

Rachael was smiling as she started back to the house. She thought of what a sight that must have been to see. She carefully leaned the stick back against the fence and picked up the overturned lemonade pitcher.

She was laughing out loud as she sat down on the edge of the porch to enjoy the fun with her daughters.

"Whew! Dawgone, that sure takes a feller's breath away!" she said smiling and fanning her face with her hand. She enjoyed the girls joke.

The girls all gathered around her and wanted to give her a hug. She was the best mama ever! When the laughter began to die down, Rachael picked up the muddy pitcher and handed it to Neva. "Sister, you and Corrine can cook supper tonight. Neva, you and Jetty make a fresh pitcher of lemonade and bring it out to the field. I think I'm going to go ride on the tractor with your papa for a while."

"But Mama," Bessie protested in shock, "what do you want us to cook?"

"I don't really know. I hadn't planned anything yet. You get to do it all by yourself today.

"Be sure you mind Laura for me, now!"

Chapter Twenty Three
Good Neighbors

At the supper table, Bessie said, "Mama, we have three new girls in school. They wear their dresses right side out one day and wrong side out the next day. And the boys tease them something awful. Corrine tries to take up for them, but she can't stop it all the time.

"They are just about the same size as Corrine and Neva and me. Can we give them some of our dresses?"

Rachael was concerned, "What is their name? I didn't know we had someone in need."

"Their name is Cooper. They are real nice girls. We all like them They have just moved out here because their daddy has asthma real bad, and the doctor told him our hot, dry climate would be better for him."

"Where do they live?"

"The other way from the schoolhouse. I don't know just where," Corrine chimed in.

"Could we give them some of our dresses, Mama? You make us pretty dresses, and we have plenty." The girls had on their best pleading faces.

Rachael looked at Epsy, "We should check into this. They may need more than just dresses. Can we drive over to Jessie and Ed's house this evening and talk to her. Maybe she will drive me and the girls to school tomorrow, so we can find out where they live. I'll make a cake tonight, and we can take it as a welcome gift."

Epsy nodded his head.

"Now, girls, while we go over to Jessie's house you can pick out the dress you want to give away. And make sure it is a pretty one, not just

315

something you want to get rid of. A gift should be something you are proud to give."

****

Next morning, Rachael and the girls walked to Jessie's house, where they all piled into her Model-T, two deep in the back seat. At the schoolhouse they waited and watched for the new girls. Rachael wanted to catch them before they got to school, so maybe they wouldn't be embarrassed.

When they saw the girls coming, Jessie drove up the road to meet them. Bessie explained, "We didn't want the boys teasing you anymore, so we want you to have one of our dresses. Is that all right?" And Bessie, Corrine and Neva pulled the dresses from behind them to show the girls.

The new girls' faces shone with delight when they saw their new dresses....Bessie had her answer. All the girls and mothers ringed around one side of the car to conceal the Cooper girls while they changed. "Now, tell us where you live. I brought a cake as a welcome gift for your mother," Rachael said.

All the girls walked toward the schoolhouse, and Jessie and Rachael drove on to the Cooper house.

"Rachael, you are so giving. To everybody!"

"Oh, pshaw," she returned softly with down cast eyes and shaking head.

****

"Epsy, that man is very frail. Even in the dryer weather, I don't think he will make it as a farmer.

"They said he has an education as a bookkeeper. Do you think you can help him find work in town?"

"Sure, we will try. Tell him to go to every store in Coahoma and ask. You never can tell who could use someone with that talent. I'll talk to the people I know in Big Spring. Maybe we can find something for him."

****

Mr. Cooper came to school one day with a bunch of big horse shoes and four pieces of small pipe he had cut into about three foot lengths. He asked Mrs. Smith if he could set up a horse shoe game for the boys, to give them something to do at recess.

"The last person who farmed where we are must have used Shire horses. I found a lot of big horse shoes beside the barn.

"I remember what it was like at that age…so much energy and they don't know what to do with it."

Mrs. Smith decided it was a good time for recess. Mr. Cooper had two hoes in his wagon, so the boys set about clearing weeds to lay out a horse shoe course. One of them got the sledge hammer to drive in the stakes. He could only lift it shoulder high, but eventually he got one driven in. Then it became a contest. Each of the older boys wanted to drive in one of the stakes.

So, for a while playing horse shoes took up most of their time at recess. They had less time to think up ways to tease the girls.

****

After Christmas when the excitement died down, the girls were getting a little bored around the house. The weather was too cold to enjoy playing outside. But not too cold to enjoy gathering mistletoe for New Years!

Rachael always enjoyed decorating the house a little for the holidays, a little, not too much. While she and the girls were out gathering mistletoe to hang in the doorways she had a wonderful idea.

"Epsy, wouldn't it be fun to have a few families over for a New Year's Eve party. I can make up a big bowl of eggnog and some tea cakes. We can ask the other women to bring something so we will have a variety of goodies.

"Do you like that idea? The girls and I have already gathered some mistletoe."

"Who would you want to invite?" he asked.

"Oh, the Woods, Myrtle and John Cox, and maybe that new family. That would be a houseful, and it would give us a chance to get to know…

"Sister, tell me again what that new family's name is?"

"Cooper," all the girls sang out from the next room.

So, after supper, while the girls did the dishes, Epsy and Rachael went for a drive to make the invitations. "Now, let's not say anything to the Coopers about bringing anything, just Jessie and Myrtle. I heard he found a job in Coahoma, but I don't know how they are doing yet. I don't want to embarrass them. I'll let Sister make that cake she has been practicing. She is getting pretty good at it."

The next day was spent with housecleaning and baking. When Epsy got home and walked in the door, Rachael was standing up in a chair trying to hang mistletoe in the doorway between the living room and the kitchen. He dropped his things into the nearest chair and ran to hold the chair for Rachael.

"Why, thank you," she said sweetly.

He stared her right in the eyes and wouldn't let her look away. Then a slight smile crept across his face. "What is the matter?" she asked, thinking something was wrong.

"When were you going to tell me?"

"Tell you what?" She straightened her dress and brushed at her skirt.

"You are getting a little tummy bulge; I could see it from the door," he grinned. "When were you going to tell me?"

She let him help her down from the chair and poured them both a cup of coffee. "Well, I wasn't sure until just the past few days, when I noticed my tummy growing.

"Epsy, I am 39 years old! I thought it could be that time of life for me starting early. Jessie and I have been talking about it, wondering; but I'm sure now that I'm pregnant. It should be here sometime in May."

Up to this time she had been very somber about all this, but now that it was said, she smiled a shy little smile and shrugged her shoulders. "Want to make bets?"

"Give it a little time to grow, then I'll tell you what it is going to be!" he said with a big grin on his face. Epsy loved his family!

They announced it at the party that night, and everybody had a good time congratulating them. "Six children! Half a dozen!" "Are you going to try for an even dozen?" "Is it going to be another girl?"

****

With Jetty in school this year, things really did get quiet around the house. Laura was the only girl at home during the day, and she had always been very quiet. She would play babies for long periods of time. By now they had a large collection of baby dolls, all sizes.

In her mind she had them talking to each other, going places together; sometimes one of them would get up on a stage and sing and dance for the others. But the sound was only in her mind. Once in a while you could hear her humming to herself.

They would all sit down to eat, and if someone spilled her milk, Laura would pretend to quickly clean it up and gently pat the shoulder of the baby who spilled it.

One day Rachael had been seeing all of this activity without getting caught actually watching. "Laura, you have such lovely babies. And they get along so well together. Do your children ever get mad at each other and have an argument?"

"Oh, no, Mama. I don't like it when people argue. My babies all like each other and play nice together." She turned to the baby dolls, "Don't we, girls?"

"Your fourth birthday is not too far away. What would you like for your birthday?"

"Oh, Mama, I would like to have a dog to play with."

"Well, I don't know about that. Your papa never has been much on having a dog around. But we will think about it."

That night after supper, while the girls were getting ready for bed, Epsy got the cards and sat down at the table. "Want to beat me in a couple of hands of Rummy?" he asked as he began shuffling. She was always ready for a game of Rummy. And she did beat him.

"I found out what Laura wants for her birthday," she said while he shuffled.

Epsy raised his eyebrows questioningly.

"A dog to play with."

"Hmmm, that will take some thinking. You go first," and he nodded toward the card he had turned up for the discard pile.

****

Two days before Laura's birthday, Epsy came home with a little dog. She was a foot and a half tall, white with brown spots. Her hair was short and slick. And she was so happy to have someone love her that her eyes fairly smiled.

"Now, the first thing we have to do is give her a bath. She is probably covered with fleas," he said as he carefully handed her into Laura's arms. The dog licked her all over her face; she closed her eyes tight and squenched up her face, but she held on tight to the dog.

Epsy got a wash tub and started filling it with water. "Rachael, do you have some hot water on the stove. This is going to be too cold without it."

All the girls were ringed around, quietly staring. This was indeed out of the ordinary. They had never had a dog on the place before.

Epsy looked at Bessie, "Sister, will you get some of your mother's washing soap for me?"

"Corrine, will you see if you can find a couple of old towels that we can use?

"Who would like to help scrub on her?" and he motioned for all the girls to come over and help.

The little dog was probably cringing inside because she was wet! But with so many loving little girls rubbing on her, she felt she was being treated like a queen. She still had that smile in her eyes.

Water was splashing everywhere and soap bubbles flying in the air. With one hand Laura reached in to wash on the dog and guarded her face with the other arm. She was delighted to be part of this, but it was a little above her ability.

Corrine was the one who got to hold the dog while Epsy emptied the tub and got some fresh water. The drenched little dog shook her hardest and drops of water went on every one of the girls. Corrine was sopping wet; yet she held on. Rachael came out with a kettle of hot water to warm the rinse water and a cup to dip clean water over her.

When the dog was all washed and dried, Epsy handed her back to Laura, and said, "Well, what do you think her name will be?"

"Spotty!" she said quietly, nodding her head.

"Well, I think that is quite descriptive," Rachael said from the kitchen steps. She had a small bowl of food for the dog and a bowl for water. She squatted down and put her arm across Laura's shoulders. "Now, since Spotty is going to be your dog, you are responsible for feeding her every day. And you must make sure that she has clean water in her bowl all the time because you never know when she will get thirsty. Can you do that?"

Epsy found a low wooden box in the barn that would work for Spotty's bed. "Let me have that towel we didn't use. That can be her bedding." He put the box in a corner made by the porch and the steps so she would have a windbreak. The food and water bowls went right beside it. And Spotty was fixed up.

"Well, everybody get washed up for supper. It's ready," Rachael called.

Laura would eat a few bites, then jump down from the table and look out the window to make sure Spotty was still there.

Epsy touched her head as she came back to the table. He reassured her, "I think she will stay here, honey. She hasn't had a home for a long time. The men working around the railroad yard have been giving her scraps from their lunches. She has been hanging around there a couple of weeks. I think she is happy to have a home."

On the way home from school the next day, the girls were inviting everyone over for Laura's birthday party on Sunday. "Daddy is going to bring home enough ice to make homemade ice cream, and Mama will make her famous chocolate cake," Corrine was saying.

Rabon ran up behind her saying, "Smarty, Smarty, had a party. Nobody came but ole black Daughtery!" Then he ran as hard as he could. He knew not to get close enough to get caught.

She shoved her things into Sister's hands and grabbed a rock. She clocked him right in the back of the head, and he went down. Everyone ran over to see if he was okay, even Corrine. Even though he always tormented her, she really did like him.

With a little help he stood up and kind of shook his head to get his bearings. Bessie was the oldest girl in the bunch, "Can you see straight, Rabon? If you see two of everything, you could have a concussion."

"Naw, I think I'm all right." But he walked the rest of the way home, instead of dancing around and cutting up the way he usually did. All the kids went in the house with him to make sure he was okay.

When all the kids came inside and Rabon was holding the back of his head, Mrs. Wood knew something was wrong. "Well, you have a nice goose egg here. It is bleeding a little, not much. I'll get a wet cloth and the iodine.

Mrs. Wood didn't even ask how it happened or who; she just knew it was Corrine. "What did she hit you with?" she called from the other room.

"A rock."

She had heard that sound in his voice before. She knew his head was not hurt as bad as his pride. He wanted so bad to tease Corrine and make her cry like Neva did, but she got the best of him every time.

"Okay, everybody into the car, we will go talk to Rachael."

Rachael was surprised to see Jessie's car drive up and all the kids piling out.

"What happened this time?" Rachael asked.

"Rabon would like to tell you," Jessie said.

All eyes turned to Rabon. "Corrine was inviting us to your party Sunday, and I teased her," he said in a down-cast tone of voice.

"What did you say to her, son?"

He looked down and his eyes quickly darted right then left. "Smarty, Smarty, had a party. Nobody came but ole black Daughtry." He sort of mumbled it in a very low voice.

"Then what did Corrine do?" Jessie prompted.

"She chunked a rock at me and hit me in the back of the head."

"Why do you think she keeps hurting you, son?" Jessie asked. This was just like pulling teeth.

"Because I keep teasing her, Mama."

It was grueling to witness. This young man was admitting he did wrong, in front of God and everybody. And he was taking it like a man.

Before Jessie could grill him any further, Rachael put her arm across his shoulders…a half hug. "You know, Rabon, I used to think that little saying was funny because it was a put-down and because it rhymed. But, really, some of the nicest people in my young life were black, and it would hurt me if they ever heard me say something like that."

By now she was walking him toward the door; she wanted to get him out of this situation. "Would you like to come to our party, Rabon? I make a very good chocolate cake, and Epsy might like to have someone help turn the crank on the ice cream freezer." She raised her eyebrows and tipped her head forward, waiting for an answer.

"Sure, Mrs. Hale, I'd be happy to help with the cranking."

He turned back toward the kitchen and said, "I'm sorry, Corrine."

"I'm sorry, too, Rabon."

He looked up at Rachael then at Corrine, "I'm just glad you weren't throwing horse shoes!"

****

For her birthday party on Sunday Laura wore her very best Sunday dress. Mama had starched the sash very stiff so that it made a big, pretty bow in the back. Mama had found a piece of the same material as the dress to tie a big bow around Spotty's neck. "Look everybody, we are dressed alike!"

Ten or twelve kids from school came over for the party. It was not every day they got a chance to eat ice cream. Several of them even brought Laura a little present. But when they missed Laura, they found her sitting on the back steps feeding Spotty chocolate cake and ice cream.

"One bite for you and one bite for me." Spotty had a hard time eating off that spoon, but she licked it clean every time.

****

Laura came into the kitchen one day saying, "Mama, Spotty is getting fat."

Rachael went out to look at Spotty. It was very true; Spotty was getting fat, but just in her tummy.

When Epsy came home Rachael asked him, "Did you notice that we are going to have puppies?"

"No, I didn't. But I'm not too surprised. That is probably how she got separated from her last family. Her manners are too good to have grown up as a stray. "I'll see if I can find a bigger box. She will need more room for puppies."

And did she have puppies! Seven of them!

"Laura, tell Papa what you have named the puppies."

She touched each puppy with her finger, "There is Blackie, Whitey, Brownie, Gray, Spot, Two Colors, and James."

"Ha, ha, ha. Tell me why you picked those names."

"Well, Blackie is mostly black. Whitey is mostly white. Brownie is mostly brown. Gray has black and white hair mixed up so he looks gray. Spot looks like his mama. Two Colors has a white front end and a black back end."

"What about this one? Why did you name him James?"

"Because he is my favorite, and Daddy really likes Uncle James."

Epsy pulled her to him giving her a big hug. "Just wait until I tell Uncle James. He will be so proud."

Chapter Twenty Four
Six Girls!

"Rachael, what will we name this baby? I've run completely out of ideas."

"Are you sure this is another girl?"

"It's a girl!"

"Well, we don't have a Mary yet. Seems as if every family eventually has a Mary."

"That might be nice. We can think on another name to put with it."

"Frances might be nice. Mary Frances? I know everyone will think we are Catholic, but that is okay, too."

And when the time came, it was, indeed, another little girl. Mary Frances! Six girls!

****

Suddenly Laura was not the baby of the family. And what a difference it made in her life. She was no longer the 'baby of the family' with privileges that go along with being the youngest. But now she wasn't so alone when everyone else was in school. She could help Mama take care of the baby. She could hardly wait for Mary to grow big enough to play with her.

But in the mean time she had Spotty and the puppies. Well, she had most of the puppies. Seems like every few days someone came over and wanted one of them. So now there were only four…and they had teeth! And sharp claws! Sometimes they didn't want to be held and cuddled; sometimes they wanted to fight with each other. Laura soon learned that she would only watch while they fought; she could not control them like she could her babies.

Then before she realized it, she was down to just Spotty again. And Spotty was ready to be just Laura's dog...ready to get all that loving attention.

School was out for the summer and the older girls were doing 'big girl' things....things that scared Laura. So she and Spotty walked around outside and played 'make believe'. Sometimes Laura threw a stick for Spotty to fetch until Spotty got tired of that.

They dug together in the cool, soft sand. Laura used a can to dig. She tried pouring the sand on Spotty; sand went all over Laura as Spotty shook, trying to get the sand off, and Spotty began to scratch. Laura wondered if the sand had tickled Spotty, so she poured sand on her own head. It did tickle as it trickled down through her hair, so she shook her head real hard. It made her dizzy, but all the sand did not come out. And her head still itched.

Laura began to whine and try to shake the sand out of her hair with her hands as she ran toward the back steps. As she ran around the corner of the house, she came near a Lantana bush, one of the few flowers Rachael could get to grow in this alkaline soil.

Suddenly Spotty began barking wildly and ran up next to Laura's leg just in time to take the fangs of a rattlesnake that had been hiding under the Lantana. And Laura screamed and ran!

Rachael and all the girls ran to see what Spotty was so upset about. Spotty did not bark this way at a lizard or horny toad. "Corrine, go get me the hoe, while I watch where this rattler crawls off to! We don't want to let him get away!

"Now you girls stay way back! Sister, keep Laura with you. And all of you girls stay back! You can see him after he is dead!"

Corrine was back with the hoe and soon the rattler was dead. Rachael did not mess around about it; she had done this before! After she cut off his head and threw it in the burn pit, she stretched him out for everyone to see.

The girls looked at the snake and said things like, "Oohhh." "Ugh!" He was not an especially large snake, but seeing one up this close was scary.

Rachael looked around to make sure all of her girls were safe; then she looked for Spotty. "Laura, where did Spotty go?"

They found Spotty out by the barn lying down in the shade. She was lying on her side, and when they reached her, she only raised her head a little bit.

Seeing the fang marks on her shoulder, Rachael raced into the house and scrambled around the medicine box. She came out of the house chewing on something, something that made her mouth water, and she was making an awful face.

The girls tried to ask her what was in her mouth, but she only shook her head and waved her arm telling them to move out of her way. She was fairly running when she got to the barn and Spotty.

With Epsy's straight razor she shaved a small area, cut between the fang marks on Spotty's shoulder and spit tobacco juice on it. Then she dug the chewing tobacco out of her mouth and spread it over the cut. Out of her pocket she pulled a piece of material she had grabbed from the 'rag bag.' She folded one into a square and placed it over the chewing tobacco and tore off strips to wrap around Spotty. "Corrine, lift up her head and shoulders while I wrap these strips around her to hold the tobacco in place."

Just as she tied a tight knot to hold the bandage in place, Rachael jumped up and ran to the water faucet on the water tank pipe. She scooped handfuls of water into her mouth, rinsed and spit for several minutes.

"Ohhh, that stuff stings!" she finally said. She walked over and sat on the back steps. "Whoo, hoo my head is spinning. You see, girls, why I don't like tobacco? That is probably the worst thing the devil ever came up with!

"Come here, Laura. Sit in Mama's lap a minute and let me love on you, baby." She enveloped Laura in her arms and squeezed her tightly for a long minute, thinking to herself, "If it weren't for that little dog, I might have lost you today, darling."

"Sister, Corrine, would you two start supper for me. I feel like I may be sick; I think I swallowed some of that tobacco juice. I probably need to sit here awhile.

"Sister, make a pan of cornbread. Corrine, you can peel a bunch of potatoes and cut them up to fry. I have a pan of black-eyed peas sitting on the back of the stove. You might boil some of that fresh squash and cut up several tomatoes. That would be a good supper on a day like this.

"Laura, do you want to go over and pet Spotty for a little while? She just saved your life, darling."

Laura was sobbing, but she started toward the little dog, rubbing her eyes.

"Don't be too upset, Laura," Rachael called. "Dogs have glands in their throat area that absorb snake poison. She most likely will live over it, but you most likely would not have."

And right on cue, Epsy pulled up in the drive way just in time to see Rachael walk away from the house and upchuck. He ran to her with a puzzled look on his face.

"I'll be okay. I just swallowed some tobacco juice, and it's got to come up. Still bent over, she pointed to the barn without lifting her head. "Go check on Spotty, though."

Laura, Jetty, and Neva sat petting the little dog and crying. "The girls can tell you what happened."

****

When Epsy came home the next day, he noticed immediately that there was a change in the outside of the house. All of the Lantana, that Rachael had worked so hard to grow, was gone. He could see several places where the dirt was still damp and freshly disturbed.

"What happened to your flowers?" he asked innocently.

Rachael, who was normally calm and resourceful about every incident, flew apart like an alarm clock wound too tightly. "I hoed them all down!

"Epsy, do you realize how close we came to losing one of our babies yesterday? If it hadn't been for that little dog, Laura would have been bitten by that rattlesnake.

"Epsy, this is the first time in my life I have not had geese on the place! I just got used to depending on them to keep snakes away, and I got careless! I know that snakes like flower beds because they are cool and the snake is concealed! I just let myself be too busy with other things to think about that possibility! And I nearly lost one of my babies! I cannot have flowers around the house anymore!"

When it looked as if she had run out of steam, he held out his arms and she wilted into them, sobbing on his shoulder. These were deep, painful sobs that racked her whole body.

****

A soft summer breeze blew in the bedroom window, waving the lace curtains at them and filling the bedroom with the scent of Rosemary. While they waited for sleep to come, Rachael said softly, "Epsy, I couldn't bring myself to cut down the Rosemary bush outside our window. Do you think you can put up some kind of fence so the girls won't get too close to it?"

****

Because of the snake bite, Rachael checked on Spotty regularly. "Epsy, I believe that Spotty is coming in heat. Can we put her up in that little room in the barn? I'll help Laura feed her so that she doesn't get out."

Laura sadly stepped up on the back porch and looked through the screen door. She had her hands up to each side of her face to shade the light, so she could see through the screen wire. "Mama, why does Spotty have to stay in the barn? Was she bad?"

"No, honey, Spotty was not bad. Come on in and I'll get you a cookie and some milk." Rachael wiped the dust from the screen off Laura's nose and forehead.

Laura sat at the table eating her cookie, but her mind was still working. "If Spotty was not bad, why does she have to stay in the barn?"

"Well, honey, she is in season. And if we don't keep her pinned up for a week or so, she will run off looking for boy dogs to help her have puppies again. We don't want her to run off, so the best thing to do is keep her pinned up for a few days. Does that make sense to you?"

"I guess. But I miss playing with her."

"You know before I can turn around twice it will be time to start making school dresses. I will have a lot of dresses to make this year. Would you like to get the Sears Roebuck catalog and show me the dresses you like for when you start to school next year?"

****

On Sunday afternoon, Bessie and Corrine walked over to visit with Imogene. They told Imogene and Jessie all about Spotty saving Laura from the rattlesnake, and about Mama and the chewing tobacco. "Mama was kinda sick all that evening. It looks like Spotty is going to be okay, though."

They were still asking questions when Rabon and his cousin, Joe, came inside. The whole story had to be told again. "Man, your mother knows a lot about a lot of things, doesn't she?" Rabon asked, with respect in his voice. Rachael had become his friend.

"Yeah, she grew up on a horse farm in Oklahoma. She learned how to do a lot of things," Corrine answered. Bessie seemed to be dumb struck and she was even quieter than usual. She let Corrine do all the talking.

"What is the matter with you, Bessie?" Imogene asked. "You are always pretty quiet, but you did not say a word while the boys were in the house."

"Who was that tall boy with Rabon?" Bessie asked sort of looking at the floor.

"He is our cousin, Joe. He lives in Big Spring." Seeing that Bessie really seemed interested, Imogene continued. "He is already out of school and working at a restaurant. He is already 18 years old. He comes out to visit sometimes on Sunday when the restaurant is closed."

"Ohh," was Bessie's best comment.

****

"Mama, you should have seen how Bessie acted when Rabon and Joe came in the house. She kind of stood behind me and mostly looked at the floor. She never said a word!"

"Oh, is that so?" Rachael asked and cut her eyes at Bessie, who was blushing.

Corrine looked at Bessie mischievously, "Maybe they will invite him to Imogene's birthday party next month!" and she danced around Bessie, making her blush again.

****

"Well, yeah, I guess Bessie is kind of pretty," Rabon said. "I think she is 14 or 15 years old, one year older than Imogene. Yeah, she is starting to grow…up," he caught himself. "She is awful quiet, though. But, she is no fun to tease."

"Rabon, is teasing all you think about?"

"No, but Corrine is fun to tease because she always fights back. I like her best."

Joe raised his eyebrows and shook his head. "Aunt Jessie, when did you say you are having Imogene's birthday party?"

*****

One summer morning Jetty followed quietly behind Epsy as he went about his morning chores. Epsy began to walk around the edge of the field. "What are you going to do today, Papa?"

"Oh, nothing big. I thought I would begin by just cleaning up around here. When I am working hard…on something that needs to be done quickly, sometimes I lay a tool down where I was working, then I forget to go back and put it away. Help me look for things around the edge of the field."

She stopped and picked some pea-sized yellow berries off a weed and began to chunk them at fence posts and things. "Papa, is there something I can do to earn some money?"

"What do you need to buy, honey?"

"I want to buy a present for Mama. Teacher told us that there is a lady trying to get people to remember their mothers on the 'second Sunday in

May'. She calls it Mother's Day. When we went to the store last time I found a little mirror to go in Mama's purse. It costs a quarter. What can I do to earn a quarter, Papa?"

"Well, those iron weeds that you are throwing are a particular bother to me. They grow when there is not enough moisture for anything else, and those berries have about 20 seeds inside them. It is really hard to keep them out of the fields.

"Would you want to hoe down those iron weeds to earn some money?"

She was delighted and her eyes brightened. "Oh, yes, Papa!"

"Okay, you have a job, then. We need to set out your responsibilities for your job. You need to hoe down only iron weeds, but if you leave them lying there, the seeds will sprout and make more weeds; so I want you to carry them to the burning pit. When you finish I will burn them for you.

"You should not try to stay out in the sun all day. Plan to work early in the morning until it gets hot. Get Mama to find you a bonnet and a pair of her work gloves. And ask her to fix you a jar of lemonade to drink when you get thirsty. Is that agreeable to you?"

With a big smile on her face, she nodded her head eagerly.

"Walk with me to the barn; I think I still have a hoe with a broken handle that should be just about the right size. Here it is. Hand me that saw hanging on the wall; and I will cut this handle off flat for you."

He held up the rusty hoe and looked at the blade, "Maybe I should sharpen it a little, too. Here; hang up the saw and hand me the file hanging over there."

He propped the hoe against his knee and began to file a little bit of an edge on it. "See that barrel in the corner? That is where I stuff toe sacks. Take one of them with you to put the weeds in…but be sure you jab your hoe down in there a couple of times before you reach in to get a toe sack. Rattlers like to climb into places like that to sleep."

Jetty's demeanor had now changed from that of a child asking for money. She was now more confident; she had a job to do and she would be a good worker. She was taking on new responsibility, and she listened carefully to every word he said.

"At the end of the week, I will pay you a quarter. Now, do you think you are lined out for your job?"

"Thank you, Papa," she said as she hugged him around the waist.

"Jetty, why do you always call me Papa? All the other girls call me Daddy."

"I just like the way it sounds. I think it is more special." She smiled at him lovingly, and then dashed off to get dressed for her new job.

Jetty faithfully worked every morning until it began to get hot, then she went in to play with her sisters. Several times one of them asked why Daddy was making her hoe weeds. She smiled a big, confident smile and said, "He is paying me a quarter!" None of the rest of the girls seemed that interested in money.

When they went to town on Saturday, Epsy gave Jetty her quarter. She hurried to the corner of the store where women's toiletries were kept, and she selected what she considered to be the prettiest little mirror on the display rack. She asked the clerk, "Put it in a small sack, please. I want to keep it a secret."

As Jetty set out plates for breakfast Sunday morning, she placed the small sack in Mama's plate and continued setting out silverware, butter, jelly, sugar bowl and salt and pepper just as usual. But there was a big smile on her face.

Rachael finally finished cooking and turned to look at the table to see if everything was in place. Bessie was pouring coffee for Mama at the time so Rachael did not notice the gift in her plate. When she sat down and saw the little sack, she drew in a quick breath and a puzzled look came on her face. "What is this?" she asked and looked around the table from face to face. She knew it was from Jetty because of the great big smile on her face.

"Open it, Mama! Open it!" Jetty said. She could hardly contain her excitement.

As Rachael took the little mirror out of the sack, Jetty's happiness burst out. "Happy Mother's Day, Mama! It is for you to carry in your purse, so you can check your hair when we get to where we are going."

"Mother's Day? Oh, it is very nice. Come here, Darling, and let me give you a hug. This is so thoughtful."

The other girls looked from one to another with puzzled looks. This was a new concept they knew nothing about. How did Jetty get ahead of them?

Jetty saw their stunned expressions. "Now they know why I was working so hard hoeing weeds," she thought. She looked at her papa and they smiled a satisfied smile.

After breakfast, Epsy walked outside and as soon as Jetty finished scraping and stacking dishes, she followed him out. "Papa, I really do hate those old iron weeds! I know now why you call them 'iron weeds'; when you try to hoe them down, they are just like iron!"

She watched him at his work a few minutes. "Why do you think God made those ole iron weeds, anyway?"

Epsy laughed a big enjoyable laugh. "I suppose to make us appreciate the good plants that He grows." Then he laughed some more…they both had a good laugh about those old iron weeds.

*****

"Mama, can Mary come outside and play with me. It is so quiet since school started."

"No, honey, she is just now crawling. She would put dirt and rocks in her mouth. Why don't you come inside and play with her?"

"Well, she doesn't play babies very well. She just tries to chew on their feet."

"Well, is Spotty not feeling good enough to play yet?" Laura shook her head slowly and sadly.

"I know what! You can pull a chair up here and help me stir up this cake. Do you want to learn how to sift flour and break eggs? That is the way Sister started and now she is a pretty good cook."

Laura pushed the chair up to the cabinet and climbed up in it. And Rachael handed her a measuring cup.

"Open that cabinet door and pull out the flour bin. Now, put the cup underneath the spout and turn that little handle on the side.

"See how the flour comes out like snowflakes? It is so soft and fluffy. Now, slow down turning when the cup gets nearly full.

"Okay, that is full enough. Pour that gently into this bowl and fill it with flour again."

While Laura turned the sifter crank, Rachael put in other necessary ingredients like salt and soda.

"Okay, that is about a cupful. Gently pour it into the bowl, and fill it one more time. Isn't this fun, working together?"

Rachael had been mixing sugar and cocoa. "Got that one full? Good girl. Now we are through with the flour, so you can push the flour bin back inside the cabinet and close the door.

"Do you see what I am working on? The cocoa mixes best with the sugar. It takes a long time to get all the cocoa mixed, but we have to get all those little brown lumps mixed in.

"Next we mix the eggs into the cocoa and sugar. Let me put my hands over your hands, and I'll teach you how to break eggs. She put her hands over Laura's and guided her movements.

"Tap it lightly on the edge of this cup, just so it cracks the egg shell a little bit. Then put your thumbs in the center of the break in the shell and sort of push in. That's it. Now, pull out towards each end, like this.

"Very good! Gently pull the eggshell apart and let the egg drop into the cup. Okay! Pour that egg into this little bowl, and break another egg. I'll let you try it by yourself this time.

"That's okay, you just pushed your thumbs into the shell a little too hard. It takes a little practice to know just how hard to press. Don't worry about that little piece of shell in there. I'll show you how to scoop it out with the eggshell.

"Pour that into the bowl and break another one, now. Yes, you did great that time. Now is that three? Count the yellows. Now comes the really fun part." She reached into the drawer and brought out the rotary beater. "Have you seen me use this before?

"We stand the beater up straight in the bowl of eggs. Put your left hand on this handle across the top and hold it tight." She put her hand over Laura's to steady it. "Now, with your right hand you turn the little crank on the side. That makes the beaters go around. See how it draws the yellows into the beaters and pops them? We have to do this until the white and yellow is all mixed together really good. Isn't this fun?

"That should be enough. Now, we pour the eggs into this chocolate and sugar mixture. See how nicely the eggs mix in with the sugar? We want to mix a little smidge of cinnamon and ground hazel nuts in with that.

"Now, we will stir the flour mixture gently to be sure the soda and salt are mixed in well. Then I'll put about three big spoons of flour in here and stir until it is mixed. Do you want to do the stirring?

"Ha, ha, ha, ha. Don't worry about that, honey. A little flour on your face just lets folks know that you did the cooking. That's good. Almost all the flour is mixed.

"Next, I will put about three spoonfuls of buttermilk, and you keep stirring. Are you getting tired? Want me to stir awhile? Okay.

"Now you can put three spoons of flour in for me. What if I get flour in my face? Ha, ha, ha.

"You know the most important thing is that while we are making the cake, we are loving the people we are making it for: Papa, Sister, Corrine, Neva, Jetty and little Mary.

"We just keep mixing like this until all the flour and buttermilk are used up.

"Now, I've already greased and floured the pans. Let me check the oven." She opened the oven door and carefully put her hand and forearm into the center of the oven. "Yes, I believe it is hot enough. I'll divide the batter between the two pans, spread the batter around evenly, gently pat each pan twice on the bottom so that any large air bubbles will float to the top, and into the oven it goes!

"Now, let's check the time so we will know when to take it out of the oven. And while it cooks, we can get these things washed and our mess cleaned up. Isn't it fun cooking together?

"Ah-oh. Mary's is waking up. Let's go change her diaper and she can come into the kitchen with us."

****

"If you girls will clear the table and scrape the plates, Laura is going to serve everyone a piece of the cake she helped make today. Take Papa one first, honey. Let's see if he likes our cake.

"No, Mary doesn't need a whole piece by herself. I'll give her bites of mine. Okay, I think this one is for you. Let's try it, now. I'll bet it's good because it was made with a lot of love!"

****

"Mama, make Laura give me a piece of her gum," Jetty said with a whine in her voice.

"Come here, darling, let's talk." Rachael stopped darning socks and put her arm around Jetty's waist, pulling her close in a half-way hug. "What did you buy when Laura got her Teaberry gum?"

"I got a Hershey, Mama."

"And did you offer to trade some of your Hershey for some of her gum?"

"No. I ate it all."

"Would you like to offer her some of your Hershey next time we go to town if she will share her gum, now?"

Jetty nodded her head.

"Laura, come here, baby. If Jetty will give you two squares of her Hershey next time we go to town, will you share your gum with her now?"

Laura looked at Jetty for a moment, trying to determine if she was telling the truth. Then she nodded her head and held out the package of her favorite gum: Teaberry fruit flavor gum!

When they arrived home from their next shopping trip, the girls helped put things away and started to disappear, one by one. As Jetty started to leave the kitchen, Rachael called her back.

"Sweetheart, did you give Laura some of your Hershey?" "Yes, ma'am."

"How much did you give her?"

"Two squares, just like you said, Mama."

"Which squares did you give her, darling?"

"What do you mean?"

"What was the letter on the ones you gave Laura?"

"I gave her the 'H's, Mama, right off the top."

Rachael smiled and nodded her approval. "Thank you, baby."

Jetty grinned and ran out the door. Rachael was still smiling to herself, "Just like it says. 'You give the first tenth.' My baby understands the principal."

****

On one cold winter day when the skies were gray and the weather was damp and dreary, the girls ran out of indoor games to play. The house was very quiet; the girls sat slumped in a chair or just lying around with solemn looks on their faces.

"Girls, I think today would be a good day to have a quilting bee!" Rachael called from the kitchen.

"What's a quilting bee, Mama?" they all tried to ask at the same time.

"That is when a group of ladies get together and sew on a quilt. I have the squares of a very pretty quilt top stitched together. I have just been waiting for the right time to put it on the frame to begin quilting it.

"Let's see, Sister, you know where I keep my sewing. Look in that cabinet and pick out the quilt top. It should be near the top. Corrine, somewhere in that cabinet is a roll of cotton batting. Neva, while they are looking, you sweep the living room floor very carefully so we can lay it all out in the floor.

"Jetty, you and Laura look under my bed and pull out the quilting frame…those long boards…and be sure you get the chains that hook to each end. You will have to dust them good…and watch Mary. She may get in the way and the boards will knock her feet out from under her.

"Okay, let's put the quilt backing down first. Each of you gather round and catch the edges and we will lay it down slowly and straighten it out. Now, hold it out flat while Sister and I will roll out the batting.

"Corrine, put your arms under the batting in the middle where it droops so it won't tear apart. Neva, you help her from this other side. It is okay if you step on the material, darling. It is just too big to reach across. We have to put down three of these strips to cover the whole thing.

"Oh, Jetty, go to the sewing machine and get my scissors and my quilting pins, those long ones. I believe they are in a little tin box. Now, hold those scissors pointed down and be careful not to trip.

"Okay, everybody gather round and help lay the quilt top down slowly without rumpling the batting. I need to pin this in place very carefully now.

"Sister, while I do this, would you take the girls into the kitchen and make some tea and put out cookies for our party? Now, make sure everybody has a job to do. It is more fun if everybody gets to help.

Soon tea was made and poured and the girls sat around the kitchen table chattering merrily as they nibbled their cookies. They used mama's good china cups with matching saucers. And each girl had a matching bread plate for her cookie. Sister made sure they used their manners, held their cookies and cups politely and took small bites. "We are practicing our company manners, now. Take only one when the cookie plate is passed." Neva laid out crisp linen napkins for everyone, knowing she would be the one who ironed them when the laundry was done this week. They pretended they were ladies at a party.

In the living room, on her hands and knees, pinning the quilt together, Rachael smiled. Her heart swelled with love as she listened to the happy sounds of her children.

"Jetty, Laura, where are those quilting frames, now? Drag them in here and put one on each side of the quilt. Corrine, I need the hammer and some small black tacks. Will you see if you can find them in the corner drawer of the kitchen cabinet? You know, where I keep string and odds and ends that I need in the house.

"Now, let's carefully slide this board under the edge of the quilt. We'll wrap the material real straight and I will tack it to the board.

"Oh, it is all right if the cotton batting sticks out a little. I left some on each edge so the binding would be padded, too.

"Now, we will do the same thing to the other side. You girls did a good job there. Let me move around there so I can tack it in place.

"Everybody get a place along the sides. Let's roll the frames under very carefully. We want the material to stay smooth, but we don't want it too tight. This side is going good. Let me come around and help get that other side started. Isn't this fun with everyone working together?

"Okay, I like the looks of that. Corrine and Sister can stand up in a chair and attach the chains to the hooks in the ceiling. The rest of us will carefully lift it up for them. Neva, get another chair and sit here so we will know how high to make it.

"Now. We need needles, thimbles and white thread, and I believe we are in business. My, we got a lot of work done with all of us working together. Everybody bring you a chair. I think I will put Mary down for her nap and have a cup of your tea, now."

There was a mad scramble for chairs and where everybody was going to sit. Jetty went back to help Laura carry her chair since she was too small to drag it by herself. The leg of the chair kept hitting her toes and she cried. "Didn't Mama tell you to put on your shoes? She doesn't like us to run around in our sock feet. Come on, now. You have to help me." But she carried the chair for her sister anyway.

"Everybody have a needle and a piece of thread? Sister, you will have to help Laura thread her needle.

"We are pretty close together here, three on each side. So everybody plan to stitch around the squares right in front of you. We rolled the quilt around the boards so we can reach the center of the quilt. Begin with the squares out in the middle and work back towards yourself. As we get really close to the boards, we will unwrap it a couple of turns and keep moving farther apart."

"Why, Mama?" Rachael looked up to see who had asked. It was Jetty. "Why must we start in the middle?"

"Well, darling, if we start on the edges, we might work our way to the center and find out that our material is a little crooked or that the quilt top or the backing is bigger than the other. There would be a big bulge in the material and nothing we could do about it. If we start in the center and see that there is slack in one place, we can adjust the pins as we go and keep it even as we move out toward the edges.

"Now, everybody remember how to anchor your thread to begin? Leave a little tag of thread hanging out and make a stitch back through the same place. Leave the needle still in the cloth. If the thread moves when you pull the tag slightly, the needle did not go through the thread underneath the material. You would need to back the needle out and try again to go through the underneath thread.

"Sister, will you anchor Laura's for her?

"Now, push the needle through the cloth just a little bit with your right hand. Hold your left hand underneath the quilt and push up just in front of the needle so that you dip up a little of the material two or three times before pulling the thread through. Now, make small stitches and be sure that you catch the quilt backing in each stitch.

"That is right. You are doing very good, girls. Now the thing that makes this such fun... makes it such a special time...is that we don't have to hurry. We can chat with each other while we sew. That is what makes it seem like a party.

"Now, Laura, be very careful or you will stick your finger under the quilt and it will hurt, baby.

"Neva, don't use your teeth to pull that needle through. You could chip a tooth, or worse, break the needle and a piece of it might go down your throat."

"But, Mama, I am trying to sew through a corner. There are so many layers of material and it is hard to get the needle to come through."

"Use your thimble to push it through a little further, honey."

"We only have three thimbles. Sister and Corrine got the other two."

Rachael cut her eyes at Corrine, who was sitting next to Neva. Corrine handed over her thimble, "I want it back, now. I am the oldest."

"Girls, remember, this is a party. We need to be pleasant to each other and make happy, polite conversation. Tell me what has been happening at school recently. Are things going good with the Cooper girls, now?"

"Mama, may I be excused? I need to go to the bathroom," Laura said in her quiet, little voice. She could hardly be heard above the chatter of the other girls.

"Of course, honey," Rachael said without looking up and without missing a stitch. She was good with a needle.

Out of the corner of her eye Rachael was watching as Laura disappeared into the other room. She leaned in slightly and said quietly, "Sister, quickly take out that stitching that Laura has done. She needs to practice quite a bit more before she becomes a quilter." She smiled kindly and looked around at all the girls.

Snickering! One girl covered her mouth, another ducked her head, but there was definite snickering all around the quilt! Rachael's head snapped up and no one wanted to look into the stern look in their mother's eyes.

In a gentle voice Rachael said, "Remember this is a quilting party! We must use our best manners and we dare not hurt someone's feelings! Now, not a word of this! If she hears about this, I will find out who told!" She raised her eyebrows and dropped her chin slightly to make an exclamation point at the end of the sentence.

"Now, you were telling me about the Cooper girls," Rachael said as Laura came back into the room.

"I thought I had done more than this," Laura said, looking around to survey the progress her sisters had made.

"Don't worry about it," Sister said. "You are still pretty small. Just make the stitches as small as you can and in a straight row. Isn't this the first time you have tried sewing?"

Laura nodded her head and began slowly making her stitches as small as she could.

"Now, isn't this fun, all of us working together? I just love it when we are all together."

Chapter Twenty Five
Girls of All Ages

On the weekends with all the girls at home, sometimes it was hard to find things to entertain themselves. Often they sat on the floor in a circle and put one hand out flat on the floor. Sister or Corrine would point to each one of their fingers, saying "Eenie, meenie, miney, moe. Catch a monkey by the toe. If he hollers, make him pay, fifty dollars every day. O-U-T spells out goes he."

Whichever finger it landed on was folded under, and the game began again with the next available finger. However, when one person finally got all five fingers folded under, that person had to go outside and run around the house by themselves. Then they would start a new game.

Rachael was used to one of the girls running out the back door and around the house, then back in the back door. Once in a while, though, Laura would come into the kitchen slowly, crying quietly, and go out the back door.

Rachael watched through the windows. Laura might go around the corner and stand there crying, but never all the way around the house. Finally, the girls got tired of waiting and came into the kitchen for a snack.

They all felt the weight of Rachael's stare, looking from one of them to another. Corrine looked up at her mother and took a deep breath, "It's always the same, Mama. If Laura is the one who runs out of fingers first, she cries because she is scared to go around the house by herself."

"Can you play something else?"

"If we play 'One potato, two potato' it is the same thing. Whenever she loses, she starts to cry."

"Well, will you step out and tell her to come back into the house for me?"

"Laura, come on back in. We have quit playing, now."

****

Toward the end of school, the girls came home talking about the 'end of school' party that the Woods are planning. Everyone had something to tell, all trying to talk at the same time. Bessie was the oldest, so she got to go first.

"Mama, they are going to have a wienie roast when school is out. The boys are going to clear a big place to build a fire and drag up the wood. And Mama, I said that Corrine would make a big batch of your lemonade, and I would bake a cake to bring. Is that okay?"

"Of course, it is, Sister. Will they need us to bring some of the things for hot dogs? Oh, I guess I can walk over and talk to Jessie about it. This will be fun."

"Mama, what would be good to wear to a wienie roast. Corrine and I want to look nice, but it won't be an inside party?"

"What is so special that you need to look real nice for a wienie roast?"

"Imogene is going to invite her cousin, Joe. Mama, I want to look real nice, but not showy."

"Well, I might make you a new dress. Let's get the catalog and get some ideas."

****

"Mama, do you like this one? Is the neck too low? I'll be 16 this fall."

Corrine came over to look at the dress, and she took over. "You won't be 16 till nearly Christmas! And, yes, that neck is too low! It will make you look too easy, and Joe will not be interested in you. He is not looking for that kind of girl, Sister. He likes you for who you are, not for what you are willing to show.

"Here, let's use this cup towel as your collar. Let's go look in Mama's big mirror so you can see, too, Sister.

"Take off your blouse. All right, now pretend this is a beautiful white collar that Mama has made you. See, now it is a round neck."

She put her finger in the center and pulled down, "Or we can make it a V-neck. We can raise it, or we can lower it.

"Now, you change it different ways. See which way it looks best on you. Hey, pull down with a finger on each side; see what a square neck looks like.

"Oh, Sister! Your face is mostly round, so I like the square neck on you.

"Sister, move your fingers further out. Good! That makes it a little higher in the front, but it lets more skin show on your shoulders. What do you think, Mama? Do you like this or the V-neck?"

Bessie had been very quiet through all of this. "Mama, are you getting any ideas?"

"Yes, but it looks so grown up. Bessie, do you really care for this Joe, whom I have never met?"

"Yes, Mama, I do."

Rachael took a deep breath and stared off at the corner. "You are so young; so serious, but so young."

She dug into her box of sewing things and pulled out several pieces of material. "Do you like this, Sister? I was able to get five of these feed sacks. I really liked this watermelon shade of pink with the little white daisies. It has just enough green stems to make it look like a pretty painting." She rubbed her hand slowly across the squares of material.

She reached back into the box and pulled out some white pique and laid it across the feed sacks. "This would make a pretty collar, and I have some narrow gathered lace to edge it.

"Five sacks would make a really full gathered skirt. Does that sound pretty to you, Sister?"

"I think it will look very pretty with your long blond hair, Sister," Corrine put in.

Bessie smiled and rushed to hug her mother. "Mama, that will make me look so pretty. Thank you, so much."

"How could he resist you?" Corrine asked and hugged her sister.

"I'll make it a little loose in the bosom. You have really developed, and early. But I would not be surprised if you grow a little more."

****

"Sister, the dress is finished. Want to try it on one last time?"

"Oh, Mama, it is beautiful! Help me get into it, would you?"

"Now, hold still so I can button you up in the back. See?" Rachael plumped up the fullness at the top of the sleeve a bit. "When I starch and iron it, I will iron a crease across the top of these gathered sleeves so they will stand up like this.

"Oh, Mama! It is beautiful!"

"Does it feel right? Is it too tight or too loose anywhere that makes it uncomfortable? The waist looks about the right length. I left it a little loose across the bosom so you can wear it throughout the summer. I think that looks all right. What do you think?"

Bessie was looking at herself in the long mirror. She touched the delicate white collar dreamily; she caught the sides of the skirt and held it out, kind of swaying. Then she spun around.

"Oh, and I made you this full petticoat to make the skirt stand out some," Rachael said. "Step into this. See, it has elastic in the waist to hold it up. It will stretch over your hips, but hold tight to your waist so it doesn't slide down. No more tying them up!

Rachael nodded her head approvingly, "Yes, that did make a difference. And it will make it stand out even more when I starch it. Now, put on your house dress and let's get busy on supper. The party is in two days. You will need to make your cake tomorrow evening."

As they walked out of the bedroom, Rachael reached out and caught Bessie by the shoulders. She pulled her close in a gentle, lingering hug. "I love you, Bessie. You were my baby! But all of your life you have been mothering and taking care of the little ones. Sometimes I think you must have been born grown up. You have been so much help to me with the little ones; but now I feel as if I am losing you. You have become a grown up young woman. And while everything looks just the same, I feel as if I have to let go. You are a woman of quiet strength, Bessie. And I am so proud of you...who you have become...who you will be."

Jetty burst into the house and the screen door banged, "Mama, make Neva let me swing. I gave her a turn; now she won't get out and let me have my turn!"

"See what you have waiting for you?" Rachael raised her eyebrows and smiled at Bessie.

****

The evening of the party Epsy was home a little earlier than usual. To his wife's puzzled look he said, "Got to get spiffed up if I'm going to the party with yall."

And there was a hub-bub with everybody getting ready at once. Everyone had to bathe, and the girls all had a special dress picked out to wear. Last minute adjustments and looking for bows to match caused a scramble. Finally with the car loaded and everybody sitting in their usual places, Epsy tooted the horn twice to encourage Bessie to hurry.

She stepped out the back door and closed it, hesitatingly. And she slowly turned around, a beautiful, poised young woman. "That's the main reason I am going tonight," Epsy said under his breath and nodded his head several times.

"Okay, Laura, you squeeze up here with us, honey. We can't have anything crushing that skirt," he said as he put the car in gear.

****

They arrived at the Wood's house about sundown. The boys already had the bonfire blazing high, and it was a spectacle in the soft shades of evening. Epsy helped Rachael and the girls carry in the food they had brought, he shook hands with Ed, and the two men drifted outside. "I'm kind of looking for a place where I can see, but not be seen," Epsy confided nodding toward Bessie. "I mean, be out of everyone's way," he grinned sheepishly. Ed understood, and they carried a couple of chairs out under the big tree beside the house.

"Now, Neva and Jetty, I want you two to kind of keep an eye on Laura and don't let her get hurt. I don't mean you can't play with your friends, but keep her near you. Let her be a part of the fun, okay?" Rachael watched for just a few seconds to see if her suggestion was going to work.

Luckily there were other younger brothers and sisters who weren't in school yet, and they kind of found each other. They played a lot quieter things, like drawing in the dirt, a little farther from the bonfire.

And the older kids were loud! Many of them running, playing tag, laughing loud. Today was the last day of school, and they were out for the summer. This was their time to howl.

"School's out, school's out. Teacher turned her mules out," could be heard frequently.

It didn't take long for Joe to notice that Bessie was there. They walked slowly around the bonfire a few times, talking. Then they stopped at the wagon Ed had backed up a little way from the bonfire. Joe took her by the waist and helped her up on the back of the wagon. They sat there watching the fire and talking most of the evening.

Ed and the boys had cut small mesquite limbs, shaved off the bark, the leaves and thorns. And they had sharpened the ends to roast wienies. Joe had a couple of sticks saved back especially for Bessie and him. They roasted wieners together, made their hot dogs, and went back to the wagon. They set down their plates and again he helped her onto the wagon.

When Joe went back to refill their lemonade glasses, Rabon met him at the table. "Joe, I think you had better go ahead and ask Mr. Hale if you can come calling on his daughter. He has been watching yall all evening."

"Where? I didn't see him."

"You haven't seen anybody but Bessie, you dummy! He is sitting over there under that tree, sharpening his knife like he always does when he is deep in thought."

On the way back to the wagon, Joe took a little better look at the landscape. "Yup, there he sits!" Then he looked back over at Bessie. She was lifting her skirt slightly and letting the air make it stand up...poofy, real pretty.

He handed Bessie the two glasses of lemonade and hopped up on the wagon. They sat in silence for a while. Then Joe said, "Bessie, would it be okay if I come to call on you some evening? Or Sunday afternoon! If I came out after work, it would be pretty late. Maybe Sunday would be better."

"I'd like that, Joe. I'd like to get to know you better. And that way my family could get to know you, too. Do you play dominoes? My daddy sure likes to play dominoes. That might be good."

"That might be good!" Joe thought as he nodded his head.

****

When the party was breaking up and Rachael had gathered up her things, she called the girls to help load the car. Joe helped Bessie off the wagon and walked her to the car. He helped Bessie into the back seat; then stood by the driver's door waiting for Epsy.

"Mr. Hale, my name is Joe Wood," Joe said holding out his hand to shake. "Forgive me for not introducing myself earlier." Epsy shook his hand slowly, his head tilted back a little, his eyes a bit narrow; but he didn't say a word.

"I'm Ed's nephew. I live in Big Spring," he said, rather hoping Epsy would let go of his hand soon. "I am fond of your daughter, sir. I would like to ask your permission to come calling on a Sunday. I work at the Palmer Hotel Restaurant, learning to be a chef. Sunday is the only day I have off work.

"Bessie said you like to play dominoes. If you would permit me, sir, I would like to be considered friend enough to play dominoes with you."

"I think that would be nice," Epsy said and finally let go of his hand. "I'd like to get to know you. Come for Sunday dinner about 11:00. Rachael usually cooks fried chicken on Sunday. She is very good at that."

Rachael was nearing the car about that time and she caught his attention. He stepped around Joe and walked over to help her into the passenger's seat. As he started the Model-T, he said, "Rachael, I have invited Mr. Wood for Sunday dinner. Is that okay with you?"

****

The summer fairly flew by. Joe came out almost every Sunday. Sunday dinner had always been special, but now Rachael and Bessie seemed to outdo themselves. Bessie was practicing her baking, so there was fresh cake or cobbler every Sunday.

It was such fun just to watch Rachael and Bessie try to beat Epsy and Joe at dominoes. There was a lot of talking and laughter. Joe would even hold Laura in his lap and sometimes let her put the dominoes out. By the end of summer, Bessie was walking him to his car when he left...and they held hands!

One Sunday morning Epsy walked up behind Bessie as she was rubbing the back of her hands and her forearms against the Rosemary bush; then she rubbed her hands against her neck. He just stood there quietly, and when she turned around, she was startled and a bit embarrassed.

He put his arm across her shoulders as they walked toward the backdoor. "Bessie, if you are interested in a young man, you need to watch him for a good while to see if he keeps his fences mended. Okay, darling?" He patted her on the shoulder and walked on.

After Joe left that evening, Bessie caught Rachael by herself and asked, "Mama, Daddy said to watch Joe and see if he keeps his fences mended. What does he mean by that?"

Rachael poured them a glass of tea and sat down at the table. "Well, you keep your fences mended to keep your livestock in, and to keep other people's livestock out. I think he means that you can tell a lot about a person's nature by how he cares for his possessions. If a man has a good pair of shoes and doesn't keep them polished, they don't weather well, or if he doesn't take good care of his car it won't last very long. If he doesn't replace damaged shingles after a high wind or hail storm, the roof will always leak.

"If he takes good care of things and makes them last, he will have money to buy other nice things, instead of constantly replacing what he already has. Does that make sense to you?

"I think Papa really means that if he takes good care of his shoes because he wants them to look nice and takes good care of his car, keeps it clean and shiny and running good, if he is quick to replace broken shingles so that the roof won't leak, he will most likely take good care of you. Provide well for you.

"No matter how much you care for a man, if your papa doesn't think he will take good care of you, Papa will not let him marry you.

"Now, I'm about worn out. Let's get ready for bed. Okay?"

****

Everybody loaded up in the T-Model for the first day of school. There was a special excitement in the air because of the new schoolhouse. More people were moving into the area all the time, and now Center Point had a two room schoolhouse. Mrs. Smith would teach the younger grades, and Mr. Smith would teach the older grades.

"I'll bet Mrs. Smith is happy not to have responsibility for keeping the older boys in line," Epsy said as they drove to school. "I am looking forward to seeing the new schoolhouse. Have you seen it yet, Rachael?"

She shook her head 'no.' Mary was sitting on her knees and Laura was standing beside her. She was brushing Laura's hair and holding ribbons in her teeth. The wind gently flipped the ribbons into her eyes occasionally and she had to shake her head to see.

"That looks good," Rachael said. She patted Laura's shoulders and looked up just in time to get her first look at the new schoolhouse. "My, doesn't that look nice. It is about twice as large as the old one and has two stove pipes."

They all went over to Mrs. Smith to introduce Laura to her. All the girls loved Mrs. Smith. Rachael turned to Neva and Jetty, "Now, yall look out for her and try to keep her from getting scared because she will cry. Okay?"

Epsy and Rachael walked to the other side of the building to meet Mr. Smith and introduce Bessie and Corrine.

The girls quickly found their friends and wandered off. "Well, I had better get on into town for work," Epsy shook hands with Mr. Smith again, and they hurried to take Rachael and Mary home.

****

Since school started, Joe still came out every Sunday, but he didn't seem as ready to play dominoes. He wanted to take Bessie for walks; sometimes he would push her in the swing. One day Rachael looked out the window just in time to see Joe stop the swing and take Bessie's hand. He slowly kneeled down on one knee.

"Epsy, come here! You have to see this!"

Epsy walked up behind her just in time to see Bessie start crying and nodding her head 'yes'. He took a deep breath and turned away from the window to hide the tears coming to his eyes. This was his baby, too; and he loved his girls.

****

"Have you bought her a ring?"

"No, sir, I wanted to ask your permission first."

"How do you plan to provide for her? Do you have any money saved?"

"Yes, sir, I have more than $2,000 in a savings account. I have been saving because I want to own my own restaurant someday. My parents have a little house across the corner from their house that they said we could live in rent free until we need more space. That will help us save money faster.

"It will need paint and we will need to buy some furniture for it. But it has good plumbing…it has an inside bathroom! "I love your daughter, Mr. Hale. I plan to take very good care of her. And I want us to have a real nice church wedding. That is really important to me. You already know that I don't attend church real regularly, but I think this is very important."

"I think you have said the right words, Joe, and I saw her reaction when you asked her. She hasn't finished school, yet. When would you plan to get married?"

"Oh, as soon as possible, sir. The sooner the better! I've waited about as long as I can stand it." Epsy frowned. "I mean seeing her every Sunday and not able to touch her….sir."

"Well, let's go talk to the women and get their take on this. Sometimes they see things we do not see." Epsy folded his knife and put it in his pocket as he stood up. He laid his hand on Joe's shoulder and steered him toward the house. "Son, I think it is time you started calling me Epsy. When do you think we can meet your parents?"

In the kitchen, Rachael and Bessie were huddled over the table, waiting. When Joe walked through the back door smiling, Bessie started to cry. "Oh, Papa, is it all right then?"

"Yes, honey. I think he will make you a fine husband. I would like for us to meet Joe's parents, and I understand he wants to get married as soon as possible. So I guess we had better get started making plans.

"Is that okay with you, Rachael?"

Joe stayed a little later that evening and Rachael and Epsy let them have some time alone.

****

Rachael walked with the girls as they left for school the next morning, however, she and Mary and Bessie stopped at Jessie's house.

Jessie was delighted to have company this morning, but she was very puzzled that Bessie stayed.

"Jessie, Joe and Bessie are going to be married," Rachael blurted out and waited for a reaction.

"Ohhh," Jessie squealed and clapped her hands. "I saw this working, and I have been hoping."

She hugged Bessie, "Joe is a real fine boy. Has his head on straight. He will do good by you. Okay, when is the wedding going to be? Tell me all about your plans."

"As soon as possible!" Rachael said. "Will you help me put this together, Jessie?"

Jessie's brow furrowed; she covered her mouth to stifle an 'ooww' sound. She involuntarily shot a glance at Bessie.

"No, she is not pregnant; it is Joe who is in a hurry. I don't think it will take long before she is, though, from what he told Epsy," Rachael laughed. She smiled at her daughter. "He must really love you, darling."

"Jessie, Mama said it will probably take her about two weeks to make me a wedding dress. Joe wants us to be married in a church, with lots of family and friends, a big cake, the works. Will you help us?"

"Of course, I will, honey. What do you need me to do?"

"First of all, Daddy wants to meet Joe's parents. Would you mind asking them and us to supper?"

"Of course! Each family should feel comfortable here, and we can keep things rolling if conversation bogs down. Would Sunday be good for yall?"

Rachael smiled and nodded. "One hurdle down. Now, Bessie show her the Sears Roebuck catalog. Show her the dresses you like, and let's start planning." Rachael lifted her coffee cup and leaned back to savor the flavor in solitude.

Between the three of them they decided on a smooth flared skirt of white pique with an inverted pleat in the center front and back. A row of lace daisies will delicately cover the seam between the skirt and bodice. And she absolutely wanted a 'sweetheart neckline' with puffed sleeves. "Yes, I think a 'sweetheart neckline will be pretty, and it is acceptable on your wedding dress, darling," Rachael counseled. "We will just have to see what kind of material they have to make the bodice. I think it would look delicate if it is sort of see-through, and I will make you a pretty fitted bodice to wear underneath. What do you think?

"Jessie, you are good at drawing. Can you sort of sketch a picture of it?"

Jessie quickly found pencil and paper and began drawing. "Do you think you want short sleeves or long puffy sleeves all the way to your wrists? Whichever way, it would be pretty to have the daisies on the ruffle of the sleeve. Now, would you like it to be made like a fitted dress or full to the waist, as if it were a blouse tucked inside? Your mama can make the fitted bodice support the weight of the skirt so that the light weight material will fluff a little at the waist."

"Oh, I don't know. This is too much to decide right now," Bessie said. "Let me think about it overnight."

"Hey, if we have Vida Mae and Joe out for supper on Sunday so yall can get acquainted, maybe we three and Vida Mae can go shopping in Big Spring on Monday. You will like her, I know. We can find a pattern that you can work from, Rachael, and pick out material. We might even stop by the jewelry store and let Bessie see what kind of ring she likes. It will be a fun day! What do you think?"

So that evening after supper Rachael sat down and wrote to Jewel and James.

"The honor of your presence is requested at the wedding of our daughter, Bessie Mae...."

*****

"Epsy, I think you should go talk to the preacher at the community church to ask if we can reserve it for the wedding."

"Mama, Joe is planning to use the Methodist Church in Big Spring." Bessie said. "That is where his family goes to church, and he knows the preacher there. Joe said he would talk to him. And they have a new flower shop in Big Spring. Joe said he will see about getting some flowers to put up at the front of the church.

"Mama, Joe took me to see our little house. It is just three rooms, but they are kind of large rooms. We need to clean it and repaint the inside. What would you think if I stay with Joe's parents, so I can clean on it during the day?"

"Most definitely not!" Epsy voiced a strong opinion. "You can ride in with me when I go to work and come home when I get off. That will give you enough time to clean and paint."

****

The night of the engagement supper at Jessie's house there were more people present than Rachael had expected to see. "Rachael and Epsy, these are Vida Mae and Joe Wood, Joe's parents. And these are his grandparents, Jetty and Raymond Wood. They are Ed's parents, too."

Rachael smiled knowingly, "Would that be Jeta Lee?"

Very puzzled, Jetty Wood nodded cautiously.

"Well, you are probably the woman we named our Jeta Lee after," Rachael said, flashing a disarming smile. "Epsy said he heard a woman's name, Jeta Lee, while he was in Big Spring once, and he liked it. It was different. Since she looks more like him than the rest of the girls, he won the honor of naming her.

"Ha, ha, ha. Isn't it so funny how things just go round in circles? Now, we have two Jettys in our family. How will we tell yall apart?" She leaned around Neva to smile at Jetty Hale.

Jetty Wood's eyes lit on her little namesake, and it was instant love. "You can call me Aunt Jetty," she said to little Jetty. And it seemed that the two families instantly melded into one. All the girls soon loved their Aunt Jetty.

****

One night after everyone was in bed and quietly waiting for sleep to come, Corrine said softly, "Sister, I sure do miss you at school. I always depended on you to help keep me from getting into trouble. Now I'm kind of on my own and it's lonely. I still have Imogene, but it's not the same.

"And I thought Mrs. Smith was going to cry when I told her you would not be coming back to school. She said you were her best student ever."

"It is really different for me, too," Bessie whispered. "I no longer have someone telling me what needs to be done next. I have to look around and see what needs to be done and do it. It really will be different when I have to start cooking meals all by myself. It was fun when I could help Mama, and make things on my own, but she did the planning. Now, I will have to do it all alone. Corrine, do you think I am a good enough cook?"

"Of course you are, Sister. I like things you cook. And you can just remember how Mama planned things so that everything gets done about the same time. You can do it."

They were quiet for a while, thinking.

"Corrine, would you stand up with me? I think Joe is going to ask Rabon because they are real good friends."

****

"Rachael, we need to have a shower for Bessie and Joe, and I think I am the logical one to give it since I am close to both of them. Would that be okay with you?"

"Oh, Jessie, that would be so nice of you! That will really help them to get started."

"Do you think next weekend would be a good time to have it? It would be good for me, and a little over a week would give us time to invite people." Rachael was nodding her head.

"I don't think Vida Mae's friends would really mind driving out here. I'll ask her when I see her tomorrow. But let's start planning for it.

"I'll make some divinity, some peanut brittle, and fudge." She grinned sheepishly. "I like to make candy. If you will make your chocolate cake and tea cakes, I'll ask Vida Mae to make lemonade; and she makes real good date loaf candy. I think that would be a lot of refreshments, don't you?

"Oh, I just love being a hostess. It brings me such happiness." Jessie was nodding as she placed her hand in the center of her chest.

****

"Ohhh, my. Epsy said he would be back by now," Rachael said looking out the window for the twentieth time. "He knows I need him to drive us over to Jessie's house for the shower. We need to be there when the guests start to arrive.

"I did not really know that man he went to town with. No telling what they are looking for or buying. Let's go ahead and load things in the Model-T so we will be completely ready when he gets here.

"Now, make sure you tuck the tea towels under the plates so they won't blow while we drive."

She busied herself for a few minutes more; then she could stand it no longer. "Well, Jessie said she learned to drive when Ed got sick from the heat, and she had to drive him to the doctor all the way into Coahoma. I guess now is a good time for me to try! Let's get in the car, girls."

Bessie and Corrine looked at each other doubtfully, kind of shaking their heads. While Rachael saw to seating the younger girls, Corrine said, "Sister, I'll set the spark and the throttle about where Papa usually sets them. You sit in the front and hold the brake. I'll turn the crank, and as soon as it starts, I'll jump out of the way and jump on the running board as the car goes by. Now, you hold back on that brake handle good and tight!"

Bessie took charge inside the auto, Girls, leave room for Corrine to sit behind the driver, okay? And leave that door open, will you? "Neva," she said quietly, "you hold on to Laura. I'll hold Mary.

Rachael sat in the driver's seat looking at the circular lever for the spark, there in the center of the steering wheel, and the knobs and dials on the dashboard. Her face went pale and she was staring like a calf looks at a new gate! It was as if she never intended to drive, so she didn't pay any attention when Epsy drove.

She grasped the steering wheel tightly with both hands and pressed her lips together hard as she took a deep breath. She looked at Corrine waiting in front of the car, her hand on the crank. Rachael kind of nodded, Corrine cranked, and the Model-T sprang to life.

"Putt, putt, ugha, ugha, chuga, chuga, chuga, chuga." Corrine jumped away from the front of the car; she reached the open door just as Bessie released her pressure on the brake handle. Corrine jumped on the running board, and the door, which opened from the front, scooped her inside.

"Turn, Mama! Turn that way so we can go behind the house and get to the road!" Bessie yelled.

Rachael began to get the idea. She turned behind the house, drove across the corner of the field, then into the bar ditch and up onto the road…and across the road, and into the bar ditch on the other side.

"Turn, Mama! Turn back the other way!" Corrine yelled.

She turned the steering wheel toward Bessie and they slowly made their way out of the bar ditch, onto the road, and into the other bar ditch.

Bessie stared at the cotton stalks coming closer and closer to her. "Turn, Mama! Turn that way!" One year old Mary began to cry because of all the yelling.

Rachael turned and headed back toward the road, only to cross it again and head into the other bar ditch.

Neva had her arms wrapped around Laura to hold her in place. In her freight she began to squeeze too tightly, and Laura began to cry.

Jetty mostly had her head hidden behind the front seats, while she tried to keep the cake and cookies from spilling as they slid one way then the other.

"Turn it back that way, Mama," Corrine said when they were in the bar ditch on her side.

In this manner they made it to Jessie's house a half mile down the road. "Turn this way, Mama. There is the drive into Jessie's house."

The Model-T pulled up in Jessie's drive, and the girls prepared to get out, but the car just kept rolling. "Make it stop, Mama! You are heading for the barn!" But they passed the barn. Bessie yelled, "Turn this way, Mama! Go around the barn!

"Oohh, straighten it up before you hit the side of the barn! Now, turn this way! Now, straighten it up! Now, turn! Now, go straight!"

Rachael finally got the wheels turned just right so that they drove a circle around the barn and didn't have to make corners. Now, all the yelling stopped, and Mary and Laura stopped crying. Everybody just sat there and watched the scenery pass by as they rode around and around the barn until the car ran out of gas.

"Whoo-hoo," Rachael said as she stepped out of the car and walked unsteadily toward Jessie and Imogene. She held out her hand for Jessie to steady her, "I think I need to sit down."

The girls carried things in from the car and had everything set up nicely when the guests started to arrive. Jessie had a beautiful white linen tablecloth on her dining table. On each end of the table, she had a two-tiered candy dish with a variety of candies. A plate for teacakes at each end kept it balanced. She had a crystal punchbowl sitting toward the center back with a space next to it for the cake plate. In the center of the table was a medium-sized, shallow, white bowl filled with the flowerets from Jessie's Lantana. Rachael smiled when she saw it, "What a lovely center piece you have created."

"Thank you. Lantana was the only flower with pretty blooms this time of year. I just snipped them all off and mixed up all the colors!" she giggled.

After a few minutes to recover, Rachael got tickled. She looked at Jessie, "I thought you said driving was easy once you got started!"

As their eyes met, they had a big, long laugh together as they thought about the ordeal of driving for the first time. Jessie was very grateful, too, that it was out in the open now and Rachael was okay to laugh out loud about it.

"I think you have done the hard part, Rachael. You made it all the way down here. We have a can of gas; we can give you some gas to go home on."

When the shower was over and it was time to go home, the girls loaded Bessie's gifts into the back seat of the car. Rachael got Mary and Laura into the car and climbed in.

"Now, remember," Jessie told her, "when you want to slow down or stop, push in a bit on the throttle…but not all the way, and pull up on the brake handle. Just pull up however hard it takes to slow it down."

Corrine turned the crank, the car started, and she jumped out of the way. The four older girls had decided to walk home. Mary and Laura didn't know they had a choice.

Finally back at home, Rachael turned into the drive and pulled up lightly on the brake handle. The car rolled past the back door. This time she pulled up hard! The car stopped on a dime and sputtered until the engine died.

Rachel nodded once, as if saying to herself that she had done a pretty good thing...over there and back. She stepped out and was lifting the girls down, as she saw Epsy step out the back door. He set his cup of coffee on the porch and came to help unload the car.

"I drove over to Jessie's house for the shower," Rachael said, nodding her head.

"Yup, I saw the ruts across the corner of the field. "Where are the girls?" he asked as he walked toward the porch, loaded with gifts.

"They decided to walk home," she said, and opened the door for him.

"Um-hum," he said, nodding his head. "Did you get home with any of that chocolate cake for me?"

He removed the cup towel from the cake plate and discovered one piece of chocolate cake...an end piece with lots of chocolate frosting.

****

And so it was that on Friday evening, October 30, 1926, Epsy walked his oldest daughter down the aisle. Tears were running down his cheeks as he hugged her, pressed his lips together and nodded to her; then he placed her hand in Joe's hand. He stepped back and sat beside Rachael and took her hand in his. He held it awfully tight.

Chapter Twenty Six
Girls Growing Up

Laura came in the back door and let it bang behind her. "Mama, I can't find Spotty. Have you seen her?"

"No, honey, I have been busy. I don't think I've seen her. Did you call her, and she didn't come?" Laura nodded her head. "Well, I'm sure she will be home in time to eat this evening."

****

"Corrine, she has been sitting out there by the barn all afternoon. Will you go out and try to cheer her up?"

Corrine sat down beside Laura, tucked her skirt up around her knees, and leaned back against the barn. For a few moments they just sat there quietly. Corrine picked a bristly head off a clump of buffalo grass and put it in her hands with the palms up. As she moved each hand back and forth, the spiny seed-head seemed to crawl toward her. When it reached the edge of her palms, she put her forearms together and the seed-head continued to crawl up her arms.

Laura quietly watched; she leaned her head over to watch the seed-head as it crawled up Corrine's arms. "Do you want to try it?" Corrine asked, picking another 'crawler'. Laura nodded her head and placed her hands together.

Corrine put the seed-head into her hands, "Now, move your hands back and forth."

It tickled Laura's hands, and she jerked them apart, letting the crawler fall on the ground. She rubbed her hands on her skirt to stop the tickling sensation. Corrine giggled, "It feels funny, doesn't it? Try it again, and maybe you won't drop it."

They played with their 'crawlers' for a while; then Neva stepped out the back door. "Mama said it is getting too cool. You had better come in. Supper will be ready soon."

Corrine jumped up, took Laura's hand and pulled her up. "Let's dust off our skirts," she said, so they walked to the house swatting at their back sides with every step and laughing at each other.

After supper, Laura put the scraps in Spotty's bowl and called her. But Spotty didn't come.

****

"Mama, will you fix my hair in French braids like you do Jetty's so it will stay out of my face?"

"Laura, honey, we can try, but I don't think it will stay. Her hair is black and coarse so it stays in the braids. Your hair is blond and silky, and fine as frog's hair. I think it will just creep out during the day. But, we will give it a try. Come, sit right here."

Rachael dipped the rat-tail comb in a glass of water and combed it through Laura's hair. "Tilt your head back." She put the comb on Laura's nose and drug it up to the hairline. That made Laura laugh. She made a part from center front all the way down to Laura's neck. As Rachael combed the hair away from the part and back from her face along the sides, the fine, blond hair packed together making a very thin amount of hair to work with. But, Rachael did her best.

The hair at the end of the braid she wrapped around her finger and made a curl to put the little hair clips over. "Yes, I know that is not the way I do Jetty's braids, but she has thicker hair. This is the only way I can make the hair clips stay on your hair.

"I think it looks kind of cute with that curl at the end, don't you?" she asked Neva, who had been watching. Over the top of Laura's head, Rachael gave Neva that look that said 'agree with me.' So Neva nodded her head. She handed Laura the hand mirror to look at herself, and Laura was satisfied. So, she hopped down and ran into the bedroom to show Jetty.

"Now, Neva, I think her fine hair will slide right out of those braids after it gets dry. If it starts looking shaggy, or gets in her face and bothers her, you take the clips off the braids and use them to pin her hair back on each side. Okay?"

"Yes, ma'am."

When the girls were finally ready and started walking to school, the house was suddenly quiet. Rachael poured herself a cup of coffee and a small glass of milk for Mary. She sat down and lifted Mary into her lap and started feeding her bites of biscuit dipped in sorghum syrup.

Mary usually didn't wake up until the girls had finished breakfast and were getting dressed. She just walked around, carrying her teddy bear, and watching all the hub-bub of four older sisters getting ready for school.

Now, it was her time for some attention from Mama.

****

Rachael heard the girls all talking as they walked in the backdoor, and the screen door slammed.

"Mama," Corrine called.

Rachael had been napping with Mary. She came out of the bedroom with her finger to her lips, "Shhhh!"

"Mama, Rabon wants to take me to the picture show on Saturday. 'The Jazz Singer' is showing at the Ritz Theater in Big Spring. You can hear the people talking and Al Jolson singing, and everything. It must be amazing!

"Jessie is going to Big Spring on Saturday, and she said it would be all right if I go, too."

Rachael looked as if she had been hit in the face with a pie. "I didn't know that you and Rabon were getting along that well. Every time he teases you, something about him bleeds!"

"Oh, he has quit teasing me so much. He is being real nice to me, now."

"Well, you will have to talk to your papa about this. I think Rabon is a really nice boy, and I think it would be all right for you to go into town with Jessie. But, you had better see what Papa has to say about it."

After supper Epsy sat at the table sharpening his knife while Rachael did the dishes. "What do you think about Corrine going to town with Jessie and her family?"

"Don't you mean, 'What do I think about Corrine going to the picture show with Rabon?'"

"Well, I was going to get around to that." "She is only 15 years old."
"She is almost as old as Bessie was when she got married. The real difference here is that Rabon is not as old as Joe was.

"This is his last year in school. I guess he has matured a little and decided it would be nice to have her on his side instead of always chunking rocks at him."

They looked out the window as they heard a flap, flap, flap.

"I wanted to tell you….that last strong wind loosened a piece of tin on the barn. I've heard it flapping for the past two days."

"I'm not too surprised. I put new tin on an old barn. The wood is dry and won't hold the nails. I'll get up there this weekend and put a few more nails in it, maybe putting some linseed oil on the wood might help. I really don't want to wait until we have some falling weather and have to get up there. Wet tin is slippery!" He hesitated.

"And you think it would be okay for her to go to the picture show with him?"

"We know him quite well after all these years. I believe him to be an honorable young man. I can't think of any other boy I'd rather see her go out with."

"Okay, then."

****

Corrine came in the kitchen door carrying Laura. "Mama, Laura bumped her "funny bone' and Neva and Jetty laughed when she started to cry."

"Well, put her down, honey. She is too heavy for you to be carrying around.

"Laura, come here and sit in my lap for a while. Let me rub it for you. What did you bump your elbow on?"

"The corner of the house," she sobbed.

"Isn't that funny how such a small bump can give you such a sharp, stinging pain?"

Laura nodded her head. "And when I was hurt, they started to laugh."

"So that made it hurt all the more, didn't it?" Laura nodded, sobbing.

"Well, it's just that they have bumped their 'funny bones' before and they know how bad that sharp stinging hurts. But it doesn't last long, and there is nothing you can do about it but laugh. That is why people call it your 'funny bone'."

She cuddled Laura for a while to sooth her feelings. Rachael sat staring off toward the corner, "You know, if you don't toughen up some, life is going to be really hard on you, baby girl," she said very softly as if to herself.

"Mama, why did Spotty run away from me? Did she stop loving me?"

"No, darling. It was just Spotty's time. She went looking for a boy dog to give her puppies again. We were so busy with Sister's wedding, that no one remembered it was time to lock her in the barn for a while. She may come home… but she may not be able to find her way back. I think that is how she came to live with us.

"Everything is for a season, darling. We got to have her with us for a season when you were a very lonely little girl. Now, you have started to school and have new friends, and she may have found a home with another lonely little girl.

"Now, tell me. What happened at school today that made you happy?"

Laura thought for a minute. "On the way home from school, Corrine showed us a 'Grandpa's Beard' that was opening up. And we watched the seeds with their fine white hairs pouring out! We touched them! They are white and round like the new cotton just out of the bowls, but they are so soft and light that you can't even feel them sitting in your hand. And when you blow on them, they fly away. Mama, they look like dandelions only bigger. Corrine said when the wind catches those long, fluffy hairs, they might fly into the next county!"

"She is very right about that. It is an amazing thing to see them come pouring out of the pod like that. I'm glad you got to see it."

Rachael started to lift Laura down from her lap. "Oh, Mama! There is something else. Mrs. Smith left the room today, and she asked me to sit at her desk on the podium and take names of people who misbehaved while she was gone," Laura said with a prim little smile and nodding her head triumphantly.

"Oh, really? She asked a first grader to take names?"

"Yes, I can spell everyone's name, and....I won't let anyone talk out without writing down their name. Like Neva does! And when Mrs. Smith came back the whole room was quiet and everyone was in their seat!"

"How did you manage that?"

"We pushed the teacher's desk to the back of the podium and Ben Nix played his French harp while I tap danced. Everybody was quiet!"

The back door slammed and Neva stormed in. "Yes, and now Laura says that Ben is her boyfriend! Mama, he has been sweet on me for a long time! Mama, make her stop saying that!"

****

"Corrine, tell us about the picture show. What is the jazz singer?"

"Oh, it was just wonderful, Mama! You could hear them speak just as their lips moved, just like in real life! And Al Jolson has a really good voice. He sings really good."

"But what was it about? What was the story?"

"Oh, it was about a young man who was Jewish. His father is the preacher....they called him a Cantor, and his father wants him to be a Cantor, too. But the young man likes to sing and dance for a crowd.

"He runs off and gets into show business, but he performs mostly with his face painted black like a Negro so people won't recognize him. Everybody likes his singing, and he gets really famous. But in the end he goes back home and sings the preaching for his church because he wanted to honor his father. And the story was really based on Al Jolson's life.

"And Mama, there was a cartoon after the movie. It was Mickey Mouse and his girlfriend, Minnie Mouse. It was so funny!"

"Then you had a good time?"

"Oh, yes, Rabon bought a bag of popcorn, and we shared it. The seats at the Ritz Theater fold up when no one is sitting in them. That gives you room to walk between the rows of seats."

She sat quietly for a moment; then she smiled. "Rabon held my hand," she said dreamily, then suddenly, "Mama, are we going to have a New Year's Eve party this year?"

For months afterward Corrine went around singing, "Toot, toot, Tootsie, good bye. Toot, toot, Tootsie, don't cry," one of the songs from the movie.

****

Before Christmas was passed, Corrine was planning for the New Year's Eve party. "Mama, can I have a new dress for the party? Will you make me a special dress like you did for Sister?"

"Oh, I guess we could manage that. If you will take over my housekeeping chores, I should have time to make you a pretty dress. You go get the catalog and show me some dresses that you like. I'll see what kind of material I have to pick from."

Rachael walked into the kitchen with two pieces of material and sat down beside Corrine, who was pouring over the dresses in the catalog. She had several pages dog-eared. "What do you think about this neckline?"

"Here, use the cup towel to see what looks good on you, like you did for Sister."

They went to the bedroom to look in the long mirror. "If we pull your hair back on each side, I could make you a bow for the back to match your dress. Do you like the way that looks?"

"And put a little sprig of mistletoe in it!" Neva said from the door. "Here, Mama, take Mary. She fell down, and she wants you to fix it."

Mary was snubbing as she reached out for her mama. "Fix what? Where is she hurt?"

"I don't know. I couldn't find anything wrong. She just wants you to hold her."

"Hey, Mama, would Daddy let me wear a sweetheart neckline like you made for Sister's wedding dress?"

"I just don't know, honey. I have seen some girls wearing that neckline, and if it is not too low, he might. It really is a pretty neckline.

"But, I can say with some certainty that he will not let you wear one of those 'flapper' dresses. That is for city women who want to show off everything they have!"

"Oh, Mama, I know better than to even ask," she smiled at her mother. "That could even get our party canceled; couldn't it?"

"Here, see which material you like best. I have this royal blue corduroy and a piece of solid red cotton chintz. See, this is kind of shiny. That is all that I have on hand that is enough yardage to make a dress. "I think the blue would look good on you."

"Mama, is there enough of the red to make a circle skirt instead of just a gathered skirt?"

"I guess there might be enough. Since it is a solid color, I wouldn't have to match the pattern or the weave."

"Can you make long sleeves and still make them puff up high like you did for Sister's dress? Well, yes. You made her wedding dress sleeves like that. Do you have some white to make a little collar?

"Mama, if you can swing that, I wouldn't be unhappy if Daddy won't let me wear a sweetheart neckline. Do you think this oval neck looks good? That would give it a special look without being low."

****

Epsy was buttering biscuits when Rachael sat down at the table. She had been sewing all day, and it was restful to sit down to a full dinner that someone else had cooked. He passed the biscuit pan first to Rachael. She took a biscuit, passed the pan across Mary's head to Neva, and took a bite of her biscuit.

Everyone was guardedly watching for her reaction. "Ummm, Corrine these biscuits are delightful! They rose just perfectly, so tender, and this is absolutely delicious!"

Then the normal chatter at the supper table began. Rachael fixed a plate for Mary, and Neva helped Laura. She wanted to help her own plate; so Neva supervised and passed the big bowls on to Jetty. Corrine sighed, a tired but satisfied sigh, and sat down opposite Rachael...close enough to the stove and cabinet to get up easily if there was something she had forgotten.

When supper was finished, everyone complimented Corrine on a delicious meal and started to leave the table.

"Neva, Jetty, why don't you clean off the table and do the dishes? Corrine has worked hard getting this meal all by herself. And I need her to try on her dress before I go any farther."

"Aw, Mama," they chimed in unison."

"Now, everybody has to do their part. You'll be wanting me to sew something special for you one of these days."

****

The dress and petticoat were finished just the day before New Year's Eve. Rachael starched it in heavy starch to make the top of the sleeves stand up and the petticoat stand out.

It was a busy day, with everybody cleaning house and ironing their favorite dresses for the party. Corrine had made Mama's chocolate cake for the party. This was the ultimate test! It was one thing to have Mama brag on her biscuits, but to try to duplicate Mama's chocolate cake…well!?!

Neva had made teacakes; Jetty was responsible for the lemonade. And together they arranged the table to hold all the goodies the ladies would bring.

True to her word, Neva found a way to attach a sprig of mistletoe to the red bow in the back of Corrine's hair. The girls had put mistletoe with red ribbons over every doorway and giggled the whole time.

Everyone was still busy with last minute things just before time for people to begin arriving.

"Girls! Come here and look!" Rachael called from the bedroom. All the girls gathered at the bedroom door.

"Ohhh." "Oh, my." "Oh, Corrine, you look lovely!"

"Fetching, absolutely fetching!" was Rachael's comment. The smile on her face showed happiness and love for her daughter, her grown-up daughter. It tugged at her heart to see her daughters grow up.

As they walked from the bedroom, Epsy was coming in the back door. The red dress quickly caught his eye, and he smiled. At the kitchen door, he grabbed Corrine and danced her around in a circle, stopping beneath the mistletoe. He gave her a quick kiss on the cheek; then held her by the shoulders at arm's length. "Are you wearing lip rouge?"

"Epsy, have you been drinking already? You had better wait until the party starts. There will be enough of that when everybody gets here!"

A car drove up in the drive, and Bessie and Joe walked in the back door. All eyes focused on Bessie in dismay. She was wearing a maternity dress! She was not showing very much, but Rachael could see that she could no longer wear her regular clothes.

"Do you like it, Mama?" she asked, holding her arms out to the side and turning around. "I made it myself on Vida Mae's sewing machine!"

"Oh, Sister, this is wonderful! And, yes, I do like your dress. It looks as if you did an excellent job on it.

"It is just that you hadn't said anything! You kept this a secret from us. What a surprise! When is it due?"

"Mama, I wanted to surprise you! Late May or early June," she said as the girls came out of shock and rushed to hug her all at once.

Epsy shook Joe's hand and winked.

More people began coming in the back door and the front door. Suddenly the house was full and the table was filled with goodies. Corrine tuned on the radio and found a program called, "New Year's Eve with Duke Ellington, coming to you from the Crystal Ballroom in New York City." Smooth, swing music filled the house and set the mood for a happy party.

Neva and Jetty were in charge of greeting people and taking coats to the bedroom. Laura and Mary were hostesses for the smaller children. They had their toys set out and ready to play. Corrine had dipped several cups of lemonade to have ready for guests. She was cutting cakes when Jessie and her family arrived.

When Rabon spotted her, fixed up so pretty and looking just fetching in that bright red dress, a smile broke across his face. Everybody who happened to see it knew that he was in love with her.

A few people were dancing in the living room, so Rabon asked Corrine to dance. The volume of the chatter became much lower as everyone stopped to watch them. They were an eye-catching couple, all right.

After a while Epsy missed his beauty in the red dress. Glancing out the window of the back door, he saw Corrine and Rabon sitting on the steps. "Neva, will you get me Rabon's jacket and a sweater or something for Corrine?"

When the back door opened, Rabon quickly dropped his arm from around Corrine's shoulders, and they turned around to see who was coming out. "Thought yall might need your jackets; it's pretty chilly tonight," Epsy said.

As he stepped back inside and the door closed, they started giggling. "That is quite a scare...for your papa to walk up like that," Rabon said.

"Oh, I don't think you need to worry. He already approves or he would have said so. And he wouldn't have brought us our coats. That is just his way of letting you know you had better ask if you can come calling!" She smiled at him, and they began to giggle again.

****

As the weather got colder, you could tell it was going to be a wet, icy winter. Several days it was hard for Epsy to get in to work because the roads were so icy.

He waited a lot later to have the crew move out of the yard on mornings when it was so slick. He didn't want to leave before some of the men could make it into town. And there was the possibility of wrecking the crew truck when the roads were so slick.

He always found things for the men to do in the yard to keep them busy. If they put forth the effort to show up, Epsy would give them a full day's work cleaning out toolboxes, cleaning tools, sharpening hoes and shovels.... there was always busy work to do that no one wanted to keep done up.

One icy day, when all the men had finally shown up, Epsy was getting them ready to leave the yard when he missed the two youngest of his hands. They were both in their late teens. Epsy thought they needed a baby sitter, but he was trying to teach them to work...trying to teach them to take on some responsibility.

When he found them, they were squatted down behind some crates. He found them because they were laughing so hard.

"Do you think you will get a day's pay when I find you over here hiding? Why aren't you working with the other hands?"

"We didn't really mean to be hiding, Mr. Hale. We were using these crates to block the cold wind."

That was not exactly a satisfactory answer, and Epsy squinted his eyes, glaring at them. "What do you see that is so funny, then?"

"We were watching the people trying to get across the via-duct. When there is enough ice on the roads, not very many cars can climb up that steep bridge across the railroad tracks." They were still giggling and pointing as they explained. "Most of the people who live on the north side of town, work on the south side of town. Most cars can't make it up that steep grade, but they have to try. They get up a little ways; then the car starts to turn sideways and slides back down." One of the boys slapped his leg and bent double with laughter, pointing to the via-duct.

"Once in a while one will make it to the top of the via-duct, then they can't control the car on its way down the other side, and they slide all over the street. You should see the looks on their faces once they get over the top and start picking up speed!"

"And you should see the people who are walking scamper out of the way when those cars start to slide sideways!"

Inwardly, Epsy could see how a person could laugh until he cried at such a funny sight, but it just wasn't right to laugh at someone else's plight. He glanced up at the via-duct and said, "So you boys think it is funny to laugh at someone's misfortune, do you? Well, if you want to continue working for the railroad, you had better get into the gang truck fast. We'll see how you like slipping and sliding when it is you doing it."

And true to his word, Epsy had the two boys carrying heavy, sooty, smudge pots a long way up the road to warn drivers that a crew was working on the railroad.

****

The, last few months of school seemed to pass pretty fast. Because the family was so excited about Bessie's baby and watching to see how big her stomach was getting. Everyone was guessing which would happen first: the end of school or the baby being born.

School was out first, and Jessie had a graduation party for Rabon and the rest of his class, well, it was a wienie roast since it was summer, but a party none the less.

Epsy shook his hand and congratulated Rabon on finishing the 11th grade; not too many boys stay in school that long, you know. "What do you plan to do now, Rabon?"

"I am seriously thinking about joining the Marines for a couple of years. I am only 17, and I don't really know what kind of work I want to do. I know I don't want to farm. A couple of years should give me some time to figure out what I want to do, don't you think?"

"Is that going to be okay with your parents?'

Rabon nodded, "I've been talking to them about it."

"Does Corrine know?"

"Well, not exactly. I've dropped a couple of hints…talked about the Marines fighting in Nicaragua and China, but I haven't said anything definite, yet. But I think it would be a good use of my time while she finishes her last year of school. I'd like to hear your thoughts, Mr. Hale?"

"Well, fighting in a war is serious business. Wouldn't be anything glamorous about it; could get you hurt or even killed. But if you live through it, it would give you some good experience, hard experience, I think. A man has to do what he thinks best," Epsy looked him straight in the eyes, "after he has thought it over really well."

Rachael rushed up behind him and patted him on the shoulder. He could tell there was urgency in her demeanor. "Bessie's water broke. I have to go. She is planning to have the baby at Vida Mae's house. They have everything all set up and ready, but I want to be there with her.

"I will ride in with Bessie and Joe, and I may stay a couple of nights. Corrine can take care of the girls and the house for a few days. I think she will do fine." She gave him a quick kiss on the cheek. "Bring me some clothes when you come into town tomorrow, Grandpa!" She smiled a quick smile, and she was gone.

"Grandpa!" he thought. "How did I get to be that old?" he chuckled to himself.

****

"Dorothy Fae! They named her Dorothy Fae, after Corrine. The baby is asleep, but Bessie is awake. Come on in and see them," Vida Mae beamed. This was her first grandbaby, too.

Bessie was sitting up in bed, and Rachael was brushing her hair. They both looked tired, but their smiles spread all across their faces. "Oh, come and see her, Papa. Isn't she just perfect?"

He kissed his daughter's cheek; then he looked at the baby. She had dark brown hair, and they had her dressed in a white batiste gown that Bessie had embroidered with tiny green leaves and pale pink flowers made of French knots. She really did look precious lying in the bassinet with its ruffled pink liner.

"I can only stay a minute or I'll be late for work," Epsy said. "Rachael, here are your clean dress and things."

He stood at the foot of the bed smiling at Bessie; then his eyes drifted to the sleeping baby. He gently pinched Bessie's toes, and there were tears in his eyes. "You did good, baby girl."

Rachael walked him to the door. "She didn't have it so hard for a first baby, Epsy. We played Rummy all night until she finally got to where she needed to walk around. Joe walked with her for about an hour; then the baby came pretty soon.

"How is Corrine doing running the house?"

"She is doing very well. In fact, she has everyone lined out about what chores they are supposed to do, and she won't allow any whining or back talk. She would make a pretty good drill sergeant!"

"Well, I am going to stay another night, then. See you when you get off work this evening?"

Chapter Twenty Seven
Marines!

When Epsy brought Rachael home next evening, Rabon was sitting at the kitchen table talking with Corrine. She was cooking supper, but you could see very quickly that she had been crying. The air was charged with electricity.

Epsy quickly surveyed the scene and thought he understood the situation. "Do you have fresh coffee made, baby girl?" He sat two cups on the table, and she filled them.

He made small talk with Rabon as they waited for the coffee to cool a bit. Then Epsy drank his coffee quickly and pushed his chair back.

"Rabon, want to walk out with me to do the chores?"

Rachael laid her hand on Corrine's shoulder. "What is the matter, honey?" she asked as soon as the men were off the porch.

Corrine spun around and threw her arms around her mother, hugging her tightly. "Mama, Rabon is going to join the Marines!"

"When?" Rachael was startled. She sat the food to the back of the stove and pulled out a chair for each of them to sit down. "Now, tell me. What exactly did he say?"

"That he wants to marry me, but right now he is too young to make a good living for me. He said if he joins the Marines for two years, maybe he will know what he really wants to do for a living.

"By that time I will be out of school. He said he wants me to finish school. But, Mama, he will be gone for two years! And he could be killed!"

"Now, baby, haven't I taught you not to look for the worst in things? Let's try to look at it from a different way.

"He is not 18 years old, yet. Around here, his only options are farming with his dad, working on the railroad gang with your papa, or maybe a job as a mechanic's helper. Or, maybe Joe could get him on at the restaurant. But, I guess he has thought of all of those options and isn't very interested in them.

"There is one thing I know for sure, if a man is not happy in his work, he is not happy at all.

"People sort of get their identity from what they do in life. I am a wife, a mother and a homemaker. That is what I am. That is who I am. I would not be happy doing anything else. I cannot imagine doing anything else. If I had to go to work for someone, my heart would be back here, longing for the things and the people I love. Does that make sense to you?"

Corrine had quit sobbing now and was snubbing once in a while as Rachael talked. "I guess it does. It makes a lot of sense. But why does he have to go away?"

"Corrine, if you really care for this man, if you are thinking of marrying him, you had best learn to let him make the important decisions. If he really loves you, he will take your feelings and your wellbeing into consideration. Honey, Rabon needs some time to grow up. And some time apart will let both of you know exactly how you feel about each other.

"Now, let's finish cooking supper. Yall can have some time after supper to talk about this without so much emotion. Okay?"

****

So it was, that on July 1, 1928, everyone went to Big Spring to watch Rabon and seven other young men sworn into the Marines. Corrine wore her red dress, even though it had long sleeves.

"Corrine, you are going to burn up in those long sleeves," Rachael said as they were about ready to get into the car.

"I don't care if I am hot, Mama. This is the dress I was wearing when I first knew that Rabon loved me. This is how I want him to remember me while he is gone. Besides hot, do I look okay?"

There was a brief period after the swearing in ceremony when the men could visit with family while they waited for the train. Epsy swept off the bed of one of the railroad's flat-bed gang trucks and drove it around to the front of the station.

The ladies spread table cloths across the end of the truck bed and spread out their picnic lunches. Some people set their plates on the truck fenders; some made a place for their plates around the edges of the truck bed. Rachael sat little Mary and her plate on the bed of the truck, well away from the edge so she wouldn't fall. There were two park benches out near Second Street where some of the people could sit to eat. Corrine and Rabon sat on the steps to the depot away from the crowd, holding their plates on their knees.

Epsy noticed three of the newly sworn Marines standing off by themselves. No family had come to see them off. He walked over and introduced himself. After learning their names and where they were from, he said, "Men, we have a large family here, and all of these women are very good cooks. I'll wager there are no less than five fried chickens plus all the trimmings. My wife and daughters baked two cakes and a peach cobbler.

"Let's go see how many pies the other ladies brought."

Everybody chattered gaily, reaching to dip their plates; then slowly groups drifted off to find a place to sit. The three young men felt most comfortable staying around Epsy and his family.

When they heard the train whistle blow announcing the train was approaching the station, a sudden look of apprehension crossed everyone's faces. People began to move away from the truck, food was no longer on their minds. Little Mary, afraid she might be left, called out loudly, "Mama, may I please be excused from the truck?"

Corrine and Rabon set down their plates and held hands, as if they would not let go. He helped her up, and they walked over to the bench where his parents were sitting. It was awfully hard for them to let him go, too.

Rabon shook hands with his dad; then hugged him. He hugged Imogene, and chucked her under the chin because she was beginning to cry. He held his mother in his arms for a long minute. "Write to us, son." They had already said their 'good-byes'.

Neva walked over and handed Corrine a box tied with red ribbon. "Oh, yes," Corrine said. "I baked you some tea cakes to take with you," and she handed the box to Rabon.

Everyone began to gravitate toward the depot, each one patting Rabon on the shoulder as they got a chance to reach him. At the steps to the train, Rabon finally let go of Corrine's hand and hugged her, a passionate, desperate hug. Part of him knew he needed to get on the train, but part of him couldn't leave.

The engineer blew two warning toots of the whistle. "All aboard!" the conductor called loudly. They were used to witnessing heart-wrenching good-byes, and they had waited as long as they could. Steam hissed as the engineer released the brake, and Rabon grabbed the handle beside the door to the passenger car and swung aboard as the train began moving.

Eight new Marines stood waving from the door of the Pullman car as the train pulled out of Big Spring and headed west toward San Diego.

Chapter Twenty Eight
Joe's Cafe

Jetty and Neva walked from the girls' bedroom into the kitchen; Neva's hands were on Jetty's shoulders, straightening her collar, arranging the long, pointed end of her old-fashioned sleeping cap. "What do you think about Jetty's costume, Mama?" She patted Jetty's shoulder. "I tried to make her look like 'Jack be nimble, Jack be quick. Jack jump over the candle stick.'

Jetty wore a long night shirt and bedroom slippers. Her black braids looked adorable hanging below the sleeping cap with a tassel on the point. She carried a candle holder with a bright red candle.

Rachael looked at her and smiled. "Tell me again what nursery rhyme she is portraying."

"Say your poem for Mama," Neva patted Jetty's shoulder and sat down beside Mama.

Jetty took a deep breath:

"To bed, to bed,' said Sleepy Head. 'Tarry awhile,' said Slow. 'Put on the pan,' said Greedy Nan, 'We'll sup before we go."

Then, holding the candlestick holder in one hand and holding the side of her nightshirt out with the other, she gave a deep curtsey.

Rachael clapped her hands and cheered. "Perfect! Perfect!" she said with an adoring smile. "Jetty, you said your poem very well, darling. And I think the costume portrays the perfect setting for the poem. You girls did a very good job.

"Where is Laura? How is her costume coming along?"

"Corrine is still trying to get enough stuffing in it," Neva explained. "What?"

Corrine and Laura came out of the girls' bedroom. Laura was almost in tears. "I know it is scratchy, but it's cute. You will just have to get tough and live with it," Corrine was saying.

"Mama, do we have any more old newspapers that I can crumple up to stuff this toe sack? I think it looks a little like a rock, don't you?"

"Oh, a rock? Well, I can see the similarity. Sugar, you did a good job shaping it and making the neck and arm holes. And it fits tight enough at the bottom to keep the newspaper stuffing in!

"Let me hear your poem, Laura. Do you know it, honey?"

Nodding her head with each meter of the poem, Laura began reciting: "I wish I was a little rock a sittin' on a hill, A doin' nothin' all day long, but just a sittin' still. I wouldn't eat; I wouldn't drink; I wouldn't even wash. I wouldn't do a thing all day but rest myself by gosh!"

Immediately Laura began scratching where the toe sack rubbed her neck and around her arms. Rachael smiled and clapped her hands. "Very good, Laura! You said your poem very well. And I think your costume is a very good likeness of a rock.

"Corrine you might have her put on a long sleeved, white blouse and pull the collar out over the neck of the toe sack. That will stop most of the itching, and I think it will make the costume show up more, too. I'll see if I have any more newspapers put away somewhere.

"You girls did really good thinking up that costume!"

"There is another verse to her poem," Jetty spoke up, "but she can't remember it. So the teacher said to just stop there.

"And the teacher wants her to just sit on a very low stool while she says her poem. But you need to teach her how to sit because you can see her panties the way she sits down on the stool."

"When is this play? This Friday night? At the schoolhouse?

"We will have to ask Papa to come home a bit early that day. Am I supposed to make any refreshments?

"Corrine, who is Imogene helping?"

"The youngest Cooper girl. Both of her older sisters have married and quit school. She is saying 'Little Miss Muffett'. Imogene doesn't need to make her a costume; she is going to wear her best Sunday dress. Imogene's only problem is making a great big spider so the people in the back of the room can see it. I think Jessie is helping on that.

"Mama, do you think Bessie and Joe will come to the school play? We hardly see them anymore."

"Well, since Joe bought that little diner across from the Railroad Station, they have been working hard cleaning and repainting it. Did you know that Bessie covered the counter stools in bright red oil cloth? She says it is real showy! They want to get it open as quickly as possible because he doesn't have any money coming in now that he quit his job at the hotel restaurant.

"Maybe Papa will go across the street tomorrow and invite them out. I'm sure a little rest and socializing would be good for them. And we haven't seen little Dorothy in two weeks, I guess. Maybe Vida Mae and Joe would like to come, too."

****

The evening of the play, Epsy came home a little early and handed Rachael a small paper sack. "This is the best I could do. I hope it fits her. The teacher at that new dance school said it is the smallest size she can get."

Rachael took something out of the sack and held it up. It looked like a small pair of panties with stockings attached, all in one piece.

"Laura, come here, baby. Let me try this up against you. Yes, it looks like it will be just a fit."

"What is it, Mama?" Laura asked.

"It is called tights! It is what the ballerinas wear when they are on stage so no one in the audience can see their panties. This is for your play costume, honey. These will cover your legs, and your panties won't show. Isn't that nice? Later, I guess you can wear them to church.

"Now, we are just snacking for supper tonight; so everybody can eat whenever they have time. Laura and Jetty, I want you to eat right now

before you put on your costumes. Wash your hands and I'll fix you each a plate."

Epsy walked into the living room. "Corrine," he called. "Bessie was pleased that you remembered to ask her and Joe to the play. They will be out later. I told her that you will be busy all during the play announcing the players, but you could visit with her afterwards."

"Good! We are all invited to Jessie's house for a while after the play."

****

Corrine fairly ran up the back steps and let the back door slam behind her. "Mama, Rabon will get to come home for Christmas! Mama? Mama, did you hear? Imogene said Rabon will be home for Christmas!"

She grabbed Rachael by the hands and pulled her down into a chair at the kitchen table. "He is finishing 'boot camp' the middle of December, and he has to leave right after Christmas!"

"Where is he going to be stationed?"

Corrine's excitement faded quickly, her chest fell and she looked down. "He is going overseas. He doesn't know where yet, but he does know they are going somewhere overseas.

"Oh, Mama!" she buried her head in her hands and began to cry.

"Now, Corrine," Rachael put her hand on her daughter's shoulder. "Don't go looking for the worst to happen. You will make yourself old before your time if you only see the bad things that could happen.

"Wouldn't it be fun if he got stationed in Hawaii? They say it is such a beautiful place Let's think good thoughts until we really have something to worry about. Okay?

"Now, honey, I think we need to get with Jessie and find out what plans they have. Find out where and when they will be willing to share Rabon with you. You know that his parents come first, don't you, dear? Their hearts are tied up in him in a way you cannot begin to understand right now."

"What do you mean, Mama?"

Rachael hesitated a moment while she searched for the right way to frame this so Corrine could understand. "Do you remember how your papa cries every time something big happens to your girls? Be it good or bad, he tears up."

Corrine rolled her eyes over to the side while she remembered. "Yes, Mama. He seems to cry about everything. Things that make me happy make him cry."

Rachael nodded her head, "That is just it! It is the love rolling out of his eyes, baby. You girls are a very big part of his world. When something good happens, his heart swells so big it overflows and tears come to his eyes. When something bad happens to you girls, it is happening to the deepest and best part of him, and he cries for you."

"I had never thought about it that way, Mama. Wow, having six girls he really does cry a lot, doesn't he?"

Rachael leaned back and nodded silently.

****

"No, Rachael, we don't have any big plans for when Rabon comes home. We just want to be around him and let him be himself. If he wants Corrine over here all the time he is home, that is okay with us. We can all enjoy him together. And that way he won't feel we are keeping him captive.

"We will just see what he wants to do when he gets here and then make plans on how to share him. What do you think about that?"

"Jessie, Corrine is so blessed to have you in her life. Now, let us know when you know exactly when he will arrive. We will go with you to meet him at the train and make a big welcome home for him."

*****

Epsy and Rachael hardly saw Corrine while Rabon was home, only when he brought her home each night. He looked good in his uniform. He was filling out in his chest and shoulders as he matured; everybody noticed that. He seemed much more confident and settled, too. He was going to be a company clerk. He laughed and said he was probably the only one in his company that finished school, so they were issuing him a typewriter instead of a rifle.

That news made Corrine feel a lot better. If he were going to be in an office, that meant he wouldn't be doing any fighting, wherever he was sent.

All too soon his leave was over and Rabon was gone again. Corrine had a hard time going back to her studies. She had begun to realize the difference in love and a crush or 'puppy love' as her mother called it. Now, she realized that love was interwoven with responsibility.

She knew that for the next year and a half she had to finish school; then get a job. She had to find things to fill up her time while Rabon was gone.

With stoic resolve she dove into helping Rachael with the housework and helping with the younger girls. She began to do more of the sewing, not only for herself; she ventured into making dresses for Mary and Laura. Jetty and Neva felt she might not do as good a job as Rachael, so they held out for Mama to make their dresses.

She wrote a short letter to Rabon almost every night, and he answered promptly once a week. He had been sent to China, where the Marines were protecting US citizens who were there and their property. It was hard for him to separate what he could tell her about his life in the Marines and what was confidential. But she was grateful for any word from him.

****

Finally school was over for the year. Jessie had her usual wienie roast for the end of school. Imogene and Corrine and their class were the honorees. It was a fun party. The bonfire was not quite as big without Rabon to encourage the boys to drag up wood. And it seemed strange to be the oldest at a school party. Somehow Corrine felt disconnected from her peers; the end of school did not mean 'freedom' as it had in the past. It was just a hurdle she had crossed, and then she was on to the next one.

****

"Hi, Sister," Corrine said as she sat down on the stool nearest the door. "I would like to have a Coca Cola, please," and she laid a nickel on the counter.

Bessie set a bottle of Coke and a glass of ice in front of her. She stood there smiling at her younger sister. "Well, what are you doing in town today?"

"I rode in with Daddy this morning. I have been looking for a job all morning. Daddy told me several places to go where he would approve of my working. I really mean men that he trusted enough to have me work for them."

"Have you found anything promising?"

"Two said they would give it some thought, but I don't think anybody in town is actually looking for someone to hire right now."

Corrine had been pouring her Coca Cola slowly into the glass to keep the foam from overflowing. Now she reached for the cylindrical, glass container of straws that was neatly grouped with the napkins, salt, pepper and catsup at the back side of the counter. She pulled up the knob on top; a rod connected the lid and the bottom, so that it lifted all the straws. The straws spread out from the mouth of the container in a circle, offering Corrine her choice of all the straws. After admiring the charming flower that had opened for her, she selected one and gently twisted it between her fingers.

"Sister, is your café business good, now? Are you and Joe able to take care of all the customers?"

Bessie was quietly running over these things in her mind.

Corrine took hold of her hands and looked deep into her eyes. "Sister, now that I am out of school, I need to find a job. I had rather work for you and Joe... if it could work, if it could help you," she said wistfully. "Mama says I am a pretty good cook, if that would help."

On the other side of the counter, Bessie stood quietly for a moment, staring at the wall behind Corrine. "Well, Joe does almost all the cooking, let me talk to him. We will see if it could work."

****

During a lull in business in midafternoon, Bessie said, "Joe, did you see Corrine when she was here this afternoon? She is looking for a job, and she wanted to know if our business is good enough that we could use her help."

Joe sat on the stool nearest the kitchen. Unless the café was completely full, this stool was reserved for the cook. Although Joe had installed an electric suction fan in the back wall of the kitchen to pull the heat and smell of hot grease out the back, it still stayed hot…very hot in the kitchen. And if they had a really busy day, he was on his feet continuously from 6:00 AM to 8:00 PM. He took advantage of every chance to sit down.

While they talked, Bessie was filling napkin holders, salt shakers and catsup bottles. These things had to be cleaned and refilled at least twice a day.

"We have been working some long hours. We hardly get to see Dorothy." She stopped and thought a minute. "I'm so thankful that we have your mother so close and that she is willing to keep her for us."

She sat the things she had refilled on a tray and carried them to the front of the café and exchanged them for the partially empty ones on the tables. The café was slender and long, with a counter and stools on one side and small tables along the other wall. Each table had a red and white checked oil cloth table cloth that complemented the red seats of the stools along the counter.

Bessie rinsed the bar towel she was using in very hot water and walked back to a table near where Joe was sitting. "If Corrine waited tables from 6:00 to 2:00, I could work from 12:00 to 8:00. That way I wouldn't be so tired all the time, and I could spend some time with Dorothy."

Silence hung in the air for a while. "What do you think? Are we making enough money to hire someone? Maybe we could pay her 25¢ an hour plus her tips?

****

So it was arranged, Corrine would work the morning shift, and Bessie would work the evening shift. "Joe, we are coming up in this world!"

He looked at her quizzically for a moment. "We have two shifts working in our café! We are a success!"

And Corrine was a good employee. She was energetic and handled the work well. She was a hit with all the customers because she was always cheerful and snappy.

Bessie was astonished at the money Corrine made in tips. Bessie had always been friendly, but quiet. People liked her and appreciated her reliability. But Corrine was energetic and bouncy. She always had something funny to say and she made people laugh a lot. She quickly learned people, knew what they usually ordered and called them by name; she remembered to ask about their families.

It was no surprise, then, that the coffee break and lunch crowd began to increase. Joe's doubts about hiring an extra employee faded into a small satisfied smile.

****

Epsy and Corrine arrived at the railroad station early one summer morning. He smiled as he watched her half walk, half skip across Second Street to the café; then he walked into the railroad yard to line out the day's work for his crew.

His two young problems were standing in the large, covered breezeway between the passenger station and the baggage storage. He wasn't trying to be quiet, but they were oblivious to his presence. Instead of calling to them, Epsy walked up behind them to see what they were watching so intently.

Looking over their shoulders, he saw Corrine framed in the space between their heads. "Now there is a pretty little heifer," one of them said dreamily. "Wouldn't you just love to be the bull in her pasture?"

"I wonder who she is," the other one puzzled. "How old do you think she is? Do you think her dad lets her date?" they mused.

"She is 17," Epsy said quietly.

The two young men spun their heads around quickly to see their boss standing so close behind them. "Her name is Corrine Hale, and 'NO', her father does not allow her date!"

He pulled his pocket watch from its little pocket at the top of his right hand pants pocket and looked at the time.

"I suggest that you two get your tools ready for work. We will be leaving the yard in five minutes."

When paychecks came out at the end of the week, the two young men signed their time card and walked away counting the money in their envelopes. They were surprised to find pink slips at the back of the dollar bills in their envelopes.

****

Corrine sat at one of the central tables refilling the condiment containers and cleaning the tops of catsup bottles. This was what she called her 'morning break'.

A man walked up to the big plate glass window that covered almost the whole front of the diner and began setting down the cumbersome load he was carrying. A more curious sight, she had never seen.

He sat down a bucket of soapy water, a bucket of clean water, a fold out table frame with legs that scissored and had webbing that held the two legs together at the top. He laid a flat wooden box across the top of the portable table; then he leaned a tall wooden pole against the window frame.

He wore a short apron made of blue and white pillow ticking that had slender pockets of various sizes across his chest and large square pockets below his waist. Rags of various kinds of cloth hung from his back pockets.

Corrine's attention was glued to this thin man whose hair had probably not been cut in three months. He was very thin, and his back bowed forward a little. His shirt was a dingy white and had not been ironed.

He glanced around at the work area he had set up. Satisfied that everything was in place, he took a medium sized, very soft-bristled brush from one pocket and screwed it onto the end of his wooden stick. Dipping it into the soapy water, he soaped the window from top to bottom with a fairly thick lather of bubbles.

As the rivulets of bubbles hurriedly slid down the window, she could only see the silhouette of a man unscrew the brush and lay it on the sidewalk. From one of his chest pockets he took what appeared to be a blade with a rubber edge and screwed it onto the stick. Then he began at the upper left corner, next to the door, and pulled the blade down the window.

Corrine looked around and saw that Joe had come out of the kitchen and was leaning against the doorway. "It's like he is erasing the bubbles!" Corrine said.

"Wait until he rinses it," Joe said. "It will look as if there is no glass there."

When the bubbles were all gone, the man reattached the brush, dipped it into the clean water and went over the window again. He did this several times until there were no bubbles left.

"What is that thing he uses to dry off the water?" Corrine asked.

"It's called a squeegee. The rubber on the edge of the blade gets all of the water off the window."

As Joe had predicted, the window now was so clean that it absolutely looked as if there were no glass in it. The man pulled a very soft rag from one pocket and touched up a few places where there was a little moisture left; then he began rearranging his work space.

He moved the buckets far to the side, rinsed and replaced the brush and blade in his apron, and centered the folding table with his wooden box in front of the window.

He selected a brush from his wooden box and gently flexed the bristles. It was a paint brush! An artist's paint brush! He dipped the fairly large, long handled brush into his white paint; and with very measured and deliberate strokes, he painted a 'C'. And what a 'C' it was! It was big and round with a long flourish extending from the bottom. With a smaller brush he made capitols at the beginning and the end of the "C" that made Corrine think of mermaids' tails.

In smaller letters, but with the same flourish, he painted the rest of the letters of the word 'Café', being careful to place the accent over the 'e'. The word 'Café' was very large and sloped up, taking up almost the whole window.

It just took her breath away to watch him paint with such mastery and assurance. It seemed he painted the majestic letters with no more forethought than if he were simply signing his name to a piece of paper.

The man took a rag from his hind pocket and cleaned the white paint from his brushes. He put them into a jar of turpentine to set. All the while he was studying his handiwork.

He selected a small thin brush and dipped it into red paint. He outlined the bottom of the top part of the letters in red; then he outlined the bottom of the bottom part of the letters, making it seem as if you were seeing a shadow behind the letters.

Again he surveyed his work as he gently cleaned the brush. The next brush, he dipped in a very soft gray paint and quickly, but deftly, painted a stripe through the center of the big white 'C'. Taking a dry brush, he began to feather the gray so that it looked exactly as if the big white 'C' were carved…it actually looked as if the center of the 'C' were raised!

The man stood back and appraised his work. Satisfied with his masterpiece, above it he wrote 'Joe's Railroad' in red, still with the beautiful flourishes, but smaller. With a touch of white to the red letters to make them show up, he was done.

He delicately signed his name at the lower left side of the 'C'. Then he began cleaning his brushes.

Seeing how awed Corrine was, Joe said, "You should pay me for that performance!" and he laughed.

Corrine came out of her trance and laughed with him. She began to put all the bottles back on the tables where they belonged, and Joe turned back toward the kitchen.

"He will be in here in a minute. I'd better get my grill hot so I can cook him a meal."

Soon the man had arranged his equipment neatly against the inside of the front window, all except the wooden box of paints and brushes. This was a dear possession, and he kept this near him wherever he went.

He walked to the back of the café and sat on the next to last stool so he and Joe could talk. Corrine brought a glass of water and poured him a cup of coffee. "That was indeed a privilege to watch you paint. I have never seen such artistry, Mr….."

"Folks just call me Jimmy," he said and nodded his head to her. Then he sat there quietly until Joe rang the bell for a pick-up from the kitchen. It was a big platter full of chicken fried steak, with French fries and everything swimming in gravy. With it she brought a whole basket of biscuits.

Jimmy began to eat hungrily, and when he had begun to slow down, so that he would not be embarrassed, Joe sat down beside him on the end stool. Corrine took Joe a cup of coffee and refilled Jimmy's cup. They talked quietly while Jimmy ate.

Other customers began to drift into the café, and Joe had to go back to work. "Give him five one dollar bills when he starts to leave," he told Corrine. As he walked back past Jimmy, Joe patted the counter and said, "Yes, Jimmy, I am very pleased with the sign. Come back tomorrow for breakfast, okay?"

Bessie arrived just in time for the noon rush. She didn't have time to admire the new sign until the afternoon lull. While they sat at one of the back tables refilling things, Corrine said, "Boy, you should have been here to see the sign painter work, Bessie! It was just like an artist painting on canvass!"

Joe turned a chair around backwards and sat down with a cup of coffee in his hand. "That is exactly what you watched, Corrine.

"Jimmy is actually a very good artist. He is not much older than me. He has some paintings that I believe may be famous someday. But he got to drinking heavy. Now he only paints signs on windows when he needs money for another bottle," Joe related with sadness in his voice.

Chapter Twenty Nine
1929!

Corrine had a long wait until Epsy got off work and she had a ride home, but today there was a lot of conversation with the customers about the new sign.

On the way home Epsy let Corrine off at the row of mail boxes at the corner. Since she and Rabon had been writing, it was her job to get the mail every day. She started walking toward the house as she read the front of each letter.

Suddenly she flung her arms up in the air, clutching letters in both hands and yelled. Then she ran the rest of the way to the house. "I got a letter from Rabon," she said as the backdoor slammed. She tossed the rest of the mail on the table and went to her bedroom to read it.

"Oh, Mama," she squealed. "Rabon will be home in October, and he wants us to get married!" She danced around the kitchen table, still trying to read the rest of the letter.

"Oh, Mama! He is back in the states, and he will be home on furlough the middle of October. That is not very long. Can we have a wedding put together by then? One like Bessie's?"

Rachael sat down in the nearest chair. She knew this was coming, but not so sudden. She drew a deep breath and smiled at her daughter. Happy memories of her life flashed through her mind and happily brought her back to this moment. She patted her fingers on the edge of the table, nodded her head and pushed up from the chair.

"We will talk to Jessie tomorrow. He should have written to her at the same time. We will have fun planning this wedding, honey."

Corrine had finished dancing all over the kitchen, and she hugged her mother. "Oh, Mama!" and then she was off again.

****

Life for the Hale family was really a hub-bub for the next three weeks. Rachael had to make Corrine's dress, white voile, with a sweetheart neckline, long fitted sleeves and a full flowing skirt.

Corrine wanted the wedding to be in their community church at Center Point with the reception at Jessie's house. Jessie was such a wonderful hostess; she managed to make everything special.

Everything for the wedding worked out easily: Jessie bought some beautiful flowers from the flower shop in Big Spring. Several women wanted to make their special candy or cake for the reception. Imogene was to be the bride's maid, and Rabon was bringing a Marine buddy home with him to be the best man. Preparations were non-stop!

Suddenly, Rabon was home. Everyone met him at the railroad station in Big Spring. He looked so handsome stepping off the train in his dress uniform. He took off his cap and swept Corrine into his arms for a long hug, as if he were absorbing warmth and strength from her. He finally kissed her; then he said, "It's been a long time since you chunked a rock at me!" and smiled a warm, glowing smile. She giggled.

****

"Well, I am going to be stationed here in Big Spring," Rabon explained after all the congratulations were said. "I will be the Marine Recruiter, and I will have an office in the Post Office building."

"Oh, that's perfect!" Corrine squealed. "I didn't know where we could live, so I rented a little house in Big Spring. I only paid two weeks rent because I didn't know where you were going to be stationed. But, now it's perfect! It is not too far for us to walk to work while we save our money for a car." She was so excited that all of this fairly spewed from her mouth.

"We have the wedding set for two days from now. Is that okay?

"Oh Rabon, wait until you see me in the beautiful wedding dress Mama made me. I look just like a princess," she beamed.

****

On the day of the wedding there was a bigger crowd at the little community church than ever before. Cars parked out as far as the cotton field, and people walked through weeds to get to the church.

All of their friends from the community came to welcome Rabon home and to see them finally get married. This had been the talk of the whole community.

Friends of Bessie and Joe and his family came out from Big Spring. And some of the businessmen who regularly ate lunch at the café came and brought their families to meet the perky little waitress that had become such a part of everyone's lives.

In the cloak room of the little church, Rachael and Neva helped Corrine put on the finishing touches. "Mama, it's almost time! You had better go sit in your seat. Neva can help me from here."

As Neva started to close the door, she spotted Albert NcNew sitting by the aisle on the back pew. He was motioning for her to sit by him.

"Neva, come help me here. You can play kneesies with Albert after I start down the aisle, okay?" Neva shot her a defiant look; then she realized that Corrine was smiling. "I know how it feels, little sister. Now close the door, will you?"

All the church pews were filled, Rabon and his friend stood at the front of the church wearing their dress uniforms, and Imogene walked slowly down the aisle in a lovely dress of pink voile with muted flowers. Then the pianist played loudly, "Dum, da-da, dum, dum, dum, and everybody looked toward the back of the church.

Corrine was standing at the open double doors of the church. She was silhouetted by the evening sunlight. Her dark brown hair was a beautiful contrast to the white dress, as rays of the evening sun managed to glimmer through the many layers of white voile. She carried an oversized bouquet. It was a beautiful blend of every red rose the florist had in her shop. Red ribbon streamers hung down the front of her skirt. This was a loving gift from her mother-in-law.

Epsy stepped up beside her holding out his left arm, and they started down the aisle. Rabon was mesmerized. She did, indeed, look like a princess! His princess!

Epsy, too, was lost in his thoughts, "My second daughter! My brood was shrinking!" And tears filled his eyes.

****

Hardly had they recovered from the wedding until they heard the evening news on the radio, "The Wall Street Stock Market has crashed!" Between October 24th (Black Thursday) and 29th (Black Tuesday) in 1929, $30 billion dollars was lost...a good portion of it by small investors who had their life savings invested in stocks.

This trend had started several years back. The economy had been very good for a long time; businesses had become used to using credit to finance large acquisitions. Banks loaned huge amounts to large, newly formed, holding companies and trading companies like Goldman Sachs Trading Corporation. The whole business strata had learned the meaning of 'leverage', small down payment with monthly payments strung out over several years. That way they were operating on someone else's money instead of the investment coming out of their own pocket. But in reality, they are over-extended. As long as the economy is good, it works!

Prohibition had hit the country hard. Well-meaning voters had intended to stop the flow of money away from the support of families and into liquor and gambling. However, instead of cutting off the dragon's head, it was forced underground.

Large American breweries like AnHauser Busch and American distilleries like Jack Daniel's were forced to close their doors, laying off workers. Importers of wine suddenly found themselves with no legal livelihood. But prohibition did not stop people from drinking! They still spent just as much for liquor as always; they just turned to another source.

Breweries and distilleries went underground; bathtub gin became a common commodity; it was poorly made and often deadly. Suddenly bootleggers were supplying the product and making the money, and 'speak easies' in basements replaced supper clubs, supplying entertainment for people who wanted to drink.

The government lost the income from the liquor tax, and it had absolutely no control over the sale of liquor. A task force on crime, headed by Elliot Ness, was formed strictly to combat bootlegging and the growing menace of organized crime.

People became accustomed to breaking the law, not realizing that their 'just buying a pint' was feeding the monster of organized crime. Throwing scruples to the wayside, their consciences became calloused.

As lawlessness became more accepted, crime lords, who were becoming wealthy from prohibition, began to socialize with the wealthy elite, legitimizing their flaunting of the law.

The St. Valentine's Day Massacre in Chicago on February 14, 1929, should have been a wakeup call. A rival crime organization ambushed Al Capone and his well-dressed henchmen in a drive-by shooting. Although these small wars between rival gangsters, for control over territory, were not altogether unusual, this one made headlines as a number of people lay dead on the streets of Chicago in broad daylight! It made it hard to look the other way.

And so the country had run headlong, building a house of cards, not realizing that disaster was lurking in the shadows.

****

It took a while for the immensity of the news of the 'crash' to soak in. One minute people felt secure and confident; then slowly they began to realize they were on their own, like a row boat just cut loose from a ship. They were powerless! They had nothing to depend on but their next paycheck.

Then it really became personal with the realization that, "If everybody lost their operating capital, what would the railroad have to haul? They would not shut down so big an operation as the railroads, but they certainly would not be building short lines to smaller towns. They would only need a skeleton crew to do cleanup and maintenance. They will lay off a bunch of the men in the yards."

Epsy sat beside the radio quietly thinking as all this ran through his head. "What does this mean for us, Epsy?" Rachael interrupted his thoughts.

"I don't know," he answered quietly. "I heard that stock market prices were starting to fall late last week. I started trying to get my broker on the telephone, but his line was always busy. I finally got to talk to him on Monday and told him to sell all our stocks. But I don't know if anybody was willing to buy at that time, or for what price. I don't even know if he had time to try to sell, with the telephone lines all busy like that.

"We will just have to wait for them to sort this all out to see if we have a little bit of money in the bank or just a worthless handful of stock certificates.

"I had some money in RCA and General Motors; they may be big enough to come through this, I don't know. And I had some money in government bonds. Those should still be good, but the government could simply say they are not going to redeem any bonds or pay any interest while the economy is bad. Who knows? We will just have to ride it out and see.

"Tomorrow morning early I'll to go the bank and withdraw the money we have there. I have heard of banks closing their doors when something like this happens."

****

Epsy was not the first in line when the bank opened its doors, but there were just a few ahead of him.

When he asked to withdraw all that was in his accounts, checking and savings, the president of the bank, himself, said, "Epsy, you have been a trusted and valued customer. I am very sorry to lose you."

"It has been a pleasure knowing that I could depend on you, Richard. I don't intend for this to end our dealings. But I believe you are going to be hit hard by this Stock Market Crash. It is bound to trickle down. I have heard of banks having to close their doors during times like this. I thought that I had better be early in case that happens."

By late afternoon, Monday of the next week, Epsy heard that the bank had indeed run out of cash on hand and closed its doors. In times like this people feel they can't trust even what they can see. So much money had been withdrawn that the bank was no longer solvent. They had no choice.

"It starts with the smaller banks; then it goes up the ladder. The larger banks will be caught in the squeeze next."

Chapter Thirty
1930

When Epsy arrived at work Monday morning after the Crash, he found most all of the men had come in early. They were milling around, gathering in groups of three or four mostly looking at the ground, many were nervously chain smoking.

Epsy nodded to those who would look up and walked inside to talk to his boss. "You're a little late this morning, aren't you? You are usually the first one on the yard."

"I went by the bank as soon as it opened. There wasn't much of a line then."

"Why did you need to go to the bank?"

"You never know what is going to happen in times like this. I wanted to get my money while they still had some to give. You know they don't keep money on hand to cover all of their depositors at one time."

His boss shot him a questioning look.

"A certain percent of it is loaned out to earn interest. I'd rather be safe than sorry. What is the news concerning the railroad?" He ambled over and poured half a cup of coffee.

"I haven't heard it officially, yet. But talk is that they will be curtailing all unnecessary expense. You needn't worry. Yours will be the crew that I keep for cleanup and repairs. You never can tell about our wages, though."

"You know the big boys will keep getting their fat share, and they might cut our rate of pay to do it. We'll just have to wait and see how it goes."

"Well, I'll get my crew lined out then." He drained his coffee cup and turned to the door. He took his assignment slip off the bulletin board and nodded, "See you, Jim."

Epsy could see the questions in the eyes of his men, though no one actually asked. He noticed that even the ones who normally grumbled about all forms of work, grabbed their tools and got loaded quickly today. There was a little pep in their pace all day…it might come down to only the most productive workers get to stay on.

As the weeks of uncertainty rolled by, one crew was laid off, then another. On pay day at the end of November, the last crew received pink slips. Epsy's crew was the only one left to work the whole Big Spring area. On December 2, 1929, it was official. The country had entered the Great Depression that didn't bottom out until July of 1932.

****

Epsy pulled out two kitchen chairs. "Rachael, pour us a cup of coffee. Let's sit down and talk.

He looked down at the coffee in his cup, "I talked to B.T.'s son, Ben, and told him I am not going to lease the land this year." He picked up his spoon and stirred, lifting spoonfuls of coffee about an inch and slowly dripping it back into the cup. "With the economy like it is, it probably won't be very profitable to farm now."

"I told him I would find us a house in Big Spring, but he said he had rather we stay here than let the house set empty. You know how things go down when no one is looking after them." He picked up his cup and took a tiny sip to test it. He studied Rachael's face, trying to read her reaction.

Taking a couple more quick sips, he set the cup down. "I think I am going to start looking for us a house in town, just the same. We won't need to be in a hurry, but I believe it will be the best way to go. There is still no guarantee that my job with the railroad is secure, and it would be better for us to be in town than way out here."

At first Rachael sat looking at her coffee cup; then she picked up the cup with both hands and propped her elbows on the table, tipping the cup just enough to take a sip. Her face held no expression as she stared off across the room. By nature she did not like change, but she would not protest...it did no good to get riled or complain. She was an adapter; she would make the best of it.

"Then you think the girls can at least finish this year in school at Center Point? If so, we needn't even mention it to them. No sense getting them upset."

The back door opened, and Neva rushed in to escape the cold wind. She was followed by a tall, slender, dark haired young man who did not look familiar to Epsy and Rachael. He let the screen door close quietly and carefully closed the kitchen door. Rachael was immediately impressed and studied the young man carefully.

His angular face was tanned from the sun. He had dark brown hair and soft brown eyes that smiled at you even before his mouth did. Rachael liked this man. He had an easy spirit about him.

"Mama, Papa, this is Albert McNew. He drove me home from school. I invited him for cake and coffee."

Epsy stood up and shook hands with the young man. He pointed to the chair next to him, "Have a seat."

Neva had taken off her coat and put her books away. "Is there enough coffee in the pot or do I need to make some more?" She lifted the pot and decided there was enough. She hurried to the cabinet, took down four small plates, and uncovered the chocolate cake she had made the evening before.

"Where are the other girls?" Rachael asked.

"They are walking home. They will be here in a minute." She shot a quick, concerned look at Rachael, "I told them I was riding with Albert, Mama." Neva set cake in front of her daddy and Albert; then, across the table, she sat cake for her mother and herself. She poured two more cups of coffee and offered to refill for her parents. They both shook their heads.

Neva sat down and smiled at Albert, "Go ahead, try it. I told you I am a good cook!"

Rachael and Neva both cut their eyes to look at Epsy. He was supposed to welcome this guest to their home. "Uch, uch, uch," he cleared his throat. "You did a good job on this cake, Neva. You are getting better all the time." He smiled across the table at her.

"Albert, is it? You had better try this cake; I think it will be delicious. I don't recall seeing you before. Are you from around here?"

"Yes, sir. I was in Bessie's class at school. My family farms north of Center Point. I have been farming with my dad for a couple of years….waiting for Neva to grow up." He smiled a soft little smile and cut his eyes at Neva. Rachael could see the love in those eyes.

"Mr. Hale, I would like your permission to come calling on her. And I know you need to get to know me, too."

Epsy glanced at Rachael, who had a cute little half-smile on her face. He knew that she already had a good opinion of this young man. He glanced at Neva. She was all smiles and giddy.

"Well, in that case, we would be pleased to have you for Sunday dinner. Rachael cooks a fine fried chicken.

"Course, it gets a little loud around here with so many girls at the table," he smiled a broad smile. These girls were his pride and joy! "It would be nice to have another man at the table."

****

The preacher at the Center Point church also had three other churches that he pastored, and he was away this Sunday. But the Hale family was busy this Sunday morning. While Rachael and Neva cooked, the younger girls were getting the house straightened up for company. It was cold outside, and when Epsy came in with the milk, he was quite aware of the temperature change. The windows were fogged over so that they looked like waxed paper. Mary was drawing on one of the kitchen windows. She would draw a picture; then wipe off what she had drawn to erase it and move to another window to try again.

"Mary, go brush your hair better. There are still tangles in the back," Neva said. She wanted everything to look its best.

When Albert showed up, he brought a large bunch of beets from his mother's garden. "I didn't know if you had a winter garden, Mrs. Hale. But my mother's beets are ready to pull right now."

There was a big smile on Rachael's face as she took the beets from him and took them to the sink to rinse off the dirt still clinging to them. "Yes, this young man is very thoughtful, indeed," she was thinking.

Albert became a regular fixture at Sunday dinner. The whole family learned to enjoy his company. Rachael invited him and his family to the annual New Year's Eve party. His family was very quiet and not as easy to get acquainted with as Albert, himself; but they were nice people. He had a little sister about Neva's age, and the girls enjoyed her company.

After the beginning of the New Year, Albert approached Epsy one day, "Mr. Hale, Neva tells me that you are not going to lease this land this year."

"You can call me Epsy. No, I have been farming on the side, and it really has been a bit too much for me to work two jobs. At my age I am beginning to feel it. And not being too confident in the economy, I decided it might not be worth it."

"Would you mind if I talk to Ben about leasing it? I would not need the house, just the land. It would be nice to have yall living here. I could see Neva every day," he sort of mumbled under his breath.

"That could work well for both of us, Albert. What do you plant? Cotton?"

Albert nodded his head. "Cotton is all I have ever worked with."

"Just to give you something to think on…if I were to keep farming during this time of economic instability, this would be the time that I would plant peanuts."

Albert gave him a questioning look.

"We don't know if anybody will have money to buy cotton. They can wear last year's clothes; but they can't eat cotton. If they have only money enough for food, they can eat peanuts."

Albert furrowed his brow, thoughtfully considering this new information. "I don't know anything about planting peanuts, Mr. Ha…Epsy."

"If you decide you want to grow peanuts, I can give you a little helpful information. I have never grown peanuts, but I have studied my friends who did. I will help you.

"One thing, though. When you talk to Ben, don't let him take advantage of your youth and inexperience. No matter what he got for the lease last year, he is not going to get much for it this year. Make him a low offer; make him deal with you!"

Several weeks later when Albert came to Sunday dinner, there was a big smile on his face. It fairly lit up his face to a glow. "Well, I leased it, Epsy."

"All right! Good for you!" Epsy shook his hand in congratulations.

"I need you to show me where I can set up a barn and pens for my horses."

"Horses? Do you have your own equipment? Or will you be using your dad's?"

"Well, my dad is not too happy about me farming on my own. He sort of expected me to farm with him, and … Well, the horses are mine, but I am going to have to buy equipment."

"Well, I have a perfectly good tractor that is going to set out there and go to ruin with nobody using it and keeping it up. Let me loan you a tractor. It is at least twice as fast as farming with horses and a lot less wear and tear on your body."

After dinner, the men walked out to the tractor. They spent a lot of time talking and finally fired it up for a test drive.

Rachael could see Neva's composure begin to fall as they drove off on the tractor. "Now, don't let your face get pouty, darling. You are looking at this man as a possible husband, aren't you?"

Neva nodded her head.

"Well, this is what men do. Their work is how they define who they are, and it comes first. They work to take care of us, and they want us to be here when they come home.

"He hasn't forgotten you, honey. Right now he is like a kid with a new toy. When he comes back, he will be enthusiastic and full of fun....and looking for you!

When the men came back in the house toward the end of the day, they were laughing and talking like old friends. Rachael and Neva had supper almost ready. "Let's play dominoes after supper, okay?" Epsy looked around to see if he had any takers, and quickly went to fetch the dominoes.

****

Around mid-February Albert began turning the land, preparing to plant peanuts. Epsy had given him a new idea, and he wanted to try it. Why not now, when he was starting to farm for himself? He was very happy to be doing this on his own. There had been some good rains during the past winter and this soil seemed to be holding the moisture really good. He could see, now, why Epsy usually did so good farming here.

Now that he was working this land, he seemed to be a regular for supper. He even took time out to spade Rachael's garden for her. Soon she noticed that when he left to go home, he did not go up the road toward Center Point. It seemed he was going toward James and Jewel's house.

"Yes, ma'am, Albert has started 'batching' at Uncle James and Aunt Jewel's house. His dad was unhappy that he wanted to go out on his own, but when he planted peanuts, that just cooked the goose. Guess he wanted Albert to do things the old way, his way.

"You know the house is on the land he is leasing, and it was just setting there empty. He said he has a cot, a skillet and a coffee pot!"

"Well, I guess that is enough for the way most men cook," Rachael commented. "He is welcome to eat here anytime he wants."

Albert built pens for his horses at Epsy and Rachael's house. That way he didn't have to haul water for them, and he was there every day to feed them anyway with his farming...and Neva.

****

One day when Rachael was planting her garden, she stood up a little too quickly and felt a sharp twinge in the middle of her abdomen. It did not last long, and she soon forgot it.

A few days later, she woke up with an upset stomach that didn't ever really go away, but it made every morning really a hassle. She was getting concerned, but she never did develop any other symptoms to say she was really sick.

She and Mary walked over to see Jessie one afternoon. "I thought I would meet the girls here and walk home with them. Is that all right? Did you have something planned?"

"No, it has been some time since you and I have had a nice visit. Let me make us something to drink. Do you want tea or coffee?"

"Neither!" Rachael said, wrinkling up her nose. "I haven't been feeling well lately. Most everything makes me sick at my stomach. And I am so sleepy; it is all I can do to stay on my feet."

"Ahhh! Rachael," Jessie gasped as excitement covered her face, "Are you pregnant again?"

"Surely not! My time of the month isn't even regular any more. Sometimes I skip a month altogether, then everything goes back to normal for a while."

"How long has it been this time?" Jessie asked?

"Well, I've missed two in a row this time, but I was never sick at my stomach with the girls. I don't think that could be it."

By now Jessie was sitting across the corner of the table from her, hanging onto every word. She reached out and patted Rachael's hand. With one eyebrow raised in humor, she said, "Rachael, I was never sick with Imogene, but I was sick for the first several months with Rabon!" She just sat there smiling mischievously at Rachael. "Stranger things have happened!"

"Oh, Jessie! We have wanted a boy for so long! Do you really think it could be?"

"We will know soon enough, dear friend. When your dresses start getting too tight in the waist, we will know for sure."

Mary had been playing on the porch waiting for her sisters. She squealed with glee when she saw them and ran to meet them. "We were waiting for you. We are going to walk home with you today."

Jessie gave all the girls a glass of lemonade, and then they were on their way home.

****

In about another month Rachael's clothes began to get tight, so when the girls were getting ready for bed, she poured two cups of coffee and sat down at the table. When Epsy found her sitting there alone, he sat down to find out what she had to talk over with him.

He sat there quietly for a minute. "Well?" He was curious now.

"Epsy, I know that it is way late in our lives." She sat looking off in space; then she cut her eyes to the left, then to the right.

"Yes?"

"Well, there is just the tiniest little chance." She looked down at the table and stirred her coffee.

"Chance of what?"

"That I might be pregnant again," she said very quietly, but did not look up.

"What?" he shouted. "Another baby?...another baby!" Delight filled his eyes as he took hold of her arms, lifted her from her chair, and danced her around the kitchen. "Another baby! Girls, we are going to have another baby!" he called toward the living room, and he gave Rachael a sharp pat on the rear.

"When? When will it be due?"

"I guess late in September," she said. By now she was beginning to smile every time she thought of it. Epsy had made it okay.

"I have been sick at my stomach for about three months now, and I've had no time of the month. But now, my dresses are getting tight in the waist, so I'm... pretty sure." She raised her eyebrows, smiled and nodded.

As they were waiting for sleep to come, Epsy suddenly said, "Rachael, I have never known of your being sick to your stomach before."

"I know. Jessie said that might mean it is a boy," she said quietly without lifting her head.

"What? A boy?" Instant excitement took hold of him. "Could it possibly be? Could it possibly be?" He hugged her, he kissed her, and he couldn't stop patting her. "Do you think it could possibly be?"

"Jessie said 'Stranger things have happened.' She could be right. We will just have to wait and see."

****

Over the next few months, Rachael's tummy did grow, indeed. "Rachael, you seem to be carrying the baby out in front this time. I don't remember you sticking out so much in front even when the baby was almost due."

She just smiled at him, a cute little smile as if she had a secret and was not going to tell. He patted her on the rear and went outside to do the chores.

He seemed to be patting her on the behind a lot here lately!

Early in June Neva had taken the younger girls with her to visit Imogene, and Jetty stayed to help Rachael. They were hoeing weeds in the garden before the sun was too hot. It was nearing noon when Rachael began to feel a twinge in her stomach. Instead of quickly going away, it began to sting very deep in her tummy.

She chopped a few more times while she thought about it. Then her back began to hurt, began to hurt a lot!

"Jetty, help me to the house. I think the baby is coming!"

They both dropped their hoes, and Jetty did her best to support her mother as they started toward the house.

"I can't go any farther, honey. Run to get help! Quickly!"

The nearest neighbor was her papa's cousin, Bitsy, so Jetty ran east to her house. She banged on the door, but no one answered. She got a glimpse of Bitsy peeking out the window so she banged more, but still no answer. "Bitsy, Mama is having the baby!" she shouted. "We need help!" Still no answer.

Jetty ran back to where her mother lay in the garden. "Mama, Bitsy wouldn't answer her door. I'll go to Jessie's. I'll hurry, Mama! I'll hurry!"

Jetty ran as fast as she could, but it was half a mile to Jessie's house. Jessie drove as fast as she could to try to help her friend. But by the time Jessie and Neva arrived, Rachael was unconscious. The baby had been born and was lying in the sun.

Jessie quickly wrapped the baby in one of the sheets she had brought and carried it into the house. She began to clean the baby with a very wet cloth, but it seemed so very hot and dehydrated.

Neva brought water to bath her mother's face. When Rachael began to wake up, Neva helped her to Jessie's car. She had laid a sheet across the back seat so that Rachael could lie down.

"Neva, you take the baby, and keep squeezing drops of water into the baby's mouth, just a drop at a time. I'll drive as fast as I can to Dr. Young's office in Coahoma. Pray, darling, pray."

Dr. Young tried everything he knew to save the baby; but it did not survive. However, after Rachael was strong enough and tucked into a crisp, white hospital bed in his office, Dr. Young let her hold the baby, wrapped in a little, soft blue blanket.

"I called the railroad," Jessie told her, "They are sending someone to get Epsy in from the field. He will be here as soon as he can." She patted Rachael gently, her face showing her deeply felt sorrow. Neva sat beside the bed with tears quietly rolling down her cheeks. "Mama…"

When Epsy entered, the room was quiet and solemn. He stood beside Rachael's bed, and she held up her arms, handing him the baby. "It was our boy, Epsy," she said quietly and without expression. "I think he would have looked like you." Tears finally began to overflow her eyes and made rivulets down her cheeks. She took hold of the fullness of Epsy's pants leg, and gripped it tightly, while she sobbed quietly.

****

Driving home by himself from Dr. Young's office, Epsy replayed the events of the afternoon as Jessie and Neva had related. He remembered his elation at thinking he was finally to have a son, how his spirits soared...now to be so quickly brought to this low. The empty, hollow feeling seemed unbearable. The pain was tortuous! He needed to lash out at something! Hit his fist on something so that his fist would hurt instead of his heart.

Suddenly he realized he had turned into Bitsy's driveway. He slammed the car door with all his might, and stomped up the steps of the kitchen porch. Still his pain was too sharp.

As usual, Bitsy didn't answer when he knocked, or when he banged on the door. But when he jerked the door open, there she stood...face to face.

"Bitsy, how could you? How could you let my baby die? And Rachael could have died as well! How could you be so calloused? You probably watched the whole thing from your window!"

Hands on hips and wagging her head from side to side, "Well, Mr. Smarty Pants!" she said in a snippy fashion. "You finally got your come-upance!!

"Mr. Baseball Man. Went away and made a lot of money. You went away and left your family!

"Mr. Cotton Gin Man! Making all the money while the farmers worked and sweated growing the cotton.

"Mr. Windmill Man! Having the only windmill for miles around and running water in the house!

"Mr. Railroad Man! Farming with a tractor and working for the railroad, too, making two incomes! Driving fancy automobiles!

"Mr. Rich and Fancy Man! How do you like it now?"

All this hatred hit Epsy flat in the face. He had always known that she did not like him, but he never understood why. He had tried to be nice to her, tried to be friendly and helpful. He just could not understand why she would despise him so and even take pleasure in the death of his child. 'A bitter root grows deep, indeed.'

He slowly turned and got back into the car. He drove the two hundred yards to his house, but then he just sat in the car. He felt so drained and flat that he absolutely had no strength to move.

Neva opened the kitchen door and stood on the porch looking at him, wondering what to do. Jetty, following her, took hold of the back of her skirt. Jetty was looking for strength. Finally she could bear it no longer, and she ran to him, throwing her arms around his shoulders. She laid her head on his chest and sobbed, "Oh, Papa, I tried so hard to find someone who could help. I ran all the way to Jessie's house. I am so sorry. I am so sorry."

He put his arm around her and held her for a minute. He patted her back and talked soothingly to her, but there was nothing that could ease this child's breaking heart.

Laura and Mary joining Neva on the porch caught his attention, and Epsy realized that though his heart was breaking, he had to be the comforter, now. He slowly began getting out of the car. As he stood up, all his girls swarmed him and began to sob. "Let's go inside, girls," he said softly.

They all sat down at the table, and for a minute they looked at each other in silence. "Is there any fire in the stove? I would like a cup of coffee," he finally said.

Neva held her hand up near the stove and shook her head.

Epsy built a fire in the stove while Neva filled the coffee pot with water. "I guess we should get supper started soon," he said. "I am to go back and get Mama just before dark. Dr. Young wanted her to rest in his office for a while."

He sat back down and thought quietly, with no expression on his face. "Girls, you know your mother is a strong woman. She has been up for all situations that have come to us. This time her body just was not strong enough to make the baby strong. He did not live. And that makes us all hurt inside, but it hurts Mama most of all because it was her baby…it was her boy.

"She is going to be pretty weak for a while, and she will be sad for a while, too. We need to try our very best to make things good for her again. Will you help me?"

Everyone nodded their heads tearfully. "Mama may be tearful for a while, and we need to let her cry. We want to make her feel better. But if we all stay around her too much at a time, it may overwhelm her. Let's each one try to spend a little special time with her, but just one at a time. Then we can let her have some time alone to rest or nap. Next it will be someone else's turn to keep her company for a while. She needs time to grieve. Does that sound like a good plan to all of you?"

Everyone nodded silently. The smell of coffee perking filled the room. Neva got up and poured him a cup. "Jetty, will you help me cook supper? Mary, will you help Laura set the table, so we will have everything ready when Daddy brings Mama home."

****

When Epsy went back to work everyone seemed solemn and respectful. Everyone, except a new kid the railroad had hired and assigned to his crew while he was gone. The young man was insolent and disrespectful to everybody on the crew, but especially to Epsy. He complained about every job he was asked to do. He did his work sloppily at best, if he completed it at all.

The assistant foreman took him aside at lunch and tried to talk to him. "Don't you know that Mr. Hale lost a child last week? We all feel real bad for him, but you seem to be angry with him. Why?"

"The arrogant S.O.B. doesn't even know that he is akin to me! My mother was a Hale, but he wouldn't know. He never had anything to do with any of the family! He thinks he is so much better than everyone else!

"He fired my two half-brothers just for saying what a sweet ass that daughter of his has. Now my family is having a hard time making it, and it is all his fault. I don't care if his boy did die! He had it coming!"

The work in the field took only until about 3:00 PM. Instead of giving the men a short day, Epsy found some maintenance work on the tracks at the yard.

The assistant foremen found a chance to slip away and talk to the yard boss. "I don't think you should keep him on, Jim. I really think this kid is dangerous. The way he was talking about Epsy, I wouldn't be a bit surprised if he tried to hurt him."

The yard boss walked over to the window to look out at the crew working in the yard. Epsy had them spreading fresh crushed rock between the railroad ties.

Epsy was standing near a box car watching some men pack down the newly laid rock. The flat-bed gang truck, loaded with more rock, was backing toward the rails.

When the man on the ground, who was directing the driver, motioned for the driver to stop, the truck sped up and was going pretty fast when it hit Epsy in the back. The force knocked him into the box car, and for a minute he was pinned there.

While everybody was intent on helping Epsy, the kid driving the truck bailed out leaving the door open, and ran away. When he took his foot off the brake and ran, the truck rolled forward, and Epsy dropped to the ground.

Jim, the yard boss, ran out of his office yelling for someone to get a doctor. When the doctor arrived, Epsy was laid out on his back right where he fell. On first examination the doctor could detect no internal injuries, but Epsy's legs were paralyzed. They loaded him on a stretcher and took him to the hospital.

About a week later, Epsy began to move his feet and legs a little while he laid in bed. After a month he could support his weight for short periods of time and was slowly learning to walk with crutches.

"Mr. Hale, I believe that in time, you will be able to walk about, but I don't believe you will ever be able to go back to work. You have ruptured discs in your lower back. It is a miracle that you weren't permanently paralyzed.

"I am going to let you go home from the hospital, but with the understanding that you cannot drive or lift even a kitchen chair or a pan of water for several more months. Let this thing heal as much as it will.

"Your wife tells me that you like to play dominoes. This would be a good time to start inviting people over to play dominoes with you. Now don't sit too long at one time, and don't lie down all the time. You need to walk around some to keep it from getting stiff and freezing up, keep the blood circulation good.

"Your back is going to give you some pain. Rub your back with liniment when it hurts. Slaon's Linament is good. Watkins has a good one; but the one I like best is Absorbine. I would recommend you buy a large bottle of the horse liniment, but be careful not to blister yourself. Oh, and well-meaning people may want to massage your back…that would be a bad idea. Stick with the liniment."

****

Epsy had a hard time adjusting to having nothing to do all day long. He even taught Mary to play dominoes with him during the day.

Albert was happy to play dominoes every evening after supper, and Epsy really did look forward to it. Epsy and Albert played well together. They fairly controlled the table until Neva began to catch on and learned to block as well as playing to make count.

One evening Albert voiced a novel idea, "Epsy, wouldn't it help your situation a little if I taught Neva to drive? You have a nice car sitting out there and no one to drive it and no way of getting to town." So thereafter, while the young people went for a drive, Epsy and Rachael played dominoes when he could swing it and Rummy when she could work it.

****

Jim, Epsy's boss, came out to visit one afternoon. Rachael set out coffee and cake for the men; then she left the room so they could talk. "Epsy, I reported your accident to the police. You know that I was looking out the window and saw the whole thing. I gave the police the kid's name, and they have him in jail. I filed charges on behalf of the railroad.

"Our lawyers got their heads together and decided that, other than the accident taking place on railroad time and property, the railroad was not actually responsible. In fact, your straw boss was in my office when it happened. He was reporting to me that he thought we should get rid of the kid because he seemed to be making threats against you."

"Making threats against me?"

"Yes. Then you didn't know that he is some kin of yours, did you?"

"No."

"The best I could figure out, he is the grandson of your cousin, Bitsy. He sure is carrying a grudge against you, Epsy. From the best we could tell, it is not because of anything you did, but just that you kind of left the family. They are blaming you for everything bad that has happened to them.

"Well, since it seems to be sort of a family feud and not faulty equipment or that the railroad put you in an unusually dangerous position, the lawyers are saying that the railroad isn't liable for your accident."

He looked down at the table and stirred his coffee, letting all this information have time to soak in.

"Now, you know that if you want to, you can bring a suit against the railroad. But under the circumstances, I believe they are offering you a pretty fair settlement. They wanted me to present it to you, and let you have some time to think about it.

"Since you were hurt on railroad property and while you were on the job, they want to offer you a $5,000 settlement and a pension for the rest of your life. It would be half of what you are making now. I know that would not really be enough to live on, but it would help a whole lot.

"The police are waiting to see if you have anything to add to the charges on the kid. He will get some prison-time out of it even without your adding to the complaint against him; our lawyers will see to that."

He got up and refilled both their cups. "Now that the business is out of the way, how are you feeling by now?"

"The doctor said that I will eventually be able to walk some, but I won't be able to come back to work."

"Yes, that is what he told us. That is why the Texas & Pacific wants to make you a settlement instead of waiting for you to come back.

"I see you have a crop in. What will you be able to do about that?"

"It is not mine. I was ready to let the lease go, and a young man from north of Center Point leased it. I guess it is really a good thing, huh?

"We have been thinking about moving into Big Spring. I guess we may as well go ahead and make the move, now. We like it here, but there seems no sense in us living this far away from town when I can't drive."

"Well, when you get settled in, maybe we can get up a game of dominoes some evenings. I hear you are just about the king! I guess I had better get back to town. Think about all this, and let me know what you decide. Tell Rachael her chocolate cake can't be beat."

****

The older girls really began to be a help. Corrine and Bessie found a nice house right in the edge of the businesses in Big Spring. "It is not on a busy street, and it is close enough to town that you can walk wherever you want to go, Mama. We really like it. Only thing is, the rent is $11 a month. Can you afford that?"

"I guess so...we have never paid rent before."

"We want to show it to you before someone else rents it. We think you will be happy with it. It's a fairly new house with four really big rooms and a bath. It has running water, it is on the city sewer, and it even has a water heater! And it has gas! You can have a gas cook stove. You won't have to build a fire in the stove or heat water anymore!"

"Mama, wait till you see that porcelain bathtub with legs! And the water heater will run hot water to the bathtub and your kitchen sink, too!"

"Where is it?"

"The address is 309 South Lancaster St. Joe and Rabon and Albert will move the furniture for you. We can have you all moved in before school starts."

"Mama," Bessie said quietly, "do you think you could keep Dorothy some? I think Vida Mae would like to have a little free time, and I would like for Dorothy to get to know my parents, too."

****

Epsy and Albert were looking over things outside, deciding what Epsy would need to take with him into Big Spring and what Albert was going to inherit. In the barn the light was dim and they stood close together pointing to this and that.

"Epsy, we have gotten to know each other pretty well since I started farming this land, don't you think?"

"Yes, and I appreciate your friendship, Albert."

"I have been kind of courting Neva for some time now. I want to ask your permission to marry her."

"Have you talked to her?" He nodded.

"What did she say?"

"She said, 'You will have to ask my daddy.' I love her, Epsy, and I'm pretty sure that she loves me."

Epsy shook his head thoughtfully, "We can't afford to give her a nice wedding like we did for Bessie and Corrine. You know, our circumstances have changed so much. When would you want to get married?"

"Right now! If she says 'yes', we can go to the Justice of the Peace in Coahoma and get married. I have a little money put away to buy furniture. You won't even have to move her things to Big Spring. And I will move over to this house."

"Have you already bought her a ring?"

Albert reached into the deep front pocket of his overalls and pulled out a ring. "It was my Grandma McNew's ring. I've been carrying it around for some time, just trying to get up the nerve to ask her. Do you think she will like it?"

"I think you ought to go in and ask her. She is cooking supper. I'll go in first and clear the kitchen for you."

Epsy gathered all of the girls, "Let's go visit with Mama for a while." Rachael looked up from her crochet when they walked into the bedroom. The girls all piled on the bed beside their mother; Epsy winked at her.

"Oh, Albert!" they heard from the kitchen, "Yes, yes, yes! I have been so afraid I was going to have to move into Big Spring and leave you! Yes, yes, yes!"

She grabbed his face between her hands and kissed him quick. "Come on," she grabbed him by the hand and dragged him toward her parent's bedroom. "Let's show them my ring!"

****

"Mama, Corrine and I are almost the same size; she said I can wear her wedding dress if you will make a few alterations.

"Would that be okay to wear such a pretty wedding dress and it not be a church wedding…to a Justice of the Peace?"

"I did, darling. I think it is perfectly all right. Try it on, and let's see what I need to do to it.

"Why, it is almost a perfect fit! You are just a little bit thinner in the waist, but the bust fits fine. And your white Sunday shoes have a little bit of a heel; that will make you stand up a little taller to hold the dress up off the floor.

"Now put it on wrong side out so I can pin it. Remember now, we all want to be there. Has Albert told his parents?" Oh, Mama,… I don't know," she said in a sad voice. 'There is still hard feelings about Albert farming on his own." She was quiet for a few seconds, lost in thought; then she perked up a bit. "I really don't care. All I care about is that he is going to be mine!"

****

Moving day started early and it got a little crazy. Bessie and Corrine both came out on Sunday and helped pack all the kitchen things. Neva took her things out of the bureau that she shared with Jetty and put them into a box. Joe, Rabon, and Albert loaded all the furniture and boxes and hauled them to the house in town. Then they loaded up the furniture Neva and Albert had bought and brought it back to the house at Center Point.

Neva had a wonderful time arranging her own furniture and dishes. She put brand new sheets on the bed and a new bedspread. Oh, this was fun and didn't it all look lovely!

She packed an overnight bag, and Albert drove her into Big Spring to spend the night with her parents...until tomorrow!

On Monday evening light streamed from the windows of the Justice of the Peace's house, highlighting five or six cars parked along the street. No one was sure how they packed so many people into the JP's parlor. Most were standing behind the chairs for the parents of the bride and groom.

Corrine stepped into the parlor door and cleared her throat. Albert and Rabon stepped up beside the Justice of the Peace. The JP's wife began playing "Oh Promise Me" on the piano, and Corrine began walking toward the front of the parlor. Suddenly Neva stepped into the parlor doorway. Tall and slender, with shining, golden hair, she looked gorgeous in the beautiful wedding dress. The JP's wife had stripped her rose bushes bare making up a multicolored bouquet for Neva to carry.

It was a simple but beautiful wedding. Their happiness for their daughter helped change the sadness that had hovered over the Hales for the past few months.

Chapter Thirty One
Time Heals

As the months rolled by, Epsy's legs became stronger and stronger, but the pain remained. He nipped at his bottle of whiskey to dull the pain, so that Rachael began hiding his bottle. He became restless, wanting something more challenging to fill up his day. He tried driving the car once; but while he was backing out of the back yard, he realized that turning his head to look behind the car caused excruciating pain in his back. "Guess that doctor knew what he was talking about," he thought.

He went back into the house and poured himself a cup of coffee. "Rachael, I don't believe I will ever be able to drive again.

"Let's give the Tin-Lizzie to Corrine and Rabon. They don't have a car yet; both of them are walking to work. It only seems right to me. We gave the tractor to Neva and Albert. What do you think?"

*****

"Epsy, you need a haircut pretty bad. Do you think you can walk up to the barber shop by yourself? Or would you rather wait and let one of the girls drive you?"

Epsy stood up slowly, giving his back time to adjust to a standing position. Shuffling his feet as he walked toward the backdoor, he took his hat down off the nail where it always hung. He turned toward her, nodded his head and he was gone.

At the barbershop he waited his turn and then slowly, carefully climbed up in the chair. He made small talk while the barber worked. Almost everyone knew the story; everyone was amazed that Epsy was even walking. It was good to see him out by himself again.

As the barber was finishing his haircut, Epsy had been watching the shoeshine boy whose stand was set up in the corner of the barbershop. Well, he was definitely more than a boy; he was an older man than you usually see shining shoes. He was slight built, black and very thin; his clothes were worn very thin. He worked fast, popping the shoeshine rag with a rhythm and put a very nice shine on the shoes of the man in his chair.

Epsy surveyed the man in the chair, contrasting the two men. The man having his shoes shined was dressed in a nice suit, and he was several pounds overweight. He read a newspaper while the black man worked, and he never spoke a word to him.

The customer stepped down from the shoeshine stand, reached into his front pocket and held out a coin. The small black man thanked him, put the coin into his pocket and turned to begin straightening his work space.

"Hey, shine boy, you didn't give me my change! I gave you a dollar! You owe me 75 cents change, darky!" The customer spoke loud and harsh. He grabbed the man by the shoulder and spun him back around. A puzzled look crossed the black man's face; his jaw dropped open, but no words came out of his mouth.

Epsy pulled the apron from around his neck and stepped down from the barber chair. This time he walked very upright and determinedly toward the disturbance in the corner.

"Do you normally keep folding money in your front pocket, mister?" The irate man was blind-sided. He was flustered as he turned to look at Epsy. There was a puzzled look on his face.

Epsy pointed to the man's hip pocket. "Do you have five ones for a five?" he asked, holding up a five dollar bill.

The man was so rattled at this intrusion on his anger that he automatically reached for his wallet in his hip pocket.

"So you don't keep your bills in your front pocket! I was watching when you reached into your front pocket and handed a coin to the man. Now you are trying to make him give you money back? I don't think so!"

Looking around the barbershop, he saw that several men were watching to see the outcome. The blustery man suddenly turned and went out the door as fast as he could.

The shy, thin black man finally raised his head to look at the face of his benefactor. "Why, Mr. Epsy! Mr. Epsy!" was all he could say, but his eyes shined with love and that said it all.

Epsy held out his arms, and the two men hugged and cried together right there in the barbershop, right in front of God and everybody. Finally, when all the tears stopped flowing, Epsy patted the black man on the back a couple of times and said, "It is good to see you after all this time, Earny. I'll see you later."

He turned back to the stunned barber and asked, "How much is a haircut these days, Fred?"

"Not a dime, Mr. Hale, not a dime. I would have paid to watch that." He started to shake the apron and turned back toward his rack of hair tonic. "Not a dime," he said, shaking his head and watching in the mirror as Epsy shuffled out the door.

Rachael could tell something was wrong when he came in the back door and slumped down on her tall kitchen stool. With a puzzled look on her face she laid her hand gently on his shoulder, "What is wrong, Epsy?"

"I saw Earny today," he said softly. He buried his face in her chest and she hugged him around his shoulders while he cried.

*****

When Bessie drove up to bring Dorothy today, there was one definite thing on her mind. "Daddy, do you think you could stand on your feet for several hours at a time if you didn't have to do much walking? Would that make your back hurt?"

"I don't know. I have been on my feet quite a bit lately, but mostly when I am on my feet, I am walking somewhere. Why? What is on your mind?"

"Joe has been working 16 hours a day ever since we bought the café. It was okay at first because he could sit down when we were not so busy. But now our business is picking up all the time. Seems the harder times get, the more customers we get. You know we get all the railroad men when they change shifts and even couples sometimes when they have the money to eat out."

"Yes", he agreed, "I guess Joe really made a smart move, leaving the fancy hotel dining room and putting in a small diner."

"Daddy, would you consider being the evening cook? If you can't handle eight hours, maybe you could work six, or even four would give Joe some time to rest."

"Well, I always have liked to cook. But your mama is such a good cook; I didn't want to discourage her!" He winked at Rachael, and she smiled at him as she played with her granddaughter.

As they watched Bessie drive away, he hooked his thumbs in his galluses and reared back a little proudly. "Well, Granny, it looks like we may make it through this after all."

"Why, Epsy, I never doubted it. You know that I am a good manager. I'll make the money stretch somehow.

"And, Epsy, did you notice that Bessie's dress is awfully tight at the waist?" There was a twinkle in her eyes; she loved babies. She smiled at him contentedly, as if her life had suddenly taken on new flavor, and she turned to go back into the kitchen….her room.

Chapter Thirty Two
Granny Talk

We brought two straight-backed, kitchen chairs out to the porch to rest during the heat of the afternoon. We each had a glass of sweet tea, and there was a little breeze now and then. It was a lot cooler here than in the house.

"Granny, how do you know all of these things? You know so much about your grandparents' lives, and you really weren't around them that much. How did you learn all of this?"

"My mother told me, just like I'm telling you, child. We would sit in the porch swing in the afternoon and drink spearmint tea. She loved spearmint tea. I could never get spearmint to grow out here in west Texas, too much sand and caliche here, There is not enough acid in the soil.

"She would tell me things she remembered from when she was young. I have always treasured these memories. I hope you will, too."

"Well, you left Oklahoma in such a hurry. You didn't get to say 'goodbye' to your friend Sarah, did you?"

"No. There just wasn't time. We were afraid that if the man who won the farm got the Sheriff out there in time, he would make us leave the livestock and everything. I really did miss Sarah; we had some good times together.

"My father liked to bring pretty things to Mama and me when he came back from his trips, but he never gave much of himself. Mama's papa really gave you his time and attention. You knew that he loved you."

She smiled really big and a twinkle came into her eyes as she began to remember. "My father always brought Mama and me fine, knitted stockings from France. You know, they looked kind of like real fine, soft fish net.

"They looked real pretty, but they hurt your heels where your shoes rubbed. And they were not very warm in the winter. One time I traded Sarah a pair of them for a pair of her cotton stockings. They were much warmer.

"And you know, once he brought me a very pretty glass powder bowl with pretty smelling powder; lilac I think it was. It was pale pink, frosted glass, and the design on it was raised and shaded from pink into white right on the top. The powder puff was made of some sort of fine, white fur that was long and fluffy. It might have been ermine.

"I wanted to share with Sarah. So, I found a pretty little box with a picture of baby angels on top and put some of my powder in it for her." She held up her fingers to measure out the size of the box.

"When I saw her trying to put some powder on by dipping her fingers in it, I realized she needed a powder puff. So we went out to the barn, and I cut a square corner off my father's sheep skin saddle blanket that just fit in the box. It worked really well for a powder puff. Ha, ha, ha, ha." She leaned her chair back on two legs as she laughed.

"And for Christmas every year, I'd hang one of my father's big socks on the edge of the fireplace mantle. Christmas morning it would be full of oranges and apples, and several kinds of nuts and hard Christmas candies that looked like a wavy ribbon. And it would have a special little gift right in the top. I always gave Sarah her pick of my fruit and nuts and candy because she didn't get a Christmas stocking."

She fell silent as she relived those good memories. We watched a little whirlwind dance across the bare ground in front of the house, and as it came near the house, it changed its course. But it came close enough to cover us with the powdery West Texas dust. "Close your eyes and put your hand over your tea glass," Granny said. When it had passed, she sat down her tea. She flipped up the hem of her skirt and cleaned her glasses on her slip. I could see the top of her stockings rolled on round garters just above her knees.

"What about the horses, Granny. With your mother so weak, who handled the horses?"

"Yes, you love horses, too, don't you, sweetheart? Oh, the ones that were already saddle horses Bob and I kept ridden down. But mostly we just bred them and sold the colts as yearlings. Let someone else break them to ride. Mama loved to walk out and brush on them some, kind of gentle the foals while they were young, but that would tire her pretty fast."

"I love the smell of horses."

"For a few years she had a little strength to go to town occasionally. Most women around that time were working for the Temperance Movement or Women's Right to Vote. Mama worked real hard to gain the right for women to own land in their own name, so their husbands wouldn't be able to sell land that the wife had inherited or had bought on her own. Since there were several attorneys in her family, she made a little progress on it, got a little notice. She had a nice little group of women helping there for a while. They attracted some attention from the lawmakers.

"She enjoyed working on that for a time. It was kind of a personal issue for her. She had experienced a real need for a woman to own the property! But then she just got too tired to go anywhere."

"She and Bun came to live with us at Rising Star. She lived about two more years. We buried her at Longbranch Cemetery just a little way outside of Eastland." I could hear the sadness in Granny's voice.

"When Mama died, my father's sisters came and took Bun away from me. He was about eight years old. But he didn't like them; he kept running away and coming back to me. But they would always come get him again. When he was eleven, he hopped a train and ran away to California. Ended up married to a really wealthy woman. Her brother was a doctor and an Admiral in the Navy. He was President Roosevelt's doctor."

A gentle breeze blowing through the mesquite tree in the front yard stirred the leaves so that they rippled. We could hear the 'whoosh' it made as it blew between the leaves.

"Well, how did you meet Granddad? If your daddy sent young men that he liked to court you and you didn't like any of them, how did you meet Granddad?"

"Well, Epsy was something special. All the girls in Bell County were after him. He had played semi-pro baseball, and he had traveled around all over the country. He had such interesting stories to tell.

"Honey, did you know he played baseball against Ty Cobb?"

"Who is that?"

"He was about the best baseball player of that time! He was a friend of Babe Ruth. He was a good batter and he liked to steal bases when the pitcher wasn't looking. There were tells that he sharpened his cleats with a file to make them razor sharp. And I guess it was true.

"Your granddad played second base, and when Ty Cobb tried to steal second, Epsy tagged him out. But in the fracas, Cobb cleated him in the ankle and crippled him too bad to ever play baseball again. Haven't you noticed that he walks with a little bit of a limp? It's because of that," she said nodding her head.

"Well, he came home to Bell County wearing the latest fashion clothes and driving a fancy four-wheeled buggy with gold fringe around the top. He had a really showy buggy horse, too. All the rest of the men that came to court me brought an extra horse with sidesaddle for me to ride.

"He talked real slow and soft. And I loved hearing him talk about all the places he had been. Well, my father didn't like him for some reason and forbade me to go out with him. "Ha, ha!" That was just like waving a red flag in front of a bull!!"

"Ha, ha, ha," she laughed as she remembered. "My girlfriend and I locked ourselves in the outdoor toilet, and I was telling her I was going to run away with Epsy. Bun wanted to come in, but we wouldn't let him. There was a barrel of lime behind the outhouse, and he climbed up on that. Then he got up on top of the outhouse and peed. And it leaked through the roof and dripped down on us! Ha, ha, ha, ha." She sure did love her little brother!

"The next time Epsy came to pick me up in his buggy, I told him that if I went with him this time, I couldn't come back home or my father was going to cause a lot of trouble. If he wanted me to go, he would just have to marry me. He said that sounded good to him!

"I told my little brother to bring the valise I had hidden behind a shrub and put it in the back of the buggy. I told Bun to tell Mama we were running off to get married; and we did.

"Problem was, a lot of people knew my father and were scared to cross him. I was 23 years old. Old enough to do what I wanted to! But, we ended up driving all the way from Bell County to Weatherford. Mama's uncle was a judge there, and even he wouldn't marry us!

"Epsy had a twin brother who lived in Coahoma. He had gotten married just two years earlier, so we went to see him. Even people out here in West Texas had heard of my father! We finally found a Methodist lay-preacher; I think he was from Stanton. He said, 'He served the Lord; and he wasn't scared of Jeff Dodd or anyone else, for that matter.' He married us."

She thought for a little, then continued, "You should have seen Big Spring then, honey. It was a wide open little town!"

"What do you mean, 'wide open'?"

"Well, this used to be called the 'Crossroads of West Texas' because this was the main route for people headed west, and the Indians had a well-known trail that ran through here. They traveled going north and south as the seasons changed. I think highway 87 pretty much follows that trail.

"A long time ago this was a major stop for the Indians because of the big spring out there south of town. That is how the town got its name, Big Spring.

"Well, when we came in 1908, the population of the whole country was shifting toward the west. A lot of people were going to New Mexico, Arizona and California. Big Spring was a major stop for the Texas & Pacific Railroad.

"I don't have any idea what the permanent population of Big Spring was, but with so many migrant people moving through here, at one time there were 19 saloons. If there was trouble, the law was slow to get there. That's what we mean by 'wide open'.

"Let me see, I think there were four churches that actually had church buildings. The Methodist church right up the street here was the largest, and that preacher also pastored two other smaller congregations."

She rocked her chair on the two back legs in silence for a while, "I had to get back home to help take care of Mama and Bun. Epsy bought the cotton gin at Rising Star in Eastland County. He made a lot of money for several years until the farmers around Rising Star realized the land was well suited to grow peanuts and they didn't have to worry so much about the weather and boll weevils.

"Epsy sold the gin when he realized that peanuts were starting to replace cotton in that area. We came out here to Big Spring because Epsy had a lot of folks around here, and there was work because of the railroad station.

"After several years the weather got so dry people couldn't raise a crop. It was the beginning of the big drought. You remember hearing about the Dust Bowl, don't you, honey? Actually the dust was the result of people breaking up the natural sod and trying to farm prairie land. It was a very long dry spell. Times got real hard for everyone.

"If it hadn't been for the spring and the railroad having a busy station here, Big Spring probably would have dried up and blown away, too."

That was a lot of information for a little girl to absorb. After I thought about it for a while, I asked, "Granny, before you married Granddad, you were sort of the 'Belle of Bell County', weren't you?"

"Why, no...I don't guess so, darling. I just kept refusing all the young men who came courting until I found the one I wanted. I didn't think I was anything special."

She rocked for a little while, remembering. "Don't scratch that smallpox vaccination, honey; just rub it when it itches. So you will be starting school this Fall, huh?

"They started giving those vaccinations when Bun was starting school. He watched the doctor scrape a place on his arm and put the medicine on the scraped place, just like they did yours. Later when Bun was outside playing, he used his pocket knife and scraped several places on both arms. He sharpened a twig and scratched it on the real vaccination, then he touched it on the places he had scraped. He was pretending he was the doctor.

"Well, every one of those places took. He had five or six of those big scabs on his arms, and he ran a very high fever for several days. We had to bathe his whole body in cool water to keep his temperature down. The doctor said it was just about like him having the real smallpox. It could have killed him."

"Ha, ha, ha. The things that kid didn't do."

"Granny, you were born in Georgia, weren't you? I was born in Big Spring, right here in this house, wasn't I?" She nodded her head. "Well, where was Uncle Bun born?'

She was very thoughtful for a long time. "Well... Grandpa Barnett didn't think it was good for it to be known, because we lived in Indian Territory. When it was time for the United States Census in 1910, Grandpa told them that Mama and me and Bun were living with them in Rome Georgia. And that both of us were born in Georgia."

"But, why? Where was he born?" It became important to me to know, now.

There was silence! She was clearly agitated. She finally made a snap decision. "He was born in Idabell, Oklahoma, in 1904. But Oklahoma was not a state at that time. It became a state in 1907! Grandpa said someone might try to say that Bun was not a United States citizen."

"But he is, isn't he? He is my uncle! He is, isn't he?" She smiled gently and nodded.

We watched a butterfly sampling the hardy, yellow-flowering weeds that grew next to the yard fence, hardly missing a one. But, she couldn't fly in a straight line. Her path went up and down, to the right and then left. I guess even the gentle breeze carried her off course.

"Oh, Granny, look. There are two lizards under those flowers. They have green bodies and long, red tails. Can I catch them?"

"It will be all right, if you can catch them. They are not poisonous."

But I couldn't catch them; every time I got close, they darted a different way. So I sat back down in my chair.

Granny sipped her tea and her false teeth became unsettled and clacked together.

"How long have you had false teeth, Granny?"

"Oh, that is a kind of funny story. We were in town for 4th of July. I had a bad toothache, so I went to see the dentist. He said I had several cavities, but one tooth had a very big cavity, and it needed to be pulled.

"He said he would have to ask my father first. You see, my father didn't live with us anymore, but he kept pretty close tabs on me anyway.

"I told that dentist that I was 20 years old and if I wanted to have a tooth pulled, I would have it pulled! 'In fact,' I said, 'just go ahead and pull them all!'

"My teeth were kind of crooked anyway. You know the way your two front teeth overlap there in the front? Well, my mama's, and mine, and your mama's and Mary's all did that very same thing. I guess maybe Grandma Barnett's did, too.

"Well, that dentist took me at my word. He gave me some kind of gas and put me to sleep. And when I woke up they were all gone!

"It made me so weak, they had to lay me out in the wagon bed and take me home. I was so sick! It was several days before I could get up and around. Ha, ha, ha, ha!

"So I have had false teeth since I was 20 years old.

"See where you get your rambunkousness? All of my girls had a high spirit, wouldn't back down from anybody. All except your mother. I guess she got her mild spirit from your granddad. He has always talked kind of slow and quiet. He never would say anything that didn't absolutely need to be said.

"When the girls were in school at Center Point, the boys used to tease your aunt Corrine. They would say, 'Corrine Hale, sitting on a rail, picking her teeth with the end of her tail.' And she would chase after them. And whip up on any of them she could catch.

"It was a two room school house. The teacher for the younger grades was a woman, and her husband taught the older kids. Sometimes, when she had to leave the room, she asked your mother to come up to her desk on the podium and take names of the kids who talked or misbehaved.

"Once when she came back the room was so quiet and orderly, she could not believe it. They had pushed the teacher's desk to the back of the podium. Ben Nix was playing his French harp and Laura was tap dancing," She smiled. "She always said Ben was her first boyfriend. Did you know your mother could tap dance?

"Hoyle Nix and Corrine were sweet on each other for a while, too."

I fidgeted in my chair. Seems I just could not find a comfortable way to sit in those chairs. I scooted back so I could lean against the back of the chair, but my feet stuck straight out in front. After a while, I scooted forward until my knees were at the front edge of the chair. I rested my feet on the rung that ran between the chair legs. But soon my back started getting tired, and I slumped with a rounded back. I much preferred the long bench that ran the length of her big kitchen table.

"Ha, ha, ha. Your knees just bend in the wrong place to fit in the chair, don't they, hon? Why don't you try sitting on the porch steps? Maybe that would be more comfortable."

So I took my tea and sat on the porch steps. It was much better.

On my fingers, I counted my mama's sisters. "You had six girls, and no boys?"

She thought about that one for a long time. "When Mary was about six years old, I was pregnant again. A change of life baby, do you understand?" I shook my head 'no'. "Well, my child bearing years were just about over, and my body wasn't strong enough to build a healthy baby. It was born way too early and didn't live. It was my boy." Her eyes misted up; then she took another sip of tea, leaned her chair back again and rocked for a while.

A mocking bird flew up and sat on a low limb of the big mesquite tree. He sang several melodious songs for us; then turned his head from side to side looking at us. "I guess he wants us to clap," I said; so we clapped. The mocking bird flew away.

I felt bad that we had chased the mocking bird away. We sat in silence. "Granny, sometimes I see Granddad start to walk across the room, but he stops and just stands there for a minute. Is that because of his hurt ankle?"

"No, honey. When that truck ran into him and pinned him to the boxcar, his back was hurt really bad. Over time it got quite a bit better, but he still has some ruptured discs in his spine. Sometimes when he has been sitting for a long time, it slips over to a bad place and paralyzes his legs for just a short while. But then it gets adjusted, and he can walk again."

"Granny, there are a lot of Hales around Big Spring. One time I asked Granddad if they were kin to us, and he said, 'No! None of them are kin to me!' It didn't sound like I should ask any more about it. Why aren't any of them kin to us? I know Mama and all the girls are always happy to see Tollie when he comes to see us. He is a Hale, isn't he?"

"Oh, well. Yes, Tollie is a cousin of my girls, and since they don't have any brothers, they are all real fond of him. They are all kin to us, honey. They just got all cross-ways a long time ago; that's all." And she sat thinking again, sipping her tea.

"Well, what ever happened to your daddy, Granny?"

"Oh, Jeff Dodd? Well, his baby with Dora died. I don't know what happened to Dora. My father came through here when you were about four. He didn't stay long. I let him spend one night and gave him a meal; then I told him to leave. Do you remember? You came in from the bedroom trying to walk in his big old shoes."

"I do remember! Those shoes were heavy! And he looked like a giant to me! But you told me to give him his shoes so he could go."

"Yes, I guess he did look like a giant to you. He was six foot, four inches tall. He wore a size 52 coat, and he had to have his shoes special made."

She was silent and thoughtful. "I heard he went to California, probably looking for Bun. I heard he died out there."

She was quiet for a while. She had a faraway look in her eyes. She was seeing pictures from the past, and there was a little sadness about her. I know it hurt her to feel the way she did about her daddy.

I left my tea sitting by the porch steps and walked over to her chair. Our heads were just about the same level as I stood beside her. I put my arms around her neck and hugged her for a long time. She reached her arm around my waist and patted my back gently. I loved hugging her with our heads touching. I could smell her powder.

"I love you, Granny. You sure do smell good. I really like your powder."

"Ha, ha, ha. You always have! One time while your daddy was in the Navy and your mama was working at Sister and Joe's café, I told Granddad to watch you while I walked up to the grocery store. When I came back, you were sitting in the middle of the kitchen floor with my brand new box of Pond's body powder. You were white as a little ghost from head to toe and still patting your face with the powder puff. There was a little cloud of powder all around your head and a ring of powder around you on the floor about two feet on each side.

"I asked, 'Epsy, why are you letting her play with my powder?' He said you cried so hard after I left that he thought you were going to get sick He carried you around, but you wouldn't hush. You finally saw my powder and 'wanted to smell of Granny'. That stopped your crying, so he let you have it. 'She thinks she smells like Granny now!' he said. And he laughed more than I had heard him laugh in a long time.

"And he just sat there watching you puff powder everywhere and smiling at you. I guess if you had wanted matches, it would have been the same! He sure does love you!"

"But, Granny! Most of the time he talks so gruff. I thought he did not like me!"

"Honey, he lives with such pain in his back, most of the time he can't think of anything friendly to say. His mind just seems to run to the bad things that happen, but it's because of the pain. He wasn't always that way. He loves you, honey."

"Granny, I remember when I was little you used to hold me in your lap and feed me breakfast. You would pinch off a little piece of buttered toast and dip it in a plate of sorghum syrup. You would give me a bite then you would get a bite. I really miss that. It doesn't taste as good when I do it.

"And remember how you used to scrape an apple with a spoon and give me a bite of applesauce? Well, I've tried that, too, and it just isn't the same."

"It's the love, honey."

Granny seemed to be all talked out, and the silence felt strange and heavy. She patted both hands down on her knees, "Well, one of these days you are going to want to look up all of this. When you do, you will find there was a picture made of all the women around Big Spring in 1920. It was taken on the front steps of the Methodist Church. Well, don't look for me there. I wouldn't be in it because I didn't have a new bonnet to wear!"

Granny rocked in silence for a while. Finally, she said, "Now you have some tales of times past to tell your children and grandchildren." She caressed the side of my face with her hand and gently rubbed her hand down my hair that was blond with just a ting of red. "Child, you do remind me of my mother, with your fair skin and that same indomitable spirit."

We started moving our chairs inside the house and Granny held the screen door open for me. "Granny, do you have any apricots?"

"I think I have some. Why?"

Can we make some fried pies? I sure love your apricot fried pies!"

"Let's do that tomorrow, honey."

*****

Rachael rode to school on horseback. As a young woman she dated riding side-saddle or in a horse-drawn buggy. She lived to see the first man walk on the moon. She never did learn to drive a car!

Made in the USA
Columbia, SC
18 April 2025